A Time in Their Lives

writings from personal experience

Edited by

Jerry Herman
Laney College

Canfield Press
San Francisco

A Department of Harper & Row, Publishers, Inc.

New York • Evanston • London

acknowledgments

I wish to thank the following people for their aid and encouragement in the preparation of this book: Robert J. Griffin, Vicki Kahan, Carmen Rezendes, Elaine Sharpe, Janet Wall, and my wife Harriet. I am grateful to Ted Ricks, English editor at Canfield Press, for his assistance and to Pearl C. Vapnek, my production editor, for her diligence in assuring that this book be published properly and well. Finally, gratitude alone is insufficient to express my appreciation to Marlene Griffith and Myrna Harrison for their large contributions to this book.

Cover: "Hand with Reflecting Globe," lithograph by M. C. Escher. Reproduced by permission of the Escher Foundation, Haags Gemeentemuseum, The Hague. "A reflecting globe rests in the artist's hand . . . His head, or to be more precise the point between his eyes, comes in the absolute centre. Whichever way he turns he remains at the centre. The ego is the unshakable core of his world."—Escher.

Cover design: j. sidonie tillinger

808.04275
H 42 t
129950
Sept. 1984

A Time in Their Lives: Writings from Personal Experience

International Standard Book Number: 0-06-383630-0

Library of Congress Catalog Card Number: 73-7191

74 75 10 9 8 7 6 5 4 3 2 1

contents_____

introduction ———————————————————————

The unexamined life is not worth living.—*Socrates*

There is no description so difficult as describing oneself.—*Montaigne*

Experience is the best teacher.—*Anonymous*

This book began as an idea. That idea began in experience. As a teacher of college composition for ten years, I have always emphasized ideas as the basis of writing, but true to my own formal education, I failed to look for the source of ideas. The ideas in my students' writing were too often shallow clichés; though in class discussion and in speaking with the students personally, I saw that most of them were bright, interesting people. I tried a multitude of methods to get them to think more deeply and originally in working out their assignments, and one day I recognized what it was I myself was doing. My experience in teaching was leading me to generate ideas, ideas which—though not always successful—meant something to me because they were related to my life. I didn't immediately grasp the connection between this notion and my experience that generally the liveliest and best writing my students produced was the "throw-away" essay on personal experience I assigned early in the semester to "warm students up," let them get a good grade easily, and "feel good" about writing. After that initial soft touch the "real work" began, the crunch of writing about the unfamiliar and the abstract from essay collections that ranged in material from "Sex in the Sixties" to "Goals and Gods." The life and uniqueness in the writing of the students' personal-experience essays faded away, yielding to stale commonplaces and pseudo-academic language. The sections of the textbooks, incidentally, which most interested students were those on "The Self" or "Identity," in which the editor would include a few personal-experience essays. At last I got the point.

I began to have students write about their own experiences and to read essays of personal experience as a large part of the semester's work, and I saw them become more interested in their writing and reading. I was able to teach them more effectively because they had become engaged as they had not been before. Instead of easy clichés that didn't fit the unique situations of each student's life, I began to get writing and thought that was fresh and interesting. Not only was I seeing evidence that their writing improved, but also many students told me they learned about themselves because they now had to confront themselves in their writing as they had never been asked to do in school before.

As the concept of this book evolved in my mind, I thought about the nature of ideas and experience. I concluded that most—if not all—ideas are derived

1

from experience, and that one of the inadvertent disservices of schools has been abstracting ideas from experience and presenting them in a vacuum as though the experiences that were their foundation didn't matter or didn't exist. I gained a new insight into why so many of a generation of students, acknowledged to be the best-informed and brightest of all student generations, found school to be, in that damning epithet, irrelevant.

This phenomenon of separating ideas from experience fit into a twentieth-century American pattern of fragmenting life which, by the mid-sixties, was being rejected by large numbers of young people. For too long they had been taught to separate themselves from what lay outside themselves, to discard wholeness in favor of compartmentalization. The young probably realized before any other sociological group not only that the divisions were false, but also that they formed one of the root systems of the alienation that has plagued the twentieth century and that, ironically, has been discussed for so long in classrooms.

Where the young lead, their teachers will often find it wise to follow. A collection of essays from personal experience, I decided, would be based on the principle of wholeness, on the integration of human qualities rather than their separation. I was encouraged by writers like Theodore Roszak who, in *The Making of a Counter-Culture* (1969), argues that if we are to regain the humanity we have lost by deifying science and worshipping technology, the idol science has created, we must tear down the screen which separates the "subjective" from the "objective":

It is precisely this sense of person which we should look for in all those who purport to teach us. We should ask, "Show us this person you have made of yourself. Let us see its full size. For how can we judge what you know, what you say, what you make, unless in the context of the whole person?" It is a matter of saying, perhaps, that truth ought not to be seen as a property of a proposition, but of the person.

My choice of essays has been guided by that principle of wholeness. I want the students and teachers who read these essays consciously to see the author in the writing because he has consciously put himself there. I hope the selections demonstrate that writing an essay is not a function of severing one's intellect from the rest of himself, but that experience, feelings, and ideas interact in complex and fascinating mutuality. The abstract theory of today evolved from a feeling in someone's guts yesterday and will affect someone's life tomorrow. Ideas should not only be understood; they can live. James Baldwin and George Orwell are illuminating examples of writers whose essays invite us into their lives to show how their convictions and intellectual positions were developed.

In the spirit of wholeness of mankind as well as of individual men, I have included selections that not only are intrinsically interesting and instructive but also show the commonality of experience among people of different cultures, vocations, and historical periods. Because students share in this commonality of men, selections of their writing, too, have been included.

The book is organized in chapters reflecting the range of human experience. Naturally, I have made no attempt to be comprehensive since this would be impossible, and the organization is not airtight; it couldn't be. An essay in one chapter might fit thematically into another as well.

The selections can well serve as models for student writing. The styles of the authors are sufficiently diverse for students to appreciate a wide range of rhetorical approaches to various subjects, and all the writers are concrete, precise, and vigorous in their use of language.

chapter one

Self-Discovery

introduction

One of the most useful but difficult prescriptions for living contains just two words: "Know thyself." Socrates' maxim, echoed by thoughtful men throughout the centuries, is as valid today as when he uttered it 2500 years ago. But in an age when men and machines hurtle into outer space, man knows little more about his inner space than he did when Plato recorded his teacher's words. Indeed, many avoid self-analysis, fearing what they might find beneath the surface of their daily lives. There is no sure path to self-discovery. Curiosity might launch one on a journey of self-examination, or emotional distress might generate the search. Sometimes self-discovery is unsought, triggered by a dramatic incident or revealed in someone's idle remark which shocks us to self-recognition.

The irrepressible Montaigne begins this chapter, striking a keynote in his essay "Why I Paint My Own Portrait" when he says of self-analysis: ". . . if a man begins to think of himself, he will find nothing to make him proud which doesn't at the same time cast into the scales something to make him humble; and, in the end, the balance can always be tipped by the insignificance of human existence."

Montaigne's reflections about his life are followed by Walt Raintree's impressionistic memories of events and people that have woven the fabric of his life from the plains of Oklahoma to the streets of San Francisco. He sees the continuum of his life as a process of self-discovery which begins early and does not end until death.

Jean Shepherd and Gerald Brock write of traumatic social incidents which shock them out of self-satisfied complacency into disturbing insights about themselves.

"On Becoming" shows Eldridge Cleaver working the changes in his life on the basis of a self-analysis that reveals a deep-seated hatred and longing for white women which he could not suppress.

As psychiatry institutionalized individual analysis of the self, the Esalen Institute in California has pioneered self-examination through groups. Leo Litwak's essay describes his experiences at Esalen and the techniques used to liberate him from a painful incident whose memory he had repressed.

Cathy Sterbentz realizes she has changed in subtle ways when she attends a Joan Baez concert and finds that her reaction to it is disenchantingly different from her expectations.

Why I Paint My Own Portrait

The originator of the personal essay, Michel de Montaigne (1533–1592) was born to a prominent and prosperous family in the town of Montaigne in southwestern France. His education was strongly classical, in keeping with the New Learning of the Renaissance then in full flower in France. He studied law and held several important posts in the parliament of Bordeaux. At thirty-seven he retired to his chateau to embark on one of history's most important literary projects, the writing of his *Essays,* the first two volumes of which were published in 1580. Emerging from retirement, he took a leisurely trip to Rome and was informed while there that he had been elected mayor of Bordeaux. He served in that post until 1585, when he again retired to continue his writing. The third volume of his *Essays* was published posthumously in 1595. Skeptical of extreme opinions and dogma, he saw mankind as a bundle of contradictions, slightly absurd and too quick to puff itself up in self-importance. Montaigne's candor is charming, and his easy, free-flowing style engaging. Emerson said of Montaigne, ''There have been men with deeper insight; but one would say, never a man with such abundance of thoughts: he is never dull, never insincere, and has the genius to make the reader care for all he cares for.''

It was a melancholy humor, very much an enemy to my natural disposition and born of the solitude in which I had taken refuge, that first put into my head this notion of writing. And because I found I had nothing else to write about, I presented myself as a subject. When I wrote of anything else I wandered and lost the way.

One day I was at Bar-le-Duc when King Francis II was presented a portrait that King René of Sicily had made of himself. Why, in a like manner, isn't it lawful for every one of us to paint himself with his pen, as René drew himself with a crayon?

If the novelty and strangeness of my design—which are wont to give value to a thing—do not save me, I shall never come off with honor in this foolish attempt. It is the only book of its kind in the world. Yet the subject is so vain and trivial, the best workman could not bring it to esteem; and there

From *The Autobiography of Michel de Montaigne,* translated by Marvin Lowenthal. Copyright 1935 and renewed 1963 by Marvin Lowenthal. Reprinted by permission of Alfred A. Knopf, Inc.

is nothing in it worth remark but its extravagancy. Still, it is so fantastic and out of the ordinary that perhaps it will pass.

I have no other aim but to disclose myself. However inconsiderable these essays of myself may be, I will not conceal them any more than my old bald pate, where the painter has set before you not a perfect face, but my own. And tomorrow I shall perhaps have another self, if by chance a new lesson will change me.

I write my book for few men and few years. Considering how rapidly our language changes—it slips through our fingers every day and since I was born has more than half-transformed itself—I do not fear to use it for a number of private messages which will die with men now living, or which concern such minds as look further into a thing than ordinary.

I do not want men to say of me, as I often hear them say of the dead: "This is how he lived and thought—that is what he meant—if he could have spoken on his death-bed, he would have said so-and-so and given such-and-such—I know him better than anyone else." If people are to talk, I want it with truth and justice. I'll gladly come back from the other world to give the lie to anyone who will shape me other than I was, even though to honor me.

If I had not defended with all my might a friend whom I had lost,[1] they would have torn him into a thousand contrary shapes. I know I shall leave no one behind me to do for me what I did for him, nor anyone to whom I can fully confide the painting of my portrait. He alone knew my true face, and he took it with him. That is why I paint myself with such care. And what I can't express, I point at with my finger.

Everyone, says Pliny, has a good curriculum in himself, provided he can spy closely into his own mind. What I offer here is not my teaching, but my study; not a lesson for others, but for myself. If I pass it on, do not take it amiss; for what is useful to me may perhaps serve someone else. For the rest, I do no harm. I make use of nothing but what is mine; and if I play the fool, it is at my own expense. It is a folly that dies with me, and there are no heirs.

We hear of one or two ancients who took this road, though I cannot say if it was in my manner; for I know nothing of them but their names. Since then, no one has trod in their tracks.

It is a thorny enterprise, harder than it seems, to pursue the rambling trail of the mind and penetrate its opaque depths—choosing and fixing in your grasp its countless fugitive reflections. It is a new and unusual entertainment, which lures me from the ordinary business of the world, even that which is in most repute.

For many years now, my thoughts have dwelt only on myself. The world

[1]La Boétie.

CHAPTER ONE / *Self-Discovery*

looks out and across: I turn my gaze within. I am always meditating on myself, trying and considering. Others, if they stop to think of it, will find that they send their mind abroad; it moves on ahead. As for me, I am forever revolving in myself. If I study something else, it is merely to apply it to, or rather in, myself. And I do not hold it improper if, as others do with less profitable knowledge, I tell what I have learned—though I am little satisfied with my progress. There is no description so difficult as describing oneself.

Custom has ruled all talk of oneself to be vicious, and prohibits it because of the boasting that seems inseparable from it. Instead of giving a child a handkerchief, this is to cut off its nose. I think that condemning wine because some persons get drunk is itself condemnable. These are muzzles for puppies, with which neither the saints whom we hear speak so highly of themselves, nor philosophers, nor divines ever muzzle themselves. And neither will I, who am as little one as the other.

My trade and art is to live my life. The man who forbids me to speak of my experience, feeling, and practice of it might as well forbid an architect to speak of building as he, and not another, knows it.

Perhaps they mean I ought to show myself in action and accomplishments, and not in words. But since my chief business is to paint my thoughts—formless things that cannot be rendered palpable—I have trouble enough to clothe them in the airy robe of the voice. The wisest and most devout men have shunned to put their life in visible deeds. My actions would tell more of my luck than of myself. They would witness their own role, and not mine—save by conjecture and guess. They are samples of their own showing.

But I show myself in my entirety: at one view the skeleton, muscles, and veins—here a cough and there a heartbeat, and their elusive effects. It is not my deeds I write—it is I and my essence.

Men fancy that to think of themselves means to be pleased with what they think—that to cultivate the self is to overindulge it. This is true only of those who skim the surface, who look on themselves as a stranger within, who see their real selves in their business, and for whom inner meditation means daydreaming and building castles in Spain.

While we should be prudent in the estimation of what we are, we must, I think, be no less conscientious in giving a report of it, for good or evil. To belittle yourself is not modesty so much as stupidity. If I thought I was altogether good and wise, I'd trumpet it abroad. But to overpraise yourself is not only presumption, but folly. However, the cure for it is not to forbid people to talk of themselves; for that will likewise stop them from thinking of themselves.

And if a man begins to think of himself, he will find nothing to make him proud which doesn't at the same time cast into the scales something to make him humble; and, in the end, the balance can always be tipped by the insignificance of human existence. Because Socrates alone chewed to the core that precept of his god: "Know thyself," he alone has been found worthy of the title of a sage. Whoever knows himself in this fashion, let him boldly speak out.

But someone may tell me: this design to make yourself the subject of your pen is excusable only in a great and famous man whose reputation has whetted our desire to know more about him. A mechanic, I confess, will hardly lift his eyes from his tools to look at an ordinary passer-by; whereas, when a prominent personage comes to town, every store and workshop is deserted. Only a man worth imitating, I know, should describe his own character; and it is a pity we have not the diaries of Alexander the Great and other men whose mere statues in bronze and marble we like to contemplate.

The objection is sound, but, so far as I am concerned, it is hardly to the point. In this book I am not casting a statue to set up at the crossroads, or in a public square or church. It is meant for some corner of a library, or to entertain a friend or neighbor who has a mind to renew and deepen his acquaintance with me.

Others have been encouraged to speak of themselves because the subject was rich and worthy—I, on the contrary, because I find it so lean and sterile there can be no suspicion of ostentation. I don't find such goodness in myself that I cannot tell it without blushing. My one relation to the public is that I borrow the public tools of printing; and, as a reward, my pages may perhaps serve in the market-place to keep a pound of butter from melting in the sun.

And if no one reads me, have I lost my time entertaining myself with pleasant and useful thoughts? Our most delicious pleasures, when enjoyed within themselves, shun the touch of the world's hand or leaving a trace behind. How often has this preoccupation diverted me from troublesome thoughts, and all frivolous thoughts should be accounted troublesome. Nature has given us ample means of diverting ourselves with ourselves, and often invites us to use them, in order that we may learn we owe only a part of us to society—and not the best nor the most.

A man has to comb his hair and brush up before he appears in public. Just so I am forever dressing myself, for I am my own public. Drawing this portrait after my own model, I have often been forced to drape and rearrange myself in order that the pose may offer a truer likeness, with the result that I have created for myself a fresher and brighter complexion than I began with. My book has made me as much as I have made my book. It is of the same stuff as the author, a limb of my body, devoted to its own being and not to the concerns of its reader, as are other books.

What, too, if I read other books a little more attentively, watching to see if I can't steal something to adorn or support my own? For I have not studied in order to make a book; but because I had to make one I somehow studied—if

CHAPTER ONE / *Self-Discovery*

it be studying to scratch and pinch this author and that, by the head or heels, not to form my opinions but to test them.

And how many times, when I am displeased with some action which I cannot, in decency and reason, openly reprove, I unburden myself here—not without the hope of bringing it to the public ear! These rhapsodical lashes lay themselves better on paper than on flesh.

We do not reform the man we hang: we hope to reform others through him. I do the same. My errors are either natural or incorrigible; but the good that virtuous men perform by setting a model before the public, I may do by setting a warning. There may be people of my cast who learn more by avoiding than imitating. The horror I have of cruelty more inclines me to clemency than any example of kindliness. An expert riding-master can't improve my seat so well as my merely looking at a lawyer or a Venetian in the saddle.

Moreover, the times are appropriate for us to reform backwards: by dissent rather than accord. Since I profit little by the good examples, which are rare, I make use of the bad, which are plentiful enough. I try to become as agreeable as I see others offensive, as constant as others are fickle, as gentle as others are gruff, and as decent as others are unspeakable. But I have set myself an impossible goal.

I find this unsuspected advantage in the publication of my memoirs. It serves in some sort as a check. Now and then it occurs to me not to betray my own story, not to belie the picture I have drawn. Moreover, I believe I have furnished enough targets so that whoever would attack me can satisfy his malice without shooting in the air. Even if he turns my evil roots into full-grown trees, a free confession disarms slander.

Besides this profit, I am in hopes that if my humors should please some honest man before I die, he will desire to seek my company. I have surrendered him a great deal of territory without battle. All he could learn of me by long years of acquaintance he can now have in three days' reading, and more certain and exact. A droll idea! Things I would not whisper to any individual I tell to the public, and send my best friends to the bookseller to inform themselves of my most intimate thoughts.

If I knew by sure report of someone after my own heart, I would go a long way indeed to seek him out. The sweetness of a companion cannot, in my mind, be bought too dear. Oh, for a friend! How true is the old saying: "Friendship is sweeter and more necessary than fire or water."

walt raintree ———————————————————————————————

Bits of Yesterday, Pieces of Now

Born in Altus, Oklahoma, Walt Raintree (1935–   ) prefers to have the essay below fill in the significant details of his life. He has been a student at Laney College in Oakland, California, since 1971. Eventually he wants to establish himself as a professional writer.

For most of his life he knew nothing of himself. Years ago, without remembering it, he had fallen into a reverie and a remembrance of some other life and had set aside the factual and infectious memoir of his own. Loneliness and anxiety were the most of him, for in all his actions, both willful and forced, there was himself standing next to himself, observing everything that came to him, and everything that left him . . . sometimes with amusement, more often with wonder and pity.

The enigmatic key lies in the day he arrived home from school at the very moment his parents, the result of a morning and afternoon of serious drinking, had attacked each other physically. He watched in horror as the man and the woman who made his life tumbled about the house trying to kill each other. They succeeded only in the final killing of their one son, who was heard by no one to mumble one word only. "No," the small boy said. "No." The day was a culmination and a beginning. The small boy went to sleep forever, to dream another life, and I myself came as a replacement, also to dream. I have since dreamed all the days of the intransigent life that is living me. That is why I can evoke the bittersweet past in all its terror and triviality, its paradox and parable, which may be nothing more than the anxious imaginings of a small boy, born in a tar-and-paper shack on the prairie, who is still dreaming.

My grandmother, with whom I lived from that day on—mahogany, hawk-faced, blue-black hair (she was Choctaw and black), strong eyes I could not look into and lie—operated a crude eating place that was also our home. It stood on what I came to realize was merely an open vastness of the prairie on the border of Oklahoma and the Texas Panhandle. Red River Country. Sunrise and sunsets, extremes of weather, the unnameable hot and dry, the cold and the wet, the freezing snow and ice that left cattle frozen-stiff as

Original publication in this volume, by permission of the author.

they stood. Nightfall and star-rise, and huge intimate moons that swallowed the forlorn nights, creating a timeless universe neither dark nor light. In this vastness of space and time, the glorious "Te Deum" of crickets, the mournful lowing of cattle, and the sweet smell of cow-dung. A shabby barn containing the births, deaths, and all the secrets animals hide from men. The sudden pow of the angry wind balling its heavy fist and punching hard against the closed windows of my room. I knew (though I was too young and ignorant to know) the erotic earth, the symphony of plants and grass, the smell and the feel of prairie flowers, the wandering spoor of small animals, and the ever-rolling brush. There was a horse I loved and cared for (a gentle, sway-backed mare named Celeste), and an old, evil bull kept in a brown pasture. There was the feel and weight of ghostly events, for history passed this way just yesterday. I played on the very spot where my grandfather was killed by a group of ranch-hands, farmers, and wild-catters. Where I played with other small boys (Osage, Choctaw, white, black, and mixed blood), wagon trails still rutted dirt roads. There were the remnants of forgotten cabins and farmhouses, and here and there a crumbling wall of what was once a barn. I had a gun (the rusted barrel and frame of an ancient Colt), and among my fiercest treasures was a worn and rotting mule trace belonging to my grandfather when he was alive—and over it all the endless sky full of endless changes that are a stunning symbol of the unknowable and unanswerable life all men must lead.

I remember (I have tried to forget) the history of my life. I remember the first time I was called a nigger (by a black man who resembled my father). I was a paper boy on the busy corners of Vernon and Central Avenues in Los Angeles. A reeking wino demanded I give him a coin. I hesitated, confused and afraid. "You're a nigger. That's why you won't give me a dime," the man said. I remember my boy's soprano screaming back at him, "No, I'm not either. . . . I'm a Catholic!" I still see the startled look that floated across the drunken face of that man as I shuffled my papers and strolled unhappily away—for without his knowledge he awakened yet another dream (perhaps a nightmare) that perversely is the most compelling of all my dreams. What can I say to you? I suppose it is easiest to tell you that I find being black in America one of the many manifestations of a grim joke played by a whimsical God (or of many gods) on everyone, both black and white. I look at other blacks (as I have come to look at everyone) as through a glass darkly, through a phantasmal haze with a stunning mixture of love, wonder, famil-iarity, pity, and sometimes hate. I see my father, I see my mother and sisters. I see schoolmates and friends, and everyday people who bear a striking resemblance to me. I see my old friend Shallerhorn (dead and buried at thirty-two from heartbreak, though his certificate shouts alcoholism). I see the face and form of big, black, beautiful Paddy Joe from North Carolina,

Bobby Walker from Harlem, Harry Hardisty (who, like me, was from Oklahoma and hated both his black and Indian blood). I remember good Louie Wise from the Chicago ghetto, and tough Gene Blueford from California. All the black, brown, red, tan, yellow, and white faces from time visit my memory and come alive with an appeal that is timeless. I am once again with old Shallerhorn on that dark day we crouched, afraid and unknowing, beneath a frozen shelf of ice and snow while watching with frozen bowels a dozen or more North Korean or Chinese soldiers (we never knew which, for we got the hell out of there) advance on our dug-in position.

I see little Geechie Smith, in his saki and beer stupor, pissing on our rations stored in the corner of our tent against the cold Korean wind. I see Bobby Walker (a street-fighting man from Harlem, he was); because of me, he married a girl he did not really want and fathered three unhappy babies. I see and hear our white Captain Morgan, who cared not a damn that we were black soldiers, only that we were good, bawling us out in his curiously pleasant Southern drawl. (He stepped on a mine and lost a foot and a leg.) I see and remember my white brother Neal, who always claimed to be pure Castillian. I recall with love and warmth, Charlotte, blonde and Irish, and from Biloxi. She gave me a son, and offered me a love I could not return. I see my own mahogany hands before me and in spite of my vision still do not know what it means to me or anyone else. What does it mean, really mean, to be black? I confess I do not know. I reveal to you that I am not certain it is the most important thing of all. To claim I have been forced to lead the subhuman life of a black man in America is banal. To relate to you an unending series of harsh and evil events, to catalogue and define a growing list of grievances, and to describe my anger, hopelessness, frustrations, and hatred is, to me, pointless and ineffectual. What I can relate to you is the ineffable thrill, revelation, and terror transcending that strange circumstance of birth to the inevitable discovery that no matter what one's color, one is ultimately and utterly alone in the phantasmal universe.

Alone, yes, but in Los Angeles years later I dreamed a lovely girl and loved and was loved beyond all telling. I lost her, of course, and in retrospect can tell you only that to stay with her meant abandoning the singular and absorbing dream that is living me. In San Francisco, another love appeared, and though I meant only the grand gesture, ended by taking the ultimate one-on-one experience with a woman. We both survived—never to speak to each other again, bent irrevocably out of original shape, never to be the same again, never to forget. I tell you the most telling days of my life have been spent on the streets of San Francisco. It is there, though already a man, I grew up to life. Everything came to me, everything left me. I knew friendships large—loves, hates strong enough to kill. I dreamed myself of a time of being and receiving that has remained unequaled in the lesser dreams that followed.

I rushed to life, and life rushed to me. Discovery and revelation revealed and oppressed me. I embraced the fulminating life of the street, the outcast and the narcotic. Among my friends were the liveliest of the lowly; pimps, prostitutes, addicts, thieves, alcoholics, derelicts, and the dispossessed lumpen numbered my everyday companions.

From them, from their degradation and misery, from them whose lives are distorted, twisted, and corrupt—whose lives are intensely short, hungry, and despicable—I learned how precious a thing life is, how wondrous and ephemeral is each moment of it. I learned to treasure the numbered moments of my own life, no matter how grim and unseeming they may be. From those streets and alleys of the human spirit, I came away with a compelling awareness of the sweet brevity of life. From the dung heap of the outcast life, I emerged with a vision of the sanctity of all life. I learned to embrace life, to seek out life, even at its most pathetic, and even now though I remain the briefest part of what appears to be merely a strange and interesting dream, it is my hope that dream of life will continue to intrigue me, to repel me, to fascinate me, to enthrall me, and to remind me always that as long as I dare to dream, I am.

The Endless Streetcar Ride
into the Night, and the Tinfoil Noose

Best-known as a satirist, Jean Shepherd (1921–   ) has been lampooning the American scene on radio and television and in magazines and books for years. The son of a cartoonist, he was raised in Hammond, Indiana. In his college days at Indiana State College and at the University of Maryland, he was a radio actor and disc jockey. After serving in the Signal Corps during World War II, he continued his radio and acting career in New York. He has his own weekly radio and television shows and has acted on the Broadway stage. A prolific writer, Shepherd has written articles and short stories for many publications. His shorter pieces have been collected in *The America of George Ade* (1962), *Wanda Hickey's Night of Golden Memories and Other Disasters* (1971), and *In God We Trust, All Others Pay Cash* (1966), from which the following selection is reprinted.

Mewling, puking babes. That's the way we all start. Damply clinging to someone's shoulder, burping weakly, clawing our way into life. *All* of us. Then gradually, surely, we begin to divide into two streams, all marching together up that long yellow brick road of life, but on opposite sides of the street. One crowd goes on to become the Official people, peering out at us from television screens, magazine covers. They are forever appearing in newsreels, carrying attaché cases, surrounded by banks of microphones while the world waits for their decisions and statements. And the rest of us go on to become . . . just us.

They are the Prime Ministers, the Presidents, Cabinet members, Stars, dynamic molders of the Universe, while we remain forever the onlookers, the applauders of their real lives.

Forever down in the dark dungeons of our souls we ask ourselves:

"How did they get away from me? When did I make that first misstep that took me forever to the wrong side of the street, to become eternally part of the accursed, anonymous Audience?"

It seems like one minute we're all playing around back of the garage, kicking tin cans and yelling at girls, and the next instant you find yourself doomed to exist as an office boy in the Mail Room of Life, while another ex-mewling, puking babe sends down Dicta, says "No comment" to the Press, and lives a real, genuine *Life* on the screen of the world.

Countless sufferers at this hour are spending billions of dollars and endless man hours lying on analysts' couches, trying to pinpoint the exact moment that they stepped off the track and into the bushes forever.

It all hinges on one sinister reality that is rarely mentioned, no doubt due to its implacable, irreversible inevitability. These decisions cannot be changed, no matter how many brightly cheerful, buoyantly optimistic books on HOW TO ACHIEVE A RICHER, FULLER, MORE BOUNTIFUL LIFE or SEVEN MAGIC GOLDEN KEYS TO INSTANT DYNAMIC SUCCESS or THE SECRET OF HOW TO BECOME A BILLIONAIRE we read, or how many classes are attended for instruction in handshaking, back-slapping, grinning, and making After-Dinner speeches. Joseph Stalin was not a Dale Carnegie graduate. He went all the way. It is an unpleasant truth that is swallowed, if at all, like a rancid, bitter pill. A star is a star; a numberless cipher is a numberless cipher.

Even more eerie a fact is that the Great Divide is rarely a matter of talent or personality. Or even luck. Adolf Hitler had a notoriously weak handshake. His smile was, if anything, a vapid mockery. But inevitably his star zoomed higher and higher. Cinema luminaries of the first order are rarely blessed with even the modicum of Talent, and often their physical beauty leaves much to be desired. What is the difference between Us and Them, We and They, the Big Ones and the great, teeming rabble?

There are about four times in a man's life, or a woman's, too, for that matter, when unexpectedly, from out of the darkness, the blazing carbon lamp, the cosmic searchlight of Truth shines full upon them. It is how we react to those moments that forever seals our fate. One crowd simply puts on its sunglasses, lights another cigar, and heads for the nearest plush French restaurant in the jazziest section of town, sits down and orders a drink, and ignores the whole thing. While we, the Doomed, caught in the brilliant glare of illumination, see ourselves inescapably for what we are, and from that day on skulk in the weeds, hoping no one else will spot us.

Those moments happen when we are least able to fend them off. I caught the first one full in the face when I was fourteen. The fourteenth summer is a magic one for all kids. You have just slid out of the pupa stage, leaving your old baby skin behind, and have not yet become a grizzled, hardened, tax-paying beetle. At fourteen you are made of cellophane. You curl easily and everyone can see through you.

When I was fourteen, Life was flowing through me in a deep, rich torrent of Castoria. How did I know that the first rocks were just ahead, and I was about to have my keel ripped out on the reef? Sometimes you feel as though you are alone in a rented rowboat, bailing like mad in the darkness with a leaky bailing can. It is important to know that there are at least two billion other ciphers in the same boat, bailing with the same leaky can. They all think they are alone and are crossed with an evil star. They are right.

I'm fourteen years old, in my sophomore year at high school. One day Schwartz, my purported best friend, sidled up to me edgily outside of school while we were waiting on the steps to come in after lunch. He proceeded to outline his plan:

"Helen's old man won't let me take her out on a date on Saturday night unless I get a date for her girlfriend. A double date. The old coot figures, I guess, that if there are four of us there won't be no monkey business. Well, how about it? Do you want to go on a blind date with this chick? I never seen her."

Well. For years I had this principle—absolutely *no* blind dates. I was a man of perception and taste, and life was short. But there is a time in your life when you have to stop taking and begin to give just a little. For the first time the warmth of sweet Human Charity brought the roses to my cheeks. After all, Schwartz was my friend. It was little enough to do, have a blind date with some no doubt skinny, pimply girl for your best friend. I would do it for Schwartz. He would do as much for me.

"Okay. Okay, Schwartz."

Then followed the usual ribald remarks, reckless boasting, and dirty jokes about dates in general and girls in particular. It was decided that next Saturday we would go all the way. I had a morning paper route at the time, and my life savings stood at about $1.80. I was all set to blow it on one big night.

I will never forget that particular Saturday as long as I live. The air was as soft as the finest of spun silk. The scent of lilacs hung heavy. The catalpa trees rustled in the early evening breeze from off the Lake. The inner Me itched in that nameless way, that indescribable way that only the fourteen-year-old Male fully knows.

All that afternoon I had carefully gone over my wardrobe to select the proper symphony of sartorial brilliance. That night I set out wearing my magnificent electric blue sport coat, whose shoulders were so wide that they hung out over my frame like vast, drooping eaves, so wide I had difficulty going through an ordinary door head-on. The electric blue sport coat that draped voluminously almost to my knees, its wide lapels flapping soundlessly in the slightest breeze. My pleated gray flannel slacks began just below my breastbone and indeed chafed my armpits. High-belted, cascading down finally to grasp my ankles in a vise-like grip. My tie, indeed one of my most prized possessions, had been a gift from my Aunt Glenn upon the state occasion of graduation from eighth grade. It was of a beautiful silky fabric, silvery pearly colored, four inches wide at the fulcrum, and of such a length to endanger occasionally my zipper in moments of haste. Hand-painted upon it was a magnificent blood-red snail.

I had spent fully two hours carefully arranging and rearranging my great mop of wavy hair, into which I had rubbed fully a pound and a half of Greasy Kid Stuff.

Helen and Schwartz waited on the corner under the streetlight at the streetcar stop near Junie Jo's home. Her name was Junie Jo Prewitt. I won't forget it quickly, although she has, no doubt, forgotten mine. I walked down the dark street alone, past houses set back off the street, through the darkness, past privet hedges, under elm trees, through air rich and ripe with promise. Her house stood back from the street even farther than the others. It sort of crouched in the darkness, looking out at me, kneeling. Pregnant with Girldom. A real Girlfriend house.

The first faint touch of nervousness filtered through the marrow of my skullbone as I knocked on the door of the screen-enclosed porch. No answer. I knocked again, louder. Through the murky screens I could see faint lights in the house itself. Still no answer. Then I found a small doorbell button buried in the sash. I pressed. From far off in the bowels of the house I heard two chimes "Bong" politely. It sure didn't sound like our doorbell. We had a real ripper that went off like a broken buzz saw, more of a BRRRAAAAKKK than a muffled Bong. This was a rich people's doorbell.

The door opened and there stood a real, genuine, gold-plated Father: potbelly, underwear shirt, suspenders, and all.

"Well?" he asked.

For one blinding moment of embarrassment I couldn't remember her name. After all, she was a blind date. I couldn't just say:

"I'm here to pick up some girl."

He turned back into the house and hollered:

"JUNIE JO! SOME KID'S HERE!"

"Heh, heh. . . ." I countered.

He led me into the living room. It was an itchy house, sticky stucco walls of a dull orange color, and all over the floor this Oriental rug with the design crawling around, making loops and sworls. I sat on an overstuffed chair covered in stiff green mohair that scratched even through my slacks. Little twisty bridge lamps stood everywhere. I instantly began to sweat down the back of my clean white shirt. Like I said, it was a very itchy house. It had little lamps sticking out of the walls that looked like phony candles, with phony glass orange flames. The rug started moaning to itself.

I sat on the edge of the chair and tried to talk to this Father. He was a Cub fan. We struggled under water for what seemed like an hour and a half, when suddenly I heard someone coming down the stairs. First the feet; then those legs, and there she was. She was magnificent! The greatest-looking girl I ever saw in my life! I have hit the double jackpot! And on a blind date! Great Scot!

My senses actually reeled as I clutched the arm of that bilge-green chair for support. Junie Jo Prewitt made Cleopatra look like a Girl Scout!

Five minutes later we are sitting in the streetcar, heading toward the bowling alley. I am sitting next to the most fantastic creation in the Feminine department known to Western man. There are the four of us in that long, yellow-lit streetcar. No one else was aboard; just us four. I, naturally, being a trained gentleman, sat on the aisle to protect her from candy wrappers and cigar butts and such. Directly ahead of me, also on the aisle, sat Schwartz, his arm already flung affectionately in a death grip around Helen's neck as we boomed and rattled through the night.

I casually flung my right foot up onto my left knee so that she could see my crepe-soled, perforated, wing-toed, Scotch bluchers with the two-toned laces. I started to work my famous charm on her. Casually, with my practiced offhand, cynical, cutting, sardonic humor I told her about how my Old Man had cracked the block in the Oldsmobile, how the White Sox were going to have a good year this year, how my kid brother wet his pants when he saw a snake, how I figured it was going to rain, what a great guy Schwartz was, what a good second baseman I was, how I figured I might go out for football. On and on I rolled, like Old Man River, pausing significantly for her to pick up the conversation. Nothing.

Ahead of us Schwartz and Helen were almost indistinguishable one from the other. They giggled, bit each other's ears, whispered, clasped hands, and in general made me itch even more.

From time to time Junie Jo would bend forward stiffly from the waist and say something I could never quite catch into Helen's right ear.

I told her my great story of the time that Uncle Carl lost his false teeth down the airshaft. Still nothing. Out of the corner of my eye I could see that she had her coat collar turned up, hiding most of her face as she sat silently, looking forward past Helen Weathers into nothingness.

I told her about this old lady on my paper route who chews tobacco, and roller skates in the backyard every morning. I still couldn't get through to her. Casually I inched my right arm up over the back of the seat behind her shoulders. The acid test. She leaned forward, avoiding my arm, and stayed that way.

"Heh, heh, heh. . . ."

As nonchalantly as I could, I retrieved it, battling a giant cramp in my right shoulder blade. I sat in silence for a few seconds, sweating heavily as ahead Schwartz and Helen are going at it hot and heavy.

It was then that I became aware of someone saying something to me. It was an empty car. There was no one else but us. I glanced around, and there it was. Above us a line of car cards looked down on the empty streetcar. One was speaking directly to me, to me alone.

DO YOU OFFEND?

Do I *offend?!*

With no warning, from up near the front of the car where the motorman is steering I see this thing coming down the aisle directly toward *me*. It's coming closer and closer. I can't escape it. It's this blinding, fantastic, brilliant, screaming blue light. I am spread-eagled in it. There's a pin sticking through my thorax. I see it all now.

I AM THE BLIND DATE!

ME!!

I'M the one they're being nice to!

I'm suddenly getting fatter, more itchy. My new shoes are like bowling balls with laces; thick, rubber-crepe bowling balls. My great tie that Aunt Glenn gave me is two feet wide, hanging down to the floor like some crinkly tinfoil noose. My beautiful hand-painted snail is seven feet high, sitting up on my shoulder, burping. Great Scot! It is all clear to me in the searing white light of Truth. My friend Schwartz, I can see him saying to Junie Jo:

"I got this crummy fat friend who never has a date. Let's give him a break and. . . ."

I AM THE BLIND DATE!

They are being nice to *me!* She is the one who is out on a Blind Date. A Blind Date that didn't make it.

In the seat ahead, the merriment rose to a crescendo. Helen tittered; Schwartz cackled. The marble statue next to me stared gloomily out into the darkness as our streetcar rattled on. The ride went on and on.

I AM THE BLIND DATE!

I didn't say much the rest of the night. There wasn't much to be said.

gerald brock ─────────────────────────────

The Shades of Night Were Falling, but I Got a Good Look Anyway

Born in Des Moines, Iowa, Gerald Brock (1943–   ) didn't remain anyplace for long as a child since his father, a career military man, kept being transferred—from Iowa to Missouri to Tennessee to France to Washington, D.C., and so on. Brock describes his education during those years as terrible. After graduating from high school, he tried college twice, but ended up enlisting in the army and spending most of 1968 in what he calls a state of apathy in Vietnam, splitting his time between his assignment in a communications center and the beach. On returning from service, he joined his family in Alameda, California, and enrolled at Laney College in Oakland. He later transferred to the University of California, Berkeley, on a scholarship. He would like to spend his life writing in areas of his interest and working at jobs that would add to his experience as a writer. The following essay was written for a freshman English class at Laney in response to an assignment to write about a personal prejudice.

─────────────────────────────

This is what I told her, that it's far better to squander your love than to hide it away, and that love exists only to serve itself and to be served as often as possible. I told her that people had done her a great disservice in erecting a wall around natural impulses like love by placing thousands of conditions to grow like weeds in her little garden and choke out all the sun. And I told her that love was giving, and that nongiving was nonloving, and that nonloving was nonliving. You have the right to say no, but you're really saying no to yourself, and it's not even you that is saying no; it's really a decision you were never allowed to make. If you're free, you can say yes or no and know what it is that you've lost or gained, or at least know you listened to the messages of your heart and the secret symbols of life.

I told her many things, using words like keys to open doors to dark empty rooms, hoping to find the place where she'd been locked away in her prison mind. I was basking in the warm sun of righteous purpose, words of persuasion flowing riverlike off my tongue to cleanse away the original sin of guilt. I think she listened, but didn't believe that my intentions were not completely self-serving. She said she'd think about it, but she never did.

Original publication in this volume, by permission of the author.

It had been a frustrating summer. My campaign to get C___ into bed had been going rather badly despite a few signs of encouragement. I'd exhausted all my usual routines and, after a period of self-searching, had settled into a desperate program of sincerity and honesty. I'd even raised the level of my intentions from the attainment of a brief sexual encounter to a long-term affair, which meant that I was kidding myself rather badly. Santayana defined a fanatic as "a person who redoubles his efforts after losing sight of his goals," and that's an apt definition of the pattern of thought I'd sunken into.

My infatuation with C___ was the result of an overburdened sexual preoccupation which caused me to overlook all of her obvious shortcomings. I'd gotten a little desperate after my last affair had come to a rather abrupt conclusion, and in a hasty effort to regain my sexual footing, I had violated a few canons of acceptable behavior and taste with the next few girls I took out. As a result, I carried a heavy burden of notoriety around with me. So I went through a period of masturbatory monotony and occasional drunken sprees until I met C___ and began my active pursuit of her young body. I don't know why I settled on her specifically. It's possible that opportunity was the most significant factor; it's difficult to be alone during desperate moments when you feel the need to reach out and feel something substantial in your hands. I needed acres of flesh to quiet the madness in my mind, and I'd spend hours imagining us grappling around naked together while feverishly working to make my fantasies real.

To my credit, though, I was not, even then, a completely self-serving individual. Perhaps I might be criticized for having a sexual interlude as my primary goal, but it was the only real goal I had at the time, and I was, to no small extent, interested in C___'s well-being. I wanted the relationship to be mutually satisfactory right from the beginning, and if Victorian attitudes toward sex are so prevalent as to cast me in the role of the villain, then at least credit me with the honesty of my purpose.

As previously mentioned though, I'd been having a frustrating time realizing my goal. She liked me very much, which meant that she'd go out with me all the time, put up with my eccentricities, go to the weird places I liked to go, and fend off my amorous advancements with a bemused tolerance. I remember days spent driving her around to various places, plying her with laughter and rich experiences, and formulating desperate plans of seduction. Then, later, a few minutes of encouragement in the back seat of a car or an open door would be sufficient to convince me that with patience I might yet be rewarded, but I never was.

I've gone into a somewhat lengthy presentation of our relationship to serve as a background to a specific incident. I've hoped to show that even though my motives and actions might be criticized, I was nonetheless attempting to live my philosophical convictions, and I'd credited myself with doing an admirable job, if not an altogether successful one. One night C___'s brother climbed into bed with me while I was sleeping, guestlike, on the living-room couch and attempted a seduction of his own. He was about as successful as I had been with his sister. Although he had a certain surprise advantage, coupled with my sleepy condition that refused to accept what was happening, I managed to get rid of him with a minimum of fuss, but the experience had a shattering effect on me.

I'd had an almost unconscious liking for C___'s brother that had been obscured by my fanatical devotion to his sister. We did a lot of talking together when I was a guest at their house, the three of us sitting around over coffee and getting into conversations about psychic phenomena, movies, music, and metaphysics. In no time at all, C___ would either turn on the television, begin to file her nails, or fall asleep in her chair. Even though I enjoyed these conversations, I was slightly resentful of this brother who forced me to suspend my program of seduction, and perhaps I was also aware that he was all the things that C___ was not. It's obvious to me now that he and I were very much alike and that she and I had practically nothing in common, not even a real sexual interest, for hers was always predicated on an unstated demand for permanence, and she never really trusted me, wisely crediting me with temporary interests and short-term goals.

So I rejected her brother's advances and put the episode out of my mind until a later time when I could handle it better. And now I realize that my choice, like C___'s, was made not by me, but by the same ideas that governed her rejection of my advances. If you really believe in love, then how can you say no to some of its forms just because they lie outside the realms of convention? Is a homosexual who would hate to go to bed with a woman any worse than a heterosexual who has the same revulsion in going to bed with a man, and is masturbation the only alternative to a conventional sexual relationship? I confess that I've never been sexually excited by a man, which is nothing more than an admission of my own lack of freedom of choice since I had nothing to do with the formation of feelings of extreme distaste for homosexual relationships. The infinitely worse realization is that one is not even supposed to feel love for another member of the same sex. Somehow I feel a sense of loss that I'm unable to reconcile. Obviously, it's easier to be conventional in matters of sex, and I've never really encountered a similar situation where I've had a chance to make a choice. Like C___, I was left in waiting at the altar, only partially oblivious to doors locked and bolted by the alien caretakers of our lives, with the bridegroom forever left in waiting outside.

My relationship with C___ lasted a few more weeks, long enough for me to realize that whatever my tastes, her brother would have been an infinitely better partner than she, and I couldn't carry on with that comparison in my mind. When I told her that I thought it was pointless to continue our relationship, I saw a gleam of triumph in her eyes—the confirmation that she had, after all, correctly determined my intentions, and she let me pass wordlessly out of her life.

eldridge cleaver _____

On Becoming

Eldridge Cleaver (1935–   ) was born in Arkansas, but spent most of his childhood and youth in Watts, California. He ran afoul of the law in junior high school when he was sent to a reformatory for bicycle theft. Later, in California State Prison at Soledad, he completed his high school education and read omnivorously such writers as Voltaire, Thomas Paine, Karl Marx, Richard Wright, and W. E. B. Du Bois. A year after his release, he was convicted of assault with intent to commit murder. In prison at San Quentin and Folsom, Cleaver began to examine what it means to be a black man in white America and to write pieces which were later collected in *Soul on Ice* (1968). He was paroled in 1965 with the guarantee of an editorial job on *Ramparts* magazine. In 1967 he joined the Black Panther Party and became its Minister of Information. He ran for President of the United States in 1968, a candidate of the Peace and Freedom Party, a coalition of the New Left and radical minority organizations. Because he was involved in a shootout with Oakland, California, police earlier that year, his parole was rescinded late in 1968. Rather than return to prison, Cleaver went underground and surfaced in Algeria, where he has remained. In 1969 Cleaver's *Post-Prison Writings and Speeches* was published. "On Becoming" is one of the essays in *Soul on Ice.*

_____

Folsom Prison
June 25, 1965

Nineteen fifty-four, when I was eighteen years old, is held to be a crucial turning point in the history of the Afro-American—for the U.S.A. as a whole— the year segregation was outlawed by the U.S. Supreme Court. It was also a crucial year for me because on June 18, 1954, I began serving a sentence in state prison for possession of marijuana.

The Supreme Court decision was only one month old when I entered prison, and I do not believe that I had even the vaguest idea of its importance or historical significance. But later, the acrimonious controversy ignited by the end of the separate-but-equal doctrine was to have a profound effect on me. This controversy awakened me to my position in America and I began to form a concept of what it meant to be black in white America.

Of course I'd always known that I was black, but I'd never really stopped to take stock of what I was involved in. I met life as an individual and took my chances. Prior to 1954, we lived in an atmosphere of novocain. Negroes found it necessary, in order to maintain whatever sanity they could, to remain somewhat aloof and detached from "the problem." We accepted indignities and the mechanics of the apparatus of oppression without reacting by sitting-in or holding mass demonstrations. Nurtured by the fires of the controversy over segregation, I was soon aflame with indignation over my newly discovered social status, and inwardly I turned away from America with horror, disgust and outrage.

In Soledad state prison, I fell in with a group of young blacks who, like myself, were in vociferous rebellion against what we perceived as a continuation of slavery on a higher plane. We cursed everything American—including baseball and hot dogs. All respect we may have had for politicians, preachers, lawyers, governors, Presidents, senators, congressmen was utterly destroyed as we watched them temporizing and compromising over right and wrong, over legality and illegality, over constitutionality and unconstitutionality. We knew that in the end what they were clashing over was us, what to do with the blacks, and whether or not to start treating us as human beings. I despised all of them.

The segregationists were condemned out of hand, without even listening to their lofty, finely woven arguments. The others I despised for wasting time in debates with the segregationists: why not just crush them, put them in prison—they were defying the law, weren't they? I defied the law and they put me in prison. So why not put those dirty mothers in prison too? I had gotten caught with a shopping bag full of marijuana, a shopping bag full of love—I was in love with the weed and I did not for one minute think that anything was wrong with getting high. I had been getting high for four or five years and was convinced, with the zeal of a crusader, that marijuana was superior to lush—yet the rulers of the land seemed all to be lushes. I could not see how they were more justified in drinking than I was in blowing the gage. I was a grasshopper, and it was natural that I felt myself to be unjustly imprisoned.

While all this was going on, our group was espousing atheism. Unsophisticated and not based on any philosophical rationale, our atheism was pragmatic. I had come to believe that there is no God; if there is, men do not know anything about him. Therefore, all religions were phony—which made all preachers and priests, in our eyes, fakers, including the ones scurrying around the prison who, curiously, could put in a good word for you with the Almighty Creator of the universe but could not get anything down with the warden or parole board—they could usher you through the Pearly Gates *after you were dead,* but not through the prison gate *while you were still alive and kicking.* Besides, men of the cloth who work in prison have an ineradicable stigma attached to them in the eyes of convicts because they escort condemned men into the gas chamber. Such men of God are powerful arguments in favor of atheism. Our atheism was a source of enormous pride to me. Later on, I bolstered our arguments by reading Thomas Paine and his devastating critique of Christianity in particular and organized religion in general.

Through reading I was amazed to discover how confused people were. I had thought that, out there beyond the horizon of my own ignorance, unanimity existed, that even though I myself didn't know what was happening in the universe, other people certainly did. Yet here I was discovering that the whole U.S.A. was in a chaos of disagreement over segregation/integration. In these circumstances I decided that the only safe thing for me to do was go for myself. It became clear that it was possible for me to take the initiative: instead of simply *reacting* I could *act.* I could unilaterally—whether anyone agreed with me or not—repudiate all allegiances, morals, values—even while continuing to exist within this society. My mind would be free and no power in the universe could force me to accept something if I didn't want to. But I would take my own sweet time. That, too, was a part of my new freedom. I would accept nothing until it was proved that it was good—for me. I became an extreme iconoclast. Any affirmative assertion made by anyone around me became a target for tirades of criticism and denunciation.

This little game got good to me and I got good at it. I attacked all forms of piety, loyalty, and sentiment: marriage, love, God, patriotism, the Constitution, the founding fathers, law, concepts of right-wrong-good-evil, all forms of ritualized and conventional behavior. As I pranced about, club in hand, seeking new idols to smash, I encountered really for the first time in my life, with any seriousness, The Ogre, rising up before me in a mist. I discovered, with alarm, that The Ogre possessed a tremendous and dreadful power over me, and I didn't understand this power or why I was at its mercy. I tried to repudiate The Ogre, root it out of my heart as I had done God, Constitution, principles, morals, and values—but The Ogre had its claws buried in the core of my being and refused to let go. I fought frantically to be free, but The Ogre only mocked me and sank its claws deeper into my soul. I knew then that I had found an important key, that if I conquered The Ogre and broke its power over me I would be free. But I also knew that it was a race against time and that if I did not win I would certainly be broken and destroyed. I, a black man, confronted The Ogre—the white woman.

In prison, those things withheld from and denied to the prisoner become precisely what he wants most of all, of course. Because we were locked up in our cells before darkness fell, I used to lie awake at night racked by painful craving to take a leisurely stroll under the stars, or to go to the beach, to drive a car on a freeway, to grow a beard, or to make love to a woman.

Since I was not married conjugal visits would not have solved my problem. I therefore denounced the idea of conjugal visits as inherently unfair; single prisoners needed and deserved *action* just as married prisoners did. I advocated establishing a system under Civil Service whereby salaried women would minister to the needs of those prisoners who maintained a record of good behavior. If a married prisoner preferred his own wife, that would be his right. Since California was not about to inaugurate either conjugal visits or the Civil Service, one could advocate either with equal enthusiasm and with the same result: nothing.

This may appear ridiculous to some people. But it was very real to me and as urgent as the need to breathe, because I was in my bull stage and lack of access to females was absolutely a form of torture. I suffered. My mistress at the time of my arrest, the beautiful and lonely wife of a serviceman stationed overseas, died unexpectedly three weeks after I entered prison; and the rigid, dehumanized rules governing correspondence between prisoners and free people prevented me from corresponding with other young ladies I knew. It left me without any contact with females except those in my family.

In the process of enduring my confinement, I decided to get myself a pin-up girl to paste on the wall of my cell. I would fall in love with her and lavish my affections upon her. She, a symbolic representative of the forbidden tribe of women, would sustain me until I was free. Out of the center of *Esquire*, I married a voluptuous bride. Our marriage went along swell for a time: no quarrels, no complaints. And then, one evening when I came in from school, I was shocked and enraged to find that the guard had entered my cell, ripped my sugar from the wall, torn her into little pieces, and left the pieces floating in the commode: it was like seeing a dead body floating in a lake. Giving her a proper burial, I flushed the commode. As the saying goes, I sent her to Long Beach. But I was genuinely beside myself with anger: almost every cell, excepting those of the homosexuals, had a pin-up girl on the wall and the guards didn't bother them. Why, I asked the guard the next day, had he singled me out for special treatment?

"Don't you know we have a rule against pasting up pictures on the walls?" he asked me.

"Later for the rules," I said. "You know as well as I do that that rule is not enforced."

"Tell you what," he said, smiling at me (the smile put me on my guard), "I'll compromise with you: get yourself a colored girl for a pinup—no white women—and I'll let it stay up. Is that a deal?"

I was more embarrassed than shocked. He was laughing in my face. I called him two or three dirty names and walked away. I can still recall his big moon-face, grinning at me over yellow teeth. The disturbing part about the whole incident was that a terrible feeling of guilt came over me as I realized that I had chosen the picture of the white girl over the available pictures of black girls. I tried to rationalize it away, but I was fascinated by the truth involved. Why hadn't I thought about it in this light before? So I took hold of the question and began to inquire into my feelings. Was it true, did I really prefer white girls over black? The conclusion was clear and inescapable: I did. I decided to check out my friends on this point and it was easy to determine, from listening to their general conversation, that the white woman occupied a peculiarly prominent place in all of our frames of reference. With what I have learned since then, this all seems terribly elementary now. But at the time, it was a tremendously intriguing adventure of discovery.

One afternoon, when a large group of Negroes was on the prison yard shooting the breeze, I grabbed the floor and posed the question: which did they prefer, white women or black? Some said Japanese women were their favorite, others said Chinese, some said European women, others said Mexican women—they all stated a preference, and they generally freely admitted their dislike for black women.

"I don't want nothing black but a Cadillac," said one.

"If money was black I wouldn't want none of it," put in another.

A short little stud, who was a very good lightweight boxer with a little man's complex that made him love to box heavyweights, jumped to his feet. He had a yellowish complexion and we called him Butterfly.

"All you niggers are sick!" Butterfly spat out. "I don't like no stinking white woman. My grandma is a white woman and I don't even like her!"

But it just so happened that Butterfly's crime partner was in the crowd, and after Butterfly had his say, his crime partner said, "Aw, sit on down and quit that lying, lil o' chump. What about that gray girl in San Jose who had your nose wide open? Did you like her, or were you just running after her with your tongue hanging out of your head because you hated her?"

Partly because he was embarrassed and partly because his crime partner was a heavyweight, Butterfly flew into him. And before we could separate them and disperse, so the guard would not know who had been fighting, Butterfly bloodied his crime partner's nose. Butterfly got away but, because of the blood, his crime partner got caught. I ate dinner with Butterfly that evening and questioned him sharply about his attitude toward white women. And after an initial evasiveness he admitted that the white woman bugged him too. "It's a sickness," he said. "All our lives we've had the white woman dangled before our eyes like a carrot on a stick before a donkey: look but don't touch." (In 1958, after I had gone out on parole and was returned to San Quentin as a parole violator with a new charge, Butterfly was still there. He had become a Black Muslim and was chiefly responsible for teaching me the Black Muslim philosophy. Upon his release from San Quentin, Butterfly joined the Los Angeles Mosque, advanced rapidly through the ranks, and

CHAPTER ONE / *Self-Discovery*

is now a full-fledged minister of one of Elijah Muhammad's mosques in another city. He successfully completed his parole, got married—to a very black girl—and is doing fine.)

From our discussion, which began that evening and has never yet ended, we went on to notice how thoroughly, as a matter of course, a black growing up in America is indoctrinated with the white race's standard of beauty. Not that the whites made a conscious, calculated effort to do this, we thought, but since they constituted the majority the whites brainwashed the blacks by the very processes the whites employed to indoctrinate themselves with their own group standards. It intensified my frustrations to know that I was indoctrinated to see the white woman as more beautiful and desirable than my own black woman. It drove me into books seeking light on the subject. In Richard Wright's *Native Son*, I found Bigger Thomas and a keen insight into the problem.

My interest in this area persisted undiminished and then, in 1955, an event took place in Mississippi which turned me inside out: Emmett Till, a young Negro down from Chicago on a visit, was murdered, allegedly for flirting with a white woman. He had been shot, his head crushed from repeated blows with a blunt instrument, and his badly decomposed body was recovered from the river with a heavy weight on it. I was, of course, angry over the whole bit, but one day I saw in a magazine a picture of the white woman with whom Emmett Till was said to have flirted. While looking at the picture, I felt that little tension in the center of my chest I experience when a woman appeals to me. I was disgusted and angry with myself. Here was a woman who had caused the death of a black, possibly because, when he looked at her, he also felt the same tensions of lust and desire in his chest—and probably for the same general reasons that I felt them. It was all unacceptable to me. I looked at the picture again and again, and in spite of everything and against my will and the hate I felt for the woman and all that she represented, she appealed to me. I flew into a rage at myself, at America, at white women, at the history that had placed those tensions of lust and desire in my chest.

Two days later, I had a "nervous breakdown." For several days I ranted and raved against the white race, against white women in particular, against white America in general. When I came to myself, I was locked in a padded cell with not even the vaguest memory of how I got there. All I could recall was an eternity of pacing back and forth in the cell, preaching to the unhearing walls.

I had several sessions with a psychiatrist. His conclusion was that I hated my mother. How he arrived at this conclusion I'll never know, because he knew nothing about my mother; and when he'd ask me questions I would answer him with absurd lies. What revolted me about him was that he had heard me denouncing the whites, yet each time he interviewed me he deliberately guided the conversation back to my family life, to my childhood. That in itself was all right, but he deliberately blocked all my attempts to bring out the racial question, and he made it clear that he was not interested in my attitude toward whites. This was a Pandora's box he did not care to open. After I ceased my diatribes against the whites, I was let out of the hospital, back into the general inmate population just as if nothing had happened. I continued to brood over these events and over the dynamics of race relations in America.

During this period I was concentrating my reading in the field of economics. Having previously dabbled in the theories and writings of Rousseau, Thomas Paine, and Voltaire, I had added a little polish to my iconoclastic stance, without, however, bothering too much to understand their affirmative positions. In economics, because everybody seemed to find it necessary to attack and condemn Karl Marx in their writings, I sought out his books, and although he kept me with a headache, I took him for my authority. I was not prepared to understand him, but I was able to see in him a thoroughgoing critique and condemnation of capitalism. It was like taking medicine for me to find that, indeed, American capitalism deserved all the hatred and contempt that I felt for it in my heart. This had a positive, stabilizing effect upon me—to an extent because I was not about to become stable—and it diverted me from my previous preoccupation: morbid broodings on the black man and the white woman. Pursuing my readings into the history of socialism, I read, with very little understanding, some of the passionate, exhortatory writings of Lenin; and I fell in love with Bakunin and Nechayev's *Catechism of the Revolutionist*—the principles of which, along with some of Machiavelli's advice, I sought to incorporate into my own behavior. I took the *Catechism* for my bible and, standing on a one-man platform that had nothing to do with the reconstruction of society, I began consciously incorporating these principles into my daily life, to employ tactics of ruthlessness in my dealings with everyone with whom I came into contact. And I began to look at white America through these new eyes.

Somehow I arrived at the conclusion that, as a matter of principle, it was of paramount importance for me to have an antagonistic, ruthless attitude toward white women. The term *outlaw* appealed to me and at the time my parole date was drawing near, I considered myself to be mentally free—I was an "outlaw." I had stepped outside of the white man's law, which I repudiated with scorn and self-satisfaction. I became a law unto myself—my own legislature, my own supreme court, my own executive. At the moment I walked out of the prison gate, my feelings toward white women in general could be summed up in the following lines:

To a White Girl

I love you
Because you're white,
Not because you're charming
Or bright.
Your whiteness
Is a silky thread
Snaking through my thoughts
In redhot patterns
Of lust and desire.

I hate you
Because you're white.
Your white meat
Is nightmare food.
White is
The skin of Evil.
You're my Moby Dick,
White Witch,
Symbol of the rope and hanging tree,
Of the burning cross.

Loving you thus
And hating you so,
My heart is torn in two.
Crucified.

I became a rapist. To refine my technique and *modus operandi*, I started out by practicing on black girls in the ghetto—in the black ghetto where dark and vicious deeds appear not as aberrations or deviations from the norm, but as part of the sufficiency of the Evil of a day—and when I considered myself smooth enough, I crossed the tracks and sought out white prey. I did this consciously, deliberately, willfully, methodically—though looking back I see that I was in a frantic, wild, and completely abandoned frame of mind.

Rape was an insurrectionary act. It delighted me that I was defying and trampling upon the white man's law, upon his system of values, and that I was defiling his women—and this point, I believe, was the most satisfying to me because I was very resentful over the historical fact of how the white man has used the black woman. I felt I was getting revenge. From the site of the act of rape, consternation spreads outwardly in concentric circles. I wanted to send waves of consternation throughout the white race. Recently, I came upon a quotation from one of LeRoi Jones' poems, taken from his book *The Dead Lecturer:*

A cult of death need of the simple striking arm under the street lamp. The cutters from under their rented earth. Come up, black dada nihilismus. Rape the white girls. Rape their fathers. Cut the mothers' throats.

I have lived those lines and I know that if I had not been apprehended I would have slit some white throats. There are, of course, many young blacks out there right now who are slitting white throats and raping the white girl. They are not doing this because they read LeRoi Jones' poetry, as some of his critics seem to believe. Rather, LeRoi is expressing the funky facts of life.

After I returned to prison, I took a long look at myself and, for the first time in my life, admitted that I was wrong, that I had gone astray—astray not so much from the white man's law as from being human, civilized—for I could not approve the act of rape. Even though I had some insight into my own motivations, I did not feel justified. I lost my self-respect. My pride as a man dissolved and my whole fragile moral structure seemed to collapse, completely shattered.

That is why I started to write. To save myself.

I realized that no one could save me but myself. The prison authorities were both uninterested and unable to help me. I had to seek out the truth and unravel the snarled web of my motivations. I had to find out who I am and what I want to be, what type of man I should be, and what I could do to become the best of which I was capable. I understood that what had happened to me had also happened to countless other blacks and it would happen to many, many more.

I learned that I had been taking the easy way out, running away from problems. I also learned that it is easier to do evil than it is to do good. And I have been terribly impressed by the youth of America, black and white. I am proud of them because they have reaffirmed my faith in humanity. I have come to feel what must be love for the young people of America and I want to be part of the good and greatness that they want for all people. From my prison cell, I have watched America slowly coming awake. It is not fully awake yet, but there is soul in the air and everywhere I see beauty. I have watched the sit-ins, the freedom raids, the Mississippi Blood Summers, demonstrations all over the country, the FSM movement, the teach-ins, and the mounting protest over Lyndon Strangelove's foreign policy—all of this, the thousands of little details, show me it is time to straighten up and fly right. That is why I decided to concentrate on my writings and efforts in this area. We are a very sick country—I, perhaps, am sicker than most. But I accept that. I told you in the beginning that I am extremist by nature—so it is only right that I should be extremely sick.

I was very familiar with the Eldridge who came to prison, but that Eldridge no longer exists. And the one I am now is in some ways a stranger to me. You may find this difficult to understand but it is very easy for one in prison to lose his sense of self. And if he has been undergoing all kinds of extreme, involved, and unregulated changes, then he ends up not knowing who he is. Take the point of being attractive to women. You can easily see how a man can lose his arrogance or certainty on that point while in prison! When he's in the free world, he gets constant feedback on how he looks from the number of female heads he turns when he walks down the street. In prison he gets only hate-stares and sour frowns. Years and years of bitter looks. Individuality is not nourished in prison, neither by the officials nor by the convicts. It is a deep hole out of which to climb.

What must be done, I believe, is that all these problems—particularly the sickness between the white woman and the black man—must be brought out into the open, dealt with and resolved. I know that the black man's sick attitude toward the white woman is a revolutionary sickness: it keeps him perpetually out of harmony with the system that is oppressing him. Many whites flatter themselves with the idea that the Negro male's lust and desire for the white dream girl is purely an esthetic attraction, but nothing could be farther from the truth. His motivation is often of such a bloody, hateful, bitter, and malignant nature that whites would really be hard pressed to find it flattering. I have discussed these points with prisoners who were convicted of rape, and their motivations are very plain. But they are very reluctant to discuss these things with white men who, by and large, make up the prison staffs. I believe that in the experience of these men lies the knowledge and wisdom that must be utilized to help other youngsters who are heading in the same direction. I think all of us, the entire nation, will be better off if we bring it all out front. A lot of people's feelings will be hurt, but that is the price that must be paid.

It may be that I can harm myself by speaking frankly and directly, but I do not care about that at all. Of course I want to get out of prison, badly, but I shall get out some day. I am more concerned with what I am going to be after I get out. I know that by following the course which I have charted I will find my salvation. If I had followed the path laid down for me by the officials, I'd undoubtedly have long since been out of prison—but I'd be less of a man. I'd be weaker and less certain of where I want to go, what I want to do, and how to go about it.

The price of hating other human beings is loving oneself less.

A Trip to Esalen Institute—
Joy Is the Prize

Born in Detroit, Leo E. Litwak (1924–   ) is currently a professor of English and creative writing at San Francisco State University. An award-winning writer of fiction, he has also written articles for such periodicals as *Look,* the *New York Times Magazine,* and *Esquire.* Litwak has published two novels, *To the Hanging Gardens* (1964) and *Waiting for the News* (1969). His latest book, co-written with his colleague Herbert Wilner, is *College Days in Earthquake Country* (1972), a nonfiction account of the student strike at San Francisco State in 1968. The following essay originally appeared in the *New York Times Magazine,* December 30, 1967.

Big Sur is an eighty-mile stretch of California coast below the Monterey Peninsula. It is approximately midway between Los Angeles and San Francisco and difficult of access from either direction. Before the coastal highway was completed in 1936, the shore was accessible only by foot. The Los Padres National Forest, one of the largest preserves in the country, extends thirty miles inland and is two hundred miles long; it occupies most of the area. Not much land is available for private ownership. There are only three hundred residents. The rugged terrain of Los Padres includes redwood canyons, barren mountain ranges, desert flora, thick forests. It is the province of mountain lions and wild boar.

Stone cliffs rise two thousand feet above the ocean. Beyond a wedge of meadow, the steeply inclined hillside begins. For great distances there is no meadow at all and the serpentine coastal highway hangs on the cliffside. It is a two-lane road, sometimes impassable after heavy rains. The fog bank wavers offshore. When it sweeps in, the traveler faces an uncanny trip, guided entirely by the few white dashes of the center line that are visible. With hairpin turns, sharp rises and declines, the road can be dangerous in bad weather. On clear days when the setting sun ignites dust particles on your windshield you are forced to drive blind for dangerous seconds.

Nonetheless, four thousand people traveled this road last year, in disregard of weather, aimed toward the Esalen Institute, famous until a few years ago under a different name, Big Sur Hot Springs. These are unlikely adventurers. They are doctors, social workers, clinical psychologists, teachers, students, business executives, engineers, housewives—or just fun lovers who have come to take the baths.

Big Sur Hot Springs was originally renowned as the Eden discovered by Henry Miller and Jack Kerouac. Joan Baez once lived there. The springs were purchased in 1910 from a man named Slade by Dr. Henry C. Murphy of Salinas. It was Dr. Murphy's intention to establish a health spa. In order to use the mineral waters he brought in two bathtubs by fishing sloop. They were hauled up the cliff and placed on a ledge at the source of the springs. But because of their inaccessibility, the springs did not flourish as a spa. Not until Dr. Murphy's grandson, Michael, assumed operation of the property in the mid-1950's did the baths begin to receive attention—attention that has grown with the development of Esalen Institute.

Michael Murphy at thirty-seven appears to be in his early twenties. He is slender and boyish and has a marvelous smile. I took part in a panel discussion at Hot Springs some years ago and I was not impressed either by the topic, my performance or the audience. I did enjoy the baths. I had misgivings about Murphy's program, yet none about him. He seemed to me generous, charming, innocent, credulous, enthusiastic and enormously sympathetic. A Stanford alumnus who had done some graduate work in psychology and philosophy, he had recently returned from an eighteen-month study of the art of meditation at the Aurobindo Ashram in Pondicherry, India, and he devoted a considerable part of each day to meditation. I believe he had—and still has—in mind some great mission, based on his Indian experience. I am not quite sure what the scope of his mission is. A friend of his told me: "Mike wants to turn on the world." Esalen Institute is his instrument for doing so. It has come a long way from the shoddy panels of a few years ago. Its spreading impact may seriously affect our methods of therapy and education.

In the course of a year, almost a thousand professional persons—social workers, psychiatrists, clinical psychologists—enroll in Esalen workshops. Close to seven hundred psychotherapists have been trained to administer techniques devised by staff members—Frederick Perls, Virginia Satir, Bernard Gunther and William Schutz. These techniques have been demonstrated at hospitals, universities and medical schools. This year Esalen has opened a San Francisco extension which in the first two months of operation has attracted an attendance in excess of ten thousand, offering the same workshops and seminars that are available at Big Sur. Esalen-type communities have begun to appear throughout the country, in Atlanta, Chicago, Los Angeles, Cleveland, La Jolla.

One has even appeared in Vancouver, Canada. Murphy offers advice and help, and permits use of his mailing list.

Consider some offerings of the Esalen winter brochure. Seminars led by Alan Watts, the Zen interpreter, and Susan Sontag, the camp interpreter. Workshops for professional therapists conducted by Frederick Perls, an early associate of Freud and Wilhelm Reich and a founder of Gestalt therapy. A lecture panel including the psychologist Carl Rogers and Herman Kahn, the "thinking about the unthinkable" man. Some of the titles are: "Kinetic Theater," "Psychotechnics," "Do You Do It? Or Does It Do You?", "Dante's Way to the Stars," "Creativity and the Daimonic," "On Deepening the Marriage Encounter," "Tibetan Book of the Dead," "Anxiety and Tension Control," "Racial Confrontation as a Transcendental Experience."

What principle guides a mélange that consists of dance workshops, therapy workshops, sensory-awareness experiments, the Tibetan Book of the Dead, Herman Kahn, Carl Rogers, Frederick Perls and Susan Sontag?

Esalen's vice president, George B. Leonard, has written a general statement of purpose. He says: "We believe that all men somehow possess a divine potentiality; that ways may be worked out—specific, systematic ways—to help, not the few, but the many toward a vastly expanded capacity to learn, to love, to feel deeply, to create. We reject the tired dualism that seeks God and human potentialities by denying the joys of the senses, the immediacy of unpostponed life." The programs, he says, are aimed toward "the joys of the senses."

I had signed up for a workshop led by Dr. William Schutz, a group therapist who has taught at Harvard and the Albert Einstein College of Medicine, among other institutions, and has served on the staff of the National Training Laboratories Interne Training Program at Bethel, Maine. His latest book, *Joy,* was published in 1967 by Grove Press.

In the brochure description of Dr. Schutz's workshop I read a warning that the experience would be more than verbal: "An encounter workshop with body movements, sensory awareness, fantasy experiments, psychodrama. Developing the ability to experience joy is the workshop's guiding theme."

Joy as the prize of a five-day workshop?

"How can we speak of joy," Leonard has written, "on this dark and suffering planet? How can we speak of anything else? We have heard enough of despair."

It was easy enough to dismiss the language. It seemed naive to promise so great a reward for so small an investment. Joy for $175 seemed cheap at the price, especially since *The New York Times* was paying. I did have considerable anxieties that some of those "body movements" might be humiliating. And what precisely was meant by "sensory awareness"?

Esalen has changed considerably since my previous visit. Rows of new cabins are ranged along terraces on the hillside. The lodge is located at the bottom of a steep incline, in a meadow. The meadow is perhaps two hundred yards deep and ends at the cliff edge. The Pacific Ocean is a hundred and fifty feet below. A staff of fifty operates the kitchen, supervises the baths, cleans the cabins and garden and works on construction.

I passed hippy laborers, stripped to the waist, long hair flowing, operating with pick and shovel. Dreamy girls in long gowns played flutes near the pool.

I was somewhat put off by what I considered to be an excessive show of affection. Men hugged men. Men hugged women. Women hugged women. These were not hippies, but older folks, like myself, who had come for the workshop. People flew into one another's arms, and it wasn't my style at all.

After dinner, thirty of us met in the gallery for our first session. We began our excursion toward joy at 9:00 P.M. of a Sunday in a woodsy room on a balmy, starry night.

William Schutz, solidly built, with bald head and muzzle beard, began by telling us that in the course of the workshop we would come to dangerous ground. At such times we ought not to resist entering, for in this area lay our greatest prospect for self-transcendence. He told us to avoid verbal manipulations and to concentrate on our feelings.

We began with exercises. A fat lady in leotards directed us to be absurd. We touched our noses with our tongues. We jumped. We ran. We clutched one another, made faces at one another. Afterward, we gathered in groups of five and were given an ambiguous instruction to discover one another by touching in any way we found agreeable. I crouched in front of a strange-looking young man with an underslung jaw and powerful shoulders. I tried unlocking his legs and he glared at me.

When Schutz asked each group of five to select one couple that seemed least close, the young man with the underslung jaw selected me. The hostile pairs were then requested to stand at opposite diagonals of the room and approach each other. They were to do whatever they felt like doing when they met in the center of the room. A burly middle-aged man marched toward a petite lady. They met, they paused, stared, then suddenly embraced. The next couple, two husky men, both frozen rigid, confronted each other, stared, then also embraced. The young man and I came next. We started at opposite diagonals. We met in the center of the room. I found myself looking into the meanest, coldest eyes I had ever seen. He pressed his hands to his sides, and it was clear to me that we were not going to embrace. I reached for his hand to shake it. He jerked free. I put my hand on his shoulder; he shrugged me off. We continued staring and finally returned to our group.

There was a general discussion of this encounter. Some feared we might start fighting. Nothing, of course, was farther from my mind. I had gone out, intending to play their game and suddenly found myself staring at a lunatic. He had very mean, cold eyes, a crazy shape to his jaw, lips so grim that his ill-feeling was unmistakable. Back in our group he said to me in a raspy, shrill voice: "You thought I was going to bat you in the face; that's why you turned away." There was a slurred quality to his speech, and it occurred to me that I might have triggered off a madman. I denied that I had turned away and I was challenged to stare him down. I was annoyed that I had been forced into something so silly.

We proceeded, on the basis of our first impressions, to give one another names, which we kept for the duration of the workshop. My nemesis accepted the name of Rebel. There was a plump, lovely girl we called Kate. A silent, powerful man with spectacles we named Clark. Our fat group leader received the name of Brigitte. A lumpy solemn man with thick spectacles we named Gary. An elegant, trim middle-aged woman we named Sheba. A buxom, mournful woman with long hair became Joan. A jovial middle-aged pipe smoker with a Jean Hersholt manner we named Hans. A fierce moustached swaggerer in Bermuda shorts was Daniel. A quiet man with a little boy's face we named Victor. I was named Lionel. We were addressed by these names at all times.

I considered this renaming of ourselves a naive attempt to create an atmosphere free of any outside reference. Many of the techniques impressed me as naive. It seemed tactless and obvious to ask so blunt and vague a question as: "What are you feeling?" Yet what happened in the course of five days was that the obvious became clarified. Clichés became significant.

I found myself discovering what had always been under my nose. I had not known how my body felt under conditions of tension or fear or grief. I discovered that I was numb. I had all sorts of tricks for avoiding encounter. I didn't particularly like to be touched. I avoided looking strangers in the eye. I took pride in my coolness and trickery. I didn't believe one should give oneself away. It seemed to me a virtue to appear cool, to be relatively immune to feeling, so that I could receive shocks without appearing to. I considered it important to keep up appearances. I'm no longer proud of what I now believe to be an incapacity rather than a talent.

I thought my group rather dull. I saw no great beauty and a great deal of weakness. I felt somewhat superior, since I was there on assignment, not by choice. I hated and feared Reb.

But in the next five days, I became enormously fond of these apparently uninteresting strangers. We encountered one another in violent and intimate ways, and I could no longer dismiss them.

I was convinced that Rebel was insane. He opened our second meeting with gratuitous insults. He referred to me as "Charley Goodguy." When

Brigitte, the leader of our group, told him not to think in stereotypes, he sneered at her: "Why don't you shut up, Fats?" It is difficult to convey the nastiness of his tone—an abrasive, jeering quality.

Daniel exploded. He called Rebel a shark and a rattlesnake. He said he wanted to quit the group because he despised this frightening, violent kid. "You scare me," he told Reb. "It's people like you who are responsible for Vietnam and Auschwitz. You're a monster and you're going to suck up all the energy of this group and it's not worth it. I want to get out."

I told Daniel his response seemed excessive. Vietnam and Auschwitz? "He's a little hostile," I said.

Reb didn't want any favors from me. "Hostile?" he sneered. "Say, I bet I know what you are. You sound to me like a professor. Or a pawnbroker. Which are you, a professor or a pawnbroker?"

Schutz intervened. He said to me and Rebel: "I feel you have something going. Why don't you have it out?" He suggested that we arm wrestle, an innocuous contest, but under the circumstances, there seemed to be a great deal invested in winning or losing. My arm felt numb, and there was some trembling in my thighs. I feared I might not have all my strength, and Rebel appeared to be a powerful kid.

I pinned him so easily, however, that the group accused him of having quit. Daniel was jubilant: "You're a loser. You're trying to get clobbered."

Rebel was teased into trying again. On the second trial, he pressed my left arm down and demanded a rematch with the right hand. We remained locked together for close to twenty minutes. It was unbearable. I lost all sensation in my hand and arm. I willed my hand not to yield. Finally, I hoped he would press me down and get it over with. It ended when Rebel squirmed around and braced his foot against the wall and the contest was called.

Daniel was delighted by the outcome. He felt as though I had won something for him. Schutz asked: "Why don't *you* wrestle Reb?" Daniel despised violence. He probably would lose and he didn't want to give that monster the satisfaction of a victory. Violence was right up that shark's alley. He refused to play his games. Nonetheless, Daniel was on the ground with Rebel a moment later, beet red with strain, trembling down to his calves. Rebel raised his elbow, pressed Daniel down and the match was called off. Daniel leaped to his feet, circled the room. He suddenly charged Rebel, who was seated, and knocked him from his chair. He then rushed at Schutz, yelling: "It's you I hate, you bastard, for making me do this." Schutz did not flinch, and Daniel backed off. I could see that his impulse was histrionic. I felt sorry for Reb, who mumbled: "I copped out. I should have hit him."

Reb later presented a different guise. Far from being an idiot, he was an extremely precocious twenty-year-old computer engineer, self-taught in the humanities. His father had abandoned the family when he was a child. His mother was a cold customer—never a sign of feeling. He didn't know where he stood with her. She taunted him in the same abrasive style which he tried with us.

Reb suffered sexual agonies that had brought him several hundred miles in search of a solution. He considered himself perverse and contemptible, the only impotent twenty-year-old kid in the world. He admitted he found women repugnant as sexual objects, and it was hardly surprising that his crude advances were rebuffed. He admitted that his strategy had been to strike out in hope that someone would strike back so that he might *feel.* He was boyish and affectionate outside the group.

My feeling for him underwent a complete reversal. He began to impress me as an intelligent kid, trying with great courage to repair terrible injuries. The monster I had seen simply vanished.

I never anticipated the effect of these revelations, as one after another of these strangers expressed his grief and was eased. I woke up one night and felt as if everything were changed. I felt as if I were about to weep. The following morning the feeling was even more intense.

Brigitte and I walked down to the cliff edge. We lay beneath a tree. She could see that I was close to weeping. I told her that I'd been thinking about my numbness, which I traced to the war. I tried to keep the tears down. I felt vulnerable and unguarded. I felt that I was about to lose all my secrets and I was ready to let them go. Not being guarded, I had no need to put anyone down, and I felt what it was to be unarmed. I could look anyone in the eyes and my eyes were open.

That night I said to Daniel: "Why do you keep diverting us with intellectual arguments? I see suffering in your eyes. You give me a glimpse of it, then you turn it off. Your eyes go dead and the intellectual stuff bores me. I feel that's part of your strategy."

Schutz suggested that the two of us sit in the center of the room and talk to each other. I told Daniel that I was close to surrender. I wanted to let go. I felt near to my grief. I wanted to release it and be purged. Daniel asked about my marriage and my work. Just when he hit a nerve, bringing me near the release I wanted, he began to speculate on the tragedy of the human condition. I told him: "You're letting me off and I don't want to be let off."

Schutz asked if I would be willing to take a fantasy trip.

It was late afternoon and the room was already dark. I lay down, Schutz beside me, and the group gathered around. I closed my eyes. Schutz asked me to imagine myself very tiny and to imagine that tiny self entering my own body. He wanted me to describe the trip.

CHAPTER ONE / *Self-Discovery*

I saw an enormous statue of myself, lying in a desert, mouth open as if I were dead. I entered my mouth. I climbed down my gullet, entering it as if it were a manhole. I climbed into my chest cavity. Schutz asked me what I saw. "It's empty," I said. "There's nothing here." I was totally absorbed by the effort to visualize entering myself and lost all sense of the group. I told Schutz there was no heart in my body. Suddenly, I felt a tremendous pressure in my chest, as if tears were going to explode. He told me to go to the vicinity of the heart and report what I saw. There, on a ledge of the chest wall, near where the heart should have been, I saw a baby buggy. He asked me to look into it. I didn't want to, because I feared I might weep, but I looked, and I saw a doll. He asked me to touch it. I was relieved to discover that it was only a doll. Schutz asked me if I could bring a heart into my body. And suddenly there it was, a heart sheathed in slime, hung with blood vessels. And that heart broke me up. I felt my chest convulse. I exploded. I *burst* into tears.

I recognized the heart. The incident had occurred more than twenty years before and had left me cold. I had written about it in a story published long ago in *Esquire*. The point of the story was that such events should have affected me but never did. The war in Germany was about over. We had just taken a German village without resistance. We had fine billets in German houses. The cellars were loaded with jams and sausages and wine. I was the aid man with the outfit, and was usually summoned by the call of "Aid man!" When I heard that call I became numb, and when I was numb I could go anywhere and do anything. I figured the battles were over. It came as a shock when I heard the call this time. There were rifle shots, then: "Aid man!" I ran to the guards and they pointed to bushes ten yards from where they had been posted. They had spotted a German soldier and called to him to surrender. He didn't answer and they fired. I went to the bushes and turned him over. He was a kid about sixteen, blond, his hair strung out in the bushes, still alive. The .30-caliber bullets had scooped out his chest and I saw his heart. It was the same heart I put in my chest 23 years later. He was still alive, gray with shock, going fast. He stared up at me—a mournful, little boy's face. He asked: "Why did you shoot? I wanted to surrender." I told him we didn't know.

Now, twenty-three years later, I wailed for that German boy who had never mattered to me and I heaved up my numbness. The trip through my body lasted more than an hour. I found wounds everywhere. I remembered a wounded friend whimpering: "Help me, Leo," which I did—a close friend, yet after he was hit no friend at all, not missed a second after I heard of his death, numb to him as I was to everyone else, preparing for losses by anesthetizing myself. And in the course of that trip through my body I started to feel again, and discovered what I'd missed. I felt wide open, lightened, ready to meet others simply and directly. No need for lies, no need to fear humiliation. I was ready to be a fool. I experienced the joy Schutz had promised to deliver. I'm grateful to him. Not even the offer of love could threaten me.

This was the transformation I underwent in the course of that fantasy trip. The force of the experience began to fade quickly, and now, writing two weeks later, I find that little remains. But I still have a vision of a possibility I had not been aware of—a simple, easy connection with my own feeling and, consequently, with others'.

I had great difficulty emerging from my body. I was pinned against my intestines, pregnant with myself. When I finally began to move and restored all the missing organs and repaired those that were damaged, I feared that all this work was temporary, that if I were to leave the heart would vanish, the stomach dry up, the intestines be exposed. Schutz asked if there was anyone who could help me get out. I said: "My daughter." So I invited my daughter to enter my body. She stood near my heart and said: "Come on out, Daddy," and led me out. I ran to a meadow in my chest. I ran through long grass, toward a gate, directly toward the sun. There I lay down and rested.

Occasionally, during my trip, I heard others crying, but I had lost track of the group. I opened my eyes. I had an initial sense of others as darts of candlelight about me. The room seemed to have shifted. It was pitch black outside. Everyone was very close to me—Reb, Daniel, Brigitte, Bill, Joan, Victor, Kate, Clark, Gary, Sheba. Sheba still wept. Brigitte directed us all to lie down and to reach out and touch one another. She turned out the lights and gave us various instructions designed to release us and finally we parted.

It was not easy leaving these people I had met only five days before. Time was distorted and we seemed to have lived years together. It was not easy leaving Big Sur. On the final morning, the entire workshop met to say good-by. Our group gathered in a tight circle, hugging and kissing, and I found myself hugging everyone, behaving like the idiots I had noticed on first arriving at Esalen. I hugged Rebel. I told him he was a great kid and that a few years from now he might not even recall his present trouble. I told him not to envy his peers. He was probably much better than they.

Schutz ended our last meeting by playing a record from *The Man of La Mancha*, "The Impossible Dream." We were at that point of sentiment where corny lyrics announced truths and we could be illuminated by the wisdom of clichés.

The condition of vulnerability is precious and very fragile. Events and people and old routines and old habits conspire to bring you down. But not all the way down. There is still the recollection of that tingling sense of being wide awake, located in the here and now, feeling freely and entirely, all constraints discarded. It remains a condition to be realized. It could change the way we live.

cathy sterbentz ———————————————————

Thirty-Three and a Third Revolutions per Minute Is a Broken Record

A native of Hayward, California, Cathy Sterbentz (1951–   ) attended Catholic schools there and in Oakland. As a child she wrote for a children's column in the Oakland *Tribune,* and she served as columnist and copy-editor of her high school newspaper. She entered the baking program at Laney College in Oakland with the hope of one day owning and operating a small-town bakery, but her interest in writing was revived in Marlene Griffith's advanced composition course at Laney in 1972. She went on from there to study journalism at San Francisco State University.

We shuffled our sandaled feet through the motorcaded streets toward the stadium, talking and laughing in the brisk October night like old friends—all fifteen thousand of us: remnants of last November's Moratorium, and last month's anti-Iranian-government midnight vigil, and last night's East Pakistan benefit showing of *The Battle of Algiers.* Rubbing elbows and political-button-brandished sleeves, we were equal in our need for melodic manna: the meek and Irish-looking men, who'd been dismissed for a night from their parish-posts as Boys' Club chairmen. For them the night was a chance to relive Joan Baez's first Newport performance of 1958. At that debut, they'd met their wives, grammar-school folk-dance instructresses, dressed tonight in floral-print dresses and blue, pilled-at-the-elbow cardigans. They smiled at us—the human ingredient of the Charles Reich revolution—through their aging eyes, tearful at all the sorrow they'd seen. We, the peaceful politicos, hair wild and frazzled or sleek and straight, asserting our individuality in purple capes or hand-embroidered knee patches. Together, the half of the world who've never been hungry, naked, or friendless, gathered with the Princess of Pacifism to bemoan the fate of the less fortunate half: a cathartic self-cleansing in a twentieth-century Greek theatre.

All seats were priced at the standard "This concert is for a good cause" price of two dollars. As well as banishing class conflict among the audience, this standard Baez price also removes her as the object of animosity if the crowd is made to wait the usual fidgety half-hour for the performance to

Original publication in this volume, by permission of the author.

begin. No chance for the classic, "I paid good money for this thing to begin on time." Two dollars is no longer considered good money.

Pamphleteers took advantage of the fated half-hour delay to litter the ground with their propaganda. Draft-dodgers and resisters confettied the stands with mimeographed flyers informing us of our legal rights in case of arrest or of the almighty strength inherent in nonviolence.

The local Jesus-Freaks (a term not coined by Miss Baez, but used by her later in a plea for them to stop stuffing her Carmel mailbox with their gospel) caught wind of the gentle person who was to grace their midst, and were poised at all entrances and exits with decrees in hand. Fully expecting an epistle announcing Joan's appointment as honorary Madonna, I was surprised to find, while waiting and sifting through my bundles of free reading material, a totally different message. Instead of a canonization, they attacked Miss Baez's mistaken notion of world change through the erasure of national boundaries and armies, rather than by trusting in Brother Jesus as the competent and rightful Ruler of Our Kingdom here on Earth. Perhaps they thought they had a better chance of attracting His much-needed attention with a celebrity on their side.

Ten minutes later, these same pamphlets were to serve as the crowd's means of sublimating its anxiety at Joan's delay. From the uppermost rows of the balcony, more ingenious members of the audience opened attack upon the groundlings with hand-crafted paper gliders. These launches were accompanied by vocal attacks, or "oohs" and "ahs" of amazement at an exceptionally well-fashioned or smooth and far-flying plane. Just as the battered groundlings were preparing to wave the torn tie-dyed T-shirt of defeat, the woman we'd all been waiting for so patiently stepped onto the stage, and the audience became as quiet as the silent space between two cuts on a record. How sad that all war games don't halt abruptly with the chanted truce of a folk singer, or that casualties consist of no more than crumpled pamphlets.

Miss Baez punctuated her sad, sweet songs with impersonations of famous people and friends, constant apologies for her constantly running nose, an occasional response to a muffled, die-hard audience request, and public meditations on current crises, meant to pinprick any consciences that may have become sleepy from an atmosphere filled with mind-numbing melodies and marijuana.

If Jesus' twentieth-century disciples hadn't felt slighted at the disrespect shown their propaganda-turned-paper-glider, their stoicism underwent its ultimate test with Joan's hymn to Bob Dylan: "Listen to the lambs, Bobby, they're crying for you. Listen to the lambs, Bobby, they're dying"—a rather blatant display of blasphemy, as Joan likened Bobby to our Savior.

I sat huddled in my purple wool cape with the rest of the lambs, knees scrunched up under my chin, leaning toward the stage and the woman who for so many years had echoed my only hopes for a New World. I sat waiting to hear the comforting songs that would tell me of marathon marches and candlelight vigils and persistent picketing changing the world. And I heard them all: how a friendly "hello" to an aged woman on the street would bring new meaning to her life, despite her impossible pension of sixty-five dollars a month; how there was no need to spend money or energy on prison reform—the only answer was to "raze them all to the ground"; and how the Vietnam War would end if only we'd erase that country's tell-tale dividing line.

Maybe it was the paper airplanes colliding with the back of my head, or the girl in the row below me, violently cursing the presence of my foot in her back; or maybe it was the couple at the end of the row who refused to move in closer in order to make room for one more aisle-stranded person. But somehow, this time I couldn't believe her; I couldn't even cry when they brought out her bouquet of roses.

chapter two

Learning

introduction _____

This chapter is divided between authors who technically might be called teachers and those who might be called students. In truth they are all learners. Each writer describes a process, usually beginning in frustration, by which he gains knowledge and insight into a subject which had previously perplexed him.

The chapter opens with Frederick Douglass' dogged struggle to learn to read and write, skills prohibited to him because he was a slave. Douglass' determination to read and write and the legal restrictions against doing so implicitly demonstrate the power that both Douglass and the slavemasters knew to reside in learning.

Norman Podhoretz's "The Brutal Bargain" begins a series of essays about student-teacher relationships. In the essay, Podhoretz shows how his English teacher's excessive zeal to mold him to her own measure was potentially destructive to him. In contrast, Carlos Castaneda enjoys nearly a father-son relationship with his teacher don Juan, even though his training to be a *brujo* (sorcerer) is highly structured and ritualized in don Juan's mind.

Ken Macrorie tells of his frustrations in teaching and of his efforts to become a more effective teacher. He discusses the evolution of his "third way" of teaching composition so as to bring humanity and vigor to student writing.

The final two essays in the chapter deal with preconceptions about learning. James Herndon's "The Dumb Class" slyly damns an educational system that defines its limits so narrowly and artificially that it condemns both students and teachers to play out static roles without hope of change. Maya Angelou writes of the excitement of her eighth-grade graduation, where the preconceptions of a white school official stun the black graduating class into proving to itself right there that he is wrong.

I Learn to Read and Write

Born a slave in Maryland, Frederick Douglass (1817–1895) rose to become one of the most influential leaders of the civil-rights struggles in nineteenth-century America. After escaping from slavery in 1838, he joined the abolitionists in the cause of emancipation. A powerful orator, he spoke extensively all over the North. Eventually, he published his own newspapers, the weekly *North Star* in 1847, and later *Douglass' Paper* and *Douglass' Monthly*. He held the post of Recorder of Deeds in Washington and served as Minister Resident and Consul General to Haiti. He wrote three versions of his autobiography, *Life and Times of Frederick Douglass* (1881), *My Bondage and My Freedom* (1855), and the earliest version, *Narrative of the Life of Frederick Douglass* (1845), from which the following selection is taken.

I lived in Master Hugh's family about seven years. During this time, I succeeded in learning to read and write. In accomplishing this, I was compelled to resort to various stratagems. I had no regular teacher. My mistress, who had kindly commenced to instruct me, had, in compliance with the advice and direction of her husband, not only ceased to instruct, but had set her face against my being instructed by any one else. It is due, however, to my mistress to say of her, that she did not adopt this course of treatment immediately. She at first lacked the depravity indispensable to shutting me up in mental darkness. It was at least necessary for her to have some training in the exercise of irresponsible power, to make her equal to the task of treating me as though I were a brute.

My mistress was, as I have said, a kind and tender-hearted woman; and in the simplicity of her soul she commenced, when I first went to live with her, to treat me as she supposed one human being ought to treat another. In entering upon the duties of a slaveholder, she did not seem to perceive that I sustained to her the relation of a mere chattel, and that for her to treat me as a human being was not only wrong, but dangerously so. Slavery proved as injurious to her as it did to me. When I went there, she was a pious, warm, and tender-hearted woman. There was no sorrow or suffering for which she had not a tear. She had bread for the hungry, clothes for the naked, and comfort for every mourner that came within her reach. Slavery

From *Narrative of the Life of Frederick Douglass*, by Frederick Douglass, published in 1845. Editor's title.

soon proved its ability to divest her of these heavenly qualities. Under its influence, the tender heart became stone, and the lamblike disposition gave way to one of tiger-like fierceness. The first step in her downward course was in her ceasing to instruct me. She now commenced to practise her husband's precepts. She finally became even more violent in her opposition than her husband himself. She was not satisfied with simply doing as well as he had commanded; she seemed anxious to do better. Nothing seemed to make her more angry than to see me with a newspaper. She seemed to think that here lay the danger. I have had her rush at me with a face made all up of fury, and snatch from me a newspaper, in a manner that fully revealed her apprehension. She was an apt woman; and a little experience soon demonstrated, to her satisfaction, that education and slavery were incompatible with each other.

From this time I was most narrowly watched. If I was in a separate room any considerable length of time, I was sure to be suspected of having a book, and was at once called to give an account of myself. All this, however, was too late. The first step had been taken. Mistress, in teaching me the alphabet, had given me the *inch,* and no precaution could prevent me from taking the *ell.*

The plan which I adopted, and the one by which I was most successful, was that of making friends of all the little white boys whom I met in the street. As many of these as I could, I converted into teachers. With their kindly aid, obtained at different times and in different places, I finally succeeded in learning to read. When I was sent on errands, I always took my book with me, and by doing one part of my errand quickly, I found time to get a lesson before my return. I used also to carry bread with me, enough of which was always in the house, and to which I was always welcome; for I was much better off in this regard than many of the poor white children in our neighborhood. This bread I used to bestow upon the hungry little urchins, who, in return, would give me that more valuable bread of knowledge. I am strongly tempted to give the names of two or three of those little boys, as a testimonial of the gratitude and affection I bear them; but prudence forbids;—not that it would injure me, but it might embarrass them; for it is almost an unpardonable offence to teach slaves to read in this Christian country. It is enough to say of the dear little fellows, that they lived on Philpot Street, very near Durgin and Bailey's ship-yard. I used to talk this matter of slavery over with them. I would sometimes say to them, I wished I could be as free as they would be when they got to be men. "You will be free as soon as you are twenty-one, *but I am a slave for life!* Have not I as good a right to be free as you have?" These words used to trouble them; they would express for me the liveliest sympathy, and console me with the hope that something would occur by which I might be free.

I was now about twelve years old, and the thought of being *a slave for life* began to bear heavily upon my heart. Just about this time, I got hold of a book entitled "The Columbian Orator." Every opportunity I got, I used to read this book. Among much of other interesting matter, I found in it a dialogue between a master and his slave. The slave was represented as having run away from his master three times. The dialogue represented the conversation which took place between them, when the slave was retaken the third time. In this dialogue, the whole argument in behalf of slavery was brought forward by the master, all of which was disposed of by the slave. The slave was made to say some very smart as well as impressive things in reply to his master—things which had the desired though unexpected effect; for the conversation resulted in the voluntary emancipation of the slave on the part of the master.

In the same book, I met with one of Sheridan's mighty speeches on and in behalf of Catholic emancipation. These were choice documents to me. I read them over and over again with unabated interest. They gave tongue to interesting thoughts of my own soul, which had frequently flashed through my mind, and died away for want of utterance. The moral which I gained from the dialogue was the power of truth over the conscience of even a slaveholder. What I got from Sheridan was a bold denunciation of slavery, and a powerful vindication of human rights. The reading of these documents enabled me to utter my thoughts, and to meet the arguments brought forward to sustain slavery; but while they relieved me of one difficulty, they brought on another even more painful than the one of which I was relieved. The more I read, the more I was led to abhor and detest my enslavers. I could regard them in no other light than a band of successful robbers, who had left their homes, and gone to Africa, and stolen us from our homes, and in a strange land reduced us to slavery. I loathed them as being the meanest as well as the most wicked of men. As I read and contemplated the subject, behold! that very discontentment which Master Hugh had predicted would follow my learning to read had already come, to torment and sting my soul to unutterable anguish. As I writhed under it, I would at times feel that learning to read had been a curse rather than a blessing. It had given me a view of my wretched condition, without the remedy. It opened my eyes to the horrible pit, but to no ladder upon which to get out. In moments of agony, I envied my fellow-slaves for their stupidity. I have often wished myself a beast. I preferred the condition of the meanest reptile to my own. Any thing, no matter what, to get rid of thinking! It was this everlasting thinking of my condition that tormented me. There was no getting rid of it. It was pressed upon me by every object within sight or hearing, animate or inanimate. The silver trump of freedom had roused my soul to eternal wakefulness. Freedom now appeared, to disappear no more forever. It was heard in every sound, and seen in every thing. It was ever present to torment me with a sense of my wretched condition. I saw nothing without seeing it, I heard nothing without hearing it, and felt nothing without feeling it. It looked from every star, it smiled in every calm, breathed in every wind, and moved in every storm.

I often found myself regretting my own existence, and wishing myself dead; and but for the hope of being free, I have no doubt but that I should have killed myself, or done something for which I should have been killed. While in this state of mind, I was eager to hear any one speak of slavery. I was a ready listener. Every little while, I could hear something about the abolitionists. It was some time before I found what the word meant. It was always used in such connections as to make it an interesting word to me. If a slave ran away and succeeded in getting clear, or if a slave killed his master, set fire to a barn, or did any thing very wrong in the mind of a slaveholder, it was spoken of as the fruit of *abolition*. Hearing the word in this connection very often, I set about learning what it meant. The dictionary afforded me little or no help. I found it was "the act of abolishing"; but then I did not know what was to be abolished. Here I was perplexed. I did not dare to ask any one about its meaning, for I was satisfied that it was something they wanted me to know very little about. After a patient waiting, I got one of our city papers, containing an account of the number of petitions from the north, praying for the abolition of slavery in the District of Columbia, and of the slave trade between the States. From this time I understood the words *abolition* and *abolitionist*, and always drew near when that word was spoken, expecting to hear something of importance to myself and fellow-slaves. The light broke in upon me by degrees. I went one day down on the wharf of Mr. Waters; and seeing two Irishmen unloading a scow of stone, I went, unasked, and helped them. When we had finished, one of them came to me and asked me if I were a slave. I told him I was. He asked, "Are ye a slave for life?" I told him that I was. The good Irishman seemed to be deeply affected by the statement. He said to the other that it was a pity so fine a little fellow as myself should be a slave for life. He said it was a shame to hold me. They both advised me to run away to the north; that I should find friends there, and that I should be free. I pretended not to be interested in what they said, and treated them as if I did not understand them; for I feared they might be treacherous. White men have been known to encourage slaves to escape, and then, to get the reward, catch them and return them to their masters. I was afraid that these seemingly good men might use me so; but I nevertheless remembered their advice, and from that time I resolved to run away. I looked forward to a time at which it would be safe for me to escape. I was too young to think of doing so immediately; besides, I wished to learn how to write, as I might have occasion to write my own pass. I consoled myself with the hope that I should one day find a good chance. Meanwhile, I would learn to write.

The idea as to how I might learn to write was suggested to me by being in Durgin and Bailey's ship-yard, and frequently seeing the ship carpenters, after hewing, and getting a piece of timber ready for use, write on the timber the name of that part of the ship for which it was intended. When a piece of timber was intended for the larboard side, it would be marked thus—"L." When a piece was for the starboard side, it would be marked thus—"S." A piece for the larboard side forward would be marked thus—"L. F." When a piece was for starboard side forward, it would be marked thus—"S. F." For larboard aft, it would be marked thus—"L. A." For starboard aft, it would be marked thus—"S. A." I soon learned the names of these letters, and for what they were intended when placed upon a piece of timber in the ship-yard. I immediately commenced copying them, and in a short time was able to make the four letters named. After that, when I met with any boy who I knew could write, I would tell him I could write as well as he. The next word would be, "I don't believe you. Let me see you try it." I would then make the letters which I had been so fortunate as to learn, and ask him to beat that. In this way I got a good many lessons in writing, which it is quite possible I should never have gotten in any other way. During this time, my copy-book was the board fence, brick wall, and pavement; my pen and ink was a lump of chalk. With these, I learned mainly how to write. I then commenced and continued copying the Italics in Webster's Spelling Book, until I could make them all without looking on the book. By this time, my little Master Thomas had gone to school, and learned how to write, and had written over a number of copy-books. These had been brought home, and shown to some of our near neighbors, and then laid aside. My mistress used to go to class meeting at the Wilk Street meetinghouse every Monday afternoon, and leave me to take care of the house. When left thus, I used to spend the time in writing in the spaces left in Master Thomas's copy-book, copying what he had written. I continued to do this until I could write a hand very similar to that of Master Thomas. Thus, after a long, tedious effort for years, I finally succeeded in learning how to write.

norman podhoretz _____

The Brutal Bargain

A brilliant student first at Columbia, then at Cambridge, editor of the respected intellectual magazine *Commentary* when he was thirty, and a controversial literary celebrity soon after that, Norman Podhoretz (1930–   ) appears to have attained the success and fame he unabashedly admits, in his candid autobiography, that he sought. His outspoken essays on literary and social topics have been collected in *Doings and Undoings* (1964), and he has also written for *Harper's, The New Yorker,* and *Partisan Review.* The following essay is the first chapter of his autobiography, *Making It.*

One of the longest journeys in the world is the journey from Brooklyn to Manhattan—or at least from certain neighborhoods in Brooklyn to certain parts of Manhattan. I have made that journey, but it is not from the experience of having made it that I know how very great the distance is, for I started on the road many years before I realized what I was doing, and by the time I did realize it I was for all practical purposes already there. At so imperceptible a pace did I travel, and with so little awareness, that I never felt footsore or out of breath or weary at the thought of how far I still had to go. Yet whenever anyone who has remained back there where I started—remained not physically but socially and culturally, for the neighborhood is now a Negro ghetto and the Jews who have "remained" in it mostly reside in the less affluent areas of Long Island—whenever anyone like that happens into the world in which I now live with such perfect ease, I can see that in his eyes I have become a fully acculturated citizen of a country as foreign to him as China and infinitely more frightening.

That country is sometimes called the upper middle class; and indeed I am a member of that class, less by virtue of my income than by virtue of the way my speech is accented, the way I dress, the way I furnish my home, the way I entertain and am entertained, the way I educate my children—the way, quite simply, I look and I live. It appalls me to think what an immense transformation I had to work on myself in order to become what I have become: if I had known what I was doing I would surely not have been able to do it, I would surely not have wanted to. No wonder the choice had to be blind; there was a kind of treason in it: treason toward my family, treason toward my friends. In choosing the road I chose, I was pronouncing a judgment upon them, and the fact that they themselves concurred in the judgment makes the whole thing sadder but no less cruel.

When I say that the choice was blind, I mean that I was never aware—obviously not as a small child, certainly not as an adolescent, and not even as a young man already writing for publication and working on the staff of an important intellectual magazine in New York—how inextricably my "noblest" ambitions were tied to the vulgar desire to rise above the class into which I was born; nor did I understand to what an astonishing extent these ambitions were shaped and defined by the standards and values and tastes of the class into which I did not know I wanted to move. It is not that I was or am a social climber as the term is commonly used. High society interests me, if at all, only as a curiosity; I do not wish to be a member of it; and in any case, it is not, as I have learned from a small experience of contact with the very rich and fashionable, my "scene." Yet precisely because social climbing is not one of my vices (unless what might be called celebrity climbing, which very definitely *is* one of my vices, can be considered the contemporary variant of social climbing), I think there may be more than a merely personal significance in the fact that class has played so large a part both in my life and in my career.

But whether or not the significance is there, I feel certain that my long-time blindness to the part class was playing in my life was not altogether idiosyncratic. "Privilege," Robert L. Heilbroner has shrewdly observed in *The Limits of American Capitalism*, "is not an attribute we are accustomed to stress when we consider the construction of *our* social order." For a variety of reasons, says Heilbroner, "privilege under capitalism is much less 'visible,' especially to the favored groups, than privilege under other systems" like feudalism. This "invisibility" extends in America to class as well.

No one, of course, is so naïve as to believe that America is a classless society or that the force of egalitarianism, powerful as it has been in some respects, has ever been powerful enough to wipe out class distinctions altogether. There was a moment during the 1950's, to be sure, when social thought hovered on the brink of saying that the country had to all intents and purposes become a wholly middle-class society. But the emergence of the civil-rights movement in the 1960's and the concomitant discovery of the poor—to whom, in helping to discover them, Michael Harrington interestingly enough applied, in *The Other America*, the very word ("invisible") that Heilbroner later used with reference to the rich—has put at least a temporary end to that kind of talk. And yet if class has become visible again, it is only in its grossest outlines—mainly, that is, in terms of income levels—and to the degree that manners and style of life are perceived as relevant at all, it is generally in the crudest of terms. There is something in us, it would seem, which resists the idea of class. Even our novelists, working in a genre for which class has traditionally been a supreme reality, are largely indifferent to it—which is to say, blind to its importance as a factor in the life of the individual.

In my own case, the blindness to class always expressed itself in an outright and very often belligerent refusal to believe that it had anything to do with me at all. I no longer remember when or in what form I first discovered that there was such a thing as class, but whenever it was and whatever form the discovery took, it could only have coincided with the recognition that criteria existed by which I and everyone I knew were stamped as inferior: we were in the *lower* class. This was not a proposition I was willing to accept, and my way of not accepting it was to dismiss the whole idea of class as a prissy triviality.

Given the fact that I had literary ambitions even as a small boy, it was inevitable that the issue of class would sooner or later arise for me with a sharpness it would never acquire for most of my friends. But given the fact also that I was on the whole very happy to be growing up where I was, that I was fiercely patriotic about Brownsville (the spawning-ground of so many famous athletes and gangsters), and that I felt genuinely patronizing toward other neighborhoods, especially the "better" ones like Crown Heights and East Flatbush which seemed by comparison colorless and unexciting— given the fact, in other words, that I was not, for all that I wrote poetry and read books, an "alienated" boy dreaming of escape—my confrontation with the issue of class would probably have come later rather than sooner if not for an English teacher in high school who decided that I was a gem in the rough and who took it upon herself to polish me to as high a sheen as she could manage and I would permit.

I resisted—far less effectively, I can see now, than I then thought, though even then I knew that she was wearing me down far more than I would ever give her the satisfaction of admitting. Famous throughout the school for her altogether outspoken snobbery, which stopped short by only a hair, and sometimes did not stop short at all, of an old-fashioned kind of patrician anti-Semitism, Mrs. K. was also famous for being an extremely good teacher; indeed, I am sure that she saw no distinction between the hopeless task of teaching the proper use of English to the young Jewish barbarians whom fate had so unkindly deposited into her charge and the equally hopeless task of teaching them the proper "manners." (There were as many young Negro barbarians in her charge as Jewish ones, but I doubt that she could ever bring herself to pay very much attention to them. As she never hesitated to make clear, it was punishment enough for a woman of her background—her family was old-Brooklyn and, she would have us understand, extremely distinguished—to have fallen among the sons of East European immigrant Jews.)

For three years, from the age of thirteen to the age of sixteen, I was her special pet, though that word is scarcely adequate to suggest the intensity of the relationship which developed between us. It was a relationship right out of *The Corn Is Green,* which may, for all I know, have served as her model; at any rate, her objective was much the same as the Welsh teacher's in that play: she was determined that I should win a scholarship to Harvard. But whereas (an irony much to the point here) the problem the teacher had in *The Corn Is Green* with her coal-miner pupil in the traditional class society of Edwardian England was strictly academic, Mrs. K.'s problem with me in the putatively egalitarian society of New Deal America was strictly social. My grades were very high and would obviously remain so, but what would they avail me if I continued to go about looking and sounding like a "filthy little slum child" (the epithet she would invariably hurl at me whenever we had an argument about "manners")?

Childless herself, she worked on me like a dementedly ambitious mother with a somewhat recalcitrant son; married to a solemn and elderly man (she was then in her early forties or thereabouts), she treated me like a callous, ungrateful adolescent lover on whom she had humiliatingly bestowed her favors. She flirted with me and flattered me, she scolded me and insulted me. Slum child, filthy little slum child, so beautiful a mind and so vulgar a personality, so exquisite in sensibility and so coarse in manner. What would she do with me, what would become of me if I persisted out of stubbornness and perversity in the disgusting ways they had taught me at home and on the streets?

To her the most offensive of these ways was the style in which I dressed: a tee shirt, tightly pegged pants, and a red satin jacket with the legend "Cherokees, S.A.C." (social-athletic club) stitched in large white letters across the back. This was bad enough, but when on certain days I would appear in school wearing, as a particular ceremonial occasion required, a suit and tie, the sight of those immense padded shoulders and my white-on-white shirt would drive her to even greater heights of contempt and even lower depths of loving despair than usual. *Slum child, filthy little slum child.* I was beyond saving; I deserved no better than to wind up with all the other horrible little Jewboys in the gutter (by which she meant Brooklyn College). If only I would listen to her, the whole world could be mine: I could win a scholarship to Harvard, I could get to know the best people, I could grow up into a life of elegance and refinement and taste. Why was I so stupid as not to understand?

In those days it was very unusual, and possibly even against the rules, for teachers in public high schools to associate with their students after hours. Nevertheless, Mrs. K. sometimes invited me to her home, a beautiful old brownstone located in what was perhaps the only section in the whole of Brooklyn fashionable enough to be intimidating. I would read her my poems and she would tell me about her family, about the schools she had gone to, about Vassar, about writers she had met, while her husband, of whom I was frightened to death and who to my utter astonishment turned out to be Jewish (but not, as Mrs. K. quite unnecessarily hastened to inform me, *my* kind of Jewish), sat stiffly and silently in an armchair across the room, squinting at his newspaper through the first *pince-nez* I had ever seen outside the movies. He spoke to me but once, and that was after I had read Mrs. K. my tearful editorial for the school newspaper on the death of Roosevelt—an effusion which provoked him into a full five-minute harangue whose blasphemous contents would certainly have shocked me into insensibility if I had not been even more shocked to discover that he actually had a voice.

But Mrs. K. not only had me to her house; she also—what was even more unusual—took me out a few times, to the Frick Gallery and the Metropolitan Museum, and once to the theater, where we saw a dramatization of *The Late George Apley,* a play I imagine she deliberately chose with the not wholly mistaken idea that it would impress upon me the glories of aristocratic Boston.

One of our excursions into Manhattan I remember with particular vividness because she used it to bring the struggle between us to rather a dramatic head. The familiar argument began this time on the subway. Why, knowing that we would be spending the afternoon together "in public," had I come to school that morning improperly dressed? (I was, as usual, wearing my red satin club jacket over a white tee shirt.) She realized, of course, that I owned only one suit (this said not in compassion but in derision) and that my poor parents had, God only knew where, picked up the idea that it was too precious to be worn except at one of those bar mitzvahs I was always going to. Though why, if my parents were so worried about clothes, they had permitted me to buy a suit which made me look like a young hoodlum she found it very difficult to imagine. Still, much as she would have been embarrassed to be seen in public with a boy whose parents allowed him to wear a zoot suit, she would have been somewhat less embarrassed than she was now by the ridiculous costume I had on. Had I no consideration for her? Had I no consideration for myself? Did I want everyone who laid eyes on me to think that I was nothing but an ill-bred little slum child?

My standard ploy in these arguments was to take the position that such things were of no concern to me: I was a poet and I had more important matters to think about than clothes. Besides, I would feel silly coming to school on an ordinary day dressed in a suit. Did Mrs. K. want me to look like one of those "creeps" from Crown Heights who were all going to become doctors? This was usually an effective counter, since Mrs. K. despised her middle-class Jewish students even more than she did the "slum children," but probably because she was growing desperate at the thought of how I would strike a Harvard interviewer (it was my senior year), she did not respond according to form on that particular occasion. "At least," she snapped, "they reflect well on their parents."

I was accustomed to her bantering gibes at my parents, and sensing, probably, that they arose out of jealousy, I was rarely troubled by them. But this one bothered me; it went beyond banter and I did not know how to deal with it. I remember flushing, but I cannot remember what if anything I said in protest. It was the beginning of a very bad afternoon for both of us.

We had been heading for the Museum of Modern Art, but as we got off the subway, Mrs. K. announced that she had changed her mind about the museum. She was going to show me something else instead, just down the street on Fifth Avenue. This mysterious "something else" to which we proceeded in silence turned out to be the college department of an expensive clothing store, de Pinna. I do not exaggerate when I say that an actual physical dread seized me as I followed her into the store. I had never been inside such a store; it was not a store, it was enemy territory, every inch of it mined with humiliations. "I am," Mrs. K. declared in the coldest human voice I hope I shall ever hear, "going to buy you a suit that you will be able to wear at your Harvard interview." I had guessed, of course, that this was what she had in mind, and even at fifteen I understood what a fantastic act of aggression she was planning to commit against my parents and asking me to participate in. Oh no, I said in a panic (suddenly realizing that I *wanted* her to buy me that suit), I can't, my mother wouldn't like it. "You can tell her it's a birthday present. Or else I will tell her. If I tell her, I'm sure she won't object." The idea of Mrs. K. meeting my mother was more than I could bear: my mother, who spoke with a Yiddish accent and of whom, until that sickening moment, I had never known I was ashamed and so ready to betray.

To my immense relief and my equally immense disappointment, we left the store, finally, without buying a suit, but it was not to be the end of clothing or "manners" for me that day—not yet. There was still the ordeal of a restaurant to go through. Where I came from, people rarely ate in restaurants, not so much because most of them were too poor to afford such a luxury—although most of them certainly were—as because eating in restaurants was not regarded as a luxury at all; it was, rather, a necessity to which bachelors were pitiably condemned. A home-cooked meal was assumed to be better than anything one could possibly get in a restaurant, and considering the class of restaurants in question (they were really diners or luncheonettes), the assumption was probably correct. In the case of my own family, myself included until my late teens, the business of going to restaurants was complicated by the fact that we observed the Jewish dietary laws, and except in certain neighborhoods, few places could be found which served kosher food; in midtown Manhattan in the 1940's, I believe there were only two and both were relatively expensive. All this is by way of explaining why I had had so little experience of restaurants up to the age of fifteen and why I grew apprehensive once more when Mrs. K. decided after we left de Pinna that we should have something to eat.

The restaurant she chose was not at all an elegant one—I have, like a criminal, revisited it since—but it seemed very elegant indeed to me: enemy territory again, and this time a mine exploded in my face the minute I set foot through the door. The hostess was very sorry, but she could not seat the young gentleman without a coat and tie. If the lady wished, however, something could be arranged. The lady (visibly pleased by this unexpected—or was it expected?—object lesson) did wish, and the so recently defiant but by now utterly docile young gentleman was forthwith divested of his so recently beloved but by now thoroughly loathsome red satin jacket and provided with a much oversized white waiter's coat and a tie—which, there being no collar to a tee shirt, had to be worn around his bare neck. Thus attired, and with his face supplying the touch of red which had moments earlier been supplied by his jacket, he was led into the dining room, there to be taught the importance of proper table manners through the same pedagogic instrumentality that had worked so well in impressing him with the importance of proper dress.

Like any other pedagogic technique, however, humiliation has its limits, and Mrs. K. was to make no further progress with it that day. For I had had enough, and I was not about to risk stepping on another mine. Knowing she would subject me to still more ridicule if I made a point of my revulsion at the prospect of eating nonkosher food, I resolved to let her order for me and then to feign lack of appetite or possibly even illness when the meal was served. She did order—duck for both of us, undoubtedly because it would be a hard dish for me to manage without using my fingers.

The two portions came in deep oval-shaped dishes, swimming in a brown sauce and each with a sprig of parsley sitting on top. I had not the faintest idea of what to do—should the food be eaten directly from the oval dish or not?—nor which of the many implements on the table to do it with. But remembering that Mrs. K. herself had once advised me to watch my hostess in such a situation and then to do exactly as she did, I sat perfectly still and waited for her to make the first move. Unfortunately, Mrs. K. also remembered having taught me that trick, and determined as she was that I should be given a lesson that would force me to mend my ways, she waited too. And so we both waited, chatting amiably, pretending not to notice the food while it sat there getting colder and colder by the minute. Thanks partly to the fact that I would probably have gagged on the duck if I had tried to eat it—dietary taboos are very powerful if one has been conditioned to them —I was prepared to wait forever. And in fact it was Mrs. K. who broke first.

"Why aren't you eating?" she suddenly said after something like fifteen minutes had passed. "Aren't you hungry?" Not very, I answered. "Well," she said, "I think we'd better eat. The food is getting cold." Whereupon, as I watched with great fascination, she deftly captured the sprig of parsley between the prongs of her serving fork, set it aside, took up her serving spoon and delicately used those two esoteric implements to transfer a piece of duck from the oval dish to her plate. I imitated the whole operation as best I could, but not well enough to avoid splattering some partly congealed sauce onto my borrowed coat in the process. Still, things could have been worse, and having more or less successfully negotiated my way around that particular mine, I now had to cope with the problem of how to get out of eating the duck. But I need not have worried. Mrs. K. took one bite, pronounced it inedible (it must have been frozen by then), and called in quiet fury for the check.

Several months later, wearing an altered but respectably conservative suit which had been handed down to me in good condition by a bachelor uncle, I presented myself on two different occasions before interviewers from Harvard and from the Pulitzer Scholarship Committee. Some months after that, Mrs. K. had her triumph: I won the Harvard scholarship on which her heart had been so passionately set. It was not, however, large enough to cover all expenses, and since my parents could not afford to make up the difference, I was unable to accept it. My parents felt wretched but not, I think, quite as wretched as Mrs. K. For a while it looked as though I would wind up in the "gutter" of Brooklyn College after all, but then the news arrived that I had also won a Pulitzer Scholarship which paid full tuition if used at Columbia and a small stipend besides. Everyone was consoled, even Mrs. K.: Columbia was at least in the Ivy League.

The last time I saw her was shortly before my graduation from Columbia and just after a story had appeared in the *Times* announcing that I had been awarded a fellowship which was to send me to Cambridge University. Mrs. K. had passionately wanted to see me in Cambridge, Massachusetts, but Cambridge, England was even better. We met somewhere near Columbia for a drink, and her happiness over my fellowship, it seemed to me, was if anything exceeded by her delight at discovering that I now knew enough to know that the right thing to order in a cocktail lounge was a very dry martini with lemon peel, please.

The Promise

A native of São Paulo, Brazil, Carlos Castaneda (1931–   ) was a graduate student in anthropology at the University of California, Los Angeles, in 1960. While in the Southwest doing research on medicinal plants used by Indians of the area, Castaneda met Juan Matus, a Yaqui Indian *brujo* (sorcerer), in a bus station and began a sometimes terrifying, often puzzling, but always fascinating ten-year apprenticeship to learn to be a *brujo*. Largely through the ritual use of plants with hallucinogenic properties (peyote, jimson weed), don Juan attempted to teach Castaneda to perceive reality differently from the rationalistic way of modern Western man. Castaneda wrote his master's thesis about the first several years of his experiences with don Juan and published it as *The Teachings of Don Juan: A Yaqui Way of Knowledge* (1968). Continuing his apprenticeship until 1970, Castaneda has written two more accounts of his later experiences and relationship with don Juan, *A Separate Reality: Further Conversations with Don Juan* (1971), from which the following selection is reprinted, and *Journey to Ixtlan: The Lessons of Don Juan* (1972).

For three months don Juan systematically avoided talking about the guardian. I paid him four visits during these months; he involved me in running errands for him every time, and when I had performed the errands he simply told me to go home. On April 24, 1969, the fourth time I was at his house, I finally confronted him after we had eaten dinner and were sitting next to his earthen stove. I told him that he was doing something incongruous to me; I was ready to learn and yet he did not even want me around. I had had to struggle very hard to overcome my aversion to using his hallucinogenic mushrooms and I felt, as he had said himself, that I had no time to lose.

Don Juan patiently listened to my complaints.

"You're too weak," he said. "You hurry when you should wait, but you wait when you should hurry. You think too much. Now you think that there is no time to waste. A while back you thought you didn't want to smoke any more. Your life is too damn loose; you're not tight enough to meet the little smoke. I am responsible for you and I don't want you to die like a goddamn fool."

I felt embarrassed.

"What can I do, don Juan? I'm very impatient."

"Live like a warrior! I've told you already, a warrior takes responsibility for his acts; for the most trivial of his acts. You act out your thoughts and that's wrong. You failed with the guardian because of your thoughts."

"How did I fail, don Juan?"

"You think about everything. You thought about the guardian and thus you couldn't overcome it.

"First you must live like a warrior. I think you understand that very well."

I wanted to interject something in my defense, but he gestured with his hand to be quiet.

"Your life is fairly tight," he continued. "In fact, your life is tighter than Pablito's or Nestor's, Genaro's apprentices, and yet they *see* and you don't. Your life is tighter than Eligio's and he'll probably *see* before you do. This baffles me. Even Genaro cannot get over that. You've faithfully carried out everything I have told you to do. Everything that my benefactor taught me, in the first stage of learning, I have passed on to you. The rule is right, the steps cannot be changed. You have done everything one has to do and yet you don't *see;* but to those who *see,* like Genaro, you appear as though you *see.* I rely on that and I am fooled. You always turn around and behave like an idiot who doesn't *see,* which of course is right for you."

Don Juan's words distressed me profoundly. I don't know why but I was close to tears. I began to talk about my childhood and a wave of self-pity enveloped me. Don Juan stared at me for a brief moment and then moved his eyes away. It was a penetrating glance. I felt he had actually grabbed me with his eyes. I had the sensation of two fingers gently clasping me and I acknowledged a weird agitation, an itching, a pleasant despair in the area of my solar plexus. I became aware of my abdominal region. I sensed its heat. I could not speak coherently any more and I mumbled, then stopped talking altogether.

"Perhaps it's the promise," don Juan said after a long pause.

"I beg your pardon."

"A promise you once made, long ago."

"What promise?"

"Maybe you can tell me that. You do remember it, don't you?"

"I don't."

"You promised something very important once. I thought that perhaps your promise was keeping you from *seeing.*"

"I don't know what you're talking about."

"I'm talking about a promise you made! You must remember it."

"If you know what the promise was, why don't you tell me, don Juan?"

"No. It won't do any good to tell you."

"Was it a promise I made to myself?"

For a moment I thought he might be referring to my resolution to quit the apprenticeship.

"No. This is something that took place a long time ago," he said.

I laughed because I was certain don Juan was playing some sort of game with me. I felt mischievous. I had a sensation of elation at the idea that I could fool don Juan, who, I was convinced, knew as little as I did about the alleged promise. I was sure he was fishing in the dark and trying to improvise. The idea of humoring him delighted me.

"Was it something I promised to my grandpa?"

"No," he said, and his eyes glittered. "Neither was it something you promised to your little grandma."

The ludicrous intonation he gave to the word "grandma" made me laugh. I thought don Juan was setting some sort of trap for me, but I was willing to play the game to the end. I began enumerating all the possible individuals to whom I could have promised something of great importance. He said no to each. Then he steered the conversation to my childhood.

"Why was your childhood sad?" he asked with a serious expression.

I told him that my childhood had not really been sad, but perhaps a bit difficult.

"Everybody feels that way," he said, looking at me again. "I too was very unhappy and afraid when I was a child. To be an Indian child is hard, very hard. But the memory of that time no longer has meaning for me, beyond that it was hard. I had ceased to think about the hardship of my life even before I had learned to *see*."

"I don't think about my childhood either," I said.

"Why does it make you sad, then? Why do you want to weep?"

"I don't know. Perhaps when I think of myself as a child I feel sorry for myself and for all my fellow men. I feel helpless and sad."

He looked at me fixedly and again my abdominal region registered the weird sensation of two gentle fingers clasping it. I moved my eyes away and then glanced back at him. He was looking into the distance, past me; his eyes were foggy, out of focus.

"It was a promise of your childhood," he said after a moment's silence.

"What did I promise?"

He did not answer. His eyes were closed. I smiled involuntarily; I knew he was feeling his way in the dark; however, I had lost some of my original impetus to humor him.

"I was a skinny child," he went on, "and I was always afraid."

"So was I," I said.

"What I remember the most is the terror and sadness that fell upon me when the Mexican soldiers killed my mother," he said softly, as if the memory was still painful. "She was a poor and humble Indian. Perhaps it was better that her life was over then. I wanted to be killed with her, because I was a child. But the soldiers picked me up and beat me. When I grabbed onto my mother's body they hit my fingers with a horsewhip and broke them. I didn't feel any pain, but I couldn't grasp any more, and then they dragged me away."

He stopped talking. His eyes were still closed and I could detect a very slight tremor in his lips. A profound sadness began to overtake me. Images of my own childhood started to flood my mind.

"How old were you, don Juan?" I asked, just to offset the sadness in me.

"Maybe seven. That was the time of the great Yaqui wars. The Mexican soldiers came upon us unexpectedly while my mother was cooking some food. She was a helpless woman. They killed her for no reason at all. It doesn't make any difference that she died that way, not really, and yet for me it does. I cannot tell myself why, though; it just does. I thought they had killed my father too, but they hadn't. He was wounded. Later on they put us in a train like cattle and closed the door. For days they kept us there in the dark, like animals. They kept us alive with bits of food they threw into the wagon from time to time.

"My father died of his wounds in that wagon. He became delirious with pain and fever and went on telling me that I had to survive. He kept on telling me that until the very last moment of his life.

"The people took care of me; they gave me food; an old woman curer fixed the broken bones of my hand. And as you can see, I lived. Life has been neither good nor bad to me; life has been hard. Life is hard and for a child it is sometimes horror itself."

We did not speak for a very long time. Perhaps an hour went by in complete silence. I had very confusing feelings. I was somewhat dejected and yet I could not tell why. I experienced a sense of remorse. A while before I had been willing to humor don Juan, but he had suddenly turned the tables with his direct account. It had been simple and concise and had produced a strange feeling in me. The idea of a child undergoing pain had always been a touchy subject for me. In an instant my feelings of empathy for don Juan gave way to a sensation of disgust with myself. I had actually taken notes, as if don Juan's life were merely a clinical case. I was on the verge of ripping up my notes when don Juan poked my calf with his toe to attract my attention. He said he was "seeing" a light of violence around me and wondered whether I was going to start beating him. His laughter was a delightful break. He said that I was given to outbursts of violent behavior but that I was not really mean and that most of the time the violence was against myself.

"You're right, don Juan," I said.

"Of course," he said, laughing.

He urged me to talk about my childhood. I began to tell him about my years of fear and loneliness and got involved in describing to him what I thought to be my overwhelming struggle to survive and maintain my spirit. He laughed at the metaphor of "maintaining my spirit."

I talked for a long time. He listened with a serious expression. Then, at a given moment his eyes "clasped" me again and I stopped talking. After a moment's pause he said that nobody had ever humiliated me and that was the reason I was not really mean.

"You haven't been defeated yet," he said.

He repeated the statement four or five times so I felt obliged to ask him what he meant by that. He explained that to be defeated was a condition of life which was unavoidable. Men were either victorious or defeated and, depending on that, they became persecutors or victims. These two conditions were prevalent as long as one did not "see"; "seeing" dispelled the illusion of victory, or defeat, or suffering. He added that I should learn to "see" while I was victorious to avoid ever having the memory of being humiliated.

I protested that I was not and had never been victorious at anything; and that my life was, if anything, a defeat.

He laughed and threw his hat on the floor.

"If your life is such a defeat, step on my hat," he dared me in jest.

I sincerely argued my point. Don Juan became serious. His eyes squinted to a fine slit. He said that I thought my life was a defeat for reasons other than defeat itself. Then in a very quick and thoroughly unexpected manner he took my head in his hands by placing his palms against my temples. His eyes became fierce as he looked into mine. Out of fright I took an involuntary deep breath through my mouth. He let my head go and reclined against the wall, still gazing at me. He had performed his movements with such a speed that by the time he had relaxed and reclined comfortably against the wall, I was still in the middle of my deep breath. I felt dizzy, ill at ease.

"I *see* a little boy crying," don Juan said after a pause.

He repeated it various times as if I did not understand. I had the feeling he was talking about me as a little boy crying, so I did not really pay attention to it.

"Hey!" he said, demanding my full concentration. "I *see* a little boy crying."

I asked him if that boy was me. He said no. Then I asked him if it was a vision of my life or just a memory of his own life. He did not answer.

"I *see* a little boy," he continued saying. "And he is crying and crying."

"Is he a boy I know?" I asked.

"Yes."

"Is he my little boy?"

"No."

"Is he crying now?"

"He's crying now," he said with conviction.

I thought don Juan was having a vision of someone I knew who was a little boy and who was at that very moment crying. I voiced the names of all the children I knew, but he said those children were irrelevant to my promise and the child who was crying was very important to it.

Don Juan's statements seemed to be incongruous. He had said that I had promised something to someone during my childhood, and that the child who was crying at that very moment was important to my promise. I told him he was not making sense. He calmly repeated that he "saw" a little boy crying at that moment, and that the little boy was hurt.

I seriously struggled to fit his statements into some sort of orderly pattern, but I could not relate them to anything I was aware of.

"I give up," I said, "because I can't remember making an important promise to anybody, least of all to a child."

He squinted his eyes again and said that this particular child who was crying at that precise moment was a child of my childhood.

"He was a child during my childhood and is still crying now?" I asked.

"He is a child crying now," he insisted.

"Do you realize what you're saying, don Juan?"

"I do."

"It doesn't make sense. How can he be a child now if he was one when I was a child myself?"

"He's a child and he's crying now," he said stubbornly.

"Explain it to me, don Juan."

"No. *You* must explain it to me."

For the life of me I could not fathom what he was referring to.

"He's crying! He's crying!" don Juan kept on saying in a mesmerizing tone. "And he's hugging you now. He's hurt! He's hurt! And he's looking at you. Do you feel his eyes? He's kneeling and hugging you. He's younger than you. He has come running to you. But his arm is broken. Do you feel his arm? That little boy has a nose that looks like a button. Yes! That's a button nose."

My ears began to buzz and I lost the sensation of being at don Juan's house. The words "button nose" plunged me at once into a scene out of my childhood. I knew a button-nose boy! Don Juan had edged his way into one of the most recondite places of my life. I knew then the promise he was talking about. I had a sensation of elation, of despair, of awe for don Juan and his splendid maneuver. How in the devil did he know about the button-nose boy of my childhood? I became so agitated by the memory don Juan had evoked in me that my power to remember took me back to a time when I was eight years old. My mother had left two years before and I had spent the most hellish years of my life circulating among my mother's sisters, who served as dutiful mother surrogates and took care of me a couple of months at a time. Each of my aunts had a large family, and no matter how careful and protective the aunts were toward me, I had twenty-two cousins to contend with. Their cruelty was sometimes truly bizarre. I felt then that I was surrounded by enemies, and in the excruciating years that followed I waged a desperate and sordid war. Finally, through means I still do not know to this day, I succeeded in subduing all my cousins. I was indeed victorious. I had no more competitors who counted. However, I did not know that, nor did I know how to stop my war, which logically was extended to the school grounds.

The classrooms of the rural school where I went were mixed and the first and third grades were separated only by a space between the desks. It was there that I met a little boy with a flat nose, who was teased with the nickname "Button-nose." He was a first-grader. I used to pick on him haphazardly, not really intending to. But he seemed to like me in spite of everything I did to him. He used to follow me around and even kept the secret that I was responsible for some of the pranks that baffled the principal. And yet I still teased him. One day I deliberately toppled over a heavy standing blackboard; it fell on him; the desk in which he was sitting absorbed some of the impact, but still the blow broke his collarbone. He fell down. I helped him up and saw the pain and fright in his eyes as he looked at me and held on to me. The shock of seeing him in pain, with a mangled arm, was more than I could bear. For years I had viciously battled against my cousins and I had won; I had vanquished my foes; I had felt good and powerful up to the moment when the sight of the button-nose little boy crying demolished my victories. Right there I quit the battle. In whatever way I was capable of, I made a resolution not to win ever again. I thought his arm would have to be cut off, and I promised that if the little boy was cured I would never again be victorious. I gave up my victories for him. That was the way I understood it then.

Don Juan had opened a festered sore in my life. I felt dizzy, overwhelmed. A well of unmitigated sadness beckoned me and I succumbed to it. I felt the weight of my acts on me. The memory of that little button-nose boy, whose name was Joaquín, produced in me such a vivid anguish that I wept. I told don Juan of my sadness for that boy who never had anything, that little Joaquín who did not have money to go to a doctor and whose arm never set properly. And all I had to give him were my childish victories. I felt so ashamed.

"Be in peace, you funny bird," don Juan said imperatively. "You gave enough. Your victories were strong and they were yours. You gave enough. Now you must change your promise."

"How do I change it? Do I just say so?"

"A promise like that cannot be changed by just saying so. Perhaps very soon you'll be able to know what to do about changing it. Then perhaps you'll even get to *see.*"

"Can you give me any suggestions, don Juan?"

"You must wait patiently, knowing that you're waiting, and knowing what you're waiting for. That is the warrior's way. And if it is a matter of fulfilling your promise then you must be aware that you are fulfilling it. Then a time will come when your waiting will be over and you will no longer have to honor your promise. There is nothing you can do for that little boy's life. Only he could cancel that act."

"But how can he?"

"By learning to reduce his wants to nothing. As long as he thinks that he was a victim, his life will be hell. And as long as you think the same your promise will be valid. What makes us unhappy is to want. Yet if we would learn to cut our wants to nothing, the smallest thing we'd get would be a true gift. Be in peace, you made a good gift to Joaquín. To be poor or wanting is only a thought; and so is to hate, or to be hungry, or to be in pain."

"I cannot truly believe that, don Juan. How could hunger and pain be only thoughts?"

"They are only thoughts for me now. That's all I know. I have accomplished that feat. The power to do that is all we have, mind you, to oppose the forces of our lives; without that power we are dregs, dust in the wind."

"I have no doubt that you have done it, don Juan, but how can a simple man like myself or little Joaquín accomplish that?"

"It is up to us as single individuals to oppose the forces of our lives. I have said this to you countless times: Only a warrior can survive. A warrior knows that he is waiting and what he is waiting for; and while he waits he wants nothing and thus whatever little thing he gets is more than he can take. If he needs to eat he finds a way, because he is not hungry; if something hurts his body he finds a way to stop it, because he is not in pain. To be hungry or to be in pain means that the man has abandoned himself and is no longer a warrior; and the forces of his hunger and pain will destroy him."

I wanted to go on arguing my point, but I stopped because I realized that by arguing I was making a barrier to protect myself from the devastating force of don Juan's superb feat which had touched me so deeply and with such a power. How did he know? I thought that perhaps I had told him the story of the button-nose boy during one of my deep states of nonordinary reality. I did not recollect telling him, but my not remembering under such conditions was understandable.

"How did you know about my promise, don Juan?"

"I *saw* it."

"Did you *see* it when I had taken Mescalito, or when I had smoked your mixture?"

"I *saw* it now. Today."

"Did you *see* the whole thing?"

"There you go again. I've told you, there's no point in talking about what *seeing* is like. It is nothing."

I did not pursue the point any longer. Emotionally I was convinced.

"I also made a vow once," don Juan said suddenly.

The sound of his voice made me jump.

"I promised my father that I would live to destroy his assassins. I carried that promise with me for years. Now the promise is changed. I'm no longer interested in destroying anybody. I don't hate the Mexicans. I don't hate anyone. I have learned that the countless paths one traverses in one's life are all equal. Oppressors and oppressed meet at the end, and the only thing that prevails is that life was altogether too short for both. Today I feel sad not because my mother and father died the way they did; I feel sad because they were Indians. They lived like Indians and died like Indians and never knew that they were, before anything else, men."

CHAPTER TWO / *Learning*

Engfish, Freedom, and Discipline

Born in Moline, Illinois, and educated at Oberlin, the University of North Carolina, and Columbia, Ken Macrorie (1918–   ) has taught at a number of universities. Currently he is professor of English at Western Michigan University. He has edited the periodical *College Composition and Communication* and has written articles for other professional journals and for popular periodicals. His textbooks on writing, *Writing to Be Read* (1968) and *Telling Writing* (1969), have enlivened a dull field. An innovative teacher who has dedicated himself to humanizing student writing, Macrorie charts his frustrations, follies, and failures, as well as his considerable success, in *Uptaught* (1970), from which the following excerpts are reprinted.

My Students Were Alive

September, 1947

The students in the first class I ever taught were World War II veterans. The room was never filled, usually a half dozen or so absentees, who I feared were wandering around Chapel Hill enjoying themselves. One day I ran into one of them on campus ten minutes after my class. He walked alongside unabashed, talking of the weather, then said, *"I hope you'll excuse my absences. I like the class, but I flew fighter planes in combat and still get the shakes. Every once in a while I have to bust loose. Usually I jump on a bus and ride anywhere for a few days."*

And Humorous

October, 1947

Two weeks later, I opened the classroom door—every seat occupied. Place looked bursting. I assumed mock surprise and said, "There must be some mistake. Do you realize this is English I, the University of North Carolina, Chapel Hill, North Carolina?"

From the back row, hurried and loud, came the words, "Oh, *North* Carolina!" A book cover popped shut, and a young man rushed out the door and slammed it. When the laughter subsided, he came back in and returned to his seat, wearing his triumph modestly.

But They Wrote Dead

January, 1948

Like this:

I found the characters in this story very interesting. The plot was exciting and an outstanding aspect of the story was its description.

Except for one boy, McDonald. After writing a few miserable, pretentious, academic papers, he went away for a while. He returned with a paper written in red ink. On the last page the words became indistinguishable, the letters more and more uncertain until they finally squiggled off in a wavy line. I was incensed. The red was so hard to read, and the carelessness insulting.

But as I puzzled out the paper, I found McDonald had produced a zany story of his adventures as exciting and humorous as Holden Caulfield's. Twice more McDonald turned in live, squirming papers. After the final exam he took me aside and explained he had written those papers while he was drunk.

I should have realized that a cataclysmic event was needed to break a student away from the dead language of the schools—some severe displacement or removal from the unreal world of the university, like drunkenness. But I didn't. I was beginning my teaching, and, naturally enough, developing a protective blindness.

My Ego Was Being Fulfilled

February, 1948

I had a captive audience but thought I was freeing their minds. Surely they were learning great things from me. I was only a part-time instructor but felt the weight of the trappings of academic prestige and rank. When I walked through the campus carrying my briefcase—an object few students owned in those days—or authoritatively removed a drawer from the card catalog in the library to look up a book, I imagined all the students were looking at me and saying with awe, "He's an instructor."

But the troops weren't performing their job, which was to write clearly and powerfully in my classes. I thought that was their fault.

What Teacher Wanted

March, 1948

In the columns of *The Daily Tarheel*, the student newspaper, appeared many swinging, ironic letters to the editor written by undergraduates. They carried the rhythms of human voices, the tension of anger, the dry sound of understatement. Good models of writing for my freshmen.

I tried to get my students to write like that—as if they were on fire about something—but they kept turning out phony paragraphs. Like blacks who know the white man's attitude toward them better than he does himself, they knew what Teacher really wanted, although I didn't. And they gave it to me.

I Learned How to Correct Papers, Not Read Them

September, 1948

Got a job at Michigan State and settled down to full-time teaching. I bought some red ink for my fountain pen and began writing in the margins of what we called *themes*—

too gen'l

awk

punct

agr

sp

need specific examples

One day I climbed on the table in the classroom and took a beseeching attitude. "Won't you please put down something specific in your next theme?"

No, students turned in empty paragraphs like this:

I went downtown for the first time. When I got there I was completely astonished by the hustle and the bustle that was going on. My first impression of the downtown area was quite impressive.

I Said, "They Can't Write This Dead."

October, 1948

A colleague showed me a book by a University of Minnesota professor designed to cure students who "bandy about vague uninteresting generalizations with no specific examples to back them up."

KEN MACRORIE / *Engfish, Freedom, and Discipline*

Off to the Snack Bar with my students to follow the man's prescription—make a chart for the Observation and Recording of Sensory Detail. Columns for (1) Form or Outline, (2) Motion or Position, (3) Shade or Color. Shorter columns for Sound, Smell, Touch, and Taste. Now fill the columns, combine words or phrases into sentences, construct paragraphs. Choose an Overall Impression.

In they came—papers full of bland, trite phrases like those the Minnesota man said were "by and large successful"—

Spreading elm tree,
huge gray skyscrapers,
huge gray glacial rocks . . .

I had forced the arms, guided the fingers—to a huge gray result.

I Tried Everything, Including Non-Direction

September, 1951

I would get those kids to write live. Tried general semantics, logic, tape-recorded conversations, ancient rhetoric.

Nothing worked.

I flipped all the way over from the Snack Bar guided exercises to Group Dynamics non-directed style. Got permission to teach sort of Carl Rogers' way. I sat in the back of the room, talked only about five or ten minutes of the fifty, and asked the students to run the class. They chose what to write on, decided what they thought was good writing, and graded each other's papers.

Grading bugged them. At first they wanted to give everyone A and I said no. Slipped a little into direction there. Then they discovered that spelling and other mechanics would give them a standard, and almost all the grades went down to C.

In the first weeks they didn't believe I was going to let them run the class. Halfway through the course many began to enjoy their freedom.

But nobody wrote live. Same old academic stuff—no conviction, no red-blooded sentences.

I Began Writing a Textbook

June, 1957

I tried to play down grammar and mechanics and get the students to write naturally of things that interested them. This book was going to reform the teaching of writing in America.

One thing wrong—it carried no extended examples of good student writing. But I didn't see the implications of that fact. If I could not provide a bunch of lively papers written by students using the program I espoused in my book, then I had nothing to give students and teachers substantially different from what they had been given before.

The book was published by a reputable house—Harcourt, Brace. Its editors insisted I call it *The Perceptive Writer, Reader, and Speaker.* Good title for a book by an author absolutely blind to what he was doing.

San Francisco State

September, 1960

In 1960 I left Michigan State for San Francisco State, a school then rated among the top four in the country for teaching creative writing. Although I was hired as a "communication expert" rather than a man who would teach the writing of novels, short stories, and poems, I thought the atmosphere by the beautiful bridge probably made students flower into writers even in composition courses.

I expected exotic real flowers in Golden Gate Park and found them. I expected sophisticated students (the year before, many at State and Berkeley had had their backbones bounced against the hard edges of the steps of City Hall by the police in the most publicized student rebellion up to that time) and literary artists as colleagues. I found only the latter. I joined a staff of teachers that included Walter Van Tilburg Clark (he was on leave but his influence was manifest), Mark Harris, Harvey Swados, and S. I. Hayakawa.

Indeed it was a writing place, and most of the professors I knew were three times as alive as most I had known at Michigan State. Caroline Shrodes, who had collected all the exciting writers, enchanted me. I had never before met a woman head of a department, and no professor who one day wore giant-sized blue earrings with high-heeled shoes to match, and the next day the same combination in shocking pink. She tapped her foot with a nervous energy that seemed to vibrate through that department, and I knew I had found the right place.

It was a wonder. Caroline told me that to teach one especially small class of students weak in writing, I would be given an assistant. I expected a pale, ineffectual boy and got a bright, deeply sensitive young woman who had just given up her job as the office boss for Kermit Bloomgarden on Broadway, where she helped him with the production of *The Music Man.* I began the semester with the highest of hopes.

The papers my students turned in were worse, if anything, than those I had received at Michigan State. I was down on my knees again pleading for sentences partially alive.

After a year, I left San Francisco State. I had met stimulating professors there, but not stimulating students. The city was dramatic and beautifully situated, as well as dirty in the Mission District and Walt Disneyish in the suburbs. I missed the white winters and green springs of Michigan; so I returned there to take a job in an unlikely sounding place called Kalamazoo.

I Became a Leader of Composition Teachers

February, 1962

I was appointed editor of *College Composition and Communication,* a journal published by the National Council of Teachers of English. In that job I read and edited hundreds of plans for saving the dying composition course.

I was determined to publish some bright student writing to show readers their students weren't hopeless. I looked hard for it, solicited the 3,500 teachers who subscribed to the journal, and turned up about three decent papers. I printed them and got this letter from a professor in Ohio:

> Why a new "arty" cover; and especially why undergraduate writing? . . . Why pretend that we are all undergraduates and want to read about each other's first impressions of college?

After that, I began to notice hundreds of signs suggesting that most English professors despised their students' work. They should have. It was usually terrible.

Sixteen Years Now Teaching Blind

February, 1963

I had devoted most of my career to teaching Freshman Composition because I wanted every college student to write with clarity and pezazz. Sometimes attending my class, students became worse writers, their sentences infected with more and more phoniness, and eventually stiffening in *rigor mortis.* One of my freshmen at Western Michigan University turned in this paragraph:

> *I consider experience to be an important part in the process of learning. For example, in the case of an athlete, experience plays an important role. After each game, he tends to acquire more knowledge and proficiency, thereby making him a better athlete. An athlete could also gain more knowledge by studying up on the sport, but it is doubtful he could participate for the first time in sports with study alone and without experience and still do an adequate job.*

Such language could only have been learned in school; no one anywhere else would hear it in the bones of his ear. Key university words are there:

process, experience, role, tend, knowledge, proficiency, participate, and *important* twice. But nothing is said worth listening to. I thought this paragraph acceptable—medium rotten, but all I could expect.

Maybe Outside of Class?

October, 1963

Maybe they're afraid to say what they feel. Maybe the assignments are too confining.

With the help of other professors in a communication program, I arranged a contest—$150 for the best essay on any subject touching university life, $150 to the judge of the contest. To encourage students to speak out, I asked Paul Goodman, author of *Growing Up Absurd,* to judge the essays. In a university then comprised of 11,000 students, we received eight essays in the competition. All dead. None seemed stirring enough to warrant a certification of life, much less a prize. But I sent them off to Mr. Goodman. He read them and wrote back:

> This isn't a very spirited group of essays, and I cannot award a prize to any. Nothing sends me—neither original idea, acute observation, accurate analysis, unique attitude, warm feeling, nor vivid expression. There is no sense in making a comparative judgment among the pieces. . . . My impression is that the young people have been so brainwashed by their social background and their so-called education that even their dissent is stereotyped, griping rather than radical, snobbish rather than indignant, do-goodish rather than compassionate. There is little sign of careful, painful perception, personal suffering, or felt loyalty and disgust. On the other hand, the couple of positive estimates of university experiences are not ideal, or loving, enough to be moving . . .

No Need to Examine the Body

November, 1963

Paul Goodman was right. And the incontrovertible fact was that back in 1960 the profession had become so sick of spending more money and time on the Freshman Comp course than any other that the head of the English Department of the University of Michigan, Warner Rice, proposed in a lead article in *College English* that the freshman writing course be abolished because it wasn't producing competent writing from students. Mr. Rice wasn't kidding; he's not a kidding man. Many professors who had given their lives to this effort felt insulted, but I didn't hear of one who came forward with a batch of lively student papers to prove Mr. Rice wrong.

A Name for It

A student stopped me in the hall and said, *"Do you think I should submit this to* The Review? *I have this terrible instructor who says I can't write. Therefore I shouldn't teach English. He really grinds me."*

I looked at the first two lines:

He finks it humorous to act like the Grape God Almighty, only the stridents in his glass lisdyke him immersely.

and thought they seemed like overdone James Joyce. I said I had better take the paper home and give it several readings before reacting. But she pushed, and I read the next lines,

Day each that we tumble into the glass he sez to mee, "Eets too badly that you someday fright preach Engfish."

I wanted to hug that girl. She had been studying Joyce in another class and had used his tongue to indict all of us Engfish teachers. Didn't believe I had lisdyked my students all those years, but I had indeed tumbled them into a glass every day and fright preached Engfish at them. This girl had given me a name for the bloated, pretentious language I saw everywhere around me, in the students' themes, in the textbooks on writing, in the professors' and administrators' communications to each other. A feel-nothing, say-nothing language, dead like Latin, devoid of the rhythms of contemporary speech. A dialect in which words are almost never "attached to things," as Emerson said they should be.

Freedom

The winter had been dark and spirits down. I said I could no longer face another student paper written in Engfish. I told my Advanced Writing class, "Go home and write anything that comes to your mind. Don't stop. Write for ten minutes or till you've filled a whole page." I had remembered reading about that exercise in Dorothea Brande's book *Becoming a Writer,* published in 1936, and I had used the exercise briefly with students in Chapel Hill. My advanced writers returned with papers that spoke disjointedly and fragmentarily, but in language often alive. Some natural rhythms appeared, a striking metaphor once in a while, and often a bit of reality that jarred me. Karen Feldkamp turned in this:

Bought a red ball.

Therapy. But it doesn't work. The hair on my legs still keeps growing. Sensuously round clouds, standing at attention, waiting in rows for inspection. Made me feel happy and light, young. Nature does that to me. Makes me fresh and alive. Never smoke when I'm in the woods or by a lake. It would tarnish the beauty. I want money. I want to feel rich so that I can know what nothing is like. Makes me think of Gibran. He says sorrow and joy are relative. Must know sorrow to know joy. I believe in him. I believed in a lot of things once.

I've decided to advise people on the subject of love. World, don't close your eyes when you kiss. I hope someone hears me. I've seen too many made rancid and disposed of. I wish I could act as I think. My mind knows, but my body doesn't. Does it? Some girls in Detroit attacked a girl in an alley, pierced her cheeks and legs with safety pins. I don't know why it made me laugh so hard. My breath smells. Must be from that milk. People think milk is so good for them. It's bad for their complexion, fattening, and causes hardening of the arteries. You're no damn good when your arteries get hard.

The Day We Killed Engfish

May 7, 1964

Then I asked the students to do another free writing, this time for fifteen minutes focusing on one subject. The day we met to read those papers was hot, so we went outside under a tall maple on heavy grass still new in Michigan's spring. Twelve out of the fourteen students were present, friendly and pleasant as usual, looking around abstractedly, probably hoping the Engfish they were about to hear would quickly dissipate in the outside air.

I asked the girl nearest me to read her paper. She had written about working at an ambulance service where one day she heard the doorbell ringing as if someone were leaning on it. I thought here we go with the cliché and the standard tired paper. But as she read on, I found that a person had indeed been leaning on the bell, *"a chartreuse-faced woman choking out that her husband was having a heart attack."*

That paper by Julie Oldt Maxson moved me. Not until I heard the third paper that afternoon did I realize that everyone on the grass had quit gazing around and was listening hard. Each student had written a powerful short paper and I had broken through and the students were speaking in their own voices about things that counted for them.

Progress?

May 11, 1964

Immediately I tried the same free writing in Freshman Comp and got almost as good papers. One boy who was flunking the course writing broken sentences and spelling incomprehensibly, turned in a strong account of driving home after a party. His spelling was much improved and he controlled his words. He built to the skillful rhythms of this ending:

Then out of the fog loomed a red sign—STOP. The end of the road. I had miscounted. Sign, trees, ditch, fog, brakes, beer, that's all I remembered.

A whole semester passed before I realized I should *begin* my classes with free writing. After that, they were writing complete stories in the second and third week. Their papers exhibited all the qualities Paul Goodman said were lacking in the essays he judged. The writers revealed a surprising occasional command of metaphor, forceful beginnings and endings, telling detail, word play, irony. All those years I had tried to get a student to put down a sensuous detail that would bring alive his ideas and feelings! Now I simply ask students to write freely, first recording random thoughts, then focusing on one subject, and they frequently produce what the poet Wallace Stevens called "the exquisite environment of fact."

"Recording Sensory Details"

May, 1965

In twenty minutes of free writing, a freshman girl produced this paper:

In a few minutes Mom and Dad are going out to eat. She's got on a long-sleeved yellow dress, black fish-net nylons and black heels. When she doesn't notice, Dad looks at her. Then he rests his head on the back of the red chair and closes his eyes.

Last night Bob brought me home at twelve o'clock. We had been wrestling and playing tag on the grass in the back of Sangren. We were still laughing when he let me out of the car. I pinched his buns and then he messed up my hair. We gave each other a noisy kiss under our five-watt porch light, and he left.

Mom and Dad were still up. I was relieved because I thought we might have awakened them. I started to go upstairs when Dad asked me to wait. I put my books down and sat at the desk. Mom's face was tight and her freckles were little red spots. Dad kept puffing on his pipe. He began. "Your mother and I have decided to get a divorce. But even though I'm leaving, remember you're still my daughter and you always will be."

Then he started to cry. Mom and I were crying too. I ran over and put my arms around him. His tears felt hot on my neck. Then he said, "Go to your mother. She feels bad, too."

He left tonight—to his little apartment on Copper Street. Mom helped him move, and she cried when she saw it. The bedroom is lavender with a purple bedspread. The furniture looks like Antique Barn. A big crack runs up and down the door. When he left, he took a lamp, four glasses, and an ash tray.

The details in that little paper speak the pain and tension in a man going to live without his women. Using no chart or program for recording pertinent details, this writer had found her way.

Professional Discipline

April 12, 1966

In the freshman class Millie Crandall sat at my right not saying a thing for the first two weeks, a little scared and country looking. When time came to hand in a case-history of some process the student knew well, she presented me with a story of her working day at a nearby hospital and care home. It was laconic and powerful.

The students looked at Millie wondering where she had been all that time. She let a few facts open up that world of loneliness and slidings in and out of reality, and ended the account like this:

The hall was dark. As I walked toward the time clock, I heard a few moans. Someone called out, "I want to go home." I punched the time clock, walked out the door.

Millie could walk out; they couldn't. That was the story—told in such exquisitely painful particulars that three hours after it was printed in a campus publication with an 11,000-copy press run, I received a phone call from the president of the university.

"That story in *The Review* this morning about the patients in the home. Was that written by one of your students?"

"Yes."

"Well, it's a good story, full of feeling, but there's one trouble. All the names in it are real."

"Oh, no!" I said. "I'm sure I told everybody in that class to watch out for real names." My mind raced back. Had I said that to Millie's class? I was sure I had. Maybe she had been absent that day.

"Yes," said the president. "And I just got a call from the director of the home. She's quite agitated. Things are said about the patients, personal things, that could be the basis for a libel suit. I wonder if you could get the editors of the paper and the writer together and drive down there to see the director. Maybe you could calm her down and apologize."

"What gets me is that it's such a compassionate story."

"Yes, it is, but things are said about individuals and about the home that shouldn't be publicized with real names."

He was right. I won't cite examples because the details should not be publicized again. Millie was so deeply embarrassed that I didn't think I'd be able to pull her out. The editors and she and I drove to the home and talked to the director. She was agitated, fearing her patients' personal lives would be spread around the county. But she felt comforted to know we admitted wrong. She said she would take all precautions possible to keep copies of *The Review* from reaching the patients. Neither she nor any of them pressed charges against the university. Millie said she could not return to our university next fall, but I insisted she had written a compassionate if searing report on the human condition and we needed students like her. I showed her a letter in which the president said we must not let her turn away from our university for what was only a human mistake.

She came back in the fall, joined the staff of *The Review,* and contributed good writing to it.

Never before had my students written anything alive and honest enough to be dangerous. I was going to have to treat them as potent.

james herndon ————————————————————————

The Dumb Class

After spending six years in Europe "living here and there, doing this and that," James Herndon (1926–   ) decided to come back to the United States in 1957. On his return, he began to teach in a black ghetto school near San Francisco, but was fired after a year for being "unfit to teach." He wrote about that year in his first book, *The Way It Spozed to Be* (1966), which was widely acclaimed as a damning criticism of American education. For the past twelve years, Herndon has been teaching in a suburban junior high school outside of San Francisco, and his second book, *How to Survive in Your Native Land* (1971), is an incisive description of those years and a continuation of his criticism of American education. The following selection is a chapter from that book.

One afternoon during our free seventh period someone looked around and said This faculty is the Dumb Class.

It was so. Given the community or the entire country as a school—reversing the usual image of the school as mirror of society to make society the mirror of the school—and given that community as one which is tracked or ability-grouped into high, high-average, average, low-average, high-low, low and low-low, the faculty or faculties, teachers, *educators,* are the dumb class.

We are the dumb class because we cannot learn. Cannot achieve. Why not? Cannot concentrate, have a low attention span, are culturally deprived, brain-damaged, non-verbal, unmotivated, lack skills, are anxiety-ridden, have broken homes, can't risk failure, no study habits, won't try, are lazy. . . ? Those are the reasons *kids* are in the dumb class, supposing we don't say it's because they are just dumb. But the characteristic of the dumb class is that it cannot learn how to do what it is there to do. Try as one may, one cannot make the dumb class learn to do these things, at least not as long as it is operating together as a dumb class. Even if those things are completely obvious, the dumb class cannot learn them or achieve them.

Is it so that what the dumb class is supposed to achieve is so difficult that only superior individuals can achieve it, and then only with hard work, endless practice? Is it so mysterious and opaque that only those with intelligence and energy enough to research and ferret out the mysteries of the universe can gain insight into it? Eighth period I was involved with this dumb class which was supposed to achieve adding and subtracting before it got out of the eighth grade and went to high school. Could the class achieve it? No sir. Given an adding problem to add, most of the dumb class couldn't add it. Those who did add it hadn't any notion of whether or not they'd added it correctly, even if they had. They asked me Is this right? Is this right? This ain't right, is it? What's the answer? If you don't know whether it's right or not, I'd say, then you aren't adding it. Is this right? screamed four kids, rushing me waving papers. Boy, this dumb class can't learn, I'd say to myself. Not a very sophisticated remark, perhaps.

For a while I would drop in on the Tierra Firma bowling alley, since Jay and Jack were always dying to go there. One day I ran into the dumbest kid in the dumb class. Rather, he came up to us as we were playing this baseball slot machine. Jay and Jack were not defeating the machine, to say the least, and as a result had to put in another dime each time they wanted to play again. Well the dumb kid showed us how to lift the front legs of the machine in just the right way so that the machine would run up a big score without tilting, enough for ten or so free games, all by itself. After it did that, he told us, you could go ahead and really play it for fun. Jay and Jack were pretty impressed; they thought this dumb kid was a genius. Those big kids in your school sure are smart, was how Jack put it.

Well, as Jay and Jack happily set out to strike out and pop-up to the infield on the machine for those free games, the dumb kid and I walked around and watched the bowlers and had a smoke and talked. In the end, of course, I asked him what he was doing around there. He was getting ready to go to work, he told me. Fooling around until five, when he started. What did he do? I keep score, he told me. For the leagues. He kept score for two teams at once. He made fifteen bucks for a couple of hours. He thought it was a great job, making fifteen bucks for something he liked to do anyway, perhaps would have done for nothing, just to be able to do it.

He was keeping score. Two teams, four people on each, eight bowling scores at once. Adding quickly, not making any mistakes (for no one was going to put up with errors), following the rather complicated process of scoring in the game of bowling. Get a spare, score ten plus whatever you get on the next ball, score a strike, then ten plus whatever you get on the next two balls; imagine the man gets three strikes in a row and two spares and you are the scorer, plus you are dealing with seven other guys all striking or sparing or neither one . . . The bowling league is not a welfare organization nor part of Headstart or anything like that and wasn't interested in giving some dumb kid a chance to improve himself by fucking up their bowling

CHAPTER TWO / *Learning*

scores. No, they were giving this smart kid who had proved to be fast and accurate fifteen dollars because they could use a good scorer.

I figured I had this particular dumb kid now. Back in eighth period I lectured him on how smart he was to be a league scorer in bowling. I pried admissions from the other boys, about how they had paper routes and made change. I made the girls confess that when they went to buy stuff they didn't have any difficulty deciding if those shoes cost $10.95 or whether it meant $109.50 or whether it meant $1.09 or how much change they'd get back from a twenty. Naturally I then handed out bowling-score problems and paper-route change-making problems and buying-shoes problems, and naturally everyone could choose which ones they wanted to solve, and naturally the result was that all the dumb kids immediately rushed me yelling Is this right? I don't know how to do it! What's the answer? This ain't right, is it? and What's my grade? The girls who bought shoes for $10.95 with a $20 bill came up with $400.15 for change and wanted to know if that was right? The brilliant league scorer couldn't decide whether two strikes and a third frame of eight amounted to eighteen or twenty-eight or whether it was one hundred eight and one half.

The reason they can't learn is because they are the dumb class. No other reason. Is adding difficult? No. It is the dumb class which is difficult. Are the teachers a dumb class? Well, we are supposed to teach kids to "read, write, cipher and sing," according to an old phrase. Can we do it? Mostly not. Is it difficult? Not at all. We can't do it because we are a dumb class, which by definition can't do it, whatever it is.

Yet what we are supposed to do is something which, like adding, everyone knows how to do. It isn't mysterious, nor dependent on a vast and intricate knowledge of pedagogy or technology or psychological tests or rats. Is there any man or woman on earth who knows how to read who doesn't feel quite capable of teaching his own child or children to read? Doesn't every father feel confident that his boy will come into the bathroom every morning to stand around and watch while the father shaves and play number games with the father and learn about numbers and shaving at the same time? Every person not in the dumb class feels that these things are simple. Want to know about Egypt? Mother or father or older brother or uncle or someone and the kid go down to the public library and get out a book on Egypt and the kid reads it and perhaps the uncle reads it too, and while they are shaving they may talk about Egypt. But the dumb class of teachers and public educators feel that these things are very difficult, and they must keep hiring experts and devising strategies in order that they can rush these experts and strategies with their papers asking Is this right? and What's my grade?

Yet, released from the dumb class to their private lives, teachers are marvelous gardeners, they work on ocean liners as engineers, they act in plays, win bets, go to art movies, build their own houses, they are opera fans, expert fishermen, champion skeet shooters, grand golfers, organ players, oratorio singers, hunters, mechanics . . . all just as if they were smart people. Of course it is more difficult to build a house or sing Bach than it is to teach kids to read. Of course if they operated in their lives outside of the dumb class the same way they do in it, their houses would fall down, their ships would sink, their flowers die, their cars blow up.

This very morning in the San Francisco *Chronicle* I read a scandalous report. The reporter reports the revelations of a member of the board of education, namely that 45 per cent of the *Spanish-surname children* (that is how we put it in the paper these days) who are in mentally retarded classes have been found, when retested in Spanish, to be of average or above-average intelligence. The board member thought that "the Spanish-speaking kids were shunted into classes for the mentally retarded because they did not understand English well enough to pass the examinations they were given." He figured that, just like if he was told that a bowler had a spare on the first frame and got eight on his next ball, he'd figure that the bowler's score in the first frame ought to be eighteen. Well, in this matter assume that the board member is the teacher in a dumb class. He's trying to tell the school administrators something obvious. Does the administrator learn, now he's been told it, that ten and eight are eighteen? No, the assistant superintendent for special services says that "the assumption was that they understood English well enough to be tested by the English versions of the Stanford-Binet and the WISC intelligence tests." He thought that "it wasn't so much the fault of the test as it was the cultural deprivation of the child at the time of testing" which caused these smart kids to be retarded. Asked if these smart retarded Spanish-surname kids were now going to be moved into the regular program, he *revealed* that no, that wasn't the case, for they were *"still working* with the elementary division to seek a proper *transitional* program, since these children were still *functional retardates"* no matter what their IQ.

The reporter, acting in his role as critical parent, found out that the tests *were* available in Spanish but that Spanish-speaking kids *weren't* tested, therefore, in Spanish (because of the above assumption). The tests *weren't* available in "Oriental," and the "Oriental" kids *weren't* tested, therefore, in "Oriental." Well, that made sense, so the reporter pried out the information that the school district got $550 extra a year for each kid in mentally retarded classes. The reporter implied cynically that they were doing it for the money and that if they let all these bright retarded Spanish kids out there might be a shortage of $550 kids to be retarded.

But it is the dumb class we are concerned with. Here this administrator is told something obvious, told to learn it, told to achieve this difficult knowledge that them Spanish-speaking kids are only dumb if they are tested in a language they don't understand. But being in the dumb class, he don't learn it. He may be the smartest man in the world, able to keep score for league bowling, read The Book of the Dead, go water skiing, make bell curves. But in the dumb class he can't learn anything, and there is no reason to expect that he ever will as long as he is in there.

Graduation

The diversity of Maya Angelou's (1929–   ) talents is staggering. She danced in a touring company of *Porgy and Bess,* performed in nightclubs as a calypso singer and dancer, starred in Jean Genêt's *The Blacks,* and collaborated with Godfrey Cambridge to produce the revue *Cabaret for Freedom.* The late Martin Luther King, Jr., requested that she become Northern Coordinator for the Southern Christian Leadership Conference, a post she held in 1960–1961. Subsequently she went to Africa, where she was a journalist in Cairo and a university lecturer in Ghana. She wrote her most celebrated work, her autobiography, *I Know Why the Caged Bird Sings* (1969), in London. She has also published a volume of poetry, *Just Give Me a Cool Drink of Water 'fore I Die* (1971), and has written the screenplay for *Georgia, Georgia,* a film released in 1972. The following selection is from *I Know Why the Caged Bird Sings.*

The children in Stamps trembled visibly with anticipation. Some adults were excited too, but to be certain the whole young population had come down with graduation epidemic. Large classes were graduating from both the grammar school and the high school. Even those who were years removed from their own day of glorious release were anxious to help with preparations as a kind of dry run. The junior students who were moving into the vacating classes' chairs were tradition-bound to show their talents for leadership and management. They strutted through the school and around the campus exerting pressure on the lower grades. Their authority was so new that occasionally if they pressed a little too hard it had to be overlooked. After all, next term was coming, and it never hurt a sixth grader to have a play sister in the eighth grade, or a tenth-year student to be able to call a twelfth grader Bubba. So all was endured in a spirit of shared understanding. But the graduating classes themselves were the nobility. Like travelers with exotic destinations on their minds, the graduates were remarkably forgetful. They came to school without their books, or tablets or even pencils. Volunteers fell over themselves to secure replacements for the missing equipment. When accepted, the willing workers might or might not be thanked, and it was of no importance to the pregraduation rites. Even teachers were respectful of the now quiet and aging seniors, and tended to speak to them, if not as equals, as beings only slightly lower than themselves. After tests were returned and grades given, the student body, which acted like an extended family, knew who did well, who excelled, and what piteous ones had failed.

Unlike the white high school, Lafayette County Training School distinguished itself by having neither lawn, nor hedges, nor tennis court, nor climbing ivy. Its two buildings (main classrooms, the grade school and home economics) were set on a dirt hill with no fence to limit either its boundaries or those of bordering farms. There was a large expanse to the left of the school which was used alternately as a baseball diamond or a basketball court. Rusty hoops on the swaying poles represented the permanent recreational equipment, although bats and balls could be borrowed from the P. E. teacher if the borrower was qualified and if the diamond wasn't occupied.

Over this rocky area relieved by a few shady tall persimmon trees the graduating class walked. The girls often held hands and no longer bothered to speak to the lower students. There was a sadness about them, as if this old world was not their home and they were bound for higher ground. The boys, on the other hand, had become more friendly, more outgoing. A decided change from the closed attitude they projected while studying for finals. Now they seemed not ready to give up the old school, the familiar paths and classrooms. Only a small percentage would be continuing on to college—one of the South's A & M (agricultural and mechanical) schools, which trained Negro youths to be carpenters, farmers, handymen, masons, maids, cooks and baby nurses. Their future rode heavily on their shoulders, and blinded them to the collective joy that had pervaded the lives of the boys and girls in the grammar school graduating class.

Parents who could afford it had ordered new shoes and ready-made clothes for themselves from Sears and Roebuck or Montgomery Ward. They also engaged the best seamstresses to make the floating graduating dresses and to cut down secondhand pants which would be pressed to a military slickness for the important event.

Oh, it was important, all right. Whitefolks would attend the ceremony, and two or three would speak of God and home, and the Southern way of life, and Mrs. Parsons, the principal's wife, would play the graduation march while the lower-grade graduates paraded down the aisles and took their seats below the platform. The high school seniors would wait in empty classrooms to make their dramatic entrance.

In the Store I was the person of the moment. The birthday girl. The center. Bailey had graduated the year before, although to do so he had had to forfeit all pleasures to make up for his time lost in Baton Rouge.

My class was wearing butter-yellow piqué dresses, and Momma launched out on mine. She smocked the yoke into tiny crisscrossing puckers, then shirred the rest of the bodice. Her dark fingers ducked in and out of the lemony cloth as she embroidered raised daisies around the hem. Before she considered herself finished she had added a crocheted cuff on the puff sleeves, and a pointy crocheted collar.

I was going to be lovely. A walking model of all the various styles of fine hand sewing and it didn't worry me that I was only twelve years old and merely graduating from the eighth grade. Besides, many teachers in Arkansas Negro schools had only that diploma and were licensed to impart wisdom.

The days had become longer and more noticeable. The faded beige of former times had been replaced with strong and sure colors. I began to see my classmates' clothes, their skin tones, and the dust that waved off pussy willows. Clouds that lazed across the sky were objects of great concern to me. Their shiftier shapes might have held a message that in my new happiness and with a little bit of time I'd soon decipher. During that period I looked at the arch of heaven so religiously my neck kept a steady ache. I had taken to smiling more often, and my jaws hurt from the unaccustomed activity. Between the two physical sore spots, I suppose I could have been uncomfortable, but that was not the case. As a member of the winning team (the graduating class of 1940) I had outdistanced unpleasant sensations by miles. I was headed for the freedom of open fields.

Youth and social approval allied themselves with me and we trammeled memories of slights and insults. The wind of our swift passage remodeled my features. Lost tears were pounded to mud and then to dust. Years of withdrawal were brushed aside and left behind, as hanging ropes of parasitic moss.

My work alone had awarded me a top place and I was going to be one of the first called in the graduating ceremonies. On the classroom blackboard, as well as on the bulletin board in the auditorium, there were blue stars and white stars and red stars. No absences, no tardinesses, and my academic work was among the best of the year. I could say the preamble to the Constitution even faster than Bailey. We timed ourselves often: "Wethepeopleofthe-UnitedStatesinordertoformamoreperfectunion . . ." I had memorized the Presidents of the United States from Washington to Roosevelt in chronological as well as alphabetical order.

My hair pleased me too. Gradually the black mass had lengthened and thickened, so that it kept at last to its braided pattern, and I didn't have to yank my scalp off when I tried to comb it.

Louise and I had rehearsed the exercises until we tired out ourselves. Henry Reed was class valedictorian. He was a small, very black boy with hooded eyes, a long, broad nose and an oddly shaped head. I had admired him for years because each term he and I vied for the best grades in our class. Most often he bested me, but instead of being disappointed I was pleased that we shared top places between us. Like many Southern Black children, he lived with his grandmother, who was as strict as Momma and as kind as she knew how to be. He was courteous, respectful and soft-spoken to elders, but on the playground he chose to play the roughest games. I admired him. Anyone, I reckoned, sufficiently afraid or sufficiently dull could be polite. But to be able to operate at a top level with both adults and children was admirable.

His valedictory speech was entitled "To Be or Not to Be." The rigid tenth-grade teacher had helped him write it. He'd been working on the dramatic stresses for months.

The weeks until graduation were filled with heady activities. A group of small children were to be presented in a play about buttercups and daisies and bunny rabbits. They could be heard throughout the building practicing their hops and their little songs that sounded like silver bells. The older girls (nongraduates, of course) were assigned the task of making refreshments for the night's festivities. A tangy scent of ginger, cinnamon, nutmeg and chocolate wafted around the home economics building as the budding cooks made samples for themselves and their teachers.

In every corner of the workshop, axes and saws split fresh timber as the woodshop boys made sets and stage scenery. Only the graduates were left out of the general bustle. We were free to sit in the library at the back of the building or look in quite detachedly, naturally, on the measures being taken for our event.

Even the minister preached on graduation the Sunday before. His subject was, "Let your light so shine that men will see your good works and praise your Father, Who is in Heaven." Although the sermon was purported to be addressed to us, he used the occasion to speak to backsliders, gamblers and general ne'er-do-wells. But since he had called our names at the beginning of the service we were mollified.

Among Negroes the tradition was to give presents to children going only from one grade to another. How much more important this was when the person was graduating at the top of the class. Uncle Willie and Momma had sent away for a Mickey Mouse watch like Bailey's. Louise gave me four embroidered handkerchiefs. (I gave her three crocheted doilies.) Mrs. Sneed, the minister's wife, made me an underskirt to wear for graduation, and nearly every customer gave me a nickel or maybe even a dime with the instruction "Keep on moving to higher ground," or some such encouragement.

Amazingly the great day finally dawned and I was out of bed before I knew it. I threw open the back door to see it more clearly, but Momma said, "Sister, come away from that door and put your robe on."

I hoped the memory of that morning would never leave me. Sunlight was itself still young, and the day had none of the insistence maturity would bring it in a few hours. In my robe and barefoot in the backyard, under cover of going to see about my new beans, I gave myself up to the gentle warmth and thanked God that no matter what evil I had done in my life He had allowed me to live to see this day. Somewhere in my fatalism I had expected to die, accidentally, and never have the chance to walk up the stairs in the auditorium and gracefully receive my hard-earned diploma. Out of God's merciful bosom I had won reprieve.

Bailey came out in his robe and gave me a box wrapped in Christmas paper. He said he had saved his money for months to pay for it. It felt like a box of chocolates, but I knew Bailey wouldn't save money to buy candy when we had all we could want under our noses.

He was as proud of the gift as I. It was a soft-leather-bound copy of a collection of poems by Edgar Allan Poe, or, as Bailey and I called him, "Eap." I turned to "Annabel Lee" and we walked up and down the garden rows, the cool dirt between our toes, reciting the beautifully sad lines.

Momma made a Sunday breakfast although it was only Friday. After we finished the blessing, I opened my eyes to find the watch on my plate. It was a dream of a day. Everything went smoothly and to my credit. I didn't have to be reminded or scolded for anything. Near evening I was too jittery to attend to chores, so Bailey volunteered to do all before his bath.

Days before, we had made a sign for the Store, and as we turned out the lights Momma hung the cardboard over the doorknob. It read clearly: CLOSED. GRADUATION.

My dress fitted perfectly and everyone said that I looked like a sunbeam in it. On the hill, going toward the school, Bailey walked behind with Uncle Willie, who muttered, "Go on, Ju." He wanted him to walk ahead with us because it embarrassed him to have to walk so slowly. Bailey said he'd let the ladies walk together, and the men would bring up the rear. We all laughed, nicely.

Little children dashed by out of the dark like fireflies. Their crepe-paper dresses and butterfly wings were not made for running and we heard more than one rip, dryly, and the regretful "uh uh" that followed.

The school blazed without gaiety. The windows seemed cold and unfriendly from the lower hill. A sense of ill-fated timing crept over me, and if Momma hadn't reached for my hand I would have drifted back to Bailey and Uncle Willie, and possibly beyond. She made a few slow jokes about my feet getting cold, and tugged me along to the now-strange building.

Around the front steps, assurance came back. There were my fellow "greats," the graduating class. Hair brushed back, legs oiled, new dresses and pressed pleats, fresh pocket handkerchiefs and little handbags, all homesewn. Oh, we were up to snuff, all right. I joined my comrades and didn't even see my family go in to find seats in the crowded auditorium.

The school band struck up a march and all classes filed in as had been rehearsed. We stood in front of our seats, as assigned, and on a signal from the choir director, we sat. No sooner had this been accomplished than the band started to play the national anthem. We rose again and sang the song, after which we recited the pledge of allegiance. We remained standing for a brief minute before the choir director and the principal signaled to us, rather desperately I thought, to take our seats. The command was so unusual that our carefully rehearsed and smooth-running machine was thrown off. For a full minute we fumbled for our chairs and bumped into each other awkwardly. Habits change or solidify under pressure, so in our state of nervous tension we had been ready to follow our usual assembly pattern: the American national anthem, then the pledge of allegiance, then the song every Black person I knew called the Negro National Anthem. All done in the same key, with the same passion and most often standing on the same foot.

Finding my seat at last, I was overcome with a presentiment of worse things to come. Something unrehearsed, unplanned, was going to happen, and we were going to be made to look bad. I distinctly remember being explicit in the choice of pronoun. It was "we," the graduating class, the unit, that concerned me then.

The principal welcomed "parents and friends" and asked the Baptist minister to lead us in prayer. His invocation was brief and punchy, and for a second I thought we were getting back on the high road to right action. When the principal came back to the dais, however, his voice had changed. Sounds always affected me profoundly and the principal's voice was one of my favorites. During assembly it melted and lowed weakly into the audience. It had not been in my plan to listen to him, but my curiosity was piqued and I straightened up to give him my attention.

He was talking about Booker T. Washington, our "late great leader," who said we can be as close as the fingers on the hand, etc. . . . Then he said a few vague things about friendship and the friendship of kindly people to those less fortunate than themselves. With that his voice nearly faded, thin, away. Like a river diminishing to a stream and then to a trickle. But he cleared his throat and said, "Our speaker tonight, who is also our friend, came from Texarkana to deliver the commencement address, but due to the irregularity of the train schedule, he's going to, as they say, 'speak and run.' " He said that we understood and wanted the man to know that we were most grateful for the time he was able to give us and then something about how we were willing always to adjust to another's program, and without more ado—"I give you Mr. Edward Donleavy."

Not one but two white men came through the door offstage. The shorter one walked to the speaker's platform, and the tall one moved over to the center seat and sat down. But that was our principal's seat, and already occupied. The dislodged gentleman bounced around for a long breath or two before the Baptist minister gave him his chair, then with more dignity than the situation deserved, the minister walked off the stage.

Donleavy looked at the audience once (on reflection, I'm sure that he wanted only to reassure himself that we were really there), adjusted his glasses and began to read from a sheaf of papers.

He was glad "to be here and to see the work going on just as it was in the other schools."

At the first "Amen" from the audience I willed the offender to immediate death by choking on the word. But Amens and Yes, sir's began to fall around the room like rain through a ragged umbrella.

He told us of the wonderful changes we children in Stamps had in store. The Central School (naturally, the white school was Central) had already been granted improvements that would be in use in the fall. A well-known artist was coming from Little Rock to teach art to them. They were going to have the newest microscopes and chemistry equipment for their laboratory. Mr. Donleavy didn't leave us long in the dark over who made these improvements available at Central High. Nor were we to be ignored in the general betterment scheme he had in mind.

He said that he had pointed out to people at a very high level that one of the first-line football tacklers at Arkansas Agricultural and Mechanical College had graduated from good old Lafayette County Training School. Here fewer Amen's were heard. Those few that did break through lay dully in the air with the heaviness of habit.

He went on to praise us. He went on to say how he had bragged that "one of the best basketball players at Fisk sank his first ball right here at Lafayette County Training School."

The white kids were going to have a chance to become Galileos and Madame Curies and Edisons and Gauguins, and our boys (the girls weren't even in on it) would try to be Jesse Owenses and Joe Louises.

Owens and the Brown Bomber were great heroes in our world, but what school official in the white-goddom of Little Rock had the right to decide that those two men must be our only heroes? Who decided that for Henry Reed to become a scientist he had to work like George Washington Carver, as a bootblack, to buy a lousy microscope? Bailey was obviously always going to be too small to be an athlete, so which concrete angel glued to what country seat had decided that if my brother wanted to become a lawyer he had to first pay penance for his skin by picking cotton and hoeing corn and studying correspondence books at night for twenty years?

The man's dead words fell like bricks around the auditorium and too many settled in my belly. Constrained by hard-learned manners I couldn't look behind me, but to my left and right the proud graduating class of 1940 had dropped their heads. Every girl in my row had found something new to do with her handkerchief. Some folded the tiny squares into love knots, some into triangles, but most were wadding them, then pressing them flat on their yellow laps.

On the dais, the ancient tragedy was being replayed. Professor Parsons sat, a sculptor's reject, rigid. His large, heavy body seemed devoid of will or willingness, and his eyes said he was no longer with us. The other teachers examined the flag (which was draped stage right) or their notes, or the windows which opened on our now-famous playing diamond.

Graduation, the hush-hush magic time of frills and gifts and congratulations and diplomas, was finished for me before my name was called. The accomplishment was nothing. The meticulous maps, drawn in three colors of ink, learning and spelling decasyllabic words, memorizing the whole of *The Rape of Lucrece*—it was for nothing. Donleavy had exposed us.

We were maids and farmers, handymen and washerwomen, and anything higher that we aspired to was farcical and presumptuous.

Then I wished that Gabriel Prosser and Nat Turner had killed all whitefolks in their beds and that Abraham Lincoln had been assassinated before the signing of the Emancipation Proclamation, and that Harriet Tubman had been killed by that blow on her head and Christopher Columbus had drowned in the *Santa María.*

It was awful to be Negro and have no control over my life. It was brutal to be young and already trained to sit quietly and listen to charges brought against my color with no chance of defense. We should all be dead. I thought I should like to see us all dead, one on top of the other. A pyramid of flesh with the whitefolks on the bottom, as the broad base, then the Indians with their silly tomahawks and teepees and wigwams and treaties, the Negroes with their mops and recipes and cotton sacks and spirituals sticking out of their mouths. The Dutch children should all stumble in their wooden shoes and break their necks. The French should choke to death on the Louisiana Purchase (1803) while silkworms ate all the Chinese with their stupid pigtails. As a species, we were an abomination. All of us.

Donleavy was running for election, and assured our parents that if he won we could count on having the only colored paved playing field in that part of Arkansas. Also—he never looked up to acknowledge the grunts of acceptance—also, we were bound to get some new equipment for the home economics building and the workshop.

He finished, and since there was no need to give any more than the most perfunctory thank-you's, he nodded to the men on the stage, and the tall white man who was never introduced joined him at the door. They left with the attitude that now they were off to something really important. (The graduation ceremonies at Lafayette County Training School had been a mere preliminary.)

The ugliness they left was palpable. An uninvited guest who wouldn't leave. The choir was summoned and sang a modern arrangement of "Onward, Christian Soldiers," with new words pertaining to graduates seeking their place in the world. But it didn't work. Elouise, the daughter of the Baptist minister, recited "Invictus," and I could have cried at the impertinence of "I am the master of my fate, I am the captain of my soul."

My name had lost its ring of familiarity and I had to be nudged to go and receive my diploma. All my preparations had fled. I neither marched up to the stage like a conquering Amazon, nor did I look in the audience for Bailey's nod of approval. Marguerite Johnson, I heard the name again, my honors were read, there were noises in the audience of appreciation, and I took my place on the stage as rehearsed.

I thought about colors I hated: ecru, puce, lavender, beige and black.

There was shuffling and rustling around me, then Henry Reed was giving his valedictory address, "To Be or Not to Be." Hadn't he heard the whitefolks? We couldn't *be*, so the question was a waste of time. Henry's voice came out clear and strong. I feared to look at him. Hadn't he got the message? There was no "nobler in the mind" for Negroes because the world didn't think we had minds, and they let us know it. "Outrageous fortune"? Now, that was a joke. When the ceremony was over I had to tell Henry Reed some things. That is, if I still cared. Not "rub," Henry, "erase." "Ah, there's the erase." Us.

Henry had been a good student in elocution. His voice rose on tides of promise and fell on waves of warnings. The English teacher had helped him to create a sermon winging through Hamlet's soliloquy. To be a man, a doer, a builder, a leader, or to be a tool, an unfunny joke, a crusher of funky toadstools. I marveled that Henry could go through with the speech as if we had a choice.

I had been listening and silently rebutting each sentence with my eyes closed; then there was a hush, which in an audience warns that something unplanned is happening. I looked up and saw Henry Reed, the conservative, the proper, the A student, turn his back to the audience and turn to us (the proud graduating class of 1940) and sing, nearly speaking,

> "Lift ev'ry voice and sing
> Till earth and heaven ring
> Ring with the harmonies of Liberty . . ."

"Lift Ev'ry Voice and Sing"—words by James Weldon Johnson and music by J. Rosamond Johnson. © copyright Edward B. Marks Music Corporation. Used by permission.

It was the poem written by James Weldon Johnson. It was the music composed by J. Rosamond Johnson. It was the Negro national anthem. Out of habit we were singing it.

Our mothers and fathers stood in the dark hall and joined the hymn of encouragement. A kindergarten teacher led the small children onto the stage and the buttercups and daisies and bunny rabbits marked time and tried to follow:

> "Stony the road we trod
> Bitter the chastening rod
> Felt in the days when hope, unborn, had died.
> Yet with a steady beat
> Have not our weary feet
> Come to the place for which our fathers sighed?"

Every child I knew had learned that song with his ABC's and along with "Jesus Loves Me This I Know." But I personally had never heard it before. Never heard the words, despite the thousands of times I had sung them. Never thought they had anything to do with me.

On the other hand, the words of Patrick Henry had made such an impression on me that I had been able to stretch myself tall and trembling and say, "I know not what course others may take, but as for me, give me liberty or give me death."

And now I heard, really for the first time:

> "We have come over a way that with tears has been watered,
> We have come, treading our path through the blood of the slaughtered."

While echoes of the song shivered in the air, Henry Reed bowed his head, said "Thank you," and returned to his place in the line. The tears that slipped down many faces were not wiped away in shame.

We were on top again. As always, again. We survived. The depths had been icy and dark, but now a bright sun spoke to our souls. I was no longer simply a member of the proud graduating class of 1940; I was a proud member of the wonderful, beautiful Negro race.

Oh, Black known and unknown poets, how often have your auctioned pains sustained us? Who will compute the lonely nights made less lonely by your songs, or by the empty pots made less tragic by your tales?

If we were a people much given to revealing secrets, we might raise monuments and sacrifice to the memories of our poets, but slavery cured us of that weakness. It may be enough, however, to have it said that we survive in exact relationship to the dedication of our poets (include preachers, musicians and blues singers).

chapter three ————————————————

———————————— *Commitment*

introduction _____

We live in an era when the dedicated scientist, the revolutionary bomb-thrower, and the passionate feminist share a common characteristic: a devotion to principles and beliefs, as well as a willingness to act in their name. If commitment at its worst can bring forth mindless fanaticism, intolerant absolutism, and simplistic polarization, at its best it can eradicate moral laziness and the fear of "getting involved." It can invest people with a sense of purpose and elicit from them acts that might go beyond their normal capabilities.

In the opening essay of the chapter, George Plimpton's commitment is neither long-range nor socially, politically, or morally significant. But his undertaking to play professional football as a layman is exhausting, dangerous, and, as his performance at quarterback proves, humiliating.

While Marjorie Karmel avoids the traditionally expected agonies of giving birth by committing herself to a natural-childbirth technique whose culmination she describes in "C'est Un Garçon!" the pangs Thomas Wolfe endures in giving birth to a novel are severe and long-lasting. Most writers find that their problems begin with trying to fill blank pages, but Wolfe couldn't stop the blizzard of words from coming. And once he cut off the flow of verbiage, he had to begin the torture of cutting the work down. It is only because of his editor, who acted as a literary midwife, that Wolfe and his novel survived as well as they did.

The risks Willie Morris and Anne Moody take in living up to their commitments are considerable. In Morris's fight for freedom of expression as student editor of the University of Texas daily newspaper, he is threatened directly and indirectly by some of the most powerful men in the state when he won't stop writing editorials critical of the state's oil industry. Leading a voter-registration drive in the heart of Mississippi, Anne Moody is driven into hiding for fear of her life as shotgun-wielding white bigots hunt her down. Even in the face of death, she remains steadfast and continues her campaign.

After the disillusionment of the Cambodian incursion in the war in Southeast Asia and in the midst of its disruptive aftermath on college campuses, including the killings at Kent State, Michael Rossman ruminates over his belief that the American consciousness must be changed to bring America peace and its citizens a meaningful life. He reviews his three years of work as an agent of that change on college campuses throughout America and rededicates himself to continuing it.

In contrast to the social involvement of the preceding authors, Henry David Thoreau and Thomas Merton delight in their commitments to solitude. They choose to leave the world of men and affairs to live alone in a more natural world. Merton's life as a hermit alternates between the mundane and the sublime. Rather than trying to explain his solitary life, he describes it, making no essential value distinctions between acts like spiritual meditation and washing out his coffee pot in the rain barrel. In his solitude he fulfills what he calls "the necessity of my own nature."

At Walden Pond, Thoreau has "a little world to myself," but he is not lonely. Nature fills his life, a nature whose very raindrops provide him with "an infinite and unaccountable friendliness all at once like an atmosphere sustaining me, as made the fancied advantages of human neighborhood insignificant."

To complete the chapter, Malcolm X describes a change in his commitments. On his pilgrimage to Mecca, Malcolm X confirms his suspicions about the narrowness of American Black Muslimism. From a global point of view, he realizes that whites are not inherently satanic and that the terms of his struggle must change to show blacks and whites alike the "Oneness of God" which might lead them to accept the "Oneness of Man."

At Quarterback for the Lions

Born to a wealthy and cultured family, George Plimpton (1927–   ) has said of his early life, "I had a perfectly pleasant, non-unhappy childhood. No divorces, no tragedies." He was educated at Harvard and Cambridge, and while living in Paris in 1952, he and some friends launched *The Paris Review,* now a respected literary magazine. He remains its editor-in-chief today. But George Plimpton is best known for rushing in where angels fear to tread, trying his hand (and body) at professional athletics for which he has had neither special training nor proven aptitude: boxing, baseball, football, golf, tennis, and auto racing From these endeavors which Ernest Hemingway once called "the dark side of the moon of Walter Mitty," Plimpton has fashioned articles, books, and television shows written with grace and wit. *Paper Lion* is his most widely known book. It describes his grueling summer training with the Detroit Lions in 1963. The following selection from that book represents the culmination of that experience.

Jack Benny used to say that when he stood on the stage in white tie and tails for his violin concerts and raised his bow to begin his routine—scraping through "Love in Bloom"—that he *felt* like a great violinist. He reasoned that, if he wasn't a great violinist, what was he doing dressed in tails, and about to play before a large audience?

At Pontiac I *felt* myself a football quarterback, not an interloper. My game plan was organized, and I knew what I was supposed to do. My nerves seemed steady, much steadier than they had been as I waited on the bench. I trotted along easily. I was keenly aware of what was going on around me.

I could hear Bud Erickson's voice over the loudspeaker system, a dim murmur, telling the crowd what was going on. He was telling them that number zero, coming out across the sidelines was not actually a rookie, but an amateur, a writer, who had been training with the team for three weeks and had learned five plays, which he was now going to run against the first-string Detroit defense. It was like a nightmare come true, he told them, as if one of *them,* rocking a beer around in a paper cup, with a pretty girl leaning past him to ask the hot-dog vendor in the aisle for mustard, were suddenly carried down underneath the stands by a sinister clutch of ushers. He would protest, but he would be encased in the accoutrements, the silver helmet, with the two protruding bars of the cage, jammed down over his ears, and sent out to take over the team—that was the substance of Erickson's words, drifting across the field, swayed and shredded by the steady breeze coming up across the open end of Wisner Stadium from the vanished sunset. The crowd was interested, and I was conscious, just vaguely, of a steady roar of encouragement.

The team was waiting for me, grouped in the huddle watching me come. I went in among them. Their heads came down for the signal. I called out, "Twenty-six!" forcefully, to inspire them, and a voice from one of the helmets said, "Down, down, the whole stadium can hear you."

"Twenty-six," I hissed at them. "Twenty-six near oh pinch; on three. *Break!*" Their hands cracked as one, and I wheeled and started for the line behind them.

My confidence was extreme. I ambled slowly behind Whitlow, poised down over the ball, and I had sufficient presence to pause, resting a hand at the base of his spine, as if on a windowsill—a nonchalant gesture I had admired in certain quarterbacks—and I looked out over the length of his back to fix in my mind what I saw.

Everything fine about being a quarterback—the embodiment of his power—was encompassed in those dozen seconds or so: giving the instructions to ten attentive men, breaking out of the huddle, walking for the line, and then pausing behind the center, dawdling amidst men poised and waiting under the trigger of his voice, cataleptic, until the deliverance of himself and them to the future. The pleasure of sport was so often the chance to indulge the cessation of time itself—the pitcher dawdling on the mound, the skier poised at the top of a mountain trail, the basketball player with the rough skin of the ball against his palm preparing for a foul shot, the tennis player at set point over his opponent—all of them savoring a moment before committing themselves to action.

I had the sense of a portcullis down. On the other side of the imaginary bars the linemen were poised, the light glistening off their helmets, and close in behind them were the linebackers, with Joe Schmidt just opposite me, the big number 56 shining on his white jersey, jumpjacking back and forth with quick choppy steps, his hands poised in front of him, and he was calling out defensive code words in a stream. I could sense the rage in his voice, and the tension in those rows of bodies waiting, as if coils had been wound overtight, which my voice, calling a signal, like a lever would trip to spring them all loose. "Blue! Blue! Blue" I heard Schmidt shout.

Within my helmet, the schoolmaster's voice murmured at me: "Son, nothing to it, nothing at all . . ."

I bent over the center. Quickly, I went over what was supposed to happen—I would receive the snap and take two steps straight back, and hand the ball to the number two back coming laterally across from right to left, who would then cut into the number six hole. That was what was designated by 26—the two back into the six hole. The mysterious code words "near oh pinch" referred to blocking assignments in the line, and I was never sure exactly what was meant by them. The important thing was to hang on to the ball, turn, and get the ball into the grasp of the back coming across laterally.

I cleared my throat. "Set!" I called out—my voice loud and astonishing to hear, as if it belonged to someone shouting into the earholes of my helmet. "Sixteen, sixty-five, forty-four, *hut* one, *hut* two, *hut* three," and at three the ball slapped back into my palm, and Whitlow's rump bucked up hard as he went for the defensemen opposite.

The lines cracked together with a yawp and smack of pads and gear. I had the sense of quick, heavy movement, and as I turned for the backfield, not a second having passed, I was hit hard from the side, and as I gasped the ball was jarred loose. It sailed away, and bounced once, and I stumbled after it, hauling it under me five yards back, hearing the rush of feet, and the heavy jarring and wheezing of the blockers fending off the defense, a great roar up from the crowd, and above it, a relief to hear, the shrilling of the referee's whistle. My first thought was that at the snap of the ball the right side of the line had collapsed just at the second of the handoff, and one of the tacklers, Brown or Floyd Peters, had cracked through to make me fumble. Someone, I assumed, had messed up on the assignments designated by the mysterious code words "near oh pinch." In fact, as I discovered later, my *own* man bowled me over—John Gordy, whose assignment as offensive guard was to pull from his position and join the interference on the far side of the center. He was required to pull back and travel at a great clip parallel to the line of scrimmage to get out in front of the runner, his route theoretically passing between me and the center. But the extra second it took me to control the ball, and the creaking execution of my turn, put me in his path, a rare sight for Gordy to see, his own quarterback blocking the way, like coming around a corner in a high-speed car to find a moose ambling across the center line, and he caromed off me, jarring the ball loose.

It was not new for me to be hit down by my own people. At Cranbrook I was knocked down all the time by players on the offense—the play patterns run with such speed along routes so carefully defined that if everything wasn't done right and at the proper speed, the play would break down in its making. I was often reminded of film clips in which the process of a porcelain pitcher, say, being dropped by a butler and smashed, is shown in reverse, so that the pieces pick up off the floor and soar up to the butler's hand, each piece on a predestined route, sudden perfection out of chaos. Often, it did not take more than an inch or so off line to throw a play out of kilter. On one occasion at the training camp, practicing handoff plays to the fullback, I had

CHAPTER THREE / *Commitment*

my chin hanging out just a bit too far, something wrong with my posture, and Pietrosante's shoulder pad caught it like a punch as he went by, and I spun slowly to the ground, grabbing at my jaw. Brettschneider had said that afternoon: "The defense is going to rack you up one of these days, if your own team'd let you *stand* long enough for us defense guys to get *at* you. It's aggravating to bust through and find that you've already been laid flat by your own offense guys."

My confidence had not gone. I stood up. The referee took the ball from me. He had to tug to get it away, a faint look of surprise on his face. My inner voice was assuring me that the fault in the tumble had not been mine. "They let you down," it was saying. "The blocking failed." But the main reason for my confidence was the next play on my list—the 93 pass, a play which I had worked successfully in the Cranbrook scrimmages. I walked into the huddle and I said with considerable enthusiasm, "All right! All *right!* Here we *go!*"

"Keep the voice down," said a voice. "You'll be tipping them the play."

I leaned in on them and said: "Green right" ("Green" designated a pass play, "right" put the flanker to the right side), "three right" (which put the three back to the right), "ninety-three" (indicating the two primary receivers; nine, the right end, and three, the three back) "on *three . . . Break!*"—the clap of the hands again in unison, the team streamed past me up to the line, and I walked briskly up behind Whitlow.

Again, I knew exactly how the play was going to develop—back those seven yards into the defensive pocket for the three to four seconds it was supposed to hold, and Pietrosante, the three back, would go down in his pattern, ten yards straight, then cut over the middle, and I would hit him.

"Set! . . . sixteen! . . . eighty-eight . . . fifty-five . . . *hut* one . . . *hut* two . . . *hut* three . . ."

The ball slapped into my palm at "three." I turned and started back. I could feel my balance going, and two yards behind the line of scrimmage I *fell down*—absolutely flat, as if my feet had been pinned under a trip wire stretched across the field, not a hand laid on me. I heard a great roar go up from the crowd. Suffused as I had been with confidence, I could scarcely believe what had happened. Mud cleats catching in the grass? Slipped in the dew? I felt my jaw go ajar in my helmet. "Wha'? Wha'?"—the mortification beginning to come fast. I rose hurriedly to my knees at the referee's whistle, and I could see my teammates' big silver helmets with the blue Lion decals turn toward me, some of the players rising from blocks they'd thrown to protect me, their faces masked, automaton, prognathous with the helmet bars protruding toward me, characterless, yet the dismay was in the set of their bodies as they loped back for the huddle. The schoolmaster's voice flailed at me inside my helmet. "Ox!" it cried. "Clumsy oaf."

I joined the huddle. "Sorry, sorry," I said.

"Call the play, man," came a voice from one of the helmets.

"I don't know what happened," I said.

"Call it, man."

The third play on my list was the 42, another running play, one of the simplest in football, in which the quarterback receives the snap, makes a full spin, and shoves the ball into the four back's stomach—the fullback's. He has come straight forward from his position as if off starting blocks, his knees high, and he disappears with the ball into the number two hole just to the left of the center—a straight power play, and one which seen from the stands seems to offer no difficulty.

I got into an awful jam with it. Once again, the jackrabbit-speed of the professional backfield was too much for me. The fullback—Danny Lewis—was past me and into the line before I could complete my spin and set the ball in his belly. And so I did what was required: I tucked the ball into my own belly and followed Lewis into the line, hoping that he might have budged open a small hole.

I tried, grimacing, my eyes squinted almost shut, and waiting for the impact, which came before I'd taken two steps—I was grabbed up by Roger Brown.

He tackled me high, and straightened me with his power, so that I churned against his three-hundred-pound girth like a comic bicyclist. He began to shake me. I remained upright to my surprise, flailed back and forth, and I realized that he was struggling for the ball. His arms were around it, trying to tug it free. The bars of our helmets were neatly locked, and I could look through and see him inside—the first helmeted face I recognized that evening—the small, brown eyes surprisingly peaceful, but he was grunting hard, the sweat shining, and I had time to think, "It's Brown, it's *Brown!*" before I lost the ball to him, and flung to one knee on the ground I watched him lumber ten yards into the end zone behind us for a touchdown.

The referee wouldn't allow it. He said he'd blown the ball dead while we were struggling for it. Brown was furious. "You taking that away from *me,*" he said, his voice high and squeaky. "Man, I took that ball in there good."

The referee turned and put the ball on the ten yard line. I had lost twenty yards in three attempts, and I had yet, in fact, to run off a complete play.

The veterans walked back very slowly to the next huddle.

I stood off to one side, listening to Brown rail at the referee. "I never scored like that befo'. You takin' that away from me?" His voice was peeved. He looked off toward the stands, into the heavy tumult of sound, spreading the big palms of his hands in grief.

I watched him, detached, not even moved by his insistence that I suffer the humiliation of having the ball stolen for a touchdown. If the referee had allowed him his score, I would not have protested. The shock of having the three plays go as badly as they had left me dispirited and numb, the purpose of the exercise forgotten. Even the schoolmaster's voice seemed to have gone—a bleak despair having set in so that as I stood shifting uneasily, watching Brown jawing at the referee, I was perfectly willing to trot in to the bench at that point and be done with it.

Then, by chance, I happened to see Brettschneider standing at his corner linebacker position, watching me, and beyond the bars of his cage I could see a grin working. That set my energies ticking over once again—the notion that some small measure of recompense would be mine if I could complete a pass in the Badger's territory and embarrass him. I had such a play in my series—a slant pass to the strong-side end, Jim Gibbons.

I walked back to the huddle. It was slow in forming. I said, "The Badger's asleep. He's fat and he's asleep."

No one said anything. Everyone stared down. In the silence I became suddenly aware of the feet. There are twenty-two of them in the huddle, after all, most of them very large, in a small area, and while the quarterback ruminates and the others await his instruction, there's nothing else to catch the attention. The sight pricked at my mind, the oval of twenty-two football shoes, and it may have been responsible for my error in announcing the play. I forgot to give the signal on which the ball was to be snapped back by the center. I said: "Green right nine slant *break!*" One or two of the players clapped their hands, and as the huddle broke, some of them automatically heading for the line of scrimmage, someone hissed: "Well, the *signal*, what's the signal, for Chrissake."

I had forgotten to say "on two."

I should have kept my head and formed the huddle again. Instead, I called out "Two!" in a loud stage whisper, directing my call first to one side, then the other, "*two! two!*" as we walked up to the line. For those that might have been beyond earshot, who might have missed the signal, I held out two fingers spread like a V, which I showed around furtively, trying to hide it from the defense, and hoping that my people would see.

The pass was incomplete. I took two steps back (the play was a quick pass, thrown without a protective pocket) and I saw Gibbons break from his position, then stop, buttonhooking, his hand, which I used as a target, came up, but I threw the ball over him. A yell came up from the crowd seeing the ball in the air (it was the first play of the evening which hadn't been "blown"—to use the player's expression for a missed play), but then a groan went up when the ball was overshot and bounced across the sidelines.

"Last play," George Wilson was calling. He had walked over with a clipboard in his hand and was standing by the referee. "The ball's on the ten. Let's see you take it all the way," he called out cheerfully.

One of the players asked: "Which end zone is he talking about?"

The last play of the series was a pitchout—called a flip on some teams—a long lateral to the number four back running parallel to the line and cutting for the eight hole at left end. The lateral, though long, was easy for me to do. What I had to remember was to keep on running out after the flight of the ball. The hole behind me as I lateraled was left unguarded by an offensive lineman pulling out from his position and the defensive tackle could bull through and take me from behind in his rush, not knowing I'd got rid of the ball, if I didn't clear out of the area.

I was able to get the lateral off and avoid the tackler behind me, but unfortunately the defense was keyed for the play. They knew my repertoire, which was only five plays or so, and they doubted I'd call the same play twice. One of my linemen told me later that the defensive man opposite him in the line, Floyd Peters, had said, "Well, here comes the forty-eight pitchout," and it *had* come, and they were able to throw the number four back, Pietrosante, who had received the lateral, back on the one yard line—just a yard away from the mortification of having moved a team backward from the thirty yard line into one's own end zone for a safety.

As soon as I saw Pietrosante go down, I left for the bench on the sidelines at midfield, a long run from where I'd brought my team, and I felt utterly weary, shuffling along through the grass.

Applause began to sound from the stands, and I looked up, startled, and saw people standing, and the hands going. It made no sense at the time. It was not derisive; it seemed solid and respectful. "Wha'? Wha'?" I thought, and I wondered if the applause wasn't meant for someone else—if the mayor had come into the stadium behind me and was waving from an open-topped car. But as I came up to the bench I could see the people in the stands looking at me, and the hands going.

I thought about the applause afterward. Some of it was, perhaps, in appreciation of the lunacy of my participation, and for the fortitude it took to do it; but most of it, even if subconscious, I decided was in *relief* that I had done as badly as I had: it verified the assumption that the average fan would have about an amateur blundering into the brutal world of professional football. He would get slaughtered. If by some chance I had uncorked a touchdown pass, there would have been wild acknowledgment—because I heard the groans go up at each successive disaster—but afterward the spectators would have felt uncomfortable. Their concept of things would have been upset. The outsider did not belong, and there was comfort in that being proved.

Some of the applause, as it turned out, came from people who had enjoyed the comic aspects of my stint. More than a few thought that they were being entertained by a professional comic in the tradition of baseball's Al Schacht, or the Charlie Chaplins, the clowns, of the bullfights. Bud Erickson told me that a friend of his had come up to him later: "Bud, that's one of funniest

CHAPTER THREE / *Commitment*

goddamn . . . I mean that guy's *got* it," this man said, barely able to control himself.

I did not take my helmet off when I reached the bench. It was tiring to do and there was security in having it on. I was conscious of the big zero on my back facing the crowd when I sat down. Some players came by and tapped me on the top of the helmet. Brettschneider leaned down and said, "Well, you stuck it . . . that's the big thing."

The scrimmage began. I watched it for a while, but my mind returned to my own performance. The pawky inner voice was at hand again. "You didn't stick it," it said testily. "You funked it."

At half time Wilson took the players down to the band shell at one end of the stadium. I stayed on the bench. He had his clipboards with him, and I could see him pointing and explaining, a big semicircle of players around him, sitting on the band chairs. Fireworks soared up into the sky from the other end of the field, the shells puffing out clusters of light that lit the upturned faces on the crowd in silver, then red, and then the reports would go off, reverberating sharply, and in the stands across the field I could see the children's hands flap up over their ears. Through the noise I heard someone yelling my name. I turned and saw a girl leaning over the rail of the grandstand behind me. I recognized her from the Gay Haven in Dearborn. She was wearing a mohair Italian sweater, the color of spun pink sugar, and tight pants, and she was holding a thick folding wallet in one hand along with a pair of dark glasses, and in the other a Lion banner, which she waved, her face alive with excitement, very pretty in a perishable, childlike way, and she was calling, "Beautiful; it was beautiful."

The fireworks lit her, and she looked up, her face chalk white in the swift aluminum glare.

I looked at her out of my helmet. Then I lifted a hand, just tentatively.

C'est Un Garçon!

Marjorie Karmel (1928–1964) is best known for popularizing the Lamaze method of "natural" or painless childbirth in the United States. She was born in Washington, D.C., and educated at Bryn Mawr College in Pennsylvania, where she received her master's degree in English drama in 1952. She became an actress and director in New York theatre before marrying Alex Karmel in Paris in 1953, where they lived until after the birth of their first child, Joseph (Pepi), in 1955. Upon returning to America, Mrs. Karmel collaborated with her husband on writing plays. She also wrote *Thank You, Dr. Lamaze* (1959), which is a record of her discovery and application of the natural-childbirth techniques developed by the French physician Fernand Lamaze. After the book's publication, she devoted herself to informing the American public, especially its medical establishment, about the Lamaze method. She gave birth to two daughters before her death from cancer in 1964. Joseph, whose birth is described below, entered Harvard University in 1972.

When we arrived at four A.M., the whole hospital was dark except for the front hall. A nurse was waiting for us—what efficiency for Paris! She led the way to the delivery room, and Alex followed us with the suitcase. He put it down on a stand in the corner of the room, and we stood looking at each other, wondering what to do next. The contractions were coming regularly every seven minutes, but they were very weak and didn't require any action on my part at all. As we stood there waiting, I felt another one. It was an interesting sensation, rather like the way it feels when you flex the muscle of your calf, but it didn't even seem worth sitting down for. I was very excited, thoroughly alert, and there was nothing to do. When the nurse came back, I looked to her for suggestions.

"Get out the clothes," she directed. Alex opened the suitcase, and I began to sort through the things I had put there, what seemed to be ages ago, wondering just what was the right thing to *accouche* in. "I don't want those," the nurse interrupted when she saw what I was doing. "The baby clothes!"

So there *was* going to be a real baby! The nurse went to the suitcase herself, and we watched her pick out the things she wanted and arrange them neatly on a table, all ready to receive little Marianne or Pepi, whenever she or he (I was still certain it would be she) made up her mind to put in an appearance. For all the months of anticipation and planning we had been through, I think that was the first moment that Alex or I really believed in the existence of the baby.

Before she went out again, the nurse pulled a short nightgown out of my suitcase and indicated that that was what I was to wear. As there was only one chair in the room, and Alex looked tired, I decided to get into bed to wait for things to start happening. A few minutes later a midwife came in and examined me. "Very little dilatation," she said. "Certainly not before nine in the morning. Probably not before noon."

She went out. We sat and talked for a while. Outside the city was very still. Alex began to yawn, and finally decided that as nothing was going to happen for a few hours, he might as well go home and get a little sleep. I supposed I ought to sleep too. The contractions were regular but still very weak, and Mme. Cohen had stressed the importance of rest before the delivery. Almost before Alex had shut the door behind him, I was off in a deep sleep. I hadn't realized how the past few days had exhausted me.

Sunlight was pouring in the window when I was awakened again by the increased force of the contractions. I looked at my watch and timed a few. They were coming regularly every five minutes, and they lasted nearly fifty seconds. They felt like the earlier ones, only stronger, with now and then a suggestion, or maybe only the threat, of a cramp. I found that by merely relaxing and doing the slow, deep breathing, they remained in the category of interesting muscular sensations. Nothing more. I didn't see any reason to begin the *effleurage.** The only thing that bothered me was the possibility that they might suddenly get stronger before Alex got back to the hospital. This idea kept me looking anxiously from my watch to the door.

At nine o'clock a new midwife came in to ask how I felt. Was I perfectly comfortable? I said that I was, but she still walked about the table puffing up the pillows under my head, and put a bolster under my knees to make sure that I was perfectly relaxed. She went out, promising to send in a nurse with some tea, and to come back again to see how I was getting along. I hoped she would hurry, because I was very curious to know how I was doing.

No sooner had I finished my tea, than the midwife was back again. She carefully pushed away the *traversin* she had so recently adjusted, and examined me very gently. "Well?" I asked. "Soon?"

"Is this your first?" she said in a tone that indicated that she was pretty sure it was. I nodded. "Be patient," she smiled. "Not before four in the afternoon."

*A light, self-administered massage of the abdominal region.—*Editor's note.*

"But how can that be?" I asked. "How far is the dilatation?"

In answer she showed me the tip of her forefinger. Practically nothing. I was disappointed. What on earth had been happening for all those hours? I waited, breathing slowly from the beginning of each contraction. I was terribly bored. I could feel the contractions gathering force and growing stronger. I tried out the *effleurage,* but it didn't really seem necessary. A nurse came in and put some things in the sterilizer. She looked at me thoughtfully and smiled. "You look bored," she said. "Why don't you go out for a nice walk in the garden?"

"But I don't want to walk in the garden," I said. I explained to her that the dilatation was only about the size of the tip of my forefinger, and that I was becoming discouraged. She insisted more than ever that what I really needed was a nice walk in the fresh air. "How often do you have contractions?" she asked.

"Every five minutes."

She looked at me skeptically, shrugged her shoulders and disappeared. I sat up and began to wonder where my bathrobe and slippers were. I found them, got up, and went to the sink to rinse my mouth. But at that moment the contractions became stronger, and I decided to forgo the walk in the garden, and got back in bed. The contractions kept coming and coming. I kept doing the slow breathing, concentrating on each one to learn all I could about it. If the cervix wasn't doing its part, at least I was doing mine.

Then, somehow, I drifted off to sleep. That was when I got my first practical lesson on how very important it is to stay awake. I couldn't have been sleeping long when I awoke in a kind of nightmare of throbbing pain. I tried to remember to breathe, but before I could catch up with the contraction, it stopped, and I dozed off again. This must have happened several times. The pain I felt was like the cramp you get in your side when you run right after a heavy meal. It couldn't have been very strong, because the moment it stopped I dozed off to sleep again. (I had had no drugs. I was just tired.) Fortunately Alex was there, and he soon realized what was happening. He woke me up by sponging my face with cold water, and told me to begin the rapid breathing. As soon as I was awake again, I regained my control, and the pain vanished. Alex checked my arms and legs to see that I was relaxed. I tried to go back to the slow breathing, but I found that its usefulness was past.

That was at two in the afternoon. From time to time I was examined by different midwives. They all had the same story to tell—very little progress in the dilatation. The contractions were somewhat stronger. They were coming every four minutes. I was still in control. I could sense the threat of pain under the muscular effort of my uterus, but as long as I did the breathing and the *effleurage* it was only a threat. All the same, I was tired and beginning to be discouraged. I very much regretted all the follies of the past week.

Despite all the warnings I had received, I had come to my *accouchement* in a state of general fatigue. Now that I saw that it was going to be a long, demanding affair, I wondered if I really would have the energy I needed to stay in control until the end. I was miserable at the thought that I might not see the birth of my child.

The afternoon was coming to an end. The midwives had stopped making time predictions. The daylight gradually faded, the sound of children's voices playing in a soccer field near the clinic stopped, and a drowsy calm came over me. The room slowly grew dim. I stopped thinking of anything but contractions. I had become a mechanism that concentrated, breathed rhythmically, relaxed, and performed an abstract hand movement known as *effleurage*. I wasn't even discouraged. It was all very businesslike, only tedious.

A nurse brought me some mashed potatoes and another cup of tea. I gobbled it down between contractions, and then wished there was more. Eating revived me. I felt less tired. Alex found that he was hungry too, and went out to look for a sandwich. A midwife came in and examined me. I continued my breathing right through the examination. Then she went out and returned with another midwife who also examined me. I looked at them and became interested in something outside my contractions. They had retired to a corner of the room for a whispered conversation. I listened intently, trying to pick out any words I could. Did I hear the word "Caesarian," or just something else in French that sounded like that? Then they went out together absorbed in an argument that I supposed could only concern me.

A minute or so later a nurse I hadn't seen before marched briskly into the room, and before I could say anything she injected a hypo of something into me. I remember feeling terribly confused and distressed. Then, before I realized what had happened to me, I dropped off into a state of semi-sleep and a recurrent nightmare of pain.

Alex came back and did what he could to help me. He washed my face and tried to tell me when to breathe, but the effect of whatever it was I had been given was too strong. I kept dozing off between contractions, and waking only when they were already under way. Mme. Cohen's analogy of the wave proved only too true. No matter how hard I tried, fighting against the contraction and the effect of the drug on my brain all at once was too much; I could not regain my control. The pain I felt was similar to that I had felt the last time I fell asleep; only now it was stronger and instead of throbbing it rose to a peak along with the contraction. I could truly imagine that if it got much worse, it would be unbearable. How I regretted not being in the metalworkers' clinic where *all* the personnel were trained in the principles of the method and a mistake like that of giving me a hypo would not have occurred!

The midwife came back and examined me. This time she had good news.

The dilatation was nearly at five francs. At last the contractions were doing their work. But I remained discouraged. I was sure that if things went on the way they were going, I would have to be put out before the end. I even had a moment of real doubt about the whole Pavlov method, and wondered if contractions didn't *have* to be painful before they did any good.

This time it was Mme. Cohen who saved me. She appeared in the doorway, all fresh and sparkling, took in the situation at a glance, and set about restoring my control. Her first move was to turn on all the lights, instead of just the little night light that had been on till then. She bathed my face and neck with cold water until I was thoroughly awake, and commanded me to breathe and relax. By that time I had to be told; I was still too sleepy to judge for myself. I couldn't manage to recognize the beginning of a contraction. Mme. Cohen put Alex to work sponging my face with cold water, while she directed my breathing and *effleurage* with one hand on my stomach. She was able to recognize the beginning of a contraction before I did, and she breathed along with me, stopping when it had passed its peak, so that all I had to do was imitate her. Between contractions she made sure I was totally relaxed. In a few minutes the pain stopped and my control returned. The contractions regained shape and form, and I was able to stay on top of them.

But there was very little time in between, and I was exhausted. Mme. Cohen sent for a glucose injection that, she explained, would give me the energy I needed for the expulsion.* At the very sound of the word "expulsion" my confidence returned. The next examination showed that I had passed five francs. At last, I was making progress. I was sure the baby would be born before long, and that I would be fully conscious when it was.

Dr. Lamaze arrived. He examined me carefully, and seemed entirely satisfied with my progress. By that time I was no longer talking to anyone, not even to him. I was much too busy. I didn't look at my watch again until after the delivery was over. Mme. Cohen gave me some oxygen with the plexiglass mask. I remember being surprised that it didn't have any smell or taste, and I was not able to judge its effect. The contractions had become very strong. It took all my concentration, even with Mme. Cohen directing me, to remain in control. For a while it seemed that the contractions merged into one, but Mme. Cohen kept telling me when to breathe and when to rest. Looking back on it now, I see that it was the hardest work I had ever done in my life, just as Mme. Cohen said it would be.

I remember the moment when the transition period began very clearly. For no apparent reason, I suddenly stopped breathing. My only sensation was one of extreme nervousness. For a moment I didn't know what was

---

*In some cases certain obstetricians also employ coramine-glucose, a heart and respiratory stimulant.

happening. Then I concluded that I must be experiencing a desire to push, although I couldn't exactly say that I really felt like pushing. What I really felt was a desire to do nothing at all. After a moment of that suspended state, the desire to push suddenly came on me overwhelmingly. *"Ça vient!"* I shouted.

"Pas encore," Mme. Cohen said. There was an immediate scurry of activity all about me. Dr. Lamaze adjusted a light, Mme. Cohen removed all my pillows, and a midwife and nurse arranged my feet in the stirrups. *"Pas encore,"* Mme. Cohen repeated several times. I panted and puffed and blew, and waited for the word to come. It was an unbelievable sensation, not at all painful but somewhat terrifying.

Finally Mme. Cohen told me I could push. What a relief! No matter what I had imagined about pushing during my rehearsals, I was tremendously surprised by what a satisfying sensation it was. Dr. Lamaze called the signals—*"Inspirez! Soufflez! Inspirez! Bloquez! Poussez!"*—and I performed automatically, just as Mme. Cohen said I would during the first lesson when she explained conditioned reflexes. (It must have been automatic because Alex told me later I did just what I was told, and I don't remember thinking of what to do.) But there was a new element I had not expected. From the moment I began to push, the atmosphere of the delivery room underwent a radical transformation. Where previously everyone had spoken in soft and moderate tones in deference to my state of concentration, now there was a wild encouraging cheering section, dedicated to spurring me on. I felt like a football star, headed for a touchdown. My fans on the sidelines, Dr. Lamaze, Mme. Cohen, the midwife, the nurse, all exhorted me, *"POUSSEZ! POUSSEZ! POUSSEZ! POUSSEZ! CONTINUEZ! CONTINUEZ! CONTINUEZ! ENCORE! ENCORE!"* When I ran out of breath, Mme. Cohen reminded me to exhale, inhale, and hold again. When the contraction was over, the cheering stopped. Each time a new contraction began and I started to push again, the cheering section burst forth. It was fantastically exhilarating; it made me push harder and harder. Then, finally (Alex says the pushing took twenty minutes), the head crowned.

"Ne poussez plus, madame!"

This time it was very easy. I lay back, relaxed, and began to pant. But suddenly a sharp pain shot through my left leg. I winced and turned to Mme. Cohen. "Relax your leg," she said.

"I can't."

"You have a muscle cramp." She massaged it deftly, and in a few seconds it was gone. The minute my leg stopped hurting I became aware of a sensation that momentarily horrified me. Dr. Lamaze was working at turning down the baby's head, and I could feel everything he was doing! I had no sensation of pain at all, but I was shocked by the fact that my perception of what was happening was so complete. I felt the presence of the head, but I felt it the way I had felt the existence of a hole the dentist was drilling in my novocained tooth, touching it with my tongue. It seemed immense! Frighteningly so.

At that moment the delivery sequence of the movie flashed into my mind. I saw the doctor working the head down—just as Dr. Lamaze was doing at that minute. I knew there was nothing to be frightened of. I continued to pant, watching the delivery in my mind as it progressed.

"Forehead, eyes, nose . . ." I heard Dr. Lamaze call out slowly. "Come here, monsieur, come quickly! *Venez voir votre enfant naitre!—*Come see your child is born!"

For an instant I thought of reminding Alex of his promise to stay at the head of the bed, but then I heard a tiny cry "La!" and realized how absurd I was. I felt something hot and wet on my leg. It was the baby's arm. Everyone shouted "Look!" Mme. Cohen helped me to raise my head and shoulders, and there I was looking into the face of my baby who was crying sweetly before he was completely born. A second more and Dr. Lamaze held him up for me to see. *"C'est un garçon, madame,"* he announced. He placed him on a sheet over my stomach so that I could hold him for a moment. It was incredible—he had my father's eyes, a Karmel forehead, and a cleft chin like Alex's, and yet he was obviously a real individual in his own right, from the very first moment. We named him immediately, Joseph Low, after my father. We even settled on the nickname "Pepi."

After we had admired him properly, Dr. Lamaze cut the cord and handed him to a nurse who took him off to the corner to be washed and dressed in the clothes that had been waiting for so long. It was twenty minutes past two, July the seventeenth, over twenty-four hours since I had felt the first contraction. I had forgotten all about the placenta, but Mme. Cohen reminded me to push when the contraction came, and I expelled it easily. Everyone examined it, including me; then all of them but Alex tidied up and went away. The baby, all dressed and wrapped in a blanket, French style, was in a little cradle beside my bed. Alex and I were alone with him. It was less than fifteen minutes after he had been born.

We sat and listened to the baby gurgle and hiccup in the quiet of the warm, still night. As it was so late, I was not going to be moved to my room until the morning. In spite of the tremendous exertion I had been through, I felt wonderfully exhilarated and excited. We talked quietly about the delivery and about our plans for the future, but mainly we were just happy to be there together with our newborn child. Finally Alex went off to send telegrams. I turned off the light, but for a long time I could not sleep. I lay in the dark and listened to the little noises my baby made and felt as happy as I had ever been.

The Story of a Novel

Born in Asheville, North Carolina, Thomas Wolfe (1900–1938) entered the University of North Carolina at the age of fifteen, becoming editor of the college newspaper and literary magazine before he graduated in 1920. He received his master's degree in English from Harvard. Although his chief interest was in writing, he took a teaching position at New York University only to leave after a year for Europe, where he began his first novel, *Look Homeward, Angel* (1929). On returning to America, Wolfe taught during the day to make a living and compulsively spent each night writing— existing on canned beans, coffee, and cigarettes. The autobiographical *Look Homeward, Angel* was a critical success everywhere but in Asheville, whose citizens were enraged to find the dark sides of their lives exposed behind thinly disguised characters and situations. Disappointed at Asheville's reaction, Wolfe nonetheless maintained that ''a man must use the material and experience of his own life if he is to create anything that has substantial value.'' His next novel, *Of Time and the River* (1935), when submitted to his editor, Maxwell Perkins at Scribner's, was nearly twice the length of *War and Peace*. Wolfe described the evolution of that book in ''The Story of a Novel,'' a series of articles published in the *Saturday Review of Literature* in 1935 and expanded into a book the next year. The following selection is a condensation of the three articles. His two other novels, *The Web and the Rock* (1939) and *You Can't Go Home Again* (1941), were published after his untimely death in 1938.

While my life and energy were absorbed in the emotional vortex which my first book [*Look Homeward, Angel*] had created, I was getting almost no work done on the second. And now I was faced with another fundamental problem which every young writer must meet squarely if he is to continue. How is a man to get his writing done? How long should he work at writing? and how often? What kind of method, if any, must he find in following his work? I suddenly found myself face to face with the grim necessity of constant, daily work. And as simple as this discovery may seem to everyone, I was not prepared for it. A young writer without a public does not feel the sense of necessity, the pressure of time, as does a writer who has been published and who must now begin to think of time schedules, publishing seasons, the completion of his next book. I realized suddenly with a sense of definite shock that I had let six months go by since the publication of my first book and that, save for a great many notes and fragments, I had done nothing. Meanwhile, the book continued to sell slowly but steadily, and in February 1930, about five months after its publication, I found it possible to resign from the faculty of New York University and devote my full time to the preparation of a second book. That spring I was also fortunate enough to be awarded the Guggenheim Fellowship which would enable me to live and work abroad for a year. And accordingly, at the beginning of May, I went abroad again.

I was in Paris for a couple of months, until the middle of July, and although I now compelled myself to work for four or five hours a day, my effort at composition was still confused and broken, and there was nothing yet that had the structural form and unity of a book. The life of the great city fascinated me as it had always done, but also aroused all the old feelings of naked homelessness, rootlessness, and loneliness which I have always felt there. During that summer in Paris, I think I felt this great homesickness more than ever before, and I really believe that from this emotion, this constant and almost intolerable effort of memory and desire, the material and the structure of the books I now began to write were derived.

The quality of my memory is characterized, I believe, in a more than ordinary degree by the intensity of its sense impressions, its power to evoke and bring back the odors, sounds, colors, shapes, and feel of things with concrete vividness. Now my memory was at work night and day, in a way that I could at first neither check nor control and that swarmed unbidden in a stream of blazing pageantry across my mind, with the million forms and substances of the life that I had left, which was my own, America. I would be sitting, for example, on the terrace of a café watching the flash and play of life before me on the Avenue de l'Opéra and suddenly I would remember the iron railing that goes along the boardwalk at Atlantic City. I could see it instantly just the way it was, the heavy iron pipes; its raw, galvanized look; the way the joints were fitted together. It was all so vivid and concrete that I could feel my hand upon it and know the exact dimensions, its size and weight and shape. And suddenly I would realize that I had never seen any railing that looked like this in Europe. And this utterly familiar, common thing would suddenly be revealed to me with all the wonder with which we discover a thing which we have seen all our life and yet have never known before. Or again, it would be an American street with all its jumble of a thousand ugly architectures. It would be Montague Street or Fulton Street in Brooklyn, or Eleventh Street in New York, or other streets where I had lived; and suddenly I would see the gaunt and savage webbing of the elevated structure along Fulton Street, and how the light swarmed through in dusty, broken bars, and I could remember the old, familiar rusty color, that incomparable rusty color that gets into so many things here in America. And this also would be like something I had seen a million times and lived with all my life.

I would sit there, looking out upon the Avenue de l'Opéra and my life would ache with the whole memory of it; the desire to see it again; somehow to find a word for it; a language that would tell its shape, its color, the way we have all known and felt and seen it. It was as if I had discovered a whole new universe of chemical elements and had begun to see certain relations between some of them but had by no means begun to organize the whole series into a harmonious and coherent union. From this time on, I think my efforts might be described as the effort to complete that organization, to discover that articulation for which I strove, to bring about that final coherent union. I know that I have failed thus far in doing so, but I believe I understand pretty thoroughly just where the nature of my failure lies, and of course my deepest and most earnest hope is that the time will come when I will not fail.

At any rate, from this time on the general progress of the three books which I was to write in the next four and a half years could be fairly described in somewhat this way. It was a progress that began in a whirling vortex and a creative chaos and that proceeded slowly at the expense of infinite confusion, toil, and error toward clarification and the articulation of an ordered and formal structure. An extraordinary image remains to me from that year, the year I spent abroad when the material of these books first began to take on an articulate form. It seemed that I had inside me, swelling and gathering all the time, a huge black cloud, and that this cloud was loaded with electricity, pregnant, crested, with a kind of hurricane violence that could not be held in check much longer; that the moment was approaching fast when it must break. Well, all I can say is that the storm did break. It broke that summer while I was in Switzerland. It came in torrents, and it is not over yet.

I cannot really say the book was written. It was something that took hold of me and possessed me, and before I was done with it—that is, before I finally emerged with the first completed part—it seemed to me that it had done for me. It was exactly as if this great black storm cloud I have spoken of had opened up and, mid flashes of lightning, was pouring from its depth a torrential and ungovernable flood. Upon that flood everything was swept and borne along as by a great river. And I was borne along with it.

I spent the winter of that year in England from October until March, and here perhaps because of the homely familiarity of the English life, the sense of order and repose which such a life can give one, my work moved forward still another step from this flood tide chaos of creation. For the first time the work began to take on the lineaments of design. These lineaments were still confused and broken, sometimes utterly lost, but now I really did get the sense at last that I was working on a great block of marble, shaping a figure which no one but its maker could as yet define, but which was emerging more and more into the sinewy lines of composition.

Yet I was terribly far away from the actual accomplishment of a book—how far away I could not at that time foresee. But four more years would have to pass before the first of the series of books on which I was now embarked would be ready for the press, and if I could have known that in those next four years there would be packed a hundred lives of birth and death, despair, defeat, and triumph and the sheer exhaustion of a brute fatigue, I do not know whether or not I could have found the power within myself to continue.

* * * *

So far as I can describe with any accuracy, the progress of that winter's work in England was not along the lines of planned design, but along this line that I have mentioned—writing some of the sections which I knew would have to be in the book. Meanwhile what was really going on in my whole creative consciousness, during all this time, although I did not realize it at the moment, was this: What I was really doing, what I had been doing all the time since my discovery of my America in Paris the summer before, was to explore day by day and month by month with a fanatic intensity, the whole material domain of my resources as a man and as a writer. This exploration went on for a period which I can estimate conservatively as two years and a half. . . .

In a way, I think I was like the Ancient Mariner who told the Wedding Guest that his frame was wrenched by the woeful agony which forced him to begin his tale before it left him free. In my own experience, my wedding guests were the great ledgers in which I wrote, and the tale which I told to them would have seemed, I am afraid, completely incoherent, as meaningless as Chinese characters, had any reader seen them. I could by no means hope to give a comprehensive idea of its whole extent because three years of work and perhaps a million and a half words went into these books. It included everything from gigantic and staggering lists of the towns, cities, counties, states, and countries I had been in, to minutely thorough, desperately evocative descriptions of the undercarriage, the springs, wheels, flanges, axle rods, color, weight, and quality of the day coach of an American railway train. There were lists of the rooms and houses in which I had lived or in which I had slept for at least a night, together with the most accurate and evocative descriptions of those rooms that I could write—their size, their shape, the color and design of the wallpaper, the way a towel hung down, the way a chair creaked, a streak of water rust upon the ceiling.

* * * *

In addition, one might come upon other sections under some such cryptic heading as "Where now?" Under such a heading as this, there would be brief notations of those thousands of things which all of us have seen for just a flash, a moment in our lives, which seem to be of no consequence whatever at the moment that we see them, and which live in our minds and hearts forever, which are somehow pregnant with all the joy and sorrow of the human destiny, and which we know, somehow, are therefore more important than many things of more apparent consequence. "Where now?" Some quiet steps that came and passed along a leafy night-time street in summer in a little town down South long years ago; a woman's voice, her sudden burst of low and tender laughter; then the voices and the footsteps going, silence, the leafy rustle of the trees. "Where now?" Two trains that met and paused at a little station at some little town at some unknown moment upon the huge body of the continent; a girl who looked and smiled from the window of the other train; another passing in a motor car on the streets of Norfolk; the winter boarders in a little boarding house down South twenty years ago; Miss Florrie Mangle, the trained nurse; Miss Jessie Rimmer, the cashier at Reed's drug store; Dr. Richards, the clairvoyant; the pretty girl who cracked the whip and thrust her head into the lion's mouth with Johnny J. Jones Carnival and Combined Shows.

*   *   *   *

It may be objected, it has been objected already by certain critics, that in such research as I have here attempted to describe there is a quality of intemperate excess, an almost insane hunger to devour the entire body of human experience, to attempt to include more, experience more, than the measure of one life can hold, or than the limits of a single work of art can well define. I readily admit the validity of this criticism. I think I realize as well as anyone the fatal dangers that are consequent to such a ravenous desire, the damage it may wreak upon one's life and on one's work. But having had this thing within me, it was in no way possible for me to reason it out of me, no matter how cogently my reason worked against it. The only way I could meet it was to meet it squarely not with reason, but with life.

*   *   *   *

When I returned to America in the spring of 1931, although I had three or four hundred thousand words of material, I had nothing that could be published as a novel. Almost a year and a half had elapsed since the publication of my first book and already people had begun to ask that question which is so well meant, but which as year followed year was to become more intolerable to my ears than the most deliberate mockery: "Have you finished your next book yet?" "When is it going to be published?"

At this time I was sure that a few months of steady work would bring the book to completion. I found a place, a little basement flat in the Assyrian quarter in South Brooklyn, and there I went about my task.

The spring passed into the summer; the summer, into autumn. I was working hard, day after day, and still nothing that had the unity and design of a single work appeared. October came and with it a second full year since the publication of my first book. And now, for the first time, I was irrevocably committed so far as the publication of my book was concerned. I began to feel the sensation of pressure, and of naked desperation which was to become almost maddeningly intolerable in the next three years. For the first time I began to realize that my project was much larger than I thought it was.

$$* \qquad * \qquad * \qquad *$$

As I began to realize the true nature of the task I had set for myself, the image of the river began to haunt my mind. I actually felt that I had a great river thrusting for release inside of me and that I had to find a channel into which its floodlike power could pour. I knew I had to find it or I would be destroyed in the flood of my own creation, and I am sure that every artist who ever lived has had the same experience.

Meanwhile, I was being baffled by a fixed and impossible idea whose error at the time I did not fully apprehend. I was convinced at that time that this whole gigantic plan had to be realized within the limits of a single book which would be called "The October Fair." It was not until more than a year had passed, when I realized finally that what I had to deal with was material which covered almost 150 years in history, demanded the action of more than 2,000 characters, and would in its final design include almost every racial type and social class of American life, that I realized that even the pages of a book of 200,000 words were wholly inadequate for the purpose.

$$* \qquad * \qquad * \qquad *$$

I would work furiously day after day until my creative energies were utterly exhausted. ... I reached that state of naked need and utter isolation which every artist has got to meet and conquer if he is to survive at all. Before this I had been sustained by that delightful illusion of success which we all have when we dream about the books we are going to write instead of actually doing them. Now I was face to face with it, and suddenly I realized that I had committed my life and my integrity so irrevocably to this struggle that I must conquer now or be destroyed. I was alone with my own work, and suddenly I knew that I had to be alone with it, that no one could help me with it now no matter how anyone might wish to help. For the first time I realized another naked fact which every artist must know, and that is that in a man's work there are contained not only the seeds of life, but the seeds of death, and that that power of creation which sustains us will also destroy us like a leprosy if we let it rot stillborn in our vitals. I had to get it out of me somehow. And now for the first time a terrible doubt began to creep into my mind that I might not live long enough to get it out of me, that I had created a labor so large and so impossible that the energy of a dozen lifetimes would not suffice for its accomplishment.

During this time, however, I was sustained by one piece of inestimable good fortune. I had for a friend a man who is, I believe, not only the greatest editor of his time, but a man of immense and patient wisdom and a gentle but unyielding fortitude. I think that if I was not destroyed at this time by the sense of hopelessness which these gigantic labors had awakened in me, it was largely because of the courage and patience of this man. I did not give in because he would not let me give in, and I think it is also true that at this particular time he had the advantage of being in the position of a skilled observer at a battle. I was myself engaged in that battle, covered by its dust and sweat and exhausted by its struggle, and I understood far less clearly than my friend the nature and the progress of the struggle in which I was engaged. At this time there was little that this man could do except observe, and in one way or another keep me at my task, and in many quiet and marvelous ways he succeeded in doing this.

My friend, the editor, has likened his own function at this painful time to that of a man who is trying to hang on to the fin of a plunging whale, but hang on he did, and it is to his tenacity that I owe my final release. Meanwhile, my creative power was functioning at the highest intensity it had ever known. I wrote at times without belief that I would ever finish, with nothing in me but black despair, and yet I wrote and wrote and could not give up writing.

*   *   *   *

People have sometimes asked me what happened to my life during these years. They have asked me how I ever found time to know anything that was going on in the world about me when my life was so completely absorbed by this world of writing. Well, it may seem to be an extraordinary fact, but the truth is that never in my whole life have I lived so fully, have I shared so richly in the common life of man as I did during these three years when I was struggling with the giant problem of my own work.

For one thing, my whole sensory and creative equipment, my powers of feeling and reflection—even the sense of hearing, and above all, my powers of memory, had reached the greatest degree of sharpness that they had ever known. At the end of the day of savage labor, my mind was still blazing with its effort, could by no opiate of reading, poetry, music, alcohol, or any other pleasure, be put at rest. I was unable to sleep, unable to subdue the tumult of these creative energies, and as a result of this condition, for three years I prowled the streets, explored the swarming web of the million-footed city and came to know it as I had never done before. It was a black time in the history of the nation, a black time in my own life and, I suppose, it is but natural that my own memory of it now should be a pretty grim and painful one.

Such was the state my life had come to in the early winter of 1933, and even at that moment, although I could not see it, the end of my huge labor was in sight. In the middle of December of that year the great editor, of whom I have spoken, and who, during all this tormented period, had kept a quiet watch upon me, called me to his home and calmly informed me that my book was finished. I could only look at him with stunned surprise, and finally I only could tell him out of the depth of my own hopelessness that he was mistaken, that the book was not finished, that it could never be completed, that I could write no more. He answered with the same quiet finality that the book was finished whether I knew it or not, and then he told me to go to my room and spend the next week in collecting in its proper order the manuscript which had accumulated during the last two years.

I followed his instructions, still without hope and without belief. I worked for six days sitting in the middle of the floor surrounded by mountainous stacks of typed manuscript on every side. At the end of a week I had the first part of it together, and just two days before Christmas, 1933, I delivered to him the manuscript of "The October Fair," and a few days later, the manuscript of "The Hills Beyond Pentland." The manuscript of "The Fair" was, at that time, something over 1,000,000 words in length. He had seen most of it in its dismembered fragments during the three preceding years, but now, for the first time, he was seeing them in their sequential order, and once again his marvelous intuition was right; he had told me the truth when he said that I had finished the book.

*   *   *   *

It was evident that many problems were before us, but now we had the thing, and we welcomed the labor before us with happy confidence. In the first place there was the problem of the book's gigantic length. Even in this skeletonized form the manuscript of "The October Fair" was over a million words in length, which is about twelve times the length of the average novel or twice the length of "War and Peace." It was manifest, therefore, that it would not only be utterly impossible to publish such a manuscript in a single volume, but that even if it were published in several volumes, the tremendous length of such a manuscript would practically annihilate its chances of ever finding a public which would read it.

This problem now faced us, and the editor grappled with it immediately.

As his examination of the manuscript of "The October Fair" proceeded, he found that the book did describe two complete and separate cycles. The first of these was a movement which described the period of wandering and hunger in a man's youth. The second cycle described the period of greater certitude, and was dominated by the unity of a single passion. It was obvious, therefore, that what we had in the two cyclic movements of this book was really the material of two completely different chronicles, and although the second of the two was by far the more finished, the first cycle, of course, was the one which logically we ought to complete and publish first, and we decided on this course.

We took the first part. I immediately prepared a minutely thorough synopsis which described not only the course of the book from the first to the last, but which also included an analysis of those chapters which had been completed in their entirety, of those which were completed only in part, and of those which had not been written at all, and with this synopsis before us, we set to work immediately to prepare the book for press. This work occupied me throughout the whole of the year 1934. The book was completed at the beginning of 1935, and was published in March of that year under the title of "Of Time and the River."

In the first place, the manuscript, even in its unfinished form, called for the most radical cutting, and because of the way in which the book had been written, as well as the fatigue which I now felt, I was not well prepared to do by myself the task that lay ahead of us.

Cutting had always been the most difficult and distasteful part of writing to me; my tendency had always been to write rather than to cut. Moreover, whatever critical faculty I may have had concerning my own work had been seriously impaired, for the time being at least, by the frenzied labor of the past four years. When a man's work has poured from him for almost five years like burning lava from a volcano; when all of it, however superfluous, has been given fire and passion by the white heat of his own creative energy, it is very difficult suddenly to become coldly surgical, ruthlessly detached.

To give a few concrete illustrations of the difficulties that now confronted us: The opening section of the book describes the journey of a train across the State of Virginia at night. Its function in the book is simply to introduce some of the chief characters, to indicate a central situation, to give something of the background from which the book proceeds, and perhaps through the movement of the train across the stillness of the earth to establish a certain beat, evoke a certain emotion which is inherent to the nature of the book. Such a section, therefore, undoubtedly serves an important function, but in proportion to the whole purport of the book, its function is a secondary one and must be related to the whole book in a proportionate way.

Now in the original version, the manuscript which described the journey of the train across Virginia at night was considerably longer than the average novel. What was needed was just an introductory chapter or two, and what I had written was over 100,000 words in length, and this same difficulty, this lack of proportion, was also evident in other parts of the manuscript.

What I had written about the great train was really good. But what I had to face, the very bitter lesson that everyone who wants to write has got to learn, was that a thing may in itself be the finest piece of writing one has ever done, and yet have absolutely no place in the manuscript one hopes to publish. This is a hard thing, but it must be faced, and so we faced it.

My spirit quivered at the bloody execution. My soul recoiled before the carnage of so many lovely things cut out upon which my heart was set. But it had to be done, and we did it. And so it went all up and down the line. Chapters 50,000 words long were reduced to ten or fifteen thousand words, and having faced this inevitable necessity, I finally acquired a kind of ruthlessness of my own, and once or twice, myself, did more cutting than my editor was willing to allow.

Meanwhile I was proceeding at full speed with the work of completing my design, finishing the unfinished parts and filling in the transition links which were essential.

This in itself was an enormous job and kept me writing all day long as hard as I could go for a full year. Here again the nature of my chief fault was manifest. I wrote too much again. I not only wrote what was essential, but time and time again my enthusiasm for a good scene, one of those enchanting vistas which can open up so magically to a man in the full flow of his creation would overpower me, and I would write thousands of words upon a scene which contributed nothing of vital importance to a book whose greatest need already was ruthless condensation.

During the course of this year, I must have written well over a half million words of additional manuscript, of which, of course, only a small part was finally used.

The end came suddenly—the end of those five years of torment and incessant productivity. In October I took a trip to Chicago, a two weeks' vacation, my first in over a year. When I returned I found that my editor had quietly and decisively sent the manuscript to the press, the printers were already at work on it, the proof was beginning to come in. I had not foreseen it; I was desperate, bewildered. "You can't do it," I told him, "the book is not yet finished. I must have six months more on it."

To this he answered that the book was not only finished, but that if I took six months more on it, I would then demand another six months and six months more beyond that, and that I might very well become so obsessed with this one work that I would never get it published. . . .

He told me finally that I would go on and do better work, that I would learn to work without so much confusion, waste, and useless torment, that my future books would more and more achieve the unity, sureness, and finality that every artist wants his work to have, but that I had to learn in the way I had learned, groping, struggling, finding my own way for myself, that this was the only way to learn.

In January 1935, I finished the last of my revisions on the proof; the first printed copies came from the press in February. The book was released for final publication early in March. I was not here when it came out. I had taken a ship for Europe the week before, and as the ship got farther and farther from the American shores, my spirits sank lower and lower, reaching, I think, the lowest state of hopeless depression they had ever known. This, I believe, was largely a physical reaction, the inevitable effect of relaxation upon a human organism which had for five years been strained to its utmost limit. My life seemed to me to be like a great spring which had been taut for years and which was now slowly uncoiling from its tension. I had the most extraordinary sense of desolation I had ever known when I thought about my book. I had never realized until now how close I had been to it, how much a part of me it had become, and now that it had been taken away from me, my life felt utterly futile, hollow as a shell. . . .

Now I had an overwhelming sense of shame greater than any I have felt before. I felt as if I had ruinously exposed myself as a pitiable fool who had no talent and who once and for all had completely vindicated the prophecies of the critics who had felt the first book was just a flash in the pan. It was in this frame of mind that I arrived in Paris on March 8, the day the book was to be published in America. I had come away to forget about it, and yet I thought about it all the time. I prowled the streets from night to morning, at least a dozen times in two short weeks I heard the celebration of mass at Sacré Coeur, and then would walk the streets again and come back to my hotel at ten o'clock and lie upon the bed, and still I could not sleep.

After several days of this, I steeled myself to go to the office of the travel agency where a message might be waiting for me. I found a cablegram there. It was from my publisher, and it said simply: "Magnificent reviews somewhat critical in ways expected, full of greatest praise."

anne moody

The Movement: Canton, Mississippi

The daughter of Mississippi sharecroppers, Anne Moody (1940–   ) was educated at Natchez Junior College and Tougaloo College, from which she graduated in 1964. She has been involved in the civil-rights struggles in the South and has traveled all over the country working for CORE. More recently she has been co-ordinator of civil-rights training projects for the School of Industrial and Labor Relations at Cornell University. Her autobiography, *Coming of Age in Mississippi* (1968), describes her childhood and her work for the movement in the South. The following selection is a chapter in that book.

In July, CORE opened up an office in Canton, Mississippi, to start a voter registration campaign in Madison County. By this time, I was so fed up with the fighting and bickering among the organizations in Jackson, I was ready to go almost anywhere, even Madison County, where Negroes frequently turned up dead. Shortly before Christmas a man's headless corpse had been found on the road between Canton and Tougaloo with the genitals cut off and with K's cut into the flesh all over his body. Around the time the body was found, Tougaloo College had received a lot of threats, so an inventory was made of all the males on campus to see if any were missing.

When Reverend King discovered that I had agreed to work with CORE in the area, he was very much concerned. He discussed Canton with me, telling me he thought the place was too rough for girls. Some of my girlfriends also begged me not to go. But I just had to. I don't know why I felt that way, but I did.

Because I had come from Wilkinson County, I just didn't think Madison could be any worse. Things might even be a little better, I thought, since in Madison there were three Negroes to every white. I remembered that in Jackson there had been one point when I could see the white folks actually tremble with fear. At times when we were having mass demonstrations we had them so confused they didn't know what to do. Whenever I could detect the least amount of fear in any white Mississippian, I felt good. I also felt there was a chance of winning the battle regardless of how costly it turned out to be.

Disregarding all acts of violence, Madison County was considered a place with a possible future for Negroes. In addition to the fact that our records showed that there was a population of twenty-nine thousand Negroes as against nine thousand whites, Negroes owned over 40 percent of the land in the county. However, there were only about one hundred and fifty to two hundred registered to vote, and these had registered as a result of a campaign conducted by a few local citizens a couple of years earlier. Of this number, less than half were actually voting.

I arrived in Canton with Dave Dennis one Friday evening, and was taken straight to the CORE office, a small room adjoining a Negro café. The café was owned by C. O. Chinn and his wife, a well-established Negro family. It was located on Franklin Street in the center of one of Canton's Negro sections. Dave and I were just in time to have supper there with George Raymond, the project director, and Bettye Poole, my old Tougaloo buddy.

Dave introduced me to Mrs. Chinn. She was a stout lady with a warm and friendly smile. I liked her right away. I spent the entire evening sitting around the office talking to her and George Raymond about Madison County.

The office had been open only a few weeks, and in that time, Mrs. Chinn had already had her liquor license taken away. The place had been broken into twice, and many Negroes had been physically threatened. George reported that so far mostly teen-agers were involved in the Movement. He said that about fifty dedicated teen-age canvassers showed up each day. They were sent out daily, but had little success. Most of the Negroes just didn't want to be bothered, Mrs. Chinn told me. "That's the way it is all over," I thought. "Most Negroes have been thoroughly brainwashed. If they aren't brainwashed, they are too insecure—either they work for Miss Ann or they live on Mr. Charlie's place."

I just didn't see how the Negroes in Madison County could be so badly off. They should have had everything going for them—outnumbering the whites three to one and owning just about as much land as they did. When I discussed this point with Mrs. Chinn, I discovered that, although they did own the land, they were allowed to farm only so much of it. Cotton is the main crop in Mississippi, and, as Mrs. Chinn explained that night, the federal government controls cotton by giving each state a certain allotment. Each state decides how much each county gets and each county distributes the allotments to the farmers. "It always ends up with the white people getting most of the allotments," Mrs. Chinn said. "The Negroes aren't able to get more, regardless of how much land they have." Most of the farmers in Madison County were barely living off what they made from their land. Besides, they were never clear from debt. The independent farmers were practically like sharecroppers, because they always had their crop pledged in advance. The more I thought about it, the more it seemed that the federal government was directly or indirectly responsible for most of the segregation, discrimination, and poverty in the South.

Later, I was taken to the Freedom House, which had been provided by Mrs. Chinn's brother, Sonny. The house was newly built and very nice. There were three bedrooms, a living room, dining room, and kitchen. Sonny was a young man who had recently separated from his wife. Since his brother Robert lived with him now, we kind of crowded them, forcing them to share a bed. But they didn't seem to mind. The more I saw of the Chinns, the more I began to like and respect them. They were the one Negro family in Canton who had put their necks on the chopping block. "If a couple of other families made similar commitments," I thought, "we might just get this place moving."

There was a rally that night at the CORE office. Mrs. Chinn was the only adult there among about twenty teen-agers. We sang freedom songs for about two hours. After that, George gave a brief talk, and introduced me, saying, "I want you people to meet one of my co-workers. She is going to spend some time with us here in and around Madison County. She is a real soul sister. Why don't you stand, Anne?"

As I rose, one of the boys in the back gave a wolf whistle. "I don't mean that kind of soul sister, Esco," George said. "What I mean is, she is dedicated, man. She has been beaten and kicked all over Jackson. Remember that bloody sit-in, and the other demonstrations? She was in all of them. She has been in jail four or five times, and as a result, she can't even go home again. She is all right and don't you guys go getting any notions. Anne, why don't you say a few words?"

I felt I had to say something real serious after those remarks. "Anyway," I thought, "I better take advantage of such an introduction to put those teen-age boys in their place from the get-go. If not, I might have a little trouble on my hands later." Therefore, I decided to pull the religious bit. Now that I was facing the street, I saw that outside the cops were on the ball. There they were, two carloads of them. They were taking it all in. "The watchdogs of the Klan. They wouldn't miss a meeting for anything." I was beginning to hate them with a passion. "I just might try and give them something to think about, too," I thought.

"It seems as though a few of us have the spirit tonight," I started.

"Yes, we got it all right," one of the boys said, somewhat freshly.

"A few is not enough," I continued. "If a change is gonna take place in Canton, as we just said in one of the songs, then it's gonna take more than a few believers. Where are the rest of the adults besides Mrs. Chinn? Where are your parents, sisters and brothers and your other friends? We sit back and say that we want Freedom. We believe that all men are created equal. Some of us even believe we are free just because our constitution guarantees us certain 'inalienable' rights. There are the thirteenth, fourteenth, and fifteenth amendments that make us citizens and give us the right to vote. If you are depending on the writing on the wall to free you, you better forget it, it's been there a long time. We've gotta be the ones to give it meaning. Some of us believe that once we get enough nerve, all we gotta do is walk up to Mr. Charlie and say, 'Man, I want my freedom.' Do you think that Mr. Charlie is going to dish it out to you on a silver platter?"

"No, he'll tell me that I am already free," one of the boys said.

"If he is that bold and thinks you are that crazy, then you should be bold and crazy enough to ask him a few more questions," I said.

"Questions like what?" he said.

"Like 'what am I free to do?'" I said. "Then name a few things you can't do if he continues. In fact, if you ever get enough nerve to do it, let me know what happens."

"I probably won't live to tell you about it," the boy said.

"So you see, it's not that simple, and all of you know that," I said. "Now that we know that we are not free and realize what's involved in freeing ourselves, we have to take certain positive actions to work on the problem. First of all, we have got to get together. I was told that it's twenty-nine thousand Negroes in this county to nine thousand whites. What's wrong with you? Don't you realize what you have going for you?" When I said this, those overseers outside began to pace nervously. I had touched a nerve in them and I felt good, but I decided to stop before I overdid it. I ended by saying, "I am looking forward to the work ahead of me. I will certainly do my best to help you get the message across to Mr. Charlie." Then I took a seat.

George got up and said, "See, I told you she was all right. Now let's sing a few more songs. Then go home and see what we can come up with to start on Mr. Charlie. *All right,* soul brothers and sisters."

"All right," Mrs. Chinn said. "We are going to get that freedom yet, ain't we?"

A few shouts of Amen and Sho-nuff came from the teen-agers. We sang three songs, ending with "We Shall Overcome," and everyone went home. All that night I kept thinking about that pitiful meeting. We just had to get some more adults involved somehow.

The next day, Saturday, I went to the office to check over some of the reports by previous canvassing teams. I had been working for a few hours when George came in. "Come outside. I want to show you something," he said.

I ran into the street thinking someone was being beaten by the cops or there was some other kind of Saturday night happening out there.

"Take a good look at that," George said. "Just about every Negro in Madison County for miles around."

It wasn't hard for me to believe what I was seeing. I had seen it too many times before. In Centreville, my hometown, the same thing took place. Saturday night was known as Nigger Night. That's how the whites put it.

"Come on," George said, "let's walk out on Pear Street" (the main street in Canton). As we walked there, we had to push our way through crowds of Negroes. On Pear Street itself, everything was at a standstill. There were so many Negroes, and they were packed so closely together, they could barely move.

"Look over there," I said to George.

"Where?" he asked.

"At the two white cops standing on that corner," I said.

"They look pretty lonely and stupid, huh?"

"They sure do," I said. "Look just like they are in a completely black town at this moment."

"Most whites don't even bother to come in on Saturdays, I've noticed," George said.

I stood there looking and thinking. Yes, Saturday night is Nigger Night all over Mississippi. I remembered in Centreville, when it was too cold for anyone to walk the streets, Negroes would come to town and sit in each other's cars and talk. Those that didn't believe in sitting around or hanging out in bars, like my mother, just sat or moved from car to car for four or five hours. Teen-agers who were not allowed in cafés went to a movie and watched the picture three or four times while they smooched. There was a special "lovers" section in the movie house on Saturday nights. Often you saw more stirring and arousing scenes in the lovers' section than on the screen. Some Negroes would come to town on Saturday night just to pick a fight with another Negro. Once the fight was over, they were satisfied. They beat their frustrations and discontent out on each other. I had often thought that if some of that Saturday night energy was used constructively or even directed at the right objects, it would make a tremendous difference in the life of Negroes in Mississippi.

The next week or so, things went along fairly well. Within a few days, I had gotten to know most of the canvassers. They were more energetic than any bunch of teen-agers I had known or worked with before. There were about forty or fifty that reported daily. We kept running into problems. I found it necessary to keep dividing them into smaller teams. First I divided them into two teams, one for the mornings and one for the afternoons. Most of the eligible voters worked during the day, so a third team was organized for the evenings. Some of the teen-agers were so energetic that they often went out with all the teams. I usually canvassed with the last team for a couple of hours, then rushed to the Freedom House to cook.

It didn't take me long to find out that the Negroes in Madison County

CHAPTER THREE / *Commitment*

were the same as those in most of the other counties. They were just as apathetic or indifferent about voting. Nevertheless, we had begun to get a few more adults out to rallies at night. Pretty soon the whites saw fit to move in. They wanted to make sure that more adults would not get involved. Since our recruitment and canvassing was done mostly by the teen-agers, they decided to scare the teen-agers away. One night after a rally, George, Bettye and I had just walked back to the Freedom House when C. O. Chinn came rushing in after us. He kept repeating over and over again, "Five kids were just shot. Five kids were just shot." We stood there motionless, not wanting to believe what we had just heard, afraid to ask any questions. Were they seriously hurt? Was anyone dead?

Before any of us said a word, Mr. Chinn was saying, "They are at the hospital now, George, let's go over and see how they are." George got his cap and headed for the door, with Bettye and me right behind him.

As we were all getting into Mr. Chinn's car, Mr. Chinn said, "I'm going to leave you girls by my house with Minnie Lou. Anne, you and Bettye can't go to the hospital. How do you know they weren't trying to kill one of you? Maybe one of the girls was taken for you or Bettye."

As we approached his house, we saw Mrs. Chinn standing in the doorway as if she was about to leave.

"Where do you think you're going, Minnie Lou? You're goin' to stay right here with Anne and Bettye," Mr. Chinn said.

Mrs. Chinn didn't answer—the voice of authority had spoken. Mrs. Chinn, Bettye and I simply did as we were told. We sat around the house talking until about 4 A.M., and then we all tried to get some sleep. I didn't sleep at all. I kept thinking of what might possibly happen. This was probably just a warning. Something else was coming on. I could feel it. Finally, it was daylight and Mr. Chinn and George still hadn't returned. Maybe they didn't want to face us and say So-and-so died.

"Anne! Anne!" Mrs. Chinn was calling me. "Are you asleep?"

"No," I answered.

"Let's go down to the office. Maybe C.O. and George are there," she said. We all got up and headed for the office. We arrived just as Mr. Chinn and George were getting out of the car. "They're O.K.," Mr. Chinn told us. "They were released from the hospital about five-thirty this morning." He explained that they had been hit with buckshot.

That afternoon when the five teen-agers came to the office to fill out affidavits to be sent to the Justice Department, I heard the full story. They had been walking home down Pear Street after last night's rally when the incident occurred. As they passed the service station on the opposite side of the street, Price Lewis, the white owner, had been standing in the doorway. This did not seem unusual—they generally saw him there. Then just as they were crossing the railroad tracks to the left of the service station, they heard a loud noise. They looked back and noticed that Price Lewis was now holding a shotgun pointed in their direction. At this point, one of the girls said she looked down and discovered blood was running down her legs into her shoes. She realized she had been shot and saw that the others had been wounded by buckshot pellets too.

Price Lewis had been arrested at the service station and taken to jail during the morning. Immediately he posted a small bail and was released. Within an hour or so he was back to work at the service station, carrying on as though nothing had happened. His Negro service attendant was still there too. He acted as if he really hated being there and he must have known how other Negroes were looking at him, but I knew he couldn't afford to leave his job.

The shooting really messed up our relationship with the teen-agers. Within two or three days they had stopped coming to the office. I knew that their parents were responsible for most of them not coming back. From the beginning most of the parents had not approved of their participation in the voter registration drive. Several kids had told me that they came against their parents' wishes, but they always refused to let me go home with them to talk things over with the adults. They took too much pride in the work they were doing with us to let me do that. I think they knew as well as I that it was for themselves and themselves alone that they were working—because within a few years they would be the ones who would have to deal with the whites.

Now, however, I felt I had an obligation to go and see their parents. I did so with very little success. Some flatly refused to see me. Those that did gave made-up excuses as to why their children had to stay home. One sent her little boy to the door to tell me she was not home; "Mama say she ain't heah," he said.

I hardly knew what to do. I was not prepared to cope with this situation. I kept trying to think of some way to get the teen-agers involved again. For one thing, we would not be able to get our work done without them. Bettye and I tried canvassing alone for a day or so and ended up almost dead from exhaustion.

During this lapse in the project, I got one of those weeping letters from Mama again. As usual, she was begging me to leave Mississippi, and as usual she peeved the hell out of me, but I couldn't take lightly what she said about Wilkinson County. I knew too well what I was up against.

The next day, in an attempt to forget her letter, I decided to busy myself with cleaning the office. I got the one teen-ager that still hung around to help me, and sent him to the café for a pail of water. When he came back, he said, "Anne, there are two white men outside in a car asking to see the person in charge of the office."

CHAPTER THREE / *Commitment*

"Are they from Canton or around here?" I asked.

"No," he said. "I've never seen them before."

My heart almost jumped right out of me. It was not until then that I really began to think of some of the things in Mama's letter. She had said that the white folks in Centreville had found out that I was in Canton, and that some Negro had told her he heard they planned to bump me off. She had been pleading with me this time as she had never done before. Why did I want to get myself killed? she kept asking. What was I trying to prove? Over and over again she said that after I was dead things would still be the same as they were now.

Now here I was standing in the middle of the office trembling with fear, not wanting to face the white men outside. Maybe they were here to tell me something terrible had happened. Maybe they came just to make sure I was here. George was out in the country talking to some farmers, and Bettye was cleaning the Freedom House. How I wished one of them were here now, so they could go outside instead of me. Finally I stopped shaking long enough to make myself walk out of the office. "You can't be getting scared without finding out who they are or what they want," I kept telling myself.

As I approached the car, and took a good look at the two men inside, I was almost positive I didn't recognize them from Centreville. Feeling almost limp from relief, I walked up to the driver and said, "I was told you would like to see the person in charge."

"Yes, we are from the FBI," he said, showing me his identification. "We are here to investigate the shooting. Where can we find the five kids who were involved?"

I stood there mad as hell. "The stupid bastards!" I thought. There I was getting all flustered and scared because of my mother's letter, not knowing who they were. "Why didn't you come inside and present yourselves as officials from the FBI?" I asked angrily. "We just don't happen to run out into the streets to see every white man that drives up in front of this office, you know. After all, it might just be someone ready to blow our heads off."

"Can you tell me where I could find those five kids that were shot?" he asked again, a little indignant.

"I'll see if I can find the addresses for you," I said sweetly. "Why don't you two come inside for a minute?"

I knew they weren't particularly interested in getting out of their car and coming into the office. However, I gave them a look that said, "You'll never get those addresses unless you do," so they followed me. They stood around impatiently, looking at our broken-down chairs and sofa, as if to say, "What a shame these niggers have to come into a place and open up a joint like this and cause all this trouble for us."

"I can find only three of the addresses for you," I said. "I would like that you wait and see George Raymond, our project director. He should be back soon and he'll be able to show you where they live. Why don't you two have a seat until he comes?"

"What time do you expect him?" one asked.

"Within fifteen or twenty minutes," I said. Realizing they had to wait that long, they decided to sit. They placed themselves carefully on the sofa, as if it was diseased or something. They must be from the South, I thought. "Where are you two from?" I asked.

"New Orleans," one said.

They waited restlessly until George returned. He spent a few hours driving around with them and they saw all the kids and questioned them. That was the extent of their "investigation." The same afternoon they left town and we never saw or heard from them after that.

By the beginning of August when the teen-age canvassers still had not returned, Dave Dennis decided to bring in three other workers—two girls, who were students from Jackson, and a boy called Flukie, a CORE task force worker. There were now six of us, but there was still more work than we could handle. George and Flukie went out in the country each day to talk with farmers and to scout for churches to conduct workshops in. The rest of us were left to canvass and look after the office.

So far we had only been able to send a handful of Negroes to the courthouse to attempt to register, and those few that went began to get fired from their jobs. This discouraged others who might have registered. Meanwhile, we were constantly being threatened by the whites. Almost every night someone came running by to tell us the whites planned to bump us off.

One evening just before dark, someone took a shot at a pregnant Negro woman who was walking home with her two small sons. This happened in a section where a few poor white families lived. The woman stood in the street with her children, screaming and yelling for help. A Negro truck driver picked them up and drove them to the Boyd Street housing project, which was right across the street from the Freedom House. She was still yelling and screaming when she got out of the truck, and people ran out of all the project houses. The woman stood there telling everyone what had happened. She was so big it looked as though she was ready to have the baby any minute. As I looked at the other women standing around her, I didn't like what I saw in their faces. I could tell what they were thinking—"Why don't you all get out of here before you get us all killed?"

After this incident, Negro participation dropped off to almost nothing, and things got so rough we were afraid to walk the streets. In addition, our money was cut off. We were being paid twenty dollars a week by the Voter Education Project, a Southern agency which supported voter registration for Negroes.

They said that since we were not producing registered voters, they could not continue to put money into the area. It seemed things were getting rough from every angle. We sometimes went for days without a meal. I was getting sick and losing lots of weight. When the NAACP invited me to speak at a Thursday night women's rally in Jackson, at one of the big churches, I tried to prepare a speech that would get across to them how we were suffering in Canton.

Everything went wrong the night of the rally. Ten minutes before Dave arrived to pick me up, Jean, one of the new girls, had a terrible asthma attack, and we had to drop her off at the hospital in Jackson. I arrived at the church exhausted and an hour late, still wearing the skirt and blouse I had worked in all day; they looked like I had slept in them for weeks. The mistress of ceremonies was just explaining that I was unable to make it, when I walked straight up on the stage. She turned and looked at me as if I was crazy, and didn't say another word. She just took her seat, and I walked up to the mike. By this time I had completely forgotten my prepared speech, and I don't remember exactly what I said at first. I had been standing up there I don't know how long when the mistress of ceremonies said, "You are running overtime." I got mad at her and thought I would tell the audience exactly what I was thinking. When I finished telling them about the trouble we were having in Canton, I found myself crying. Tears were running down my cheeks and I was shaking and saying, "What are we going to do? Starve to death? Look at me. I've lost about fifteen pounds in a week." I stood there going to pieces, until Reverend Ed King walked up on the platform, put his arm around me and led me away.

Outside he said, "You touched them, Anne. I think you got your message across." He was still standing with his arm around me, and I was drying my eyes when Dave came up.

"What's wrong with her?" he asked.

"She just finished a speech which I think was tremendous," Reverend King said. "But I think she needs a rest, Dave."

Dave took me to his apartment in Jackson and said I could rest there a couple of days. I didn't really think about what had happened during my speech until I was in bed trying to sleep. Then I realized I was cracking up, and I began to cry again.

When I got back to Canton on Sunday, I discovered that a tub of food had been brought in from Jackson. We arrived just in time to find Flukie helping himself to some golden brown chicken. He gave me a note that had been left with the food:

Dear Anne. Brought some food for your people. Your speech was something Thursday night. However, you need a rest. Why don't you come spend a week with me? See you next week. Let me know if the food runs out before then. You take care of yourself.

Mrs. Young

I knew Mrs. Young through her sons, who had gone to jail with me during the demonstrations in Jackson. She had nine children, five of whom had been arrested. She was a beautiful lady and I appreciated the food she brought. But I felt bad about taking it, thinking about all those children she had and no husband.

Dave and Mattie Dennis, and Jerome Smith, another CORE field secretary, moved in to Canton with us the next week. Dave felt that the only way we were going to get any money put back into the area was if we got more people registered.

Suddenly we began to get quite a lot of support from the local Negroes. Mr. Chinn began working with us almost full time. They saw that we were trying hard and that we were doing our best under the circumstances. Every day now we managed to send a few Negroes to the courthouse. Soon we had a steady flow moving daily. But the registrar was flunking them going and coming. Sometimes out of twenty or twenty-five Negroes who went to register, only one or two would pass the test. Some of them were flunked because they used a title (Mr. or Mrs.) on the application blank; others because they didn't. And most failed to interpret a section of the Mississippi constitution to the satisfaction of Foote Campbell, the Madison County circuit clerk.

All of the Negroes who flunked but should have passed the test were asked to fill out affidavits to be sent to the Justice Department. Hundreds of these were sent and finally two men came down from Washington to look at the county registrar's books. They talked with the registrar and persuaded him to register four or five people who had been flunked because of using "Mr." or "Mrs." One of them was a blind man who had failed several times, and who should not have had to take the test anyway.

To keep up the pace, Dave brought in two more workers. Now there were nine of us working full time. When this news got to the white community, and they sensed the support we must be getting, they began to threaten us again.

One Friday evening, just as we were finishing dinner, Sonny's brother Robert came running into the kitchen. He was sweating and panting as if he had been running for a long time. At first, he didn't say anything. We all sat and stared, waiting. He just stared back. He looked like he was trying to decide how to tell us something. I thought that he had been chased by someone.

"Man, what's wrong with you?" George finally asked.

"Uh . . . uh . . ." Robert began. "Man, y'all better get outta Canton *tonight!* I got a funny feelin' when I was walkin' aroun' in town tonight so I went over to that Black Tom's café to see what people were talkin' 'bout. Sho' nuff, one o' them drunk bastards sittin' up there sayin' they gonna kill all them damn freedom workers tonight."

"What? *Who* said that?" Jerome Smith yelled. "You got more sense, Robert, than to go believe what you hear some drunkard sayin' in a café."

"Man, lissen, lissen, you don't believe me, go ask Joe Lee. He was sittin' there a *long* time. He said he was just about to come over and tell y'all. They really gonna do it, they really gonna do it tonight! Did Dave go to Jackson yet? Man, y'all better get outta Canton!"

"What do you mean, Robert?" I asked. "How did that guy find out? Them whites probably spread that shit just so it'll get back to us. If they were really gonna kill us, wouldn't any nigger in town know anything about it till it was all over with."

"Moody, that man work for Howard, who's behind *all* this shit here in Canton, and if he say he heard somethin', he *heard* it."

"That's what I just said, it was intended for him to hear," I said.

"George, y'all can sit here and listen to Annie Moody if you want to, but I swear to *God,* you betta get outta here! You think that fuckin' nigger woulda said anything if he *hadn'ta* been drunk?"

It was hard for us to believe what Robert was saying; however, none of us had ever seen him this nervous before. Finally George and Jerome decided that they would go into town to see if they could find out anything. By the time they got back it was pitch black outside. As soon as Jerome burst in the door we could all see that Robert had been right.

"Them white folks in town's *together,* man, and we better do something but quick," he said, almost out of breath.

I knew we were in bad shape. Dave had taken the car into Jackson for the weekend and the only people in town that would put us up were C.O. and Minnie Lou and they weren't home. So we just sat there until after eleven, trying to figure out a way to get out of Canton. We couldn't walk because there was only one way in and one way out, and we knew they could just as well mow us down on the highway.

"We are just wastin' time sittin' here bullshittin' like this. I ain't about to go down that dark-ass road. And I ain't about to stay in this damn house either," Flukie said.

"Y'all can sit here and talk *all night* if you want to," Bettye said, suddenly appearing in the door with a blanket in her arms. "But I'm gonna take my ass out back in that tall grass and worry about gettin' outta here tomorrow."

Since Sonny's house was new, he hadn't cultivated a garden yet, so the space behind the house where the garden would have been had grown wild with tall weeds. Sonny just mowed the back lawn right up to the weeds and let them grow like hedges.

It didn't take us long to agree that the weeds were our only way out. Even so, we knew that there was still a good chance that we would be discovered back there, but we had no other choice. So we pulled open the curtains and left the lamps on dim so that anyone could see that the house was empty. We also removed the sheets and blankets and left the spreads so the beds looked made. We waited until about twelve-thirty when all the lights in the neighborhood had been turned out. Then we sneaked out back with blankets and sheets clutched in our arms. The nine of us spaced ourselves so that from a distance no one patch of grass would look mashed down. The five guys made us girls stay behind them. We agreed not to do anything but look and listen without saying a word to each other.

I was wrapped in one of the spreads and after lying still for what seemed like hours, I began to get very cold and stiff. I couldn't hear a sound not even a cricket and I began to feel like I was all alone out there. I listened for Bettye's breathing, but I heard nothing. I wondered if the others were feeling as alone and scared as I was. I could feel the grass getting wet with dew and I began to get colder and colder. I kept thinking about what might happen to us if they found us out there. I tried hard not to think about it. But I couldn't help it. I could see them stomping us in the face and shooting us. I also kept thinking about the house and whether we had left some clue that we were out back. Suddenly I heard a noise and I could almost feel everyone jump with me.

"Don't get scared, it's that damn dog next door. Just be quiet and he'll shut up," one of the guys whispered.

Now I knew we were in for it. That damn dog kept on whimpering. I could see the neighbor coming out and discovering us just when the Klan drove up. But finally the dog was quiet again.

I must have begun to doze off when I heard a car door slam.

"Quiet! Quiet! They're here," Flukie whispered as someone moved in the grass.

I couldn't even breathe. My whole chest began to hurt as I heard the mumbling voices toward the front of the house. When the mumbling got louder I knew that they were in the back. But I still couldn't make out what they were saying. As I heard them moving around in the backyard, I had a horrible feeling that they could see us as plain as daylight and I just trembled all over. But in a few minutes I heard the car door slam again and they were gone.

We lay quietly in case they had pulled a trick. Finally Jerome whispered loudly, "They think we're at C.O.'s. They'll probably be back."

Soon the roosters were crowing and it began to get light. Sure enough they drove up again but this time they must have just taken a quick look, because they were gone almost immediately. We knew they wouldn't be back because it was too light. So we sneaked back in the house before the neighbors got up.

George, who had been in a position to see and hear them, told us what happened. He said that there was a pickup truck with about eight men who had obviously been drinking. They had all sorts of weapons. They discussed burning the house down, but decided that they would come back and get us another night.

After this incident, Robert and a group of men all in their middle or late twenties formed a group to protect us. Three or four of them had already lost their jobs because they tried to register. They couldn't find other jobs so they followed us around everywhere we went, walking with us as if they were bulletproof. They also spread rumors that the Freedom House was protected by armed men. We were all still a little up tight and afraid to sleep at night, but after a while, when the whites didn't come back, we figured the rumors worked. The threats didn't bother me as much now. I began to feel almost safe with those men around all the time. Their interest, courage, and concern gave all of us that extra lift we needed.

Now every Negro church in the county was opened for workshops. The nine of us split into groups of three. Almost every night we had workshops in different churches, sometimes sixteen to thirty miles out of town.

One or two of our protective guys had cars. They were usually sent along with the girls out in the country. It was dark and dangerous driving down those long country rock roads, but now that we always had two or three of the guys riding with us, it wasn't so bad. In fact, once we got to the churches, everything was fine. Listening to those old Negroes sing freedom songs was like listening to music from heaven. They sang them as though they were singing away the chains of slavery. Sometimes I just looked at the expressions on their faces as they sang and cold chills would run down my back. Whenever God was mentioned in a song, I could tell by the way they said the word that most of them had given up here on earth. They seemed to be waiting just for God to call them home and end all the suffering.

The nightly church workshops were beginning to be the big thing going for us at this point in the campaign. However, the white folks found out about this and tried to put a stop to it. One night out in the country three carloads of whites chased George and a group of the guys all the way to Canton. George said they were shooting at them like crazy. Since George thought the whites could have killed them if they had wanted to, we took it as a warning. We were extra careful after that.

The luckiest thing that happened to us was that we had succeeded in getting C. O. Chinn to work with us. He was a powerful man, known as "bad-ass

C. O. Chinn" to the Negroes and whites alike. All of the Negroes respected him for standing up and being a man. Most of the whites feared him. He was the type of person that didn't take shit from anyone. If he was with you he was all for you. If he didn't like you that was it—in that case he just didn't have anything to do with you. Because he was respected by most of the local Negroes, he was our most effective speaker in the churches. He was in a position to speak his mind and what he said was taken without offense to anyone in particular.

Just as Mr. Chinn opened up full force, the whites cut in on him. Within a week he was forced to close his place and he began moving out most of his things. This still wasn't enough to satisfy the whites. One evening, when he was taking home the .45 he had kept around for protection, he was stopped and arrested by those damn cops that hung around the office all the time. He was immediately taken to jail and charged with carrying a concealed weapon—actually he had placed the gun on the seat beside him. His bail was set at five hundred dollars. He was in jail for a week before his family could find anyone to post a property bond. Most of the local Negroes had borrowed money on their property, which meant that it couldn't be used for bail purposes.

I think this was the beginning of C.O.'s realization of what had happened to him. Not only had he lost everything he had, he was sitting in jail with no one to go his bail. Instead of this putting the damper on his activities as the whites had expected, it increased them. He began hitting harder than ever. Often when he was speaking, he would say, "Take me, for example, they have completely put me out of business. I have lost practically everything I have. These young workers are here starving to death trying to help you people. And for what? A lot of you ain't worth it!" Not one of us working for CORE could have talked to the local people like that.

It was the middle of August now, and we had been working in the county for two months. Up until this time, not one of the ministers in Canton had committed himself to helping us. When they did give us a chance to speak in their churches, it was only for two or three minutes during the announce-ments. The biggest Negro church in Canton was pastored by Canton's biggest "Tom." Most of his congregation were middle-class bourgeois Negroes. We all knew that if we could somehow force him to move, every other large church in Canton would open its doors to us.

We set up a meeting and invited all the ministers, but since the number one minister didn't show up, all the others did was mumble to each other and tell us, "We can't do anything until Reverend Tucker says so." After that we decided to forget the ministers and go to work on their congregations. At this point the ministers started coming around. In fact, they called a meeting to talk things over with us. But the talk was fruitless. The ministers tried to play the same game the Southern white people played when things got too hot for them. That is, to find out what you are thinking and try and get you to hold off long enough for them to come up with some new strategy to use on you. Those Toms weren't as dumb as they appeared, I thought. They had learned to play Mr. Charlie's game pretty well.

We had a surprise for them, though. We had made headway with several of their most influential members, and they put us right where we wanted to go—behind the pulpits for more than five minutes. Now we could hit the Canton churches hard.

For a little while that good old Movement spirit was on the surge again. Everyone began to feel it. We still were not getting any money, but for the most part we didn't need any. The Canton Negroes began to take good care of us, and we were never hungry. A Negro service station owner even let us have gas on credit. What pleased me most was that many of our teen-agers had come back. I had really missed them.

michael rossman _____

The Day We Named Our Child
We Had Fish for Dinner

Michael Rossman (1939–   ), a central figure in the New Left and the movement's best writer, grew up in Marin County, California. He came to political consciousness, he says, when, as a high school junior, he chose to write a paper on a local woman who burned controversial books and lived on a street named Liberty Lane. He attended the University of Chicago, where, in 1958, he participated in an abortive educational reform movement. As a graduate student in mathematics at the University of California, Berkeley, he was one of the leaders of the 1964 Free Speech Movement, the landmark event in student political activity in the United States, and served a jail term for his participation. He has been involved in counterculture activities ever since, lecturing and organizing on college campuses all over America and writing eloquently about his experiences. The chief goal of his current and future activities is not only to bring about change, but also "to rediscover eternal things, things that through change do not change." Rossman's recently published *On Learning and Social Change* (1972) reflects his theories of radical educational reform. His earlier essays have been collected in *The Wedding Within the War* (1971), in which the following selection appears, under the title "Four Days After Cambodia."

"What shall I do with the filet?" asked Karen from the kitchen. "There are bones in it."

"Cook it," I said.

"I don't like it with bones."

"They come out easier after it's cooked. That's the way fish are."

"Oh, never mind." Clatter of pans, water running. Indistinctly: "Screw you, anyway."

"What was that?"

"I said, never mind."

"And what else? What after that?"

Clatter of pans, running water. I pulled myself up again, weary, and went into the kitchen. She was standing over the stove, stirring instant mashed potatoes. I couldn't read her back. I held her. "I think we're tearing ourselves apart because the world is coming apart."

"I think you're right," she said.

"Water the plants," I told her, as I went back into the front room, grimly ignoring the radio, the phone. "That's the thing to remember now, remember to water the plants."

It was the fourth night of Cambodia. I was watching the ferns when our brother Lonnie from San Diego came in. "Carol called to find out when you're coming back," I reported. "She says they're working for a school-wide strike on Thursday. The English Department already voted to go out. Farber brought them round, and the paper's agreed to support it."

"All up and down Telegraph they're talking about Kent State," he said, his face still flushed from walking, intense through his spectacles. "There's little knots of freaks just talking, all along the street. It's true, four were killed, the National Guard shot them down in the parking lots. I can't believe it."

We want to run a training program this summer, for public school teachers in the San Diego area: learn them a little political smarts to protect the learning they're learning. But Carol can't make the planning meeting, too busy with a crisis in the Woman Studies Program she's organizing in the college there. And she's hard to get hold of now: with the Minutemen at their door, they don't go back to the house much, and are learning to travel armed. Lonnie and I fumble to fix time for another meeting. Nothing will come into focus. He drifts out the door. I say, "Wait." We embrace.

Later Tom calls, from over in the next house, to tell me that Reagan has just ordered all the state colleges and universities closed through Sunday at least. Another first for California, the Golden State.

Three years before Cambodia I visited Kent, Ohio. Spring 1967. The media were just discovering the Haight and the Hippy. I was on my first round of visiting campuses, just starting to sort things out, to adjust my perspective from Berkeley-provincial to a national scope, and learn what work I could do in our ghetto. For the moment, I was writing a story on what the war was doing to what we then called the Student Movement, and I wanted some unknown dreary large public campus to play off against Antioch and Oberlin. So I chose Kent State, found a contact, and spent a couple of days there.

I mostly remember the flat apathy of the faces I met while on campus, these students of lower-class blood slack-weary from the mineral-drained hills of upland Ohio, many of them serving time for the upward mobility of the teaching credential. The buxom girls chattering in the morning Pancake House, as I sat over fourth coffee, road-grimed, hugging my sleeping bag.

Flat, that campus, flat. Some months earlier a first hiccup of antiwar protest had turned out a hundred for a lonely march. Now I found all told maybe a dozen committed to keeping active, trying to find a way to move it on. Isolated, embattled, embittered, taking refuge in an overtight group whose talk was laced with hurtful humor and flashes of longing.

They took me home for the night, the house was old and they had made their warm mark on its surfaces, they lived in what would become a commune, and then a family. Over late coffee we talked about organizing, about guerrilla theater, about holding together for warmth. Hang on, brothers and sisters, I said to them, some Spring is coming. And I left them the large *Yellow Submarine* poster I designed for Mario's birthday—an anarchist program for a disruptive festival of joy, "a generally loving retaliation against absurd attack." The poster commemorated the 1966 Second Strike at Berkeley—for us in the West, the first event in which freaks and politicos joined in public ritual, in song and an elaborate masque. We discussed community program, wild with the energy of coming together, and broke into spontaneous joy:

> We all live in a yellow submarine,
> and our friends are all on board,
> many more of them live next door,
> sky of blue and sea of green. . . .

Then next October, before I left to begin my second round of traveling campus work, we put on our feathers at dawn and marched 7,000 strong down into Oakland to block the doors of the Induction Center. After we got the shit clubbed out of 200 people, we tied up the downtown for the rest of the week, dodging the heat and chanting, "We are the people!" in the intersections.

So long ago. *Saturday in Kent they trashed the town in protest, breaking 56 windows.* I was in Rock Island, Illinois, with my brother Russell from our theater troupe, talking about the death of a culture and teaching college kids how to begin to play again, to live in their bodies. *Sunday in Kent they burned down the Army ROTC building.* I was home in Berkeley, in the house we call Dragon's Eye. Sixteen of our family were learning to play a holy gambling game together, device for pooling psychic force, handed down from the Indians through Stewart Brand of the Pranksters. *Today in Kent on the fourth of Cambodia 2,000 turned out, and they shot 4 dead in the parking lots.* O let us laugh and canter. O I will play the Fool, grant me my mad anger, I still believe that art will see us through.

October evening falling in 1964. Berkeley. I was standing in Sproul Plaza beside the police car that held Jack Weinberg captive, I was changing in the crucible that formed the Free Speech Movement, the first campus explosion. It was the thirtieth hour since a thousand had captured the car and Mario stepped on top to begin the first open public dialogue I had heard

CHAPTER THREE / *Commitment*

in America. Behind Sproul Hall 600 cops were preparing, around us the Greeks were chanting drunkenly, "We want blood! We want blood!" We were sharing our green apples and bread, waiting for them to wade in clubbing, and singing "We are not afraid" in voices shaking with fear, betrayed into life by our longing for the pure radiations of community which we first there kindled among us, bright as imagination.

And I had a heavy flash, and said it to some friend: *"Five years from now they'll be killing kids on campuses, all over America."* They began with the blacks, with the Orangeburg Three massacred in '68, and they killed the first white brother, James Rector, at People's Park in Berkeley nine months later. And now Kent State: only the first in this, the fifth Spring.

(Rewriting now on the sixth of Cambodia, the plastic "underground" radio turns real as it tells me how the girl's leg broke as they beat her and threw her off the wall, an hour ago up on campus, and how 2,000 National Guardsmen have been ordered into Urbana, Illinois. I've spent ten separate weeks in Urbana, we have family there. Vic centers it, he works in wood and is making a cradle for the baby. Last month I saw him. He was organizing a craft-food-garage cooperative. The week before he had charged the pigs for the first time to help rescue a brother, was still shaken.)

But I had that flash and said that thing, I truly did, and have five years of poems to prove it, canceled stubs on the checking account of my sorrow, a long coming to terms. Sure, I'm a prophet, my name is Michael, I've shared total consciousness and seen the magicians summon the Powers. Prophets are common in Berkeley, and I've met quite a few on the road, mixed with the saints who now walk among us. What else do you expect to appear when our energy comes somewhat truly to focus?

It is time to own up to what we are doing. Everyone knows or suspects a snatch of the holy language of Energy, via acid, confrontation, or contact. The wavelengths of our common transformations flow strongly through Berkeley: for twelve years now, what happens here and across the Bay happens a year or two later in concentric circles spreading out across the young of America. I've lived here all that time. Most leave. If you stay, you close off or go mad. Or you stay open, and are transformed into an active conduit for the common sea of our Energy: lines of its organizing come to flow through you. I think I am learning to feel them in my body. It is frightening, it is always frightening not to have a language in which to wrap the nakedness of your experience. Cold wind of the new, hanging on the tip of the rushing wave.

For three years, linked into a growing net of comrades in work, I wandered from Berkeley through our involuntary ghetto. Four hundred days on the road, 150,000 miles. I visited seventy campuses, *worked* on forty, training and organizing, trying to follow the Tao of transformation in furthering the change that is happening through us. Call me an action sociologist, a specialist in learning and student of change; and color me proud to be supported mostly by my own people, freaks and radicals, plus some rip-offs from "adult" institutions and the media. I hustled to be free to put my energy where I draw my warmth, and luck was kind. And my trip is one among many. Our own and our best are staying with us now, instead of being bought off by the stale rewards of a dying System, and our change accelerates the more.

And I know where it's going, for a little way at least. For Berkeley is truly a barometer. Every college in the country is undergoing an evolution in the culture and politics of its captive transient population; and each evolution is essentially like Berkeley's. I have watched it happening on every kind of campus, from upper-class Catholic girls' schools to working-class junior colleges. Activism begins slow, diversifies to departmental organizing, antidraft work, and guerrilla theater; the dance of confrontation proceeds in growing ranks, the administration grows slicker but finally blows its cool; dope culture spreads, the girls chuck their bras—wow, you wouldn't believe the wealth of data.

And then beyond the campus the *voluntary* ghetto forms. Freak community sinks roots and begins to generate communes, families, head shops and food co-ops, freak media, friendly dog packs and dog shit, links with the farm communes—there are ten within fifteen miles of Rock Island, micro-sample of America. O, it is happening everywhere just like in Berkeley, only faster now: long-haired kids on the street, merchants' complaints, heavy dope busts, teachers fired, kids suspended, leash laws, narcs and agents and street sweeps and riot practice for the neighboring precincts, and dynamite at the farmhouse.

Here now in Berkeley it is the fourth night of Cambodia. Kent State is catching up fast. We shall have to go some to keep ahead. But like the University we have broad strength in our Departments, their lintels display the Tao of Life and Death. The Free Bakery has opened, capacity 2,000 loaves a day, put together by a family of forty living mostly on welfare: people drop by to pick up bread or learn how to bake, and linger. The city government is trying to get $175,000 for two helicopters to maintain a full-time patrol over the city; the City Council has decided not to make its meetings public, because of disruption; we will shoot their birds down, I am sure. A thousand tenants are out on rent strike; now the evictions begin. Governor Reagan is calling for a bloodbath. Gay Liberation flames buoyant in the front lines of demonstrations. Our medics are special targets, speed and smack are spreading like crazy. Six hundred Berkeley families are linked into the Great Food Conspiracy, buying cooperative spinach and cheese. The campus has the third-largest police force in the whole county, the leaves are beginning to wilt from the tear-gas. The people who hand-deliver the high-graphic newsletter *Kaliflower* to 150 communes in Berkeley and S.F., cycling goods and needs and lore and advice, come by and leave us a rap on planting and compost. My kid brother by blood was busted on campus last week, charged with assaulting a police officer with a deadly weapon, i.e., chucking a rock at a cop, $5,000 bail. He didn't do it, no matter: the Grand Jury's seeking indictments. The leaflet from the Berkeley Labor Gift Plan says, "*Together,* brothers and sisters, we can build a new community of labor and of love." Each time we go into the streets they test some new piece of technology upon us, last week it was cars spewing pepper-fog from their exhausts. The leaflet from the Leopold Family begs the community not to rip off records from the people's own store. On the radio a brother is reporting from Kent, he says he had to drive forty miles to get out from under the phone blank-out the government has clamped over the area. Berkeley was an exemplary city, you know. She had a progressive form of government and an overtly liberal party in power for years. She dazzled the nation with thoughtful, advanced programs of curricular enrichment and racial integration. Active support for the schools was her proudest civic tradition. O, Berkeley was always noted for how she cared for her children.

Cold wind coming. Sky turning black, the missiles sulk in their cages, the green net of the ocean grows dangerous thin, the terrorism of bombs begins, the Minutemen multiply bunkers, the economy chokes and staggers, the blacks grow yet more desperate, the War is coming home. I figure I'm likely to die in this decade, perhaps in this city I love, down the street beyond the neighborhood garden, in some warm summer twilight when people sit on their porches and the joy of live music drifts out from their windows. That's a cold political judgment, without much to do with what's also true: that since I woke at fifteen I've never been able to imagine past about thirty-five, it's been only a blank in my mind, always the same through the years, down to now, when I'm thirty. Do you mind if I finger my intimate fragments in front of you, awkwardly? I can't fit them together. But what else is a man to do in this mad time, pretend that everything's only at its usual standard of incoherence? For I have also been One with the great two-headed snake of the Universe, and I have seen us begin to recover our bodies and share our will, seen us learn that realities are collective conspiracies. Now in the families forming and linking we are weaving a blank social canvas for the play of our imagination. I have seen the first sketches of group will, love, and art, and a whole life, the first organized forms of human energy liberated one more degree. They transfix me with awe. I was never taught to dream so boldly, I had to learn for myself. I was not alone. For all our failures and unfinished business, what we are pulling together is bright and well begun. If we are let live through this decade and the next, we will be strong, strong, our women will be powerful and our men beautiful.

So all of this is running through my mind on the fourth night of Cambodia, I'd just got back the night before from three months of hustling my ass around the country to pile up bread for the baby and the coming recession, in the process cutting through maybe sixty family groups in twenty cities, cross-fertilizing news and goods and paper and trinkets, a bee in the meadow of change. I came back stoned and mellow at how fast and strong it is coming together among us, even within the strain of the War, and bearing the love of a dozen fine women and men for Karen. All day now through the cottage people have been flooding with these atrocity tales, I wallow in the gloomy pleasures of verification. Diagnosis: Fascism, soft form turning hard, terminal cultural cancer. The radio tells me 258 campuses are out on strike, and then sings to me: *"Rejoice, rejoice, you have no choice."* I take another toke, last of the good stuff: been running too fast to score, and summer's customary drought is almost upon us. The typewriter beckons. Torn between life and death I calm my chattering schizophrenic, refuse, and turn to the guitar, god damn! the sweet guitar who embraces all of me in her stroking vibrations when I touch her well. *O, how I need to go to the sea!*

Music is magical, music is my balm, music suspends me and aligns the frame of my spirit. O, shit, I wish I could sing to you, I am no longer ashamed, it is time to come out with it all, nothing less will do, the child will be born. I hate these pages, hate these mechanical fingers. Sometimes I pop for a moment above the surface of sanity and grab for the floating flute or guitar, manage to clear the Breath of my energy for a time from the choking hurrying flow of vital and desperate information, rapping words healing words data words analysis words magic words maggots and birds on the acid wallpaper of my mind. And I water the plants, the ferns in particular. When I am broken jagged like tonight I think it is because I mostly cannot cry, and that I travel the crystal rapids of melody for this reason too, singing because I cannot weep. When I'm together I see it as a way of keeping in touch with the slower rhythms. Either way the ferns are grateful, and they sing to me with their green misty love, and the spiders arch their webs in the corners of the window frames.

And I sing to them back, and to the dog my familiar, and to the pregnant animal Karen crouched unseen in her den—to them all, but softly to myself—a song I have made for her from a fragment another singer left in my mind. Karen comes in from the kitchen, plate and bowl of dinner in her hand, sets it down, retreats from the shaken animal in his den. While the rock cod cools, I sing the song again, for the first time loudly.

"Now damn," I think, with bitter satisfaction, "ain't that a song to inspire pity and awe and all! Not bad for a first lullaby, opus 7. I sure would like to spend a long stretch of years writing some songs. I'd be grateful if they just kept on coming three or four a year, now that I know they're coming."

Slow, with a lagging rhythm

					"Things	might	be
					It	might	be

la — zy if they weren't so cra-zy" ___ he
bet — ter in some o — ther wea ther ___ I

tells you, I tell ___ you that too.
don't know, I'm do – ing it with you.

bridge between verses (freely):

(2)
Some say the city, a farm would be pretty,
the mountains refuse to be blue.*
Come, with me wander, while they seek us yonder;
what else could you choose to do?

(3)
But pray for the baby whose birthday is Maybe,
and meet me at two in the moon.
Keep warm if you're able and fight for the cradle,
we can't hide, let's ride this one through.

Keep warm if you're able and fight for the cradle,
we can't hide, let's ride this one through.

fuse to be blue

And I rack the guitar, pick up the plate, and wander into the bedroom to eat with Karen.

In the next room my love is curled weeping on the black leather chair, the dog is anxiously kissing her, careful of her belly. I hold the song of her sobbing. "Ah, little princess," I say, "you didn't know what it would cost to be my muse." Through my head spin Cambodia, Babylon, that five-year-old flash by the cop-car, growing up during the McCarthy years with the FBI at the door, the times we have been in the street together, our trips, our campus travels. "But there's spin-off, you know," I say. "We're maybe better prepared spiritually for what's coming than most, advantage of foresight and practice, pay of the bruises. We've been making our peace for a while." No ultimate blame: culture changing too fast for its able. But the child will be born, though they tie the mother's legs.

"Yes," she says, "but I didn't know it would be this sudden." And then: "But if the gods are stingy with time, at least they've been generous in other ways."

On my lap. I see. Wavering. The plastic plate with pink decal flowers from the Goodwill. Fresh fish filet our cousin family brought us from up the Sonoma coast. Cheese sauce, recently mastered, with chopped green onions. Dehydrated mashed potatoes. In the stoneware bowls my sister Deborah made and laid on us for our anniversary—before she went down South again to the Army-base coffee shop she helped start, to watch her successors get six years and then go off to help organize another—in my dear blood sister's bowls is fresh spinach salad, well-flavored, we are learning to tend our bodies. Anticipation of apple juice in the refrigerator. This is how it is, you see, I am sitting here eating this food, and Bull is watching us very intently while the puppy from next door chews on his dinner, and my feet are up cuddled around the ball of her belly, watermelon-hard in its last weeks. I sing to her, we share the cooking, the dog eats when we do, mostly. She is bearing our child, on the bed under the light and the ferns is the government pamphlet on how to raise a child during the first year, it's not bad.

And she says, "What do you think of Lorca?"

"I think I can dig it, for a boy," I say slowly, "I been thinking about it, and I can."

"I'm glad," she says softly, the blush of shy triumphant pleasure crowning round her eyes. "Your mother and I were having lunch, and we started to think of the names of Spanish poets. 'García Rossman,' she said, 'no, that's impossible.' 'Federico . . .' I said. And then we just looked at each other, and we *knew*. And it has a nice sound."

I sink into the thought and mirror of her love, reach for the resonances, roots in the soil, and start to cry. Is it for the first time or the tenth, on this fourth night of Cambodia? Lorca was my first song teacher, the man who opened the keys of Metaphor to me: for ten years I relived his poems into my American language. "I have lost myself many times in the sea," he sang, "with my ear full of freshly cut flowers, with my tongue full of love and of agony. Many times I have lost myself in the sea, as I lose myself in the heart of certain children. . . ." Hold on, dear heart, jagged at this four A.M., now is not the time to tear. From Federico's arms I passed through those of grandfather Neruda, and then into Vallejo's volcano, which finished for me what acid began and gave me open form to integrate my fragments.

But Lorca began me, long before I learned how death found him in a Fascist trench, how he went to sleep forever in the autumn night of the gypsies, beyond the lemon moon. Mercurial brightest spirit of the second Golden Age of his tongue's power, murdered in Granada by Franco's highwaymen, in the first summer of the Civil War. All the poets, all, all the singers were on one side in that great division, perhaps as never before since old Athens. And the schools and the hospitals of the brief flowering of Republican Spain went down under German planes and Italian artillery, the dogs of Church and Greed. And all the poets perished or fled.

Torn, my father watched the Fascists rehearse, with their scientific grace; stayed to organize at home with his trade of words and a red perspective. I was born six months after the fall of Madrid, while he was editing the Mine, Mill and Smelter Workers' Union paper in Denver. Pablo Neruda was in exile from the Fascists in Chile. Cesár Vallejo was dead of hunger and heartbreak for Spain. Lorca's grave was never found, in a hundred lands and Franco's jails the poets of his race who survived sang him their tenderest elegies. Lincoln Steffens began a new family and life at sixty, his *Autobiography* instructed my father. When he died the last lines in his typewriter read, "the Spanish Civil War is the opening battle in mankind's struggle against Fascism." Steffens' son Peter taught my sister Deborah before she went South, I have touched his children. Even the high-school babysitters I hitched home from the airport with know what's coming down.

A week before Cambodia I was at a conference in Boston, thrown by some church folk and book people, on "the religious dimension of the Movement." Indeed. It was quite a happening, believe me: a bunch of us freaks from the families got together behind some mellow mescaline and opened up some free space, some Chaos. Then someone asked about Ritual, and little incredible Raymond Mungo opened up in a musing country style, speaking the sainted baby babble.

"Well, we get up in the morning," he says, "and we look at the light and we eat, we eat together. And we go to sleep when it gets dark, sometimes alone and sometimes together, for there is no light. But sometimes at night we watch the moon. During the day we plant. We chop wood. We use the wood for fire. We eat when the sun goes down. From April to October there is very much food. We have to find ways to give it away. We have to, there is very much. There is the summer solstice, and then there is the autumn solstice, and so on. In spring the solstice was very cold, very cold. We chopped some wood and put it in a box. I made a mantra: *Equinox/sticks in box/soon it will be warm/big dog.* And a big dog came, and it grew warm. And sometimes we go out when there is no moon and run around in the grass. And then we come back to the houses we build. Last week one of our houses burned down, it was very warm. We lost four brothers and sisters. I think we're going to learn to build better chimneys."

O, I met a little saint in Boston, he organizes energy, used to be founding Czar of Liberation News Service, then he figured out the cities were dying, now in his Vermont town of 800, over a quarter live in communes, and he studies the government pamphlet to learn to build better chimneys. We're met on the fifteenth floor, overlooking the river of death called the Charles, the plastic pastries and draperies are poisoning our bodies, our minds, we've come to talk about rituals for living with fire. Mitch Goodman loves us and he's frantic with terror, sees the black sky looming, MIRV's lurking, etc., etc., he's positively yelling at Raymond, half his age and weight, scarecrow child in oversized coveralls: *"but what about Fascism?"* And somehow we can't quite get it through to him there that Raymond is not simply talking about farms, pigs, dinner, etc., but about the house burning down and learning to make better chimneys and going on in season, and about Lorca and Vallejo and my brother and my sister and two of each dead in Kent and my lover lazy with child, whose belly my baboon feet grip as if I stand on the round of the world, spinning through all time.

I was translating a poem of Lorca's when I got the call that my grandfather was suddenly dead. The poem follows a brief skit for puppet theater, in which the gypsy whose name is *Anything* is captured on the bridge of all the rivers while building a tower of candlelight, and is brought before the Lieutenant-Colonel of the Spanish Civil Guard to be interrogated.

He, Harry, my mother's father, was a Bolshevik. He organized a strike in the machine shop, was jailed, loved his tutor, she died of consumption, he fled here in 1906 to dodge the interrogations of the Czar, clerked and warehoused to send Mother through college. He wanted her to learn. I have his blue eyes. He taught me to carve, and cried with memory when I told him in '60, during that spring of Chessman and HUAC, how they beat us and hosed us down the steps of City Hall in San Francisco. "That was how it started, you know . . ." he said. And three years later the phone call came and was, and I put down the receiver and thought for a moment, and said somewhere inwardly and quite distinctly, I will file this for future reference, I will weep for you some day, grandfather. And I turned back to finish reworking the poem, for there was nothing to do but go on, I knew it would take years to comprehend that grief.

Sitting in my rocker, plate on my lap, our eyes intertwining and my feet on the future, the ferns turn to oleander and the cottage to a patio, and the song of the beaten gypsy rises up in the well of his absence.

> Twenty-four slaps,
> twenty-five slaps,
> then at night my mother
> will wrap me in silver paper.

> Civil Guard of the roads,
> give me a sip of water.
> Water with fishes and boats.
> Water, water, water.

> Aii, boss of the Guard,
> standing upstairs in your parlor!
> There'll be no silk handkerchieves
> to clean my face!

And the tears rip through me, Grandfather, deep, and out, everything opens and echoes in hers, and we touch and cling and are shaken. And the dog, our first child and familiar, pushes up anxious between us and offers her his nose and me his nads, which we take to complete the circle of energy, love, and time around the child to be born in Cambodia.

"Yes," I say, "Lorca, if it's a boy."

"Maybe even a girl," she says, "it has a nice sound."

"Maybe a girl," I say, "yes."

And she says I'm glad with her eyes.

And the radio sings, *"Rejoice, rejoice, you have no choice,"* and the acid magic of those moments, of that state we once called existential, goes on and on forever, and I go off to set down the brief notes of these thoughts, like the rib-thin eaten skeleton of the dinner fish, to flesh back out later. And then we take off for the City, to try to be with our people, our theater troupe in rehearsal coming suddenly real. For it is clearly a time for coming together with those we are dear with, and we must take care that the Wedding go on within the War.

Irreverence Stopped at the Wellhead

Born in Jackson and raised in Yazoo City, Mississippi, Willie Morris (1934–   )
was educated at the University of Texas, where he was editor-in-chief of the college
newspaper, *The Daily Texan.* He won a Rhodes scholarship and studied at Oxford
until 1960, when he returned to America to become editor of the respected muckrak-
ing newspaper *The Texas Observer.* In 1963 he was appointed an editor at *Harper's,*
and three years later he became the youngest executive editor in that magazine's
long history. His editorial innovations, though critically praised, brought him trouble.
On March 1, 1971, after a dispute over editorial policy which he has characterized
as "the money men against the literary men," he resigned from *Harper's.* His stories
and articles have appeared in numerous periodicals, including *The New Yorker,*
Commentary, and *The Texas Quarterly.* He has written two books of autobiography,
North Toward Home (1967), from which the following selection is reprinted, and
Good Old Boy (1971), an extensive account of his childhood.

A great irony occasionally besets an American state university, for it allows
and at its best encourages one to develop his critical capacities, his imagination,
his values; at the same time, in its institutional aspects, a university under
pressure can become increasingly wary of the very intent and direction of
the ideals it has helped spawn. It is too easy, too much a righteous judgment,
to call this attitude hypocrisy, for actually it is a kind of schizophrenia. This
involves more than a gap between preaching and practicing; it involves the
splitting of a university's soul. There can be something brutal about a university's teaching its young people to be alive, aware, critical, independent, and
free, and then, when a threatening turn is taken, to reject by its actual behavior
the substance of everything it claims for itself. Then ideals and critical capacities exist in a vacuum. They are sometimes ignored, and in extreme instances
victimized. And the greater society suffers as well.

For a year I had been reading heavily in politics, history, and the journalism
of the great editors. I took to my heart the memorable statement in Joseph
Pulitzer's will, now reprinted every day on the editorial pages of the *St. Louis
Post-Dispatch,* and which I subsequently tacked to the wall in my office next

to my typewriter, as I have in every office where I have worked: "that it will always fight for progress and reform, never tolerate injustice or corruption, always fight demagogues of all parties, never belong to any party, always oppose privileged classes and public plunderers, never lack sympathy for the poor, always remain devoted to the public welfare, never be satisfied merely with printing news, always be drastically independent, never be afraid to attack wrong, whether by predatory plutocracy or predatory poverty."

I read the journalism of H. L. Mencken, Lincoln Steffens, William Allen White, S. S. McClure, Bernard DeVoto, Hodding Carter, Ralph McGill, and Brann the Iconoclast. I read the files of *The Daily Texan* itself, learning of different and more alive times—the great editorials of Horace Busby, who brought sanity and courage to the campus during the Rainey disaster of the 1940s, D. B. Hardeman, Ronnie Dugger, and others. The political climate of the state had become more pointed to me, and in long and sometimes agonizing talks with the brightest and most perceptive student leaders I had thought out the huge responsibility of the largest and most prominent student newspaper in the South in a period when the integration issue was coming alive; my experience with my hometown Citizens Council had helped me judge the extent of my own personal change, and showed the sad barbarism of intransigence. I was suffused with the ideals of freedom of expression and the open marketplace. I had the most emphatic belief that this freedom should be used to positive purposes, that freedom is as freedom does, that the pages of this newspaper should reflect the great diversity of the place I had come to know, that the University of Texas was too much a part of its state and of the rest of the world to avoid editorials on significant questions beyond the campus, and that the campus itself—as so many others then—was bogged down in dullness, complacency, and the corporate mentality. My deficits, as I fully realized later, were a self-righteousness, a lack of subtlety in polemic, and an especially underdeveloped awareness of the diplomatic approach.

President Kennedy, Theodore Sorensen later wrote, liked to improvise on the passage from Ecclesiastes: "A time to weep and a time to laugh, a time to mourn and a time to dance, a time to fish and a time to cut bait." I did not know as much about bait-cutting then as I would later. But I wanted the paper which would briefly be mine to be a living thing, distinctive and meaningful, in both its own tradition and the tradition of hard-hitting, outspoken American journalism. The University of Texas itself had taught me to place a high value on these qualities; the necessity of the free marketplace of ideas was apparently high on its list of formal priorities. It was in the books in its libraries, the valedictions of its deans, administrators, commencement speakers, even on the buildings and statues around its campus. You cannot make gestures of support for all these things and expect them to have no context. They either apply to a particular setting or they do not apply at all. They are either watered down to appease the distrusts of a power faction or they are not. But uphold these ideas long enough, frequently enough, and with such inspiration, and some young people are not only going to believe in them, they are going to believe in them with the fervor of the young, and even arrange their lives and their sense of honor by them.

So it was that I came out fighting hard, and the reactions were no sooner than immediate. I erred, first of all, into editorializing occasionally about state politics, particularly its twin deities, oil and gas. I suppose the authorities had not expected a gentle-natured Southern boy to overreach into areas ruled by hidden divinities; a student editor in Texas could blaspheme the Holy Spirit and the Apostle Paul, but irreverence stopped at the wellhead. We were going against a set of scandals and money frauds that had rocked Governor Shivers' administration. We were seeking intelligence and good will on integration and lauding most Texans for their tolerant attitude. Occasionally we chided John Foster Dulles' view of the rest of the world. Against the reactions from the school administration we categorically defended student press freedom and our right to comment as we wished on controversial state and national issues. We were committing the crime of being vigorous and outspoken, naïvely idealistic and exuberantly but not radically liberal in a state that at that time had little patience with either, on a campus where exuberance was reserved for the minor furies, and in a decade which encouraged little essential ebullience in the young.

There began a series of summonses to President Logan Wilson's office, much like a grade-school student who had been caught throwing spitballs in class being called to the principal; I was immediately reminded of my tribulations with my fourth-grade teacher, the evangelical Miss Abbott. Wilson's personal secretary would telephone and say, "Mr. Morris, the President would like to confer with you. Could we see you at three?" Ushered into the offices of the principal, who ruled over an academic domain stretching from El Paso to Galveston, I would wait in the outer chamber for an appropriate five minutes and admire there the lush carpet six inches deep; then the President was ready to see me. I would be offered menthol cigarettes and dealt with soothingly, charmingly, and with the condescension befitting the occasion. These biting editorials had to stop, though for a while the issue was not presented quite that frontally. There were meetings with the corps of deans, especially the one who had been a captain in the Navy and who believed that when an order is given, people should hop-to; anyone to the political left of Eisenhower, he once told me, was stupid if not downright treacherous. At first he was baffled, but this gave way to rage; there was no bemusement in these quarters. The slight liquid film that glazed his eyes as I came into his office suggested that he was keeping himself under control with some difficulty; his apparent preference was to assign me to the brig.

A good part of the time I was scared, and Logan Wilson must have been equally miserable; he was beginning to get caught in a vicious crossfire. The political appointees who ran the University were beginning to use the old and tested dogmatisms. And in the end more people than President Wilson and I were to be involved.

Finally the Regents erupted. At a meeting with several student leaders, including good friends of mine who were president and vice-president of the student body, they declared that the student paper should not discuss controversial state and national topics, and that college students were not interested in these things anyway. *The Daily Texan,* they said, had especially gone too far astray in commenting on a piece of natural gas legislature. There, now, was the rub! A little later they handed down a censorship edict. This was based, they said, not on principle but on legal considerations. They cited the rider on state appropriations bills, which stipulated that no state money "shall be used for influencing the outcome of any election or the passage or defeat of any legislative measure." Then they advanced one step further, a major step as it turned out, and announced that "editorial preoccupation with state and national political controversy" would be prohibited.

My friends and I on the *Texan* did some painful soul-searching after that announcement. Should we give in and avoid an agonizing fight? Was a fight worth it? The next morning, as I remember it, I drove out to Lyndon Johnson's lakes, to the one my beauty queen and I liked so much; I sat around under a scrub oak for a time reading some Thomas Jefferson. Then I came back to town and talked with Bergen, our managing editor, a shy, deceptive little man with an abundance of courage, and we decided in thirty minutes what Tom Jefferson likely would have recommended all along.

That began one of the greatest controversies in the history of American college journalism. Bergen and I stayed up all night in the editor's office, planning and writing editorials under the new censorship arrangement. We submitted critical editorials the next day, attacking the implications of the Regents' order, along with a guest editorial from *The New York Times* on the natural gas legislation* and several paragraphs from Thomas Jefferson on press freedom. All were rejected. The Jefferson quotes had been included in a personal column, and when he was censored there was thunder in the heavens, fire in the sky was reported over Monticello, and a thirty-minute moratorium on bourbon was declared in Charlottesville. But the student majority on the publications board outvoted the faculty representatives, and all the editorials were printed in toto in the next issue.

We kept right on going. We authorized a brilliant young law student, the

---

*This was the Fulbright-Harris bill that Eisenhower later vetoed for the exertion of "improper influences" on the Senate.

"attorney general" for the student government, to examine the legal consequences of the Regents' order. He counselled with some of the state's most respected lawyers and legal scholars and refuted the applicability of the appropriations rider. The Regents' interpretation of this rider, he argued, had "terrifying implications" and could be used in the same way to stifle legitimate comment among students, faculty, and quasi-independent corporations housed on the campus like the alumni organization, the student government, and the law review.

In retrospect a number of things stand out clearly. One Regent saying, "The *Texan* has gone out of bounds in discussing issues pertaining to oil and gas because 66 percent of Texas tax money comes from oil and gas." And another adding, "We're just trying to hold Willie to a college yell." ("There are our young barbarians, all at play!") . . . A journalism professor coming up to me the day after the controversy began and whispering, "I just want to shake your hand. I'm proud to know you." . . . My parents phoning long-distance from Mississippi and asking, "Son, you in trouble? They won't kick you out of school so close to graduation, will they?" . . . At one of the interminable meetings of the publications board, one faculty representative saying to me, "You know what you are? You're a *propagandist,*" a gripping judgment coming from an associate professor of advertising . . . And I recall one afternoon soon after the Regents' action when I telephoned J. Frank Dobie, the indomitable and lovable old *pater familias* of Texas writers, who had lost his own teaching job at the University in the 1940s, and asked if he would consider writing to the letters column commenting on our troubles. "Hell," he said, "I been workin' on one all mornin'." The Board of Regents, Dobie's letter said, "are as much concerned with free intellectual enterprise as a razorback sow would be with Keats' 'Ode on a Grecian Urn' "—a well-known statement now despite the fact that this phrase, and many another colorful one, were deleted after I had gone home to sleep and the paper was going to press.

One day one of the few outspoken old souls on the faculty in that period, an English professor who had never ceased to fight the political appointees with scorn and satire even in the 1940s, stood up in a faculty meeting and asked what the student newspaper's troubles *meant* in terms of the entire university. "We should discuss this matter," he said, waving his walking cane at his colleagues, "and deplore a contemptuous, cynical attitude toward what the student body or what an elected student leader may say." He spoke of the "dignity of the student" as a "new citizen"; a university's funds, he said, "should not be meant to *stifle* discussion but to encourage it." There was no further discussion, however, from the faculty. I wrote a lead-editorial on his speech and entitled it "Whispers in a Sleepy Lagoon." The night of its publication, as I sat at my desk eating a cold hamburger and drinking my fourth cup of black coffee, one of the administrative deans telephoned. "You published that editorial," he said, "but do you know that professor is runnin' around on his wife?" I had barely slept in a week, and at this point the fatigue had robbed me of any semblance of cynicism or humor. "Why you old bastard!" was all I could say, and hung up the telephone.

Looking back on it now, I had forgotten what a nasty time it was, how it sapped the patience of all of us on both sides, and the sad indignity with which many decent but weak men had to try to enforce official demands that I think they would have preferred in their hearts to ignore. One grew to be sympathetic, if not respectful, of some of these men, stripped as they were of power and sometimes, I believe, ashamed.

Finally, after more troubles, after we ran blank spaces and editorials entitled "Let's Water the Pansies," or "Don't Walk on the Grass" and held to our prerogatives to publish what we wished, there was a loosening up. There were no further official orders, and we remained free. But I was obsessed with the fear that in winning the battle we had lost the war, and that we had fought back wrongly and badly—and that the fight had not been worth it.

Yet I do not believe it was coincidence that in May of that year the Regents and the administration sought to impose in the general faculty a sweeping set of restrictions on the involvement of University of Texas faculty members in politics and political issues. One of the administration's spokesmen described these restrictions as the drawing of "a little circle" around political responsibilities. "That little circle," one young professor, the philosopher John Silber, said, "happens to comprise 90 percent of my political concerns." The issue was resoundingly defeated. For whom was the bell trying to toll? I believed then there was a connection there; the contempt for an independent student voice trying to engage itself in important issues in that age of McCarthy and silence was reflected in an effort to do lasting damage to a state university's most basic civil liberties. Perhaps if the student newspaper had not chosen to meet the whole question head-on and in public, the controlling political faction would have thought anything easy and possible. Perhaps we won something more than a battle after all.

People would tell me long afterward that this sort of thing could never happen again in the later climate of the University of Texas, that everything became much better, that academic freedom, and freedom of expression, had been won, and were old issues now. I am convinced this is true. The 1960s were not the 1950s, and at our state universities these issues would become, not more straightforward, but more complex, involving considerations of the very quality of the mass society. In 1956 the issue was a direct one, and it became bigger than *The Daily Texan*, bigger than the Board of Regents, bigger than the University itself—and it could never be old-fashioned.

I have often asked myself in the years that followed, would I do all this again? I would be less than honest if I answered that question simply.

At the time, as I understood later, the tone, style, and content of public discourse meant much more to me than the practical considerations of how one arranges complicated matters in feasible, flexible terms. There could have been more subtle and practical ways of dealing with the problem that confronted us. For this kind of personal diplomacy I was too immature and too impressionable.

Yet I was twenty years old; the real antagonists were in the seats of power. To my credit I knew who the enemy was. It would be an unwarranted personal renunciation for me to say retrospectively that the indignation I felt in 1956 was unjustified. It is legitimate to assume that editors of student papers at any university have a right to arouse the authorities, and within the laws of libel to bring them down on him. It is right to be able to carry on an aggressive campaign against an ethic they consider sterile and contemptuous. The attempt to censor *The Daily Texan* in 1956 involved not a displacement of dissent, but the running roughshod over it by real power, and the more sophisticated kind of criticism that served as its forum—the kind of wealth which still encourages the idea in America that anything can be bought, including culture. A friend of mine in the state legislature would say to me a few years later, perhaps Texas can never become a truly civilized place until its great natural resources are gone.

For three years I had written my column, "The Round-Up," and in my "30" piece that spring, the last one I wrote, I said, with too many genuflections to Thomas Wolfe:

The University of Texas, I fear, has travelled all too swiftly toward beautiful buildings and sterling reputations. Its leaders, in submitting to those who relish the corporate purse, have too often, and even without reluctance, betrayed the corporation of ideas . . . It has existed at the whim of those forces which would readily crush its heart, its soul, and its mind.

The quick Texas rich, who apply the values of fast money to the values of higher education, have dealt foolishly and cruelly with the prerogatives of the spirit . . . As a result, our University condones the tyranny of the majority, and it encourages in its students sedate complacency to the national and regional arbiter.

It must lead, not follow . . . it must insist that society and the race can be made better. It must strive to show our people, our uneducated and our quick rich, that our civilization is doomed when the material can coerce the human spirit.

I believe that our University is lost, and that being lost has been silent and afraid, but that someday its destiny shall be fulfilled more courageously, more magnificently, and more humbly than we have ever imagined. It is in the bright promise of this vision that I close.

At graduation at the end of that year the air was heavy with the scents of the berry trees; most of the students were long since gone, and the campus was more lovely and still than I had ever seen it before. The chimes on the Tower rang with stirring processionals to the Class of 1956, and proud country parents stood in diffident little groups watching their children march past. I received my diploma, and before a packed audience walked out the wrong door of the auditorium. At the reception afterward a journalism professor said, "I told my wife, there goes Morris, lost again," and the mother of one of my classmates walked up to me and said, "Why, you look too *innocent* to have caused all that newspaper trouble." The next day I left the campus, my '47 Plymouth loaded with books and the paraphernalia of four years, and drove all night one final time to the place I had come from.

Solitude

Henry David Thoreau (1817–1862) was born, raised, and "traveled widely" in Concord, Massachusetts. After graduating from Harvard, which, he said, "taught all the branches and none of the roots," he worked variously as teacher, hired man, surveyor, and lecturer, and earned some money from his writing. Thoreau was a friend of Emerson and part of the Transcendentalist movement of the time. His single-minded individualism led him to spend twenty-six months living alone at Walden Pond outside of Concord in a small hut he built himself with a borrowed ax. "I went into the woods," he wrote, "because I wished to live deliberately, to front only the essential facts of life, and see if I could not learn what it had to teach, and not, when I came to die, discover that I had not lived." He spent only one night away from Walden Pond during those twenty-six months, the night he spent in jail for refusing to pay a tax which would support the Mexican War that he considered wrong. His most famous essay, "Civil Disobedience" (1849), is an argument for passive resistance in the face of unjust government action. It has directly influenced such men as Tolstoy, Gandhi, and Martin Luther King, Jr. Thoreau's first book, *A Week on the Concord and Merrimack Rivers* (1849), is a record of a canoe journey he took with his brother. *Walden* (1854), his only other book to be published in his lifetime, not only describes his life at the pond, but also develops most of his central ideas about man and nature. Despite his moral earnestness, he maintained a keen sense of humor to the end. Asked on his deathbed if he had made his peace with God, Thoreau replied that he was unaware that he and God had ever quarreled. "Solitude" is a chapter from *Walden*.

This is a delicious evening, when the whole body is one sense, and imbibes delight through every pore. I go and come with a strange liberty in Nature, a part of herself. As I walk along the stony shore of the pond in my shirt-sleeves, though it is cool as well as cloudy and windy, and I see nothing special to attract me, all the elements are unusually congenial to me. The bullfrogs trump to usher in the night, and the note of the whip-poor-will is borne on the rippling wind from over the water. Sympathy with the fluttering alder and poplar leaves almost takes away my breath; yet, like the lake, my serenity is rippled but not ruffled. These small waves raised by the evening wind are as remote from storm as the smooth reflecting surface. Though it is now

From *Walden, or Life in the Woods*, by Henry David Thoreau, published in 1854.

dark, the wind still blows and roars in the wood, the waves still dash, and some creatures lull the rest with their notes. The repose is never complete. The wildest animals do not repose, but seek their prey now; the fox, and skunk, and rabbit, now roam the fields and woods without fear. They are Nature's watchmen,—links which connect the days of animated life.

When I return to my house I find that visitors have been there and left their cards, either a bunch of flowers, or a wreath of evergreen, or a name in pencil on a yellow walnut leaf or a chip. They who come rarely to the woods take some little piece of the forest into their hands to play with by the way, which they leave, either intentionally or accidentally. One has peeled a willow wand, woven it into a ring, and dropped it on my table. I could always tell if visitors had called in my absence, either by the bended twigs or grass, or the print of their shoes, and generally of what sex or age or quality they were by some slight trace left, as a flower dropped, or a bunch of grass plucked and thrown away, even as far off as the railroad, half a mile distant, or by the lingering odor of a cigar or pipe. Nay, I was frequently notified of the passage of a traveller along the highway sixty rods off by the scent of his pipe.

There is commonly sufficient space about us. Our horizon is never quite at our elbows. The thick wood is not just at our door, nor the pond, but somewhat is always clearing, familiar and worn by us, appropriated and fenced in some way, and reclaimed from Nature. For what reason have I this vast range and circuit, some square miles of unfrequented forest, for my privacy, abandoned to me by men? My nearest neighbor is a mile distant, and no house is visible from any place but the hill-tops within half a mile of my own. I have my horizon bounded by woods all to myself; a distant view of the railroad where it touches the pond on the one hand, and of the fence which skirts the woodland road on the other. But for the most part it is as solitary where I live as on the prairies. It is as much Asia or Africa as New England. I have, as it were, my own sun and moon and stars, and a little world all to myself. At night there was never a traveller passed my house, or knocked at my door, more than if I were the first or last man; unless it were in the spring, when at long intervals some came from the village to fish for pouts,—they plainly fished much more in the Walden Pond of their own natures, and baited their hooks with darkness,—but they soon retreated, usually with light baskets, and left "the world to darkness and to me," and the black kernel of the night was never profaned by any human neighborhood. I believe that men are generally still a little afraid of the dark, though the witches are all hung, and Christianity and candles have been introduced.

Yet I experienced sometimes that the most sweet and tender, the most innocent and encouraging society may be found in any natural object, even for the poor misanthrope and most melancholy man. There can be no very black melancholy to him who lives in the midst of nature and has his senses still. There was never yet such a storm but it was Æolian music to a healthy and innocent ear. Nothing can rightly compel a simple and brave man to a vulgar sadness. While I enjoy the friendship of the seasons I trust that nothing can make life a burden to me. The gentle rain which waters my beans and keeps me in the house to-day is not drear and melancholy, but good for me too. Though it prevents my hoeing them, it is of far more worth than my hoeing. If it should continue so long as to cause the seeds to rot in the ground and destroy the potatoes in the low lands, it would still be good for the grass on the uplands, and, being good for the grass, it would be good for me. Sometimes, when I compare myself with other men, it seems as if I were more favored by the gods than they, beyond any deserts that I am conscious of; as if I had a warrant and surety at their hands which my fellows have not, and were especially guided and guarded. I do not flatter myself, but if it be possible they flatter me. I have never felt lonesome, or in the least oppressed by a sense of solitude, but once, and that was a few weeks after I came to the woods, when, for an hour, I doubted if the near neighborhood of man was not essential to a serene and healthy life. To be alone was something unpleasant. But I was at the same time conscious of a slight insanity in my mood, and seemed to foresee my recovery. In the midst of a gentle rain while these thoughts prevailed, I was suddenly sensible of such sweet and beneficent society in Nature, in the very pattering of the drops, and in every sound and sight around my house, an infinite and unaccountable friendliness all at once like an atmosphere sustaining me, as made the fancied advantages of human neighborhood insignificant, and I have never thought of them since. Every little pine needle expanded and swelled with sympathy and befriended me. I was so distinctly made aware of the presence of something kindred to me, even in scenes which we are accustomed to call wild and dreary, and also that the nearest of blood to me and humanest was not a person nor a villager, that I thought no place could ever be strange to me again.—

"Mourning untimely consumes the sad;
Few are their days in the land of the living,
Beautiful daughter of Toscar."

Some of my pleasantest hours were during the long rainstorms in the spring or fall, which confined me to the house for the afternoon as well as the forenoon, soothed by their ceaseless roar and pelting; when an early twilight ushered in a long evening in which many thoughts had time to take root and unfold themselves. In those driving northeast rains which tried the village houses so, when the maids stood ready with mop and pail in front entries

CHAPTER THREE / *Commitment*

to keep the deluge out, I sat behind my door in my little house, which was all entry, and thoroughly enjoyed its protection. In one heavy thundershower the lightning struck a large pitch pine across the pond, making a very conspicuous and perfectly regular spiral groove from top to bottom, an inch or more deep, and four or five inches wide, as you would groove a walking-stick. I passed it again the other day, and was struck with awe on looking up and beholding that mark, now more distinct than ever, where a terrific and resistless bolt came down out of the harmless sky eight years ago. Men frequently say to me, "I should think you would feel lonesome down there, and want to be nearer to folks, rainy and snowy days and nights especially." I am tempted to reply to such,—This whole earth which we inhabit is but a point in space. How far apart, think you, dwell the two most distant inhabitants of yonder star, the breadth of whose disk cannot be appreciated by our instruments? Why should I feel lonely? Is not our planet in the Milky Way? This which you put seems to me not to be the most important question. What sort of space is that which separates a man from his fellows and makes him solitary? I have found that no exertion of the legs can bring two minds much nearer to one another. What do we want most to dwell near to? Not to many men surely, the depot, the post-office, the bar-room, the meeting-house, the school-house, the grocery, Beacon Hill, or the Five Points, where men most congregate, but to the perennial source of our life, whence in all our experience we have found that to issue, as the willow stands near the water and sends out its roots in that direction. This will vary with different natures, but this is the place where a wise man will dig his cellar. . . . I one evening overtook one of my townsmen, who has accumulated what is called "a handsome property,"—though I never got a *fair* view of it,—on the Walden road, driving a pair of cattle to market, who inquired of me how I could bring my mind to give up so many of the comforts of life. I answered that I was very sure I liked it passably well; I was not joking. And so I went home to my bed, and left him to pick his way through the darkness and the mud to Brighton,—or Bright-town,—which place he would reach some time in the morning.

Any prospect of awakening or coming to life to a dead man makes indifferent all times and places. The place where that may occur is always the same, and indescribably pleasant to all our senses. For the most part we allow only outlying and transient circumstances to make our occasions. They are, in fact, the cause of our distraction. Nearest to all things is that power which fashions their being. *Next* to us the grandest laws are continually being executed. *Next* to us is not the workman whom we have hired, with whom we love so well to talk, but the workman whose work we are.

"How vast and profound is the influence of the subtle powers of Heaven and of Earth!"

HENRY DAVID THOREAU / *Solitude*

"We seek to perceive them, and we do not see them; we seek to hear them, and we do not hear them; identified with the substance of things, they cannot be separated from them."

"They cause that in all the universe men purify and sanctify their hearts, and clothe themselves in their holiday garments to offer sacrifices and oblations to their ancestors. It is an ocean of subtile intelligences. They are everywhere, above us, on our left, on our right; they environ us on all sides."

We are the subjects of an experiment which is not a little interesting to me. Can we not do without the society of our gossips a little while under these circumstances,—have our own thoughts to cheer us? Confucius says truly, "Virtue does not remain as an abandoned orphan; it must of necessity have neighbors."

With thinking we may be beside ourselves in a sane sense. By a conscious effort of the mind we can stand aloof from actions and their consequences; and all things, good and bad, go by us like a torrent. We are not wholly involved in Nature. I may be either the driftwood in the stream, or Indra in the sky looking down on it. I *may* be affected by a theatrical exhibition: on the other hand, I *may not* be affected by an actual event which appears to concern me more. I only know myself as a human entity; the scene, so to speak, of thoughts and affections; and am sensible of a certain doubleness by which I can stand as remote from myself as from another. However intense my experience, I am conscious of the presence and criticism of a part of me, which, as it were, is not a part of me, but spectator, sharing no experience, but taking note of it; and that is no more I than it is you. When the play, it may be the tragedy, of life is over, the spectator goes his way. It was a kind of fiction, a work of the imagination only, so far as he was concerned. This doubleness may easily make us poor neighbors and friends sometimes.

I find it wholesome to be alone the greater part of the time. To be in company, even with the best, is soon wearisome and dissipating. I love to be alone. I never found the companion that was so companionable as solitude. We are for the most part more lonely when we go abroad among men than when we stay in our chambers. A man thinking or working is always alone, let him be where he will. Solitude is not measured by the miles of space that intervene between a man and his fellows. The really diligent student in one of the crowded hives of Cambridge College is as solitary as a dervis in the desert. The farmer can work alone in the field or the woods all day, hoeing or chopping, and not feel lonesome, because he is employed; but when he comes home at night he cannot sit down in a room alone, at the mercy of his thoughts, but must be where he can "see the folks," and recreate, and, as he thinks, remunerate himself for his day's solitude; and hence he wonders how the student can sit alone in the house all night and most of the day without ennui and "the blues," but he does not realize that the student, though in the house, is still at work in *his* field, and chopping in *his* woods, as the farmer in his, and in turn seeks the same recreation and society that the latter does, though it may be a more condensed form of it.

Society is commonly too cheap. We meet at very short intervals, not having had time to acquire any new value for each other. We meet at meals three times a day, and give each other a new taste of that old musty cheese that we are. We have had to agree on a certain set of rules, called etiquette and politeness, to make this frequent meeting tolerable and that we need not come to open war. We meet at the post-office, and at the sociable, and about the fireside every night; we live thick and are in each other's way, and stumble over one another, and I think that we thus lose some respect for one another. Certainly less frequency would suffice for all important and hearty communications. Consider the girls in a factory,—never alone, hardly in their dreams. It would be better if there were but one inhabitant to a square mile, as where I live. The value of a man is not in his skin, that we should touch him.

I have heard of a man lost in the woods and dying of famine and exhaustion at the foot of a tree, whose loneliness was relieved by the grotesque visions with which, owing to bodily weakness, his diseased imagination surrounded him, and which he believed to be real. So also, owing to bodily and mental health and strength, we may be continually cheered by a like but more normal and natural society, and come to know that we are never alone.

I have a great deal of company in my house; especially in the morning, when nobody calls. Let me suggest a few comparisons, that some one may convey an idea of my situation. I am no more lonely than the loon in the pond that laughs so loud, or than Walden Pond itself. What company has that lonely lake, I pray? And yet it has not the blue devils, but the blue angels in it, in the azure tint of its waters. The sun is alone, except in thick weather, when there sometimes appear to be two, but one is a mock sun. God is alone,—but the devil, he is far from being alone; he sees a great deal of company; he is legion. I am no more lonely than a single mullein or dandelion in a pasture, or a bean leaf, or sorrel, or a horse-fly, or a humble-bee. I am no more lonely than the Mill Brook, or a weathercock, or the north star, or the south wind, or an April shower, or a January thaw, or the first spider in a new house.

I have occasional visits in the lone winter evenings, when the snow falls fast and the wind howls in the wood, from an old settler and original proprietor, who is reported to have dug Walden Pond, and stoned it, and fringed it with pine woods; who tells me stories of old time and of new eternity; and between us we manage to pass a cheerful evening with social mirth and pleasant views of things, even without apples or cider,—a most wise and humorous friend, whom I love much, who keeps himself more secret than ever did Goffe or Whalley; and though he is thought to be dead, none can show where he is buried. An elderly dame, too, dwells in my neighborhood, invisible to most persons, in whose odorous herb garden I love to stroll sometimes, gathering simples and listening to her fables; for she has a genius of unequalled fertility, and her memory runs back farther than mythology, and she can tell me the original of every fable, and on what fact every one is founded, for the incidents occurred when she was young. A ruddy and lusty old dame, who delights in all weathers and seasons, and is likely to outlive all her children yet.

The indescribable innocence and beneficence of Nature,—of sun and wind and rain, of summer and winter,—such health, such cheer, they afford forever! and such sympathy have they ever with our race, that all Nature would be affected, and the sun's brightness fade, and the winds would sigh humanely, and the clouds rain tears, and the woods shed their leaves and put on mourning in midsummer, if any man should ever for a just cause grieve. Shall I not have intelligence with the earth? Am I not partly leaves and vegetable mould myself?

What is the pill which will keep us well, serene, contented? Not my or thy great-grandfather's, but our great-grandmother Nature's universal, vegetable, botanic medicines, by which she has kept herself young always, outlived so many old Parrs in her day, and fed her health with their decaying fatness. For my panacea, instead of one of those quack vials of a mixture dipped from Acheron and the Dead Sea, which come out of those long shallow black-schooner looking wagons which we sometimes see made to carry bottles, let me have a draught of undiluted morning air. Morning air! If men will not drink of this at the fountain-head of the day, why, then, we must even bottle up some and sell it in the shops, for the benefit of those who have lost their subscription ticket to morning time in this world. But remember, it will not keep quite till noonday even in the coolest cellar, but drive out the stopples long ere that and follow westward the steps of Aurora. I am no worshipper of Hygeia, who was the daughter of that old herb-doctor Æsculapius, and who is represented on monuments holding a serpent in one hand, and in the other a cup out of which the serpent sometimes drinks; but rather of Hebe, cup-bearer to Jupiter, who was the daughter of Juno and wild lettuce, and who had the power of restoring gods and men to the vigor of youth. She was probably the only thoroughly sound-conditioned, healthy, and robust young lady that ever walked the globe, and wherever she came it was spring.

Day of a Stranger

The hills are blue and hot. There is a brown, dusty field in the bottom of the valley. I hear a machine, a bird, a clock. The clouds are high and enormous. Through them the inevitable jet plane passes: this time probably full of passengers from Miami to Chicago. What passengers? This I have no need to decide. They are out of my world, up there, busy sitting in their small, isolated, arbitrary lounge that does not even seem to be moving—the lounge that somehow unaccountably picked them up off the earth in Florida to suspend them for a while with timeless cocktails and then let them down in Illinois. The suspension of modern life in contemplation that *gets you somewhere!*

There are also other worlds above me. Other jets will pass over, with other contemplations and other modalities of intentness.

I have seen the SAC plane, with the bomb in it, fly low over me and I have looked up out of the woods directly at the closed bay of the metal bird with a scientific egg in its breast! A womb easily and mechanically opened! I do not consider this technological mother to be the friend of anything I believe in. However, like everyone else, I live in the shadow of the apocalyptic cherub. I am surveyed by it, impersonally. Its number recognizes my number. Are these numbers preparing at some moment to coincide in the benevolent mind of a computer? This does not concern me, for I live in the woods as a reminder that I am free not to be a number.

There is, in fact, a choice.

In an age where there is much talk about "being yourself" I reserve to myself the right to forget about being myself, since in any case there is very little chance of my being anybody else. Rather it seems to me that when one is too intent on "being himself" he runs the risk of impersonating a shadow.

Yet I cannot pride myself on special freedom, simply because I am living in the woods. I am accused of living in the woods like Thoreau instead of living in the desert like St. John the Baptist. All I can answer is that I am not living "like anybody." Or "unlike anybody." We all live somehow or other, and that's that. It is a compelling necessity for me to be free to embrace the necessity of my own nature.

I exist under trees. I walk in the woods out of necessity. I am both a prisoner and an escaped prisoner. I cannot tell you why, born in France, my journey ended here in Kentucky. I have considered going further, but it is not practical. It makes no difference. Do I have a "day"? Do I spend my "day" in a "place"? I know there are trees here. I know there are birds here. I know the birds in fact very well, for there are precise pairs of birds (two each of fifteen or twenty species) living in the immediate area of my cabin. I share this particular place with them: we form an ecological balance. This harmony gives the idea of "place" a new configuration.

As to the crows, they form part of a different pattern. They are vociferous and self-justifying, like humans. They are not two, they are many. They fight each other and the other birds, in a constant state of war.

There is a mental ecology, too, a living balance of spirits in this corner of the woods. There is room here for many other songs besides those of birds. Of Vallejo for instance. Or Rilke, or René Char, Montale, Zukofsky, Ungaretti, Edwin Muir, Quasimodo or some Greeks. Or the dry, disconcerting voice of Nicanor Parra, the poet of the sneeze. Here is also Chuang Tzu whose climate is perhaps most the climate of this silent corner of woods. A climate in which there is no need for explanations. Here is the reassuring companionship of many silent Tzu's and Fu's; Kung Tzu, Lao Tzu, Meng Tzu. Tu Fu. And Hui Neng. And Chao-Chu. And the drawings of Sengai. And a big graceful scroll from Suzuki. Here also is a Syrian hermit called Philoxenus. An Algerian cenobite called Camus. Here is heard the clanging prose of Tertullian, with the dry catarrh of Sartre. Here the voluble dissonances of Auden, with the golden sounds of John of Salisbury. Here is the deep vegetation of that more ancient forest in which the angry birds, Isaias and Jeremias, sing. Here should be, and are, feminine voices from Angela of Foligno to Flannery O'Connor, Theresa of Avila, Juliana of Norwich, and, more personally and warmly still, Raissa Maritain. It is good to choose the voices that will be heard in these woods, but they also choose themselves, and send themselves here to be present in this silence. In any case there is no lack of voices.

The hermit life is cool. It is a life of low definition in which there is little to decide, in which there are few transactions or none, in which there are no packages delivered. In which I do not bundle up packages and deliver them to myself. It is not intense. There is no give and take of questions and answers, problems and solutions. Problems begin down the hill. Over there under the water tower are the solutions. Here there are woods, foxes. Here there is no need for dark glasses. "Here" does not even warm itself up with references to "there." It is just a "here" for which there is no "there." The hermit life is that cool.

The monastic life as a whole is a hot medium. Hot with words like "must," "ought" and "should." Communities are devoted to high definition projects: "making it all clear!" The clearer it gets the clearer it has to be made. It branches out. You have to keep clearing the branches. The more branches you cut back the more branches grow. For one you cut you get three more. On the end of each branch there is a big bushy question mark. People are running all around with packages of meaning. Each is very anxious to know whether all the others have received the latest messages. Has someone else received a message that he has not received? Will they be willing to pass it on to him? Will he understand it when it is passed on? Will he have to argue about it? Will he be expected to clear his throat and stand up and say "Well the way I look at it St. Benedict said . . . ?" Saint Benedict saw that the best thing to do with the monastic life was to cool it but today everybody is heating it up. Maybe to cool it you have to be a hermit. But then they will keep thinking that *you* have got a special message. When they find out you haven't. . . . Well, that's their worry, not mine.

This is not a hermitage—it is a house. ("Who was that hermitage I seen you with last night? . . .") What I wear is pants. What I do is live. How

I pray is breathe. Who said Zen? Wash out your mouth if you said Zen. If you see a meditation going by, shoot it. Who said "Love?" Love is in the movies. The spiritual life is something that people worry about when they are so busy with something else they think they ought to be spiritual. Spiritual life is guilt. Up here in the woods is seen the New Testament: that is to say, the wind comes through the trees and you breathe it. Is it supposed to be clear? I am not inviting anybody to try it. Or suggesting that one day the message will come saying NOW. That is none of my business.

I am out of bed at two-fifteen in the morning, when the night is darkest and most silent. Perhaps this is due to some ailment or other. I find myself in the primordial lostness of night, solitude, forest, peace, a mind awake in the dark, looking for a light, not totally reconciled to being out of bed. A light appears, and in the light an ikon. There is now in the large darkness a small room of radiance with psalms in it. The psalms grow up silently by themselves without effort like plants in this light which is favorable to them. The plants hold themselves up on stems which have a single consistency, that of mercy, or rather great mercy. *Magna misericordia.* In the formlessness of night and silence a word then pronounces itself: Mercy. It is surrounded by other words of lesser consequence: "destroy iniquity" "Wash me" "purify" "I know my iniquity." *Peccavi.* Concepts without interest in the world of business, war, politics, culture, etc. Concepts also often without serious interest to ecclesiastics.

Other words: Blood. Guile. Anger. The way that is not good. The way of blood, guile, anger, war.

Out there the hills in the dark lie southward. The way over the hill is blood, guile, dark, anger, death: Selma, Birmingham, Mississippi. Nearer than these, the atomic city, from which each day a freight car of fissionable material is brought to be laid carefully beside the gold in the underground vault which is at the heart of this nation.

"Their mouth is the opening of the grave; their tongues are set in motion by lies; their heart is void."

Blood, lies, fire, hate, the opening of the grave, void. Mercy, great mercy.

The birds begin to wake. It will soon be dawn. In an hour or two the towns will wake, and men will enjoy everywhere the great luminous smiles of production and business.

—Why live in the woods?
—Well, you have to live somewhere.
—Do you get lonely?
—Yes, sometimes.

—Are you mad at people?
—No.
—Are you mad at the monastery?
—No.
—What do you think about the future of monasticism?
—Nothing. I don't think about it.
—Is it true that your bad back is due to Yoga?
—No.
—Is it true that you are practicing Zen in secret?
—Pardon me, I don't speak English.

All monks, as is well known, are unmarried, and hermits more unmarried than the rest of them. Not that I have anything against women. I see no reason why a man can't love God and a woman at the same time. If God was going to regard women with a jealous eye, why did he go and make them in the first place? There is a lot of talk about a married clergy. Interesting. So far there has not been a great deal said about married hermits. Well, anyway, I have the place full of ikons of the Holy Virgin.

One might say I had decided to marry the silence of the forest. The sweet dark warmth of the whole world will have to be my wife. Out of the heart of that dark warmth comes the secret that is heard only in silence, but it is the root of all the secrets that are whispered by all the lovers in their beds all over the world. So perhaps I have an obligation to preserve the stillness, the silence, the poverty, the virginal point of pure nothingness which is at the center of all other loves. I attempt to cultivate this plant without comment in the middle of the night and water it with psalms and prophecies in silence. It becomes the most rare of all the trees in the garden, at once the primordial paradise tree, the *axis mundi*, the cosmic axle, and the Cross. *Nulla silva talem profert.* There is only one such tree. It cannot be multiplied. It is not interesting.

It is necessary for me to see the first point of light which begins to be dawn. It is necessary to be present alone at the resurrection of Day, in the blank silence when the sun appears. In this completely neutral instant I receive from the Eastern woods, the tall oaks, the one word "DAY," which is never the same. It is never spoken in any known language.

Sermon to the birds: "Esteemed friends, birds of noble lineage, I have no message to you except this: be what you are: be *birds.* Thus you will be your own sermon to yourselves!"

Reply: "Even this is one sermon too many!"

Rituals. Washing out the coffee pot in the rain bucket. Approaching the outhouse with circumspection on account of the king snake who likes to curl up on one of the beams inside. Addressing the possible king snake in the outhouse and informing him that he should not be there. Asking the formal ritual question that is asked at this time every morning: "Are you in there, you bastard?"

More rituals: Spray bedroom (cockroaches and mosquitoes). Close all the windows on South side (heat). Leave windows open on north and east sides (cool). Leave windows open on west side until maybe June when it gets very hot on all sides. Pull down shades. Get water bottle. Rosary. Watch. Library book to be returned.

It is time to visit the human race.

I start out under the pines. The valley is already hot. Machines out there in the bottoms, perhaps planting corn. Fragrance of the woods. Cool west wind under the oaks. Here is the place on the path where I killed a copperhead. There is the place where I saw the fox run daintily and carefully for cover carrying a rabbit in his mouth. And there is the cement cross that, for no reason, the novices rescued from the corner of a destroyed wall and put up in the woods: people imagine someone is buried there. It is just a cross. Why should there not be a cement cross by itself in the middle of the woods?

A squirrel is kidding around somewhere overhead in midair. Tree to tree. The coquetry of flight.

I come out into the open over the hot hollow and the old sheep barn. Over there is the monastery, bugging with windows, humming with action.

The long yellow side of the monastery faces the sun on a sharp rise with fruit trees and beehives. This is without question one of the least interesting buildings on the face of the earth. However, in spite of the most earnest efforts to deprive it of all character and keep it ugly, it is surpassed in this respect by the vast majority of other monasteries. It is so completely plain that it ends, in spite of itself, by being at least simple. A lamentable failure of religious architecture—to come so close to non-entity and yet not fully succeed! I climb sweating into the novitiate, and put down my water bottle on the cement floor. The bell is ringing. I have duties, obligations, since here I am a monk. When I have accomplished these, I return to the woods where I am nobody. In the choir are the young monks, patient, serene, with very clear eyes, then, reflective, gentle, confused. Today perhaps I tell them of Eliot's *Little Gidding,* analyzing the first movement of the poem ("Midwinter spring in its own season"). They will listen with attention thinking some other person is talking to them about some other poem.

Chanting the *alleluia* in the second mode: strength and solidity of the Latin, seriousness of the second mode, built on the *Re* as though on a sacrament, a presence. One keeps returning to the *re* as to an inevitable center. *Sol-Re, Fa-Re, Sol-Re, Do-Re.* Many other notes in between, but suddenly one hears only the one note. *Consonantia:* all notes, in their perfect distinctness, are yet blended in one. (Through a curious oversight Gregorian chant has continued to be sung in this monastery. But not for long.)

In the refectory is read a message of the Pope, denouncing war, denouncing the bombing of civilians, reprisals on civilians, killing of hostages, torturing of prisoners (all in Vietnam). Do the people of this country realize who the Pope is talking about? They have by now become so solidly convinced that the Pope never denounces anybody but Communists that they have long since ceased to listen. The monks seem to know. The voice of the reader trembles.

In the heat of noon I return with the water bottle freshly filled, through the cornfield, past the barn under the oaks, up the hill, under the pines, to the hot cabin. Larks rise out of the long grass singing. A bumblebee hums under the wide shady eaves.

I sit in the cool back room, where words cease to resound, where all meanings are absorbed in the *consonantia* of heat, fragrant pine, quiet wind, bird song and one central tonic note that is unheard and unuttered. This is no longer a time of obligations. In the silence of the afternoon all is present and all is inscrutable in one central tonic note to which every other sound ascends or descends, to which every other meaning aspires, in order to find its true fulfillment. To ask when the note will sound is to lose the afternoon: it has already sounded, and all things now hum with the resonance of its sounding.

I sweep. I spread a blanket out in the sun. I cut grass behind the cabin. I write in the heat of the afternoon. Soon I will bring the blanket in again and make the bed. The sun is over-clouded. The day declines. Perhaps there will be rain. A bell rings in the monastery. A devout Cistercian tractor growls in the valley. Soon I will cut bread, eat supper, say psalms, sit in the back room as the sun sets, as the birds sing outside the window, as night descends on the valley. I become surrounded once again by all the silent Tzu's and Fu's (men without office and without obligation). The birds draw closer to their nests. I sit on the cool straw mat on the floor, considering the bed in which I will presently sleep alone under the ikon of the Nativity.

Meanwhile the metal cherub of the apocalypse passes over me in the clouds, treasuring its egg and its message.

Mecca

With Martin Luther King, Jr., Malcolm X (1925–1965) was the most charismatic of all twentieth-century black leaders, a hero to both blacks and whites after his death even more than in his life. The son of a militant Baptist minister, who, he said, had been assassinated by white men, he was born Malcolm Little in Omaha, Nebraska. In prison he converted from a street hustler to the Black Muslim movement, adopting a code of stern self-discipline and educating himself in the prison library. Rejecting his Christian name, Little, he chose X to symbolize his African name lost in slavery. After his release from prison, Malcolm X rose quickly to a position in the Muslim movement second only to its founder, Elijah Muhammad. An extremely effective speaker, he achieved international prominence as a spokesman for the Muslims. In 1964 he broke with Elijah Muhammad and the religion which saw all whites as "devils." During his subsequent pilgrimage to Mecca, described below, Malcolm X came to the position of "recognizing every human being as a human being" and began to organize a movement of his own. On February 21, 1965, as he was about to deliver a speech, Malcolm X was gunned down by three assassins. *The Autobiography of Malcolm X* (1964), which he wrote in collaboration with Alex Haley, has been one of the most significant and popular books of the last decade. The following selection is reprinted from it.

The pilgrimage to Mecca, known as Hajj, is a religious obligation that every orthodox Muslim fulfills, if humanly able, at least once in his or her lifetime.

The Holy Quran says it, "Pilgrimage to the Ka'ba is a duty men owe to God; those who are able, make the journey."

Allah said: "And proclaim the pilgrimage among men; they will come to you on foot and upon each lean camel, they will come from every deep ravine."

At one or another college or university, usually in the informal gatherings after I had spoken, perhaps a dozen generally white-complexioned people would come up to me, identifying themselves as Arabian, Middle Eastern or North African Muslims who happened to be visiting, studying, or living in the United States. They had said to me that, my white-indicting statements notwithstanding, they felt that I was sincere in considering myself a Muslim— and they felt if I was exposed to what they always called "true Islam," I would "understand it, and embrace it." Automatically, as a follower of Elijah Muhammad, I had bridled whenever this was said.

But in the privacy of my own thoughts after several of these experiences, I did question myself: if one was sincere in professing a religion, why should he balk at broadening his knowledge of that religion?

Once in a conversation I broached this with Wallace Muhammad, Elijah Muhammad's son. He said that yes, certainly, a Muslim should seek to learn all that he could about Islam. I had always had a high opinion of Wallace Muhammad's opinion.

Those orthodox Muslims whom I had met, one after another, had urged me to meet and talk with a Dr. Mahmoud Youssef Shawarbi. He was described to me as an eminent, learned Muslim, a University of Cairo graduate, a University of London Ph.D., a lecturer on Islam, a United Nations advisor and the author of many books. He was a full professor of the University of Cairo, on leave from there to be in New York as the Director of the Federation of Islamic Associations in the United States and Canada. Several times, driving in that part of town, I had resisted the impulse to drop in at the F.I.A. building, a brownstone at 1 Riverside Drive. Then one day Dr. Shawarbi and I were introduced by a newspaperman.

He was cordial. He said he had followed me in the press; I said I had been told of him, and we talked for fifteen or twenty minutes. We both had to leave to make appointments we had, when he dropped on me something whose logic never would get out of my head. He said, "No man has believed perfectly until he wishes for his brother what he wishes for himself."

Then, there was my sister Ella herself. I couldn't get over what she had done. I've said before, this is a *strong* big, black, Georgia-born woman. Her domineering ways had gotten her put out of the Nation of Islam's Boston Mosque Eleven; they took her back, then she left on her own. Ella had started studying under Boston orthodox Muslims, then she founded a school where Arabic was taught! *She* couldn't speak it, she hired teachers who did. That's Ella! She deals in real estate, and *she* was saving up to make the pilgrimage. Nearly all night, we talked in her living room. She told me there was no question about it; it was more important that I go. I thought about Ella the whole flight back to New York. A *strong* woman. She had broken the spirits of three husbands, more driving and dynamic than all of them combined. She had played a very significant role in my life. No other woman ever was strong enough to point me in directions; I pointed women in directions. I had brought Ella into Islam, and now she was financing me to Mecca.

Allah always gives you signs, when you are with Him, that He is with you.

When I applied for a visa to Mecca at the Saudi Arabian Consulate, the Saudi Ambassador told me that no Muslim converted in America could have a visa for the Hajj pilgrimage without the signed approval of Dr. Mahmoud

Shawarbi. But that was only the beginning of the sign from Allah. When I telephoned Dr. Shawarbi, he registered astonishment. "I was just going to get in touch with you," he said, "by all means come right over."

When I got to his office, Dr. Shawarbi handed me the signed letter approving me to make the Hajj in Mecca, and then a book. It was *The Eternal Message of Muhammad* by Abd ar-Rahman Azzam.

The author had just sent the copy of the book to be given to me, Dr. Shawarbi said, and he explained that this author was an Egyptian-born Saudi citizen, an international statesman, and one of the closest advisors of Prince Faisal, the ruler of Arabia. "He has followed you in the press very closely." It was hard for me to believe.

Dr. Shawarbi gave me the telephone number of his son, Muhammad Shawarbi, a student in Cairo, and also the number of the author's son, Omar Azzam, who lived in Jedda, "your last stop before Mecca. Call them both, by all means."

I left New York quietly (little realizing that I was going to return noisily). Few people were told I was leaving at all. I didn't want some State Department or other roadblocks put in my path at the last minute. Only my wife, Betty, and my three girls and a few close associates came with me to Kennedy International Airport. When the Lufthansa Airlines jet had taken off, my two seatrow mates and I introduced ourselves. Another sign! Both were Muslims, one was bound for Cairo, as I was, and the other was bound for Jedda, where I would be in a few days.

All the way to Frankfurt, Germany, my seatmates and I talked, or I read the book I had been given. When we landed in Frankfurt, the brother bound for Jedda said his warm good-bye to me and the Cairo-bound brother. We had a few hours layover before we would take another plane to Cairo. We decided to go sightseeing in Frankfurt.

In the men's room there at the airport, I met the first American abroad who recognized me, a white student from Rhode Island. He kept eyeing me, then he came over. "Are you X?" I laughed and said I was, I hadn't ever heard it that way. He exclaimed, "You can't be! Boy, I know no one will believe me when I tell them this!" He was attending school, he said, in France.

The brother Muslim and I both were struck by the cordial hospitality of the people in Frankfurt. We went into a lot of shops and stores, looking more than intending to buy anything. We'd walk in; any store, every store, and it would be Hello! People who never saw you before, and knew you were strangers. And the same cordiality when we left, without buying anything. In America, you walk in a store and spend a hundred dollars, and leave, and you're still a stranger. Both you and the clerks act as though you're doing each other a favor. Europeans act more human, or humane, whichever the right word is. My brother Muslim, who could speak enough German to get by, would explain that we were Muslims, and I saw something I had already experienced when I was looked upon as a Muslim and not as a Negro, right in America. People seeing you as a Muslim saw you as a human being and they had a different look, different talk, everything. In one Frankfurt store—a little shop, actually—the storekeeper leaned over his counter to us and waved his hand, indicating the German people passing by: "This way one day, that way another day—" My Muslim brother explained to me that what he meant was that the Germans would rise again.

Back at the Frankfurt airport, we took a United Arab Airlines plane on to Cairo. Throngs of people, obviously Muslims from everywhere, bound on the pilgrimage, were hugging and embracing. They were of all complexions, the whole atmosphere was of warmth and friendliness. The feeling hit me that there really wasn't any color problem here. The effect was as though I had just stepped out of a prison.

I had told my brother Muslim friend that I wanted to be a tourist in Cairo for a couple of days before continuing to Jedda. He gave me his number and asked me to call him, as he wanted to put me with a party of his friends, who could speak English, and would be going on the pilgrimage, and would be happy to look out for me.

So I spent two happy days sightseeing in Cairo. I was impressed by the modern schools, housing developments for the masses, and the highways and the industrialization that I saw. I had read and heard that President Nasser's administration had built up one of the most highly industrialized countries on the African continent. I believe what most surprised me was that in Cairo, automobiles were being manufactured, and also buses.

I had a good visit with Dr. Shawarbi's son, Muhammad Shawarbi, a nineteen-year-old, who was studying economics and political science at Cairo University. He told me that his father's dream was to build a University of Islam in the United States.

The friendly people I met were astounded when they learned I was a Muslim—from America! They included an Egyptian scientist and his wife, also on their way to Mecca for the Hajj, who insisted I go with them to dinner in a restaurant in Heliopolis, a suburb of Cairo. They were an extremely well-informed and intelligent couple. Egypt's rising industrialization was one of the reasons why the Western powers were so anti-Egypt, it was showing other African countries what they should do, the scientist said. His wife asked me, "Why are people in the world starving when America has so much surplus food? What do they do, dump it in the ocean?" I told her, "Yes, but they put some of it in the holds of surplus ships, and in subsidized granaries and refrigerated space and let it stay there, with a small army of caretakers, until it's unfit to eat. Then another army of disposal people get rid of it to make space for the next surplus batch." She looked at me in something like disbelief.

Probably she thought I was kidding. But the American taxpayer knows it's the truth. I didn't go on to tell her that right in the United States, there are hungry people.

I telephoned my Muslim friend, as he had asked, and the Hajj party of his friends was waiting for me. I made it eight of us, and they included a judge and an official of the Ministry of Education. They spoke English beautifully, and accepted me like a brother. I considered it another of Allah's signs, that wherever I turned, someone was there to help me, to guide me.

The literal meaning of Hajj in Arabic is to set out toward a definite objective. In Islamic law, it means to set out for Ka'ba, the Sacred House, and to fulfill the pilgrimage rites. The Cairo airport was where scores of Hajj groups were becoming *Muhrim*, pilgrims, upon entering the state of Ihram, the assumption of a spiritual and physical state of consecration. Upon advice, I arranged to leave in Cairo all of my luggage and four cameras, one a movie camera. I had bought in Cairo a small valise, just big enough to carry one suit, shirt, a pair of underwear sets and a pair of shoes into Arabia. Driving to the airport with our Hajj group, I began to get nervous, knowing that from there in, it was going to be watching others who knew what they were doing, and trying to do what they did.

Entering the state of Ihram, we took off our clothes and put on two white towels. One, the *Izar*, was folded around the loins. The other, the *Rida*, was thrown over the neck and shoulders, leaving the right shoulder and arm bare. A pair of simple sandals, the *na'l*, left the ankle-bones bare. Over the *Izar* waist-wrapper, a money belt was worn, and a bag, something like a woman's big handbag, with a long strap, was for carrying the passport and other valuable papers, such as the letter I had from Dr. Shawarbi.

Every one of the thousands at the airport, about to leave for Jedda, was dressed this way. You could be a king or a peasant and no one would know. Some powerful personages, who were discreetly pointed out to me, had on the same thing I had on. Once thus dressed, we all had begun intermittently calling out *"Labbayka! Labbayka!"* (Here I come, O Lord!) The airport sounded with the din of *Muhrim* expressing their intention to perform the journey of the Hajj.

Planeloads of pilgrims were taking off every few minutes, but the airport was jammed with more, and their friends and relatives waiting to see them off. Those not going were asking others to pray for them at Mecca. We were on our plane, in the air, when I learned for the first time that with the crush, there was not supposed to have been space for me, but strings had been pulled, and someone had been put off because they didn't want to disappoint an American Muslim. I felt mingled emotions of regret that I had inconvenienced and discomfited whoever was bumped off the plane for me, and, with that, an utter humility and gratefulness that I had been paid such an honor and respect.

Packed in the plane were white, black, brown, red, and yellow people, blue eyes and blond hair, and my kinky red hair—all together, brothers! All honoring the same God Allah, all in turn giving equal honor to each other.

From some in our group, the word was spreading from seat to seat that I was a Muslim from America. Faces turned, smiling toward me in greeting. A box lunch was passed out and as we ate that, the word that a Muslim from America was aboard got up into the cockpit.

The captain of the plane came back to meet me. He was an Egyptian, his complexion was darker than mine; he could have walked in Harlem and no one would have given him a second glance. He was delighted to meet an American Muslim. When he invited me to visit the cockpit, I jumped at the chance.

The co-pilot was darker than he was. I can't tell you the feeling it gave me. I had never seen a black man flying a jet. That instrument panel: no one ever could know what all of those dials meant! Both of the pilots were smiling at me, treating me with the same honor and respect I had received ever since I left America. I stood there looking through the glass at the sky ahead of us. In America, I had ridden in more planes than probably any other Negro, and I never had been invited up into the cockpit. And there I was, with two Muslim seatmates, one from Egypt, the other from Arabia, all of us bound for Mecca, with me up in the pilots' cabin. Brother, I *knew* Allah was with me.

I got back to my seat. All of the way, about an hour's flight, we pilgrims were loudly crying out, *"Labbayka! Labbayka!"* The plane landed at Jedda. It's a seaport town on the Red Sea, the arrival or disembarkation point for all pilgrims who come to Arabia to go to Mecca. Mecca is about forty miles to the east, inland.

The Jedda airport seemed even more crowded than Cairo's had been. Our party became another shuffling unit in the shifting mass with every race on earth represented. Each party was making its way toward the long line waiting to go through Customs. Before reaching Customs, each Hajj party was assigned a *Mutawaf,* who would be responsible for transferring that party from Jedda to Mecca. Some pilgrims cried *"Labbayka!"* Others, sometimes large groups, were chanting in unison a prayer that I will translate, "I submit to no one but Thee, O Allah, I submit to no one but Thee. I submit to Thee because Thou hast no partner. All praise and blessings come from Thee, and Thou art alone in Thy kingdom." The essence of the prayer is the Oneness of God.

Only officials were not wearing the *Ihram* garb, or the white skull caps, long, white, nightshirt-looking gown and the little slippers of the *Mutawaf,* those who guided each pilgrim party, and their helpers. In Arabic, an *mmmm* sound before a verb makes a verbal noun, so *"Mutawaf"* meant "the one who guides" the pilgrims on the *"Tawaf,"* which is the circumambulation of the Ka'ba in Mecca.

I was nervous, shuffling in the center of our group in the line waiting to have our passports inspected. I had an apprehensive feeling. Look what I'm handing them. I'm in the Muslim world, right at The Fountain. I'm handing them the American passport which signifies the exact opposite of what Islam stands for.

The judge in our group sensed my strain. He patted my shoulder. Love, humility, and true brotherhood was almost a physical feeling wherever I turned. Then our group reached the clerks who examined each passport and suitcase carefully and nodded to the pilgrim to move on.

I was so nervous that when I turned the key in my bag, and it didn't work, I broke open the bag, fearing that they might think I had something in the bag that I shouldn't have. Then the clerk saw that I was handing him an American passport. He held it, he looked at me and said something in Arabic. My friends around me began speaking rapid Arabic, gesturing and pointing, trying to intercede for me. The judge asked me in English for my letter from Dr. Shawarbi, and he thrust it at the clerk, who read it. He gave the letter back, protesting—I could tell that. An argument was going on, *about* me. I felt like a stupid fool, unable to say a word, I couldn't even understand what was being said. But, finally, sadly, the judge turned to me.

I had to go before the *Mahgama Sharia,* he explained. It was the Muslim high court which examined all possibly non-authentic converts to the Islamic religion seeking to enter Mecca. It was absolute that no non-Muslim could enter Mecca.

My friends were going to have to go on to Mecca without me. They seemed stricken with concern for me. And *I* was stricken. I found the words to tell them, "Don't worry, I'll be fine. Allah guides me." They said they would pray hourly in my behalf. The white-garbed *Mutawaf* was urging them on, to keep schedule in the airport's human crush. With all of us waving, I watched them go.

It was then about three in the morning, a Friday morning. I never had been in such a jammed mass of people, but I never had felt more alone, and helpless, since I was a baby. Worse, Friday in the Muslim world is a rough counterpart of Sunday in the Christian world. On Friday, all the members of a Muslim community gather, to pray together. The event is called *yaum al-jumu'a*—"the day of gathering." It meant that no courts were held on Friday. I would have to wait until Saturday, at least.

An official beckoned a young Arab *Mutawaf's* aide. In broken English, the official explained that I would be taken to a place right at the airport. My passport was kept at Customs. I wanted to object, because it is a traveler's first law never to get separated from his passport, but I didn't. In my wrapped towels and sandals, I followed the aide in his skull cap, long white gown, and slippers. I guess we were quite a sight. People passing us were speaking all kinds of languages. I couldn't speak anybody's language. I was in bad shape.

Right outside the airport was a mosque, and above the airport was a huge, dormitory-like building, four tiers high. It was semi-dark, not long before dawn, and planes were regularly taking off and landing, their landing lights sweeping the runways, or their wing and tail lights blinking in the sky. Pilgrims from Ghana, Indonesia, Japan, and Russia, to mention some, were moving to and from the dormitory where I was being taken. I don't believe that motion picture cameras ever have filmed a human spectacle more colorful than my eyes took in. We reached the dormitory and began climbing, up to the fourth, top, tier, passing members of every race on earth. Chinese, Indonesians, Afghanistanians. Many, not yet changed into the *Ihram* garb, still wore their national dress. It was like pages out of the *National Geographic* magazine.

My guide, on the fourth tier, gestured me into a compartment that contained about fifteen people. Most lay curled up on their rugs asleep. I could tell that some were women, covered head and foot. An old Russian Muslim and his wife were not asleep. They stared frankly at me. Two Egyptian Muslims and a Persian roused and also stared as my guide moved us over into a corner. With gestures, he indicated that he would demonstrate to me the proper prayer ritual postures. Imagine, being a Muslim minister, a leader in Elijah Muhammad's Nation of Islam, and not knowing the prayer ritual.

I tried to do what he did. I knew I wasn't doing it right. I could feel the other Muslims' eyes on me. Western ankles won't do what Muslim ankles have done for a lifetime. Asians squat when they sit, Westerners sit upright in chairs. When my guide was down in a posture, I tried everything I could to get down as he was, but there I was, sticking up. After about an hour, my guide left, indicating that he would return later.

I never even thought about sleeping. Watched by the Muslims, I kept practicing prayer posture. I refused to let myself think how ridiculous I must have looked to them. After a while, though, I learned a little trick that would let me get down closer to the floor. But after two or three days, my ankle was going to swell.

As the sleeping Muslims woke up, when dawn had broken, they almost instantly became aware of me, and we watched each other while they went about their business. I began to see what an important role the rug played in the overall cultural life of the Muslims. Each individual had a small prayer rug, and each man and wife, or large group, had a larger communal rug. These Muslims prayed on their rugs there in the compartment. Then they spread a tablecloth over the rug and ate, so the rug became the dining room. Removing the dishes and cloth, they sat on the rug—a living room. Then they curl up and sleep on the rug—a bedroom. In that compartment, before I was to leave it, it dawned on me for the first time why the fence had paid such a high price for Oriental rugs when I had been a burglar in Boston. It was because so much intricate care was taken to weave fine rugs in countries where rugs were so culturally versatile. Later, in Mecca, I would see yet another use of the rug. When any kind of a dispute arose, someone who was respected highly and who was not involved would sit on a rug with the disputers around him, which made the rug a courtroom. In other instances it was a classroom.

One of the Egyptian Muslims, particularly, kept watching me out of the corner of his eye. I smiled at him. He got up and came over to me. "Hel-lo—" he said. It sounded like the Gettysburg Address. I beamed at him. "Hello!" I asked his name. "Name? Name?" He was trying hard, but he didn't get it. We tried some words on each other. I'd guess his English vocabulary spanned maybe twenty words. Just enough to frustrate me. I was trying to get him to comprehend anything. "Sky." I'd point. He'd smile. "Sky," I'd say again, gesturing for him to repeat it after me. He would. "Airplane . . . rug . . . foot . . . sandal . . . eyes. . . ." Like that. Then an amazing thing happened. I was so glad I had some communication with a human being, I was just saying whatever came to mind. I said "Muhammad Ali Clay—" All of the Muslims listening lighted up like a Christmas tree. "You? You?" My friend was pointing at me. I shook my head, "No, no. Muhammad Ali Clay my friend—*friend!*" They half understood me. Some of them didn't understand, and that's how it began to get around that I was Cassius Clay, world heavy-weight champion. I was later to learn that apparently every man, woman and child in the Muslim world had heard how Sonny Liston (who in the Muslim world had the image of a man-eating ogre) had been beaten in Goliath-David fashion by Cassius Clay, who then had told the world that his name was Muhammad Ali and his religion was Islam and Allah had given him his victory.

Establishing the rapport was the best thing that could have happened in the compartment. My being an American Muslim changed the attitudes from merely watching me to wanting to look out for me. Now, the others began smiling steadily. They came closer, they were frankly looking me up and down. Inspecting me. Very friendly. I was like a man from Mars.

The *Mutawaf's* aide returned, indicating that I should go with him. He pointed from our tier down at the mosque and I knew that he had come to take me to make the morning prayer, *El Sobh*, always before sunrise. I followed him down, and we passed pilgrims by the thousands, babbling languages, everything but English. I was angry with myself for not having taken the time to learn more of the orthodox prayer rituals before leaving

America. In Elijah Muhammad's Nation of Islam, we hadn't prayed in Arabic. About a dozen or more years before, when I was in prison, a member of the orthodox Muslim movement in Boston, named Abdul Hameed, had visited me and had later sent me prayers in Arabic. At that time, I had learned those prayers phonetically. But I hadn't used them since.

I made up my mind to let the guide do everything first and I would watch him. It wasn't hard to get him to do things first. He wanted to anyway. Just outside the mosque there was a long trough with rows of faucets. Ablutions had to precede praying. I knew that. Even watching the *Mutawaf's* helper, I didn't get it right. There's an exact way that an orthodox Muslim washes, and the exact way is very important.

I followed him into the mosque, just a step behind, watching. He did his prostration, his head to the ground. I did mine. *"Bi-smi-llahi-r-Rahmain-r-Rahim—"* ("In the name of Allah, the Beneficent, the Merciful—") All Muslim prayers began that way. After that, I may not have been mumbling the right thing, but I was mumbling.

I don't mean to have any of this sound joking. It was far from a joke with me. No one who happened to be watching could tell that I wasn't saying what the others said.

After that Sunrise Prayer, my guide accompanied me back up to the fourth tier. By sign language, he said he would return within three hours, then he left.

Our tier gave an excellent daylight view of the whole airport area. I stood at the railing, watching. Planes were landing and taking off like clockwork. Thousands upon thousands of people from all over the world made colorful patterns of movement. I saw groups leaving for Mecca, in buses, trucks, cars. I saw some setting out to walk the forty miles. I wished that I could start walking. At least, I knew how to do that.

I was afraid to think what might lie ahead. Would I be rejected as a Mecca pilgrim? I wondered what the test would consist of, and when I would face the Muslim high court.

The Persian Muslim in our compartment came up to me at the rail. He greeted me, hesitantly, "Amer . . . American?" He indicated that he wanted me to come and have breakfast with him and his wife, on their rug. I knew that it was an immense offer he was making. You don't have tea with a Muslim's wife. I didn't want to impose, I don't know if the Persian understood or not when I shook my head and smiled, meaning "No, thanks." He brought me some tea and cookies, anyway. Until then, I hadn't even thought about eating.

Others made gestures. They would just come up and smile and nod at me. My first friend, the one who had spoken a little English, was gone. I didn't know it, but he was spreading the word of an American Muslim on the fourth tier. Traffic had begun to pick up, going past our compartment. Muslims in the *Ihram* garb, or still in their national dress, walked slowly past, smiling. It would go on for as long as I was there to be seen. But I hadn't yet learned that I was the attraction.

I have always been restless, and curious. The *Mutawaf's* aide didn't return in the three hours he had said, and that made me nervous. I feared that he had given up on me as beyond help. By then, too, I was really getting hungry. All of the Muslims in the compartment had offered me food, and I had refused. The trouble was, I have to admit it, at that point I didn't know if I could go for their manner of eating. Everything was in one pot on the dining-room rug, and I saw them just fall right in, using their hands.

I kept standing at the tier railing observing the courtyard below, and I decided to explore a bit on my own. I went down to the first tier. I thought, then, that maybe I shouldn't get too far, someone might come for me. So I went back up to our compartment. In about forty-five minutes, I went back down. I went further this time, feeling my way. I saw a little restaurant in the courtyard. I went straight in there. It was jammed, and babbling with languages. Using gestures, I bought a whole roasted chicken and something like thick potato chips. I got back out in the courtyard and I tore up that chicken, using my hands. Muslims were doing the same thing all around me. I saw men at least seventy years old bring both legs up under them, until they made a human knot of themselves, eating with as much aplomb and satisfaction as though they had been in a fine restaurant with waiters all over the place. All ate as One, and slept as One. Everything about the pilgrimage atmosphere accented the Oneness of Man under One God.

I made, during the day, several trips up to the compartment and back out in the courtyard, each time exploring a little further than before. Once, I nodded at two black men standing together. I nearly shouted when one spoke to me in British-accented English. Before their party approached, ready to leave for Mecca, we were able to talk enough to exchange that I was American and they were Ethiopians. I was heartsick. I had found two English-speaking Muslims at last—and they were leaving. The Ethiopians had both been schooled in Cairo, and they were living in Ryadh, the political capital of Arabia. I was later going to learn to my surprise that in Ethiopia, with eighteen million people, ten million are Muslims. Most people think Ethiopia is Christian. But only its government is Christian. The West has always helped to keep the Christian government in power.

I had just said my Sunset Prayer, *El Maghrib;* I was lying on my cot in the fourth-tier compartment, feeling blue and alone, when out of the darkness came a sudden light!

It was actually a sudden thought. On one of my venturings in the yard

CHAPTER THREE / *Commitment*

full of activity below. I had noticed four men, officials, seated at a table with a telephone. Now, I thought about seeing them there, and with *telephone,* my mind flashed to the connection that Dr. Shawarbi in New York had given me, the telephone number of the son of the author of the book which had been given to me. Omar Azzam lived right there in Jedda!

In a matter of a few minutes, I was downstairs and rushing to where I had seen the four officials. One of them spoke functional English. I excitedly showed him the letter from Dr. Shawarbi. He read it. Then he read it aloud to the other three officials. "A Muslim from America!" I could almost see it capture their imaginations and curiosity. They were very impressed. I asked the English-speaking one if he would please do me the favor of telephoning Dr. Omar Azzam at the number I had. He was glad to do it. He got someone on the phone and conversed in Arabic.

Dr. Omar Azzam came straight to the airport. With the four officials beaming, he wrung my hand in welcome, a young, tall, powerfully built man. I'd say he was six foot three. He had an extremely polished manner. In America, he would have been called a white man, but—it struck me, hard and instant-ly—from the way he acted, I had no *feeling* of him being a white man. "Why didn't you call before?" he demanded of me. He showed some identification to the four officials, and he used their phone. Speaking in Arabic, he was talking with some airport officials. "Come!" he said.

In something less than half an hour, he had gotten me released, my suitcase and passport had been retrieved from Customs, and we were in Dr. Azzam's car, driving through the city of Jedda, with me dressed in the *Ihram* two towels and sandals. I was speechless at the man's attitude, and at my own physical feeling of no difference between us as human beings. I had heard for years of Muslim hospitality, but one couldn't quite imagine such warmth. I asked questions. Dr. Azzam was a Swiss-trained engineer. His field was city planning. The Saudi Arabian government had borrowed him from the United Nations to direct all of the reconstruction work being done on Arabian holy places. And Dr. Azzam's sister was the wife of Prince Faisal's son. I was in a car with the brother-in-law of the son of the ruler of Arabia. Nor was that all that Allah had done. "My father will be so happy to meet you," said Dr. Azzam. The author who had sent me the book!

I asked questions about his father. Abd ir-Rahman Azzam was known as Azzam Pasha, or Lord Azzam, until the Egyptian revolution, when President Nasser eliminated all "Lord" and "Noble" titles. "He should be at my home when we get there," Dr. Azzam said. "He spends much time in New York with his United Nations work, and he has followed you with great interest."

I was speechless.

It was early in the morning when we reached Dr. Azzam's home. His father was there, his father's brother, a chemist, and another friend—all up that early, waiting. Each of them embraced me as though I were a long-lost child. I had never seen these men before in my life, and they treated me so good! I am going to tell you that I had never been so honored in my life, nor had I ever received such true hospitality.

A servant brought tea and coffee, and disappeared. I was urged to make myself comfortable. No women were anywhere in view. In Arabia, you could easily think there were no females.

Dr. Abd ir-Rahman Azzam dominated the conversation. Why hadn't I called before? They couldn't understand why I hadn't. Was I comfortable? They seemed embarrassed that I had spent the time at the airport; that I had been delayed in getting to Mecca. No matter how I protested that I felt no inconvenience, that I was fine, they would not hear it. "You must rest," Dr. Azzam said. He went to use the telephone.

I didn't know what this distinguished man was doing. I had no dream. When I was told that I would be brought back for dinner that evening, and that, meanwhile, I should get back in the car, how could I have realized that I was about to see the epitome of Muslim hospitality?

Abd ir-Rahman Azzam, when at home, lived in a suite at the Jedda Palace Hotel. Because I had come to them with a letter from a friend, he was going to stay at his son's home, and let me use his suite, until I could get on to Mecca.

When I found out, there was no use protesting: I was in the suite; young Dr. Azzam was gone; there was no one to protest to. The three-room suite had a bathroom that was as big as a double at the New York Hilton. It was suite number 214. There was even a porch outside, affording a beautiful view of the ancient Red Sea city.

There had never before been in my emotions such an impulse to pray—and I did, prostrating myself on the living-room rug.

Nothing in either of my two careers as a black man in America had served to give me any idealistic tendencies. My instincts automatically examined the reasons, the motives, of anyone who did anything they didn't have to do for me. Always in my life, if it was any white person, I could see a selfish motive.

But there in that hotel that morning, a telephone call and a few hours away from the cot on the fourth-floor tier of the dormitory, was one of the few times I had been so awed that I was totally without resistance. That white man—at least he would have been considered "white" in America—related to Arabia's ruler, to whom he was a close advisor, truly an international man, with nothing in the world to gain, had given up his suite to me, for my transient comfort. He had *nothing* to gain. He didn't need me. He had everything. In fact, he had more to lose than gain. He had followed the American press about me. If he did that, he knew there was only stigma attached to me. I was supposed to have horns. I was a "racist." I was "anti-white"—and he from all appearances was white. I was supposed to be a criminal; not only that, but everyone was even accusing me of using his religion of Islam as a cloak for my criminal practices and philosophies. Even if he had had some motive to use me, he knew that I was separated from Elijah Muhammad and the Nation of Islam, my "power base," according to the press in America. The only organization that I had was just a few weeks old. I had no job. I had no money. Just to get over there, I had had to borrow money from my sister.

That morning was when I first began to reappraise the "white man." It was when I first began to perceive that "white man," as commonly used, means complexion only secondarily; primarily it described attitudes and actions. In America, "white man" meant specific attitudes and actions toward the black man, and toward all other non-white men. But in the Muslim world, I had seen that men with white complexions were more genuinely brotherly than anyone else had ever been.

That morning was the start of a radical alteration in my whole outlook about "white" men.

I should quote from my notebook here. I wrote this about noon, in the hotel: "My excitement, sitting here, waiting to go before the Hajj Committee, is indescribable. My window faces to the sea westward. The streets are filled with the incoming pilgrims from all over the world. The prayers are to Allah and verses from the Quran are on the lips of everyone. Never have I seen such a beautiful sight, nor witnessed such a scene, nor felt such an atmosphere. Although I am excited, I feel safe and secure, thousands of miles from the totally different life that I have known. Imagine that twenty-four hours ago, I was in the fourth-floor room over the airport, surrounded by people with whom I could not communicate, feeling uncertain about the future, and very lonely, and then *one* phone call, following Dr. Shawarbi's instructions. I have met one of the most powerful men in the Muslim world. I will soon sleep in his bed at the Jedda Palace. I know that I am surrounded by friends whose sincerity and religious zeal I can feel. I must pray again to thank Allah for this blessing, and I must pray again that my wife and children back in America will always be blessed for their sacrifices, too."

I did pray, two more prayers, as I had told my notebook. Then I slept for about four hours, until the telephone rang. It was young Dr. Azzam. In another hour, he would pick me up to return me there for dinner. I tumbled words over one another, trying to express some of the thanks I felt for all of their actions. He cut me off. "Ma sha'a-llah"—which means, "It is as Allah has pleased."

I seized the opportunity to run down into the lobby, to see it again before Dr. Azzam arrived. When I opened my door, just across the hall from me a man in some ceremonial dress, who obviously lived there, was also headed downstairs, surrounded by attendants. I followed them down, then through the lobby. Outside, a small caravan of automobiles was waiting. My neighbor appeared through the Jedda Palace Hotel's front entrance and people rushed and crowded him, kissing his hand. I found out who he was: the Grand Mufti of Jerusalem. Later, in the hotel, I would have the opportunity to talk with him for about a half-hour. He was a cordial man of great dignity. He was well up on world affairs, and even the latest events in America.

I will never forget the dinner at the Azzam home. I quote my notebook again: "I couldn't say in my mind that these were 'white' men. Why, the men acted as if they were brothers of mine, the elder Dr. Azzam as if he were my father. His fatherly, scholarly speech. I *felt* like he was my father. He was, you could tell, a highly skilled diplomat, with a broad range of mind. His knowledge was so worldly. He was as current on world affairs as some people are to what's going on in their living room.

"The more we talked, the more his vast reservoir of knowledge and its variety seemed unlimited. He spoke of the racial lineage of the descendants of Muhammad the Prophet, and he showed how they were both black and white. He also pointed out how color, the complexities of color, and the problems of color which exist in the Muslim world, exist only where, and to the extent that, that area of the Muslim world has been influenced by the West. He said that if one encountered any differences based on attitude toward color, this directly reflected the degree of Western influence."

I learned during dinner that while I was at the hotel, the Hajj Committee Court had been notified about my case, and that in the morning I should be there. And I was.

The Judge was Sheikh Muhammad Harkon. The Court was empty except for me and a sister from India, formerly a Protestant, who had converted to Islam, and was, like me, trying to make the Hajj. She was brown-skinned, with a small face that was mostly covered. Judge Harkon was a kind, impressive man. We talked. He asked me some questions, having to do with my sincerity. I answered him as truly as I could. He not only recognized me as a true Muslim, but he gave me two books, one in English, the other in Arabic. He recorded my name in the Holy Register of true Muslims, and we were ready to part. He told me, "I hope you will become a great preacher of Islam in America." I said that I shared that hope, and I would try to fulfill it.

The Azzam family were very elated that I was qualified and accepted to go to Mecca. I had lunch at the Jedda Palace. Then I slept again for several hours, until the telephone awakened me.

It was Muhammad Abdul Azziz Maged, the Deputy Chief of Protocol for Prince Faisal. "A special car will be waiting to take you to Mecca, right after your dinner," he told me. He advised me to eat heartily, as the Hajj rituals require plenty of strength.

I was beyond astonishment by then.

Two young Arabs accompanied me to Mecca. A well-lighted, modern turn-pike highway made the trip easy. Guards at intervals along the way took one look at the car, and the driver made a sign, and we were passed through, never even having to slow down. I was, all at once, thrilled, important, humble, and thankful.

Mecca, when we entered, seemed as ancient as time itself. Our car slowed through the winding streets, lined by shops on both sides and with buses, cars, and trucks, and tens of thousands of pilgrims from all over the earth were everywhere.

The car halted briefly at a place where a *Mutawaf* was waiting for me. He wore the white skullcap and long nightshirt garb that I had seen at the airport. He was a short, dark-skinned Arab, named Muhammad. He spoke no English whatever.

We parked near the Great Mosque. We performed our ablution and entered. Pilgrims seemed to be on top of each other, there were so many, lying, sitting, sleeping, praying, walking.

My vocabulary cannot describe the new mosque that was being built around the Ka'ba. I was thrilled to realize that it was only one of the tremendous rebuilding tasks under the direction of young Dr. Azzam, who had just been my host. The Great Mosque of Mecca, when it is finished, will surpass the architectural beauty of India's Taj Mahal.

Carrying my sandals, I followed the *Mutawaf.* Then I saw the Ka'ba, a huge black stone house in the middle of the Great Mosque. It was being circumambulated by thousands upon thousands of praying pilgrims, both sexes, and every size, shape, color, and race in the world. I knew the prayer to be uttered when the pilgrim's eyes first perceive the Ka'ba. Translated, it is "O God, You are peace, and peace derives from You. So greet us, O Lord, with peace." Upon entering the Mosque, the pilgrim should try to kiss the Ka'ba if possible, but if the crowds prevent him getting that close, he touches it, and if the crowds prevent that, he raises his hand and cries out "Takbir!" ("God is great!") I could not get within yards. "Takbir!"

My feeling there in the House of God was a numbness. My *Mutawaf* led me in the crowd of praying, chanting pilgrims, moving seven times around the Ka'ba. Some were bent and wizened with age; it was a sight that stamped itself on the brain. I saw incapacitated pilgrims being carried by others. Faces were enraptured in their faith. The seventh time around, I prayed two *Rak'a,* prostrating myself, my head on the floor. The first prostration, I prayed the Quran verse "Say He is God, the one and only"; the second prostration: "Say O you who are unbelievers, I worship not that which you worship. . . ."

As I prostrated, the *Mutawaf* fended pilgrims off to keep me from being trampled.

The *Mutawaf* and I next drank water from the well of Zem Zem. Then we ran between the two hills, Safa and Marwa, where Hajar wandered over the same earth searching for water for her child Ishmael.

Three separate times, after that, I visited the Great Mosque and circumambulated the Ka'ba. The next day we set out after sunrise toward Mount Arafat, thousands of us, crying in unison: "Labbayka! Labbayka!" and "Allah Akbar!" Mecca is surrounded by the crudest-looking mountains I have ever seen; they seem to be made of the slag from a blast furnace. No vegetation is on them at all. Arriving about noon, we prayed and chanted from noon until sunset, and the *asr* (afternoon) and *Maghrib* (sunset) special prayers were performed.

Finally, we lifted our hands in prayer and thanksgiving, repeating Allah's words: "There is no God but Allah. He has no partner. His are authority and praise. Good emanates from Him, and He has power over all things."

Standing on Mount Arafat had concluded the essential rites of being a pilgrim to Mecca. No one who missed it could consider himself a pilgrim.

The *Ihram* had ended. We cast the traditional seven stones at the devil. Some had their hair and beards cut. I decided that I was going to let my beard remain. I wondered what my wife Betty, and our little daughters, were going to say when they saw me with a beard, when I got back to New York. New York seemed a million miles away. I hadn't seen a newspaper that I could read since I left New York. I had no idea what was happening there. A Negro rifle club that had been in existence for over twelve years in Harlem had been "discovered" by the police; it was being trumpeted that I was "behind it." Elijah Muhammad's Nation of Islam had a lawsuit going against me, to force me and my family to vacate the house in which we lived on Long Island.

The major press, radio, and television media in America had representatives in Cairo hunting all over, trying to locate me, to interview me about the furor in New York that I had allegedly caused—when I knew nothing about any of it.

I only knew what I had left in America, and how it contrasted with what I had found in the Muslim world. About twenty of us Muslims who had finished the Hajj were sitting in a huge tent on Mount Arafat. As a Muslim from America, I was the center of attention. They asked me what about the Hajj had impressed me the most. One of the several who spoke English asked; they translated my answers for the others. My answer to that question was not the one they expected, but it drove home my point.

I said, "The *brotherhood!* The people of all races, colors, from all over the world coming together as *one!* It has proved to me the power of the One God."

It may have been out of taste, but that gave me an opportunity, and I used it, to preach them a quick little sermon on America's racism, and its evils.

CHAPTER THREE / *Commitment*

I could tell the impact of this upon them. They had been aware that the plight of the black man in America was "bad," but they had not been aware that it was inhuman, that it was a psychological castration. These people from elsewhere around the world were shocked. As Muslims, they had a very tender heart for all unfortunates, and very sensitive feelings for truth and justice. And in everything I said to them, as long as we talked, they were aware of the yardstick that I was using to measure everything—that to me the earth's most explosive and pernicious evil is racism, the inability of God's creatures to live as One, especially in the Western world.

I have reflected since that the letter I finally sat down to compose had been subconsciously shaping itself in my mind.

The *color-blindness* of the Muslim world's religious society and the *color-blindness* of the Muslim world's human society: these two influences had each day been making a greater impact, and an increasing persuasion against my previous way of thinking.

The first letter was, of course, to my wife, Betty. I never had a moment's question that Betty, after initial amazement, would change her thinking to join mine. I had known a thousand reassurances that Betty's faith in me was total. I knew that she would see what I had seen—that in the land of Muhammad and the land of Abraham, I had been blessed by Allah with a new insight into the true religion of Islam, and a better understanding of America's entire racial dilemma.

After the letter to my wife, I wrote next essentially the same letter to my sister Ella. And I knew where Ella would stand. She had been saving to make the pilgrimage to Mecca herself.

I wrote to Dr. Shawarbi, whose belief in my sincerity had enabled me to get a passport to Mecca.

All through the night, I copied similar long letters for others who were very close to me. Among them was Elijah Muhammad's son Wallace Muhammad, who had expressed to me his conviction that the only possible salvation for the Nation of Islam would be its accepting and projecting a better understanding of Orthodox Islam.

And I wrote to my loyal assistants at my newly formed Muslim Mosque, Inc. in Harlem, with a note appended, asking that my letter be duplicated and distributed to the press.

I knew that when my letter became public knowledge back in America, many would be astounded—loved ones, friends, and enemies alike. And no less astounded would be millions whom I did not know—who had gained during my twelve years with Elijah Muhammad a "hate" image of Malcolm X.

Even I was myself astounded. But there was precedent in my life for this letter. My whole life had been a chronology of—*changes.*

Here is what I wrote . . . from my heart:

"Never have I witnessed such sincere hospitality and the overwhelming spirit of true brotherhood as is practiced by people of all colors and races here in this Ancient Holy Land, the home of Abraham, Muhammad, and all the other prophets of the Holy Scriptures. For the past week, I have been utterly speechless and spellbound by the graciousness I see displayed all around me by people *of all colors.*

"I have been blessed to visit the Holy City of Mecca. I have made my seven circuits around the Ka'ba, led by a young *Mutawaf* named Muhammad. I drank water from the well of Zem Zem. I ran seven times back and forth between the hills of Mt. Al-Safa and Al-Marwah. I have prayed in the ancient city of Mina, and I have prayed on Mt. Arafat.

"There were tens of thousands of pilgrims, from all over the world. They were of all colors, from blue-eyed blonds to black-skinned Africans. But we were all participating in the same ritual, displaying a spirit of unity and brotherhood that my experiences in America had led me to believe never could exist between the white and the non-white.

"America needs to understand Islam, because this is the one religion that erases from its society the race problem. Throughout my travels in the Muslim world, I have met, talked to, and even eaten with people who in America would have been considered 'white'—but the 'white' attitude was removed from their minds by the religion of Islam. I have never before seen *sincere* and *true* brotherhood practiced by all colors together, irrespective of their color.

"You may be shocked by these words coming from me. But on this pilgrimage, what I have seen, and experienced, has forced me to *re-arrange* much of my thought-patterns previously held, and to *toss aside* some of my previous conclusions. This was not too difficult for me. Despite my firm convictions, I have been always a man who tries to face facts, and to accept the reality of life as new experience and new knowledge unfolds it. I have always kept an open mind, which is necessary to the flexibility that must go hand in hand with every form of intelligent search for truth.

"During the past eleven days here in the Muslim world, I have eaten from the same plate, drunk from the same glass, and slept in the same bed (or on the same rug)—while praying to the *same God*—with fellow Muslims, whose eyes were the bluest of blue, whose hair was the blondest of blond, and whose skin was the whitest of white. And in the *words* and in the *actions* and in the *deeds* of the 'white' Muslims, I felt the same sincerity that I felt among the black African Muslims of Nigeria, Sudan, and Ghana.

"We were *truly* all the same (brothers)—because their belief in one God had removed the 'white' from their *minds*, the 'white' from their *behavior*, and the 'white' from their *attitude.*

"I could see from this, that perhaps if white Americans could accept the

CHAPTER THREE / *Commitment*

Oneness of God, then perhaps, too, they could accept *in reality* the Oneness of Man—and cease to measure, and hinder, and harm others in terms of their 'differences' in color.

"With racism plaguing America like an incurable cancer, the so-called 'Christian' white American heart should be more receptive to a proven solution to such a destructive problem. Perhaps it could be in time to save America from imminent disaster—the same destruction brought upon Germany by racism that eventually destroyed the Germans themselves.

"Each hour here in the Holy Land enables me to have greater spiritual insights into what is happening in America between black and white. The American Negro never can be blamed for his racial animosities—he is only reacting to four hundred years of the conscious racism of the American whites. But as racism leads America up the suicide path, I do believe, from the experiences that I have had with them, that the whites of the younger generation, in the colleges and universities, will see the handwriting on the wall and many of them will turn to the *spiritual* path of *truth*—the *only* way left to America to ward off the disaster that racism inevitably must lead to.

"Never have I been so highly honored. Never have I been made to feel more humble and unworthy. Who would believe the blessings that have been heaped upon an *American Negro?* A few nights ago, a man who would be called in America a 'white' man, a United Nations diplomat, an ambassador, a companion of kings, gave me *his* hotel suite, *his* bed. By this man, His Excellency Prince Faisal, who rules this Holy Land, was made aware of my presence here in Jedda. The very next morning, Prince Faisal's son, in person, informed me that by the will and decree of his esteemed father, I was to be a State Guest.

"The Deputy Chief of Protocol himself took me before the Hajj Court. His Holiness Sheikh Muhammad Harkon himself okayed my visit to Mecca. His Holiness gave me two books on Islam, with his personal seal and autograph, and he told me that he prayed that I would be a successful preacher of Islam in America. A car, a driver, and a guide, have been placed at my disposal, making it possible for me to travel about this Holy Land almost at will. The government provides air-conditioned quarters and servants in each city that I visit. Never would I have even thought of dreaming that I would ever be a recipient of such honors—honors that in America would be bestowed upon a King—not a Negro.

"All praise is due to Allah, the Lord of all the Worlds.

"Sincerely,

"*El-Hajj Malik El-Shabazz*
"*(Malcolm X)*"

chapter four

Survival

introduction _____

One of the supreme ironies of a century which has so prided itself on its material and intellectual progress is that so many of its people have had to spend so much of their lives struggling for physical and psychological survival. From one point of view, the twentieth century can be portrayed as a conflict between those whose greatest efforts have been exerted in the perfection of techniques—gross and refined—for destroying human life in the name of peace and freedom and those intended victims who have called on all the resources of the human spirit simply to keep body and soul together. From the Russo-Japanese War in 1904 to the continuing conflict in Vietnam, men of the twentieth century have forced each other into the heroism of survival in the face of tremendous odds. In addition to open warfare, there have been political and racial oppression, the quiet violence of poverty, and the emotional disorders generated by the pressures of contemporary life, creeping up subtly but devastatingly on their victims.

World War II was the grimmest period of the twentieth century, giving birth to the concentration camp and the nuclear bomb. The first two selections in this chapter were written by men who lived through these grotesque phenomena. Primo Levi survived Auschwitz, one of the most notorious of the Nazi death camps. "On the Bottom" relates the first stages of the macabre inhumanity by which the Nazis dehumanized their prisoners, the humiliation of stripping away individual human identity, an initial step in the ultimate degradation of both the prisoners and their jailer-executioners. With the detachment of an observer rather than a participant, Michihiko Hachiya narrates his experiences in the cataclysm of the atomic bomb dropped on Hiroshima. None of the morbid statistics whose cold precision tells one version of the death camps and Hiroshima can match the impact of the retelling of those shameful episodes which disgrace the name of humanity.

Carolina de Jesus' diary records her scramble to keep herself and her children from starving in the abject poverty of the Brazilian *favela* they inhabit. And in an American counterpoint to de Jesus' life in the *favela*, Eon Cjohn-athan's essay depicts her hardships growing up in the poverty of Harlem.

George Jackson and Feodor Dostoyevsky both write of prison: Dostoyevsky from the perspective of his release, Jackson from a hostile prison environment, reporting, in a letter to Angela Davis, the conditions to which he adapted to stay alive and the convictions he developed to retain his psychological balance.

Joan Didion depicts her psychological degeneration in the face of the pressures of living and working in contemporary New York; and from a mental institution, Vincent van Gogh writes hopefully to his brother of recuperating from the psychotic attacks which plagued his last years.

On the Bottom

Born in Turin, Italy, Primo Levi (1919–   ) was a member of the Italian Resistance during World War II. In 1943, because he was a Jew, he was arrested and interned in the notorious Auschwitz prison camp in Poland until 1945. He has written two books about his concentration camp experience, *If This Is a Man* (1958) and *The Reawakening* (1965), which he has called "a chronicle of my exile, and an attempt to understand its meaning." Currently Levi is a business executive in Torino, Italy. The following essay is from *If This Is a Man.*

The journey did not last more than twenty minutes. Then the lorry stopped, and we saw a large door, and above it a sign, brightly illuminated (its memory still strikes me in my dreams): *Arbeit Macht Frei,* work gives freedom.

We climb down, they make us enter an enormous empty room that is poorly heated. We have a terrible thirst. The weak gurgle of the water in the radiators makes us ferocious; we have had nothing to drink for four days. But there is also a tap—and above it a card which says that it is forbidden to drink as the water is dirty. Nonsense. It seems obvious that the card is a joke, "they" know that we are dying of thirst and they put us in a room, and there is a tap, and *Wassertrinken Verboten.* I drink and I incite my companions to do likewise, but I have to spit it out, the water is tepid and sweetish, with the smell of a swamp.

This is hell. Today, in our times, hell must be like this. A huge, empty room: we are tired, standing on our feet, with a tap which drips while we cannot drink the water, and we wait for something which will certainly be terrible, and nothing happens and nothing continues to happen. What can one think about? One cannot think anymore, it is like being already dead. Someone sits down on the ground. The time passes drop by drop.

We are not dead. The door is opened and an SS man enters, smoking. He looks at us slowly and asks, *"Wer kann Deutsch?"* One of us whom I have never seen, named Flesch, moves forward; he will be our interpreter. The SS man makes a long calm speech; the interpreter translates. We have to form rows of five, with intervals of two yards between man and man; then we have to undress and make a bundle of the clothes in a special manner, the woollen garments on one side, all the rest on the other; we must take off our shoes but pay great attention that they are not stolen.

Stolen by whom? Why should our shoes be stolen? And what about our documents, the few things we have in our pockets, our watches? We all look at the interpreter, and the interpreter asks the German, and the German smokes and looks him through and through as if he were transparent, as if no one had spoken.

I had never seen old men naked. Mr. Bergmann wore a truss and asked the interpreter if he should take it off, and the interpreter hesitated. But the German understood and spoke seriously to the interpreter pointing to someone. We saw the interpreter swallow and then he said: "The officer says, take off the truss, and you will be given that of Mr. Coen." One could see the words coming bitterly out of Flesch's mouth; this was the German manner of laughing.

Now another German comes and tells us to put the shoes in a certain corner, and we put them there, because now it is all over and we feel outside this world and the only thing is to obey. Someone comes with a broom and sweeps away all the shoes, outside the door in a heap. He is crazy, he is mixing them all together, ninety-six pairs, they will be all mixed up. The outside door opens, a freezing wind enters and we are naked and cover ourselves up with our arms. The wind blows and slams the door; the German reopens it and stands watching with interest how we writhe to hide from the wind, one behind the other. Then he leaves and closes it.

Now the second act begins. Four men with razors, soapbrushes and clippers burst in; they have trousers and jackets with stripes, with a number sewn on the front; perhaps they are the same sort as those others of this evening (this evening or yesterday evening?); but these are robust and flourishing. We ask many questions but they catch hold of us and in a moment we find ourselves shaved and sheared. What comic faces we have without hair! The four speak a language which does not seem of this world. It is certainly not German, for I understand a little German.

Finally another door is opened: here we are, locked in, naked, sheared and standing, with our feet in water—it is a shower-room. We are alone. Slowly the astonishment dissolves, and we speak, and everyone asks questions and no one answers. If we are naked in a shower-room, it means that we will have a shower. If we have a shower it is because they are not going to kill us yet. But why then do they keep us standing, and give us nothing to drink, while nobody explains anything, and we have no shoes or clothes, but we are all naked with our feet in the water, and we have been travelling five days and cannot even sit down.

And our women?

Mr. Levi asks me if I think that our women are like us at this moment, and where they are, and if we will be able to see them again. I say yes, because he is married and has a daughter; certainly we will see them again. But by now my belief is that all this is a game to mock and sneer at us. Clearly they will kill us, whoever thinks he is going to live is mad, it means that he has swallowed the bait, but I have not; I have understood that it will soon all be over, perhaps in this same room, when they get bored of seeing us naked, dancing from foot to foot and trying every now and again to sit down on the floor. But there are two inches of cold water and we cannot sit down.

We walk up and down without sense, and we talk, everybody talks to everybody else, we make a great noise. The door opens, and a German enters; it is the officer of before. He speaks briefly, the interpreter translates. "The officer says you must be quiet, because this is not a rabbinical school." One sees the words which are not his, the bad words, twist his mouth as they come out, as if he was spitting out a foul taste. We beg him to ask what we are waiting for, how long we will stay here, about our women, everything; but he says no, that he does not want to ask. This Flesch, who is most unwilling to translate into Italian the hard cold German phrases and refuses to turn into German our questions because he knows that it is useless, is a German Jew of about fifty, who has a large scar on his face from a wound received fighting the Italians on the Piave. He is a closed, taciturn man, for whom I feel an instinctive respect as I feel that he has begun to suffer before us.

The German goes and we remain silent, although we are a little ashamed of our silence. It is still night and we wonder if the day will ever come. The door opens again, and someone else dressed in stripes comes in. He is different from the others, older, with glasses, a more civilized face, and much less robust. He speaks to us in Italian.

By now we are tired of being amazed. We seem to be watching some mad play, one of those plays in which the witches, the Holy Spirit and the devil appear. He speaks Italian badly, with a strong foreign accent. He makes a long speech, is very polite, and tries to reply to all our questions.

We are at Monowitz, near Auschwitz, in Upper Silesia, a region inhabited by both Poles and Germans. This camp is a work-camp, in German one says *Arbeitslager;* all the prisoners (there are about ten thousand) work in a factory which produces a type of rubber called Buna, so that the camp itself is called Buna.

We will be given shoes and clothes—no, not our own—other shoes, other clothes, like his. We are naked now because we are waiting for the shower and the disinfection, which will take place immediately after the reveille, because one cannot enter the camp without being disinfected.

Certainly there will be work to do, everyone must work here. But there is work and work: he, for example, acts as doctor. He is a Hungarian doctor who studied in Italy and he is the dentist of the Lager. He has been in the Lager for four and a half years (not in this one: Buna has only been open for a year and a half), but we can see that he is still quite well, not very thin. Why is he in the Lager? Is he Jewish like us? "No," he says simply, "I am a criminal."

We ask him many questions. He laughs, replies to some and not to others, and it is clear that he avoids certain subjects. He does not speak of the women: he says they are well, that we will see them again soon, but he does not say how or where. Instead he tells us other things, strange and crazy things, perhaps he too is playing with us. Perhaps he is mad—one goes mad in the Lager. He says that every Sunday there are concerts and football matches. He says that whoever boxes well can become cook. He says that whoever works well receives prize-coupons with which to buy tobacco and soap. He says that the water is really not drinkable, and that instead a coffee substitute is distributed every day, but generally nobody drinks it as the soup itself is sufficiently watery to quench thirst. We beg him to find us something to drink, but he says that he cannot, that he has come to see us secretly, against SS orders, as we still have to be disinfected, and that he must leave at once; he has come because he has a liking for Italians, and because, he says, he "has a little heart." We ask him if there are other Italians in the camp and he says there are some, a few, he does not know how many; and he at once changes the subject. Meanwhile a bell rang and he immediately hurried off and left us stunned and disconcerted. Some feel refreshed but I do not. I still think that even this dentist, this incomprehensible person, wanted to amuse himself at our expense, and I do not want to believe a word of what he said.

At the sound of the bell, we can hear the still dark camp waking up. Unexpectedly the water gushes out boiling from the showers—five minutes of bliss; but immediately after, four men (perhaps they are the barbers) burst in yelling and shoving and drive us out, wet and steaming, into the adjoining room which is freezing; here other shouting people throw at us unrecognizable rags and thrust into our hands a pair of broken-down boots with wooden soles; we have no time to understand and we already find ourselves in the open, in the blue and icy snow of dawn, barefoot and naked, with all our clothing in our hands, with a hundred yards to run to the next hut. There we are finally allowed to get dressed.

When we finish, everyone remains in his own corner and we do not dare lift our eyes to look at one another. There is nowhere to look in a mirror, but our appearance stands in front of us, reflected in a hundred livid faces, in a hundred miserable and sordid puppets. We are transformed into the phantoms glimpsed yesterday evening.

Then for the first time we became aware that our language lacks words to express this offence, the demolition of a man. In a moment, with almost prophetic intuition, the reality was revealed to us: we had reached the bottom. It is not possible to sink lower than this; no human condition is more miserable than this, nor could it conceivably be so. Nothing belongs to us anymore; they have taken away our clothes, our shoes, even our hair; if we speak, they will not listen to us, and if they listen, they will not understand. They will even take away our name: and if we want to keep it, we will have to find in ourselves the strength to do so, to manage somehow so that behind the name something of us, of us as we were, still remains.

We know that we will have difficulty in being understood, and this is as it should be. But consider what value, what meaning is enclosed even in the smallest of our daily habits, in the hundred possessions which even the poorest beggar owns: a handkerchief, an old letter, the photo of a cherished person. These things are part of us, almost like limbs of our body; nor is it conceivable that we can be deprived of them in our world, for we immediately find others to substitute the old ones, other objects which are ours in their personification and evocation of our memories.

Imagine now a man who is deprived of everyone he loves, and at the same time of his house, his habits, his clothes, in short, of everything he possesses: he will be a hollow man, reduced to suffering and needs, forgetful of dignity and restraint, for he who loses all often easily loses himself. He will be a man whose life or death can be lightly decided with no sense of human affinity, in the most fortunate of cases, on the basis of a pure judgment of utility. It is in this way that one can understand the double sense of the term "extermination camp," and it is now clear what we seek to express with the phrase: "to lie on the bottom."

Häftling[1]: I have learnt that I am a Häftling. My number is 174517; we have been baptized, we will carry the tattoo on our left arm until we die.

The operation was slightly painful and extraordinarily rapid: they placed us all in a row, and one by one, according to the alphabetical order of our names, we filed past a skilful official, armed with a sort of pointed tool with a very short needle. It seems that this is the real, true initiation: only by "showing one's number" can one get bread and soup. Several days passed, and not a few cuffs and punches, before we became used to showing our number promptly enough not to disorder the daily operation of food-distribution; weeks and months were needed to learn its sound in the German language. And for many days, while the habits of freedom still led me to look for the time on my wristwatch, my new name ironically appeared instead, its number tattooed in bluish characters under the skin.

[1]A prisoner.

Only much later, and slowly, a few of us learnt something of the funereal science of the numbers of Auschwitz, which epitomize the stages of destruction of European Judaism. To the old hands of the camp, the numbers told everything: the period of entry into the camp, the convoy of which one formed a part, and consequently the nationality. Everyone will treat with respect the numbers from 30,000 to 80,000: there are only a few hundred left and they represent the few survivals from the Polish ghettos. It is as well to watch out in commercial dealings with a 116,000 or a 117,000: they now number only about forty, but they represent the Greeks of Salonica, so take care they do not pull the wool over your eyes. As for the high numbers, they carry an essentially comic air about them, like the words "freshman" or "conscript" in ordinary life. The typical high number is a corpulent, docile and stupid fellow: he can be convinced that leather shoes are distributed at the infirmary to all those with delicate feet, and can be persuaded to run there and leave his bowl of soup "in your custody"; you can sell him a spoon for three rations of bread; you can send him to the most ferocious of the Kapos to ask him (as happened to me!) if it is true that his is the *Kartoffelschalenkommando,* the "Potato Peeling Command," and if one can be enrolled in it.

In fact, the whole process of introduction to what was for us a new order took place in a grotesque and sarcastic manner. When the tattooing operation was finished, they shut us in a vacant hut. The bunks are made, but we are severely forbidden to touch or sit on them: so we wander around aimlessly for half the day in the limited space available, still tormented by the parching thirst of the journey. Then the door opens and a boy in a striped suit comes in, with a fairly civilized air, small, thin and blond. He speaks French and we throng around him with a flood of questions which till now we had asked each other in vain.

But he does not speak willingly; no one here speaks willingly. We are new, we have nothing and we know nothing; why waste time on us? He reluctantly explains to us that all the others are out at work and will come back in the evening. He has come out of the infirmary this morning and is exempt from work for today. I asked him (with an ingenuousness that only a few days later already seemed incredible to me) if at least they would give us back our toothbrushes. He did not laugh, but with his face animated by fierce contempt, he threw at me *"Vous n'êtes pas à la maison."* And it is this refrain that we hear repeated by everyone: you are not at home, this is not a sanatorium, the only exit is by way of the Chimney. (What did it mean? Soon we were all to learn what it meant.)

And it was in fact so. Driven by thirst, I eyed a fine icicle outside the window, within hand's reach. I opened the window and broke off the icicle but at once a large, heavy guard prowling outside brutally snatched it away from me. *"Warum?"* I asked him in my poor German. *"Hier ist kein warum"* (there is no why here), he replied, pushing me inside with a shove.

The explanation is repugnant but simple: in this place everything is forbidden, not for hidden reasons, but because the camp has been created for that purpose. If one wants to live one must learn this quickly and well:

> "No Sacred Face will help thee here! it's not
> A Serchio bathing-party. . . ."

Hour after hour, this first long day of limbo draws to its end. While the sun sets in a tumult of fierce, blood-red clouds, they finally make us come out of the hut. Will they give us something to drink? No, they place us in line again, they lead us to a huge square which takes up the centre of the camp and they arrange us meticulously in squads. Then nothing happens for another hour: it seems that we are waiting for someone.

A band begins to play, next to the entrance of the camp: it plays *Rosamunda*, the well known sentimental song, and this seems so strange to us that we look sniggering at each other; we feel a shadow of relief, perhaps all these ceremonies are nothing but a colossal farce in Teutonic taste. But the band, on finishing *Rosamunda*, continues to play other marches, one after the other, and suddenly the squads of our comrades appear, returning from work. They walk in columns of five with a strange, unnatural hard gait, like stiff puppets made of jointless bones; but they walk scrupulously in time to the band.

They also arrange themselves like us in the huge square, according to a precise order; when the last squad has returned, they count and recount us for over an hour. Long checks are made which all seem to go to a man dressed in stripes, who accounts for them to a group of SS men in full battle dress.

Finally (it is dark by now, but the camp is brightly lit by headlamps and reflectors) one hears the shout *"Absperre!"* at which all the squads break up in a confused and turbulent movement. They no longer walk stiffly and erectly as before: each one drags himself along with obvious effort. I see that all of them carry in their hand or attached to their belt a steel bowl as large as a basin.

We new arrivals also wander among the crowd, searching for a voice, a friendly face or a guide. Against the wooden wall of a hut two boys are seated on the ground: they seem very young, sixteen years old at the outside, both with their face and hands dirty with soot. One of the two, as we are passing by, calls me and asks me in German some questions which I do not understand; then he asks where we come from. *"Italien,"* I reply; I want to ask him many things, but my German vocabulary is very limited.

"Are you a Jew?" I ask him.

"Yes, a Polish Jew."

"How long have you been in the Lager?"

"Three years," and he lifts up three fingers. He must have been a child when he entered, I think with horror; on the other hand this means that at least some manage to live here.

"What is your work?"

"*Schlosser,*" he replies. I do not understand. "*Eisen, Feuer*" (iron, fire), he insists, and makes a play with his hands of someone beating with a hammer on an anvil. So he is an ironsmith.

"*Ich Chemiker,*" I state; and he nods earnestly with his head, "*Chemiker gut.*" But all this has to do with the distant future: what torments me at the moment is my thirst.

"Drink, water. We no water," I tell him.

He looks at me with a serious face, almost severe, and states clearly: "Do not drink water, comrade," and then other words that I do not understand. "*Warum?*"

"*Geschwollen,*" he replies cryptically. I shake my head, I have not understood. "*Swollen,*" he makes me understand, blowing out his cheeks and sketching with his hands a monstrous tumefaction of the face and belly. "*Warten bis heute Abend.*" "Wait until this evening," I translate word by word.

Then he says: "*Ich Schlome. Du?*" I tell him my name, and he asks me: "Where your mother?"

"In Italy." Schlome is amazed: a Jew in Italy? "Yes," I explain as best I can, "hidden, no one knows, run away, does not speak, no one sees her." He has understood; he now gets up, approaches me and timidly embraces me. The adventure is over, and I feel filled with a serene sadness that is almost joy. I have never seen Schlome since, but I have not forgotten his serious and gentle face of a child, which welcomed me on the threshold of the house of the dead.

We still have a great number of things to learn, but we have learnt many already. We already have a certain idea of the topography of the Lager; our Lager is a square of about six hundred yards in length, surrounded by two fences of barbed wire, the inner one carrying a high tension current. It consists of sixty wooden huts, which are called Blocks, ten of which are in construction. In addition, there is the body of the kitchens, which are in brick; an experimental farm, run by a detachment of privileged Häftling; the huts with the showers and the latrines, one for each group of six or eight Blocks. Besides these, certain Blocks are reserved for specific purposes. First of all, a group of eight, at the extreme eastern end of the camp, forms the infirmary and clinic; then there is Block 24 which is the *Krätzeblock,* reserved for infectious skin-diseases; Block 7 which no ordinary Häftling has ever entered, reserved for the "*Prominenz,*" that is, the aristocracy, the internees holding the highest posts; Block 47, reserved for the *Reichsdeutsche* (the Aryan Germans, 'politicals' or criminals); Block 49, for the Kapos alone; Block 12, half of which, for use of the *Reichsdeutsche* and the Kapos, serves as canteen, that is, a distribution centre for tobacco, insect powder and occasionally other articles; Block 37, which formed the Quartermaster's office and the Office for Work; and finally, Block 29, which always has its windows closed as it is the *Frauenblock*, the camp brothel, served by Polish Häftling girls, and reserved for the Reichsdeutsche.

The ordinary living Blocks are divided into two parts. In one *Tagesraum* lives the head of the hut with his friends. There is a long table, seats, benches, and on all sides a heap of strange objects in bright colours, photographs, cuttings from magazines, sketches, imitation flowers, ornaments; on the walls, great sayings, proverbs and rhymes in praise of order, discipline and hygiene; in one corner, a shelf with the tools of the *Blockfrisör* (official barber), the ladles to distribute the soup, and two rubber truncheons, one solid and one hollow, to enforce discipline should the proverbs prove insufficient. The other part is the dormitory: there are only one hundred and forty-eight bunks on three levels, fitted close to each other like the cells of a beehive, and divided by three corridors so as to utilize without wastage all the space in the room up to the roof. Here all the ordinary *Häftlinge* live, about two hundred to two hundred and fifty per hut. Consequently there are two men in most of the bunks, which are portable planks of wood, each covered by a thin straw sack and two blankets.

The corridors are so narrow that two people can barely pass together; the total area of the floor is so small that the inhabitants of the same Block cannot all stay there at the same time unless at least half are lying on their bunks. Hence the prohibition to enter a Block to which one does not belong.

In the middle of the Lager is the roll-call square, enormous, where we collect in the morning to form the work-squads and in the evening to be counted. Facing the roll-call square there is a bed of grass, carefully mown, where the gallows are erected when necessary.

We had soon learned that the guests of the Lager are divided into three categories: the criminals, the politicals and the Jews. All are clothes in stripes, all are *Häftlinge*, but the criminals wear a green triangle next to the number sewn on the jacket; the politicals wear a red triangle; and the Jews, who form the large majority, wear the Jewish star, red and yellow. SS men exist but are few and outside the camp, and are seen relatively infrequently. Our effective masters in practice are the green triangles, who have a free hand over us, as well as those of the other two categories who are ready to help them—and they are not few.

And we have learnt other things, more or less quickly, according to our intelligence: to reply *"Jawohl,"* never to ask questions, always to pretend to understand. We have learnt the value of food; now we also diligently scrape the bottom of the bowl after the ration and we hold it under our chins when we eat bread so as not to lose the crumbs. We, too, know that it is not the same thing to be given a ladleful of soup from the top or from the bottom of the vat, and we are already able to judge, according to the capacity of the various vats, what is the most suitable place to try and reach in the queue when we line up.

We have learnt that everything is useful: the wire to tie up our shoes, the rags to wrap around our feet, waste paper to (illegally) pad out our jacket against the cold. We have learnt, on the other hand, that everything can be stolen, in fact is automatically stolen as soon as attention is relaxed; and to avoid this, we had to learn the art of sleeping with our head on a bundle made up of our jacket and containing all our belongings, from the bowl to the shoes.

We already know in good part the rules of the camp, which are incredibly complicated. The prohibitions are innumerable: to approach nearer to the barbed wire than two yards; to sleep with one's jacket, or without one's pants, or with one's cap on one's head; to use certain washrooms or latrines which are *"nur für Kapos"* or *"nur für Reichsdeutsche"*; not to go for the shower on the prescribed day, or to go there on a day not prescribed; to leave the hut with one's jacket unbuttoned, or with the collar raised; to carry paper or straw under one's clothes against the cold; to wash except stripped to the waist.

The rites to be carried out were infinite and senseless: every morning one had to make the "bed" perfectly flat and smooth; smear one's muddy and repellent wooden shoes with the appropriate machine grease; scrape the mudstains off one's clothes (paint, grease and rust-stains were, however, permitted); in the evening one had to undergo the control for lice and the control of washing one's feet; on Saturday, have one's beard and hair shaved, mend or have mended one's rags; on Sunday, undergo the general control for skin diseases and the control of buttons on one's jacket, which had to be five.

In addition, there are innumerable circumstances, normally irrelevant, which here become problems. When one's nails grow long, they have to be shortened, which can only be done with one's teeth (for the toenails, the friction of the shoes is sufficient); if a button comes off, one has to tie it on with a piece of wire; if one goes to the latrine or the washroom, everything has to be carried along, always and everywhere, and while one washes one's face, the bundle of clothes has to be held tightly between one's knees; in any other manner it will be stolen in that second. If a shoe hurts, one has to go in the evening to the ceremony of the changing of the shoes: this tests the skill of the individual who, in the middle of the incredible crowd, has to be able to choose at an eye's glance one (not a pair, one) shoe, which fits. Because once the choice is made, there can be no second change.

And do not think that shoes form a factor of secondary importance in the life of the Lager. Death begins with the shoes; for most of us, they show themselves to be instruments of torture, which after a few hours of marching cause painful sores which become fatally infected. Whoever has them is forced to walk as if he was dragging a convict's chain (this explains the strange gait of the army which returns every evening on parade); he arrives last everywhere, and everywhere he receives blows. He cannot escape if they run after him; his feet swell and the more they swell, the more the friction with the wood and the cloth of the shoes becomes insupportable. Then only the hospital is left: but to enter the hospital with a diagnosis of *"dicke Füsse"* (swollen feet) is extremely dangerous, because it is well known to all, and especially to the SS, that here there is no cure for that complaint.

And in all this we have not yet mentioned the work, which in its turn is a Gordian knot of laws, taboos and problems.

We all work, except those who are ill (to be recognized as ill implies in itself an important equipment of knowledge and experience). Every morning we leave the camp in squads for the Buna; every evening, in squads, we return. As regards the work, we are divided into about two hundred *Kommandos*, each of which consists of between fifteen and one hundred and fifty men and is commanded by a Kapo. There are good and bad Kommandos; for the most part they are used as transport and the work is quite hard, especially in the winter, if for no other reason merely because it always takes place in the open. There are also skilled Kommandos (electricians, smiths, bricklayers, welders, mechanics, concrete-layers, etc.), each attached to a certain workshop or department of the Buna, and depending more directly on civilian foremen, mostly German and Polish. This naturally only applied to the hours of work; for the rest of the day the skilled workers (there are no more than three or four hundred in all) receive no different treatment from the ordinary workers. The detailing of individuals to the various Kommandos is organized by a special office of the Lager, the *Arbeitsdienst,* which is in continual touch with the civilian direction of the Buna. The *Arbeitsdienst* decided on the basis of unknown criteria, often openly on the basis of protection or corruption, so that if anyone manages to find enough to eat, he is practically certain to get a good post at Buna.

The hours of work vary with the season. All hours of light are working hours: so that from a minimum winter working day (8–12 a.m. and 12:30–4 p.m.) one rises to a maximum summer one (6:30–12 a.m. and 1–6 p.m.). Under no excuse are the Häftlinge allowed to be at work during the hours of darkness or when there is a thick fog, but they work regularly even if it rains or snows or (as occurs quite frequently) if the fierce wind of the Carpathians blows; the reason being that the darkness or fog might provide opportunities to escape.

One Sunday in every two is a regular working day; on the so-called holiday Sundays, instead of working at Buna, one works normally on the upkeep of the Lager, so that days of real rest are extremely rare.

Such will be our life. Every day, according to the established rhythm, *Ausrücken* and *Einrücken,* go out and come in; work, sleep and eat; fall ill, get better or die.

. . . And for how long? But the old ones laugh at this question: they recognize the new arrivals by this question. They laugh and they do not reply. For months and years, the problem of the remote future has grown pale to them and has lost all intensity in face of the far more urgent and concrete problems of the near future: how much one will eat today, if it will snow, if there will be coal to unload.

If we were logical, we would resign ourselves to the evidence that our fate is beyond human knowledge, that every conjecture is arbitrary and demonstrably devoid of foundation. But men are rarely logical when their own fate is at stake; on every occasion, they prefer the extreme positions. According to our character, some of us are immediately convinced that all is lost, that one cannot live here, that the end is near and sure; others are convinced that however hard the present life may be, salvation is probable and not far off, and if we have faith and strength, we will see our houses and our dear ones again. The two classes of pessimists and optimists are not so clearly defined, however, not because there are many agnostics, but because the majority, without memory or coherence, drift between the two extremes, according to the moment and the mood of the person they happen to meet.

Here I am, then, on the bottom. One learns quickly enough to wipe out the past and the future when one is forced to. A fortnight after my arrival I already had the prescribed hunger, that chronic hunger unknown to free men, which makes one dream at night, and settles in all the limbs of one's body. I have already learnt not to let myself be robbed, and in fact if I find a spoon lying around, a piece of string, a button which I can acquire without danger of punishment, I pocket them and consider them mine by full right. On the back of my feet I already have those numb sores that will not heal. I push wagons, I work with a shovel, I turn rotten in the rain, I shiver in the wind; already my own body is no longer mine: my belly is swollen, my limbs emaciated, my face is thick in the morning, hollow in the evening; some of us have yellow skin, others grey. When we do not meet for a few days we hardly recognize each other.

We Italians had decided to meet every Sunday evening in a corner of the Lager, but we stopped it at once, because it was too sad to count our numbers and find fewer each time, and to see each other ever more deformed and more squalid. And it was so tiring to walk those few steps and then, meeting each other, to remember and to think. It was better not to think.

michihiko hachiya ————————————————————————

from Hiroshima Diary

Michihiko Hachiya (1903–   ) was born in Okayama Prefecture in Japan. He was educated at Okayama Medical College, receiving his medical degree in 1929. He has taught in Japanese medical schools, and from 1939 to 1942 was the medical officer at the Hiroshima Communications Bureau. He then was appointed Director of the Hiroshima Communications Hospital, a position he retained through 1955. He has written for Japanese medical journals and published *Stray Notes of a Doctor* in 1942. *Hiroshima Diary* (1955) is a day-by-day record of the atomic-bomb attack on Hiroshima and its aftermath. The following selection is the first chapter of that book.

6 August 1945

The hour was early; the morning still, warm, and beautiful. Shimmering leaves, reflecting sunlight from a cloudless sky, made a pleasant contrast with shadows in my garden as I gazed absently through wide-flung doors opening to the south.

Clad in drawers and undershirt, I was sprawled on the living room floor exhausted because I had just spent a sleepless night on duty as an air warden in my hospital.

Suddenly, a strong flash of light startled me—and then another. So well does one recall little things that I remember vividly how a stone lantern in the garden became brilliantly lit and I debated whether this light was caused by a magnesium flare or sparks from a passing trolley.

Garden shadows disappeared. The view where a moment before all had been so bright and sunny was now dark and hazy. Through swirling dust I could barely discern a wooden column that had supported one corner of my house. It was leaning crazily and the roof sagged dangerously.

Moving instinctively, I tried to escape, but rubble and fallen timbers barred the way. By picking my way cautiously I managed to reach the *rōka* and stepped down into my garden. A profound weakness overcame me, so I stopped to regain my strength. To my surprise I discovered that I was completely naked. How odd! Where were my drawers and undershirt?

Reprinted with the permission of the University of North Carolina Press from *Hiroshima Diary* by Michihiko Hachiya, translated and edited by Warner Wells, M.D.

What had happened?

All over the right side of my body I was cut and bleeding. A large splinter was protruding from a mangled wound in my thigh, and something warm trickled into my mouth. My cheek was torn, I discovered as I felt it gingerly, with the lower lip laid wide open. Embedded in my neck was a sizable fragment of glass which I matter-of-factly dislodged, and with the detachment of one stunned and shocked I studied it and my blood-stained hand.

Where was my wife?

Suddenly thoroughly alarmed, I began to yell for her: "Yaeko-san! Yaeko-san! Where are you?"

Blood began to spurt. Had my carotid artery been cut? Would I bleed to death? Frightened and irrational, I called out again: "It's a five-hundred-ton bomb! Yaeko-san, where are you? A five-hundred-ton bomb has fallen!"

Yaeko-san, pale and frightened, her clothes torn and blood-stained, emerged from the ruins of our house holding her elbow. Seeing her, I was reassured. My own panic assuaged, I tried to reassure her.

"We'll be all right," I exclaimed. "Only let's get out of here as fast as we can."

She nodded, and I motioned for her to follow me.

The shortest path to the street lay through the house next door so through the house we went—running, stumbling, falling, and then running again until in headlong flight we tripped over something and fell sprawling into the street. Getting to my feet, I discovered that I had tripped over a man's head.

"Excuse me! Excuse me, please!" I cried hysterically.

There was no answer. The man was dead. The head had belonged to a young officer whose body was crushed beneath a massive gate.

We stood in the street, uncertain and afraid, until a house across from us began to sway and then with a rending motion fell almost at our feet. Our own house began to sway, and in a minute it, too, collapsed in a cloud of dust. Other buildings caved in or toppled. Fires sprang up and whipped by a vicious wind began to spread.

It finally dawned on us that we could not stay there in the street, so we turned our steps towards the hospital.* Our home was gone; we were wounded and needed treatment; and after all, it was my duty to be with my staff. This latter was an irrational thought—what good could I be to anyone, hurt as I was.

We started out, but after twenty or thirty steps I had to stop. My breath became short, my heart pounded, and my legs gave way under me. An overpowering thirst seized me and I begged Yaeko-san to find me some water. But there was no water to be found. After a little my strength somewhat returned and we were able to go on.

*Dr. Hachiya's home was only a few hundred meters from the hospital.

CHAPTER FOUR / *Survival*

I was still naked, and although I did not feel the least bit of shame, I was disturbed to realize that modesty had deserted me. On rounding a corner we came upon a soldier standing idly in the street. He had a towel draped across his shoulder, and I asked if he would give it to me to cover my nakedness. The soldier surrendered the towel quite willingly but said not a word. A little later I lost the towel, and Yaeko-san took off her apron and tied it around my loins.

Our progress towards the hospital was interminably slow, until finally, my legs, stiff from drying blood, refused to carry me farther. The strength, even the will, to go on deserted me, so I told my wife, who was almost as badly hurt as I, to go on alone. This she objected to, but there was no choice. She had to go ahead and try to find someone to come back for me.

Yaeko-san looked into my face for a moment, and then, without saying a word, turned away and began running towards the hospital. Once, she looked back and waved and in a moment she was swallowed up in the gloom. It was quite dark now, and with my wife gone, a feeling of dreadful loneliness overcame me.

I must have gone out of my head lying there in the road because the next thing I recall was discovering that the clot on my thigh had been dislodged and blood was again spurting from the wound. I pressed my hand to the bleeding area and after a while the bleeding stopped and I felt better.

Could I go on?

I tried. It was all a nightmare—my wounds, the darkness, the road ahead. My movements were ever so slow; only my mind was running at top speed.

In time I came to an open space where the houses had been removed to make a fire lane. Through the dim light I could make out ahead of me the hazy outlines of the Communications Bureau's big concrete building, and beyond it the hospital. My spirits rose because I knew that now someone would find me; and if I should die, at least my body would be found.

I paused to rest. Gradually things around me came into focus. There were the shadowy forms of people, some of whom looked like walking ghosts. Others moved as though in pain, like scarecrows, their arms held out from their bodies with forearms and hands dangling. These people puzzled me until I suddenly realized that they had been burned and were holding their arms out to prevent the painful friction of raw surfaces rubbing together. A naked woman carrying a naked baby came into view. I averted my gaze. Perhaps they had been in the bath. But then I saw a naked man, and it occurred to me that, like myself, some strange thing had deprived them of their clothes. An old woman lay near me with an expression of suffering on her face; but she made no sound. Indeed, one thing was common to everyone I saw— complete silence.

All who could were moving in the direction of the hospital. I joined in the dismal parade when my strength was somewhat recovered, and at last reached the gates of the Communications Bureau.

Familiar surroundings, familiar faces. There was Mr. Iguchi and Mr. Yoshihiro and my old friend, Mr. Sera, the head of the business office. They hastened to give me a hand, their expressions of pleasure changing to alarm when they saw that I was hurt. I was too happy to see them to share their concern.

No time was lost over greetings. They eased me onto a stretcher and carried me into the Communications Building, ignoring my protests that I could walk. Later, I learned that the hospital was so overrun that the Communications Bureau had to be used as an emergency hospital. The rooms and corridors were crowded with people, many of whom I recognized as neighbors. To me it seemed that the whole community was there.

My friends passed me through an open window into a janitor's room recently converted to an emergency first-aid station. The room was a shambles; fallen plaster, broken furniture, and debris littered the floor; the walls were cracked; and a heavy steel window casement was twisted and almost wrenched from its seating. What a place to dress the wounds of the injured.

To my great surprise who should appear but my private nurse, Miss Kado, and Mr. Mizoguchi, and old Mrs. Saeki. Miss Kado set about examining my wounds without speaking a word. No one spoke. I asked for a shirt and pajamas. They got them for me, but still no one spoke. Why was everyone so quiet?

Miss Kado finished the examination, and in a moment it felt as if my chest was on fire. She had begun to paint my wounds with iodine and no amount of entreaty would make her stop. With no alternative but to endure the iodine, I tried to divert myself by looking out the window.

The hospital lay directly opposite with part of the roof and the third floor sunroom in plain view, and as I looked up, I witnessed a sight which made me forget my smarting wounds. Smoke was pouring out of the sunroom windows. The hospital was afire!

"Fire!" I shouted. "Fire! Fire! The hospital is on fire!"

My friends looked up. It was true. The hospital *was* on fire.

The alarm was given and from all sides people took up the cry. The high-pitched voice of Mr. Sera, the business officer, rose above the others, and it seemed as if his was the first voice I had heard that day. The uncanny stillness was broken. Our little world was now in pandemonium.

I remember that Dr. Sasada, chief of the Pediatric Service, came in and tried to reassure me, but I could scarcely hear him above the din. I heard Dr. Hinoi's voice and then Dr. Koyama's. Both were shouting orders to evacuate the hospital and with such vigor that it sounded as though the sheer strength of their voices could hasten those who were slow to obey.

The sky became bright as flames from the hospital mounted. Soon the

Bureau was threatened and Mr. Sera gave the order to evacuate. My stretcher was moved into a rear garden and placed beneath an old cherry tree. Other patients limped into the garden or were carried until soon the entire area became so crowded that only the very ill had room to lie down. No one talked, and the ominous silence was relieved only by a subdued rustle among so many people, restless, in pain, anxious, and afraid, waiting for something else to happen.

The sky filled with black smoke and glowing sparks. Flames rose and the heat set currents of air in motion. Updrafts became so violent that sheets of zinc roofing were hurled aloft and released, humming and twirling, in erratic flight. Pieces of flaming wood soared and fell like fiery swallows. While I was trying to beat out the flames, a hot ember seared my ankle. It was all I could do to keep from being burned alive.

The Bureau started to burn, and window after window became a square of flame until the whole structure was converted into a crackling, hissing inferno.

Scorching winds howled around us, whipping dust and ashes into our eyes and up our noses. Our mouths became dry, our throats raw and sore from the biting smoke pulled into our lungs. Coughing was uncontrollable. We would have moved back, but a group of wooden barracks behind us caught fire and began to burn like tinder.

The heat finally became too intense to endure, and we were left no choice but to abandon the garden. Those who could fled; those who could not perished. Had it not been for my devoted friends, I would have died, but again, they came to the rescue and carried my stretcher to the main gate on the other side of the Bureau.

Here, a small group of people were already clustered, and here I found my wife. Dr. Sasada and Miss Kado joined us.

Fires sprang up on every side as violent winds fanned flames from one building to another. Soon, we were surrounded. The ground we held in front of the Communications Bureau became an oasis in a desert of fire. As the flames came closer the heat became more intense, and if someone in our group had not had the presence of mind to drench us with water* from a fire hose, I doubt if anyone could have survived.

Hot as it was, I began to shiver. The drenching was too much. My heart pounded; things began to whirl until all before me blurred.

"*Kurushii,*" I murmured weakly. "I am done."

The sound of voices reached my ears as though from a great distance and

---

*The water mains entered the city from the north and since the Communications Bureau was in the northern edge of the city, its water supply was not destroyed.

MICHIHIKO HACHIYA / from *Hiroshima Diary*   *219* finally became louder as if close at hand. I opened my eyes; Dr. Sasada was feeling my pulse. What had happened? Miss Kado gave me an injection. My strength gradually returned. I must have fainted.

Huge raindrops began to fall. Some thought a thunderstorm was beginning and would extinguish the fires. But these drops were capricious. A few fell and then a few more and that was all the rain we saw.*

The first floor of the Bureau was now ablaze and flames were spreading rapidly towards our little oasis by the gate. Right then, I could hardly understand the situation, much less do anything about it.

An iron window frame, loosened by fire, crashed to the ground behind us. A ball of fire whizzed by me, setting my clothes ablaze. They drenched me with water again. From then on I am confused as to what happened.

I do remember Dr. Hinoi because of the pain, the pain I felt when he jerked me to my feet. I remember being moved or rather dragged, and my whole spirit rebelling against the torment I was made to endure.

My next memory is of an open area. The fires must have receded. I was alive. My friends had somehow managed to rescue me again.

A head popped out of an air-raid dugout, and I heard the unmistakable voice of old Mrs. Saeki: "Cheer up, doctor! Everything will be all right. The north side is burnt out. We have nothing further to fear from the fire."

I might have been her son, the way the old lady calmed and reassured me. And indeed, she was right. The entire northern side of the city was completely burned. The sky was still dark, but whether it was evening or midday I could not tell. It might even have been the next day. Time had no meaning. What I had experienced might have been crowded into a moment or been endured through the monotony of eternity.

Smoke was still rising from the second floor of the hospital, but the fire had stopped. There was nothing left to burn, I thought; but later I learned that the first floor of the hospital had escaped destruction largely through the courageous efforts of Dr. Koyama and Dr. Hinoi.

The streets were deserted except for the dead. Some looked as if they had been frozen by death while in the full action of flight; others lay sprawled as though some giant had flung them to their death from a great height.

Hiroshima was no longer a city, but a burnt-over prairie. To the east and to the west everything was flattened. The distant mountains seemed nearer than I could ever remember. The hills of Ushita and the woods of Nigitsu loomed out of the haze and smoke like the nose and eyes on a face. How small Hiroshima was with its houses gone.

The wind changed and the sky again darkened with smoke.

---

*There were many reports of a scanty rainfall over the city after the bombing. The drops were described as large and dirty, and some claimed that they were laden with radioactive dust.

Suddenly, I heard someone shout: "Planes! Enemy planes!"

Could that be possible after what had already happened? What was there left to bomb? My thoughts were interrupted by the sound of a familiar name. A nurse calling Dr. Katsube.

"It is Dr. Katsube! It's him!" shouted old Mrs. Saeki, a happy ring to her voice. "Dr. Katsube has come!"

It was Dr. Katsube, our head surgeon, but he seemed completely unaware of us as he hurried past, making a straight line for the hospital. Enemy planes were forgotten, so great was our happiness that Dr. Katsube had been spared to return to us.

Before I could protest, my friends were carrying me into the hospital. The distance was only a hundred meters, but it was enough to cause my heart to pound and make me sick and faint.

I recall the hard table and the pain when my face and lip were sutured, but I have no recollection of the forty or more other wounds Dr. Katsube closed before night.

They removed me to an adjoining room, and I remember feeling relaxed and sleepy. The sun had gone down, leaving a dark red sky. The red flames of the burning city had scorched the heavens. I gazed at the sky until sleep overtook me.

Five Days in the Favela

Although she had been poor most of her life, Carolina Maria de Jesus (1913–   )
did not realize the ultimate degradation of poverty until she was forced to live in
a *favela* above São Paulo, Brazil. Built in the hills overlooking metropolitan cities,
Brazilian *favelas* are among the most squalid slums on earth. In 1947, six months
pregnant, abandoned by her lover, turned out by the white family that employed
her as a domestic, Carolina lugged boards from a church construction site five
miles from her *favela* and put up the shack that was to be her home. For twelve
years she kept herself and her three children alive, partially by foraging for food
among the garbage cans of the rich. She maintained her sanity by writing fantasies
of wealth and opulence as well as a diary of *favela* life. A local journalist heard
of the diary, read it, and recognized its power and humanity. Eventually, he saw
to it that the diary was published. *Child of the Dark: The Diary of Carolina Maria
de Jesus* (1962) was an immediate sensation, selling more copies than any other
book in Brazil's publishing history. The following selection is reprinted from it.

───────────────────────────────────────

May 23

I got up feeling sad this morning because it was raining. The shack is in
terrible disorder. And I don't have soap to wash the dishes. I say "dishes"
from force of habit. But they are really tin cans. If I had soap I would wash
the clothes. I'm really not negligent. If I walk around dirty it's because I'm
trapped in the life of a *favelado*. I've come to the conclusion that for those
who aren't going to Heaven, it doesn't help to look up. It's the same with
us who don't like the favela, but are obliged to live in one. . . . It doesn't
help to look up.

I made a meal. The grease frying in the pan was beautiful. What a dazzling
display! The children smile watching the food cooking in the pans. Still more
when it is rice and beans—it's a holiday for them.

In the old days macaroni was the most expensive dish. Now it's rice and
beans that have replaced the macaroni. They've crossed over to the side of

the nobility. Even you, rice and beans, have deserted us! You who were the friends of the marginal ones, the *favelados*, the needy. Just look. They are not within reach of the unhappy ones of the Garbage Dump. Who has not flown off is senhor cornmeal. But the children don't like cornmeal.

When I put the food on the table João smiled. He ate and didn't mention the black color of the beans.[1] Because black is our life. Everything is black around us.

In the streets and shops I see the posters with the names of candidates for deputy. Some names are already known. They are the repeaters who have already failed once at the ballot boxes. But the people are not interested in elections. Our elections are just a Trojan Horse that appears once every four years.

The sky is beautiful, worthy of contemplation because the drifting clouds are forming dazzling landscapes. Soft breezes pass by carrying the perfume of flowers. And the sun is always punctual at rising and setting. The birds travel in space, showing off in their happiness. The night brings up the sparkling stars to adorn the blue sky. There are so many beautiful things in the world that are impossible to describe. Only one thing saddens us: the prices when we go shopping. They overshadow all the beauty that exists.

Theresa, Meryi's sister, drank poison. And for no reason. They say she found a note from a woman in her lover's pocket. It ate away her mouth, her throat, and her stomach. She lost a lot of blood. The doctors say that even if she does get well she will be helpless. She has two sons, one four years old and the other nine months.

May 26

At dawn it was raining. I only have four cruzeiros, a little food left over from yesterday, and some bones. I went to look for water to boil the bones. There is still a little macaroni and I made a soup for the children. I saw a neighbor washing beans.[2] How envious I became. It's been two weeks that I haven't washed clothes because I haven't any soap. I sold some boards for 40 cruzeiros. The woman told me she'd pay today. If she pays I'll buy soap.

For days there hasn't been a policeman in the favela, but today one came

---

[1] Black beans in almost every part of Brazil, except Rio, are looked down upon as the lowest thing that can be eaten. In the northeast poor families shut their windows out of shame that neighbors will see them eating black beans rather than brown ones.

[2] Beans, like rice, must be picked over to get rid of the rotten kernels, and then washed to take away dust and pieces of dirt and other foreign matter. The *favelados* buy these staples at street fairs from huge wooden bins that are never covered over.

because Julião beat his father. He gave him such a violent blow that the old man cried and went to call the police.

May 27

It seems that the slaughterhouse threw kerosene on their garbage dump so the *favelados* would not look for meat to eat. I didn't have any breakfast and walked around half dizzy. The daze of hunger is worse than that of alcohol. The daze of alcohol makes us sing, but the one of hunger makes us shake. I know how horrible it is to only have air in the stomach.

I began to have a bitter taste in my mouth. I thought: is there no end to the bitterness of life? I think that when I was born I was marked by fate to go hungry. I filled one sack of paper. When I entered Paulo Guimarães Street, a woman gave me some newspapers. They were clean and I went to the junk yard picking up everything that I found. Steel, tin, coal, everything serves the *favelado*. Leon weighed the paper and I got six cruzeiros.

I wanted to save the money to buy beans but I couldn't because my stomach was creaming and torturing me.

I decided to do something about it and bought a bread roll. What a surprising effect food has on our organisms. Before I ate, I saw the sky, the trees, and the birds all yellow, but after I ate, everything was normal to my eyes.

Food in the stomach is like fuel in machines. I was able to work better. My body stopped weighing me down. I started to walk faster. I had the feeling that I was gliding in space. I started to smile as if I was witnessing a beautiful play. And will there ever be a drama more beautiful than that of eating? I felt that I was eating for the first time in my life.

The Radio Patrol arrived. They came to take the two Negro boys who had broken into the power station. Four and six years old. It's easy to see that they are of the favela. Favela children are the most ragged children in the city. What they can find in the streets they eat. Banana peels, melon rind, and even pineapple husks. Anything that is too tough to chew, they grind. These boys had their pockets filled with aluminum coins, that new money in circulation.

May 28

It dawned raining. I only have three cruzeiros because I loaned Leila five so she could go get her daughter in the hospital. I'm confused and don't know where to begin. I want to write, I want to work, I want to wash clothes. I'm cold and I don't have any shoes to wear. The children's shoes are worn out.

The worst thing in the favela is that there are children here. All the children of the favela know what a woman's body looks like. Because when the couples that are drunk fight, the woman, so as not to get a beating, runs naked into the street. When the fights start the *favelados* leave whatever they are doing to be present at the battle. So that when the woman goes running naked it's a real show for Joe Citizen. Afterward the comments begin among the children:

"Fernanda ran out nude when Armin was hitting her."

"Oh, I didn't see it. Damn!"

"What does a naked woman look like?"

And then the other, in order to tell him, puts his mouth near his ear. And the loud laughter echoes. Everything that is obscene or pornographic the *favelado* learns quickly.

There are some shacks where prostitutes play their love scenes right in front of the children.

The rich neighbors in the brick houses say we are protected by the politicians. They're wrong. The politicians only show up here in the Garbage Dump at election time. This year we had a visit from a candidate for deputy, Dr. Paulo de Campos Moura, who gave us beans and some wonderful blankets. He came at an opportune moment, before it got cold.

What I want to clear up about the people who live in the favela is the following: the only ones who really survive here are the *nordestinos*.[3] They work and don't squander. They buy a house or go back up north.

Here in the favela there are those who build shacks to live in and those who build them to rent. And the rents are from 500 to 700 cruzeiros. Those who make shacks to sell spend 4,000 cruzeiros and sell them for 11,000. Who made a lot of shacks to sell was Tiburcio.

May 29

It finally stopped raining. The clouds glided toward the horizon. Only the cold attacked us. Many people in the favela don't have warm clothing. When one has shoes he won't have a coat. I choke up watching the children walk in the mud. It seems that some new people have arrived in the favela. They are ragged with undernourished faces. They improvised a shack. It hurts me to see so much pain, reserved for the working class. I stared at my new companion in misfortune. She looked at the favela with its mud and sickly children. It was the saddest look I'd ever seen. Perhaps she has no more illusions. She had given her life over to misery.

There will be those who reading what I write will say—this is untrue. But misery is real.

What I revolt against is the greed of men who squeeze other men as if they were squeezing oranges.

Nordestinos: forced by land-parching droughts and almost no industry, the poor of the north swarm into cities like São Paulo and Rio looking for work. Needing a place to live, they choose the favelas and end up worse off than they were before.

All the Children Sang, "Lord, Let Me Die Easy"

Having dropped out of high school in New York in 1968 because she was "disgusted with the New York City school system," Eon Chontay Cjohnathan (1950–   ) came to San Francisco, attended night school and received her high school diploma in 1969. She is married to a painter-sculptor and started studies at Laney College in Oakland in 1971. She intends to continue both her education and her writing.

I am Black. I am a woman. Most of my life has been spent in the broken-down, rat-infested, overpriced slums of Harlem, and I am angry.

Those years spent in Harlem were not, to say the least, the happiest of my life. And because I was born there and raised on her streets until I was sixteen, I can rightly say that my childhood ended soon after I left the womb. By age five, I was solely responsible for my own wardrobe (what little there was of one), including being certain that I had clean underwear and socks. Mama worked as a domestic in some white woman's home on Fifth Avenue. She cooked, cleaned, and took care of the woman's son—all for eight dollars a day. So, with her gone from morning till early evening, I was left to dress myself, prepare my own breakfast, get to kindergarten on time, and get home when school was over.

Mama worked hard; her rewards were few. She labored long hours in a job that had neither dignity nor opportunity. Her wages were low and she always looked shabby. She never had the money to buy anything that was new, and even the hand-me-downs cleaned and pressed didn't do much for her appearance because her stockings were always raggedy. And since spending money on stockings meant that there would be less food money, she usually went in need of new ones. But beneath the tatters and the worn-out shoes was a sensitive and intelligent woman.

I missed Mama when she went away to work. It seemed wrong that she should be on some distant street caring for some plump, white baby while I was home burning my fingers on greasy frying pans, hot ovens, and steaming irons. It seemed wrong that I should be left alone to be afraid and in danger

Original publication in this volume, by permission of the author.

while she was downtown protecting and watching over some white woman's child. I needed her to be with me. I needed her every time I entered our tenement building, every time I ran the risk of being assaulted by some angry would-be robber or pounced upon by some strung-out junkie or devoured by some sexually depraved male neighbor. I needed her when I tried to cook my own bacon and egg sandwiches, but set the cheap plastic kitchen curtains on fire instead. I needed her when it was four o'clock on some wintry Harlem afternoon and someone knocked at the door and I had to shout, "My mother isn't home right now, and I'm not allowed to open the door; you'll have to come back later," and I hoped that he would. I hoped that he would go away and not try to break the lock and force his way in, whoever he was. I needed her when I was coughing, shivering, and vomiting from some illness at a time when she could not leave work in order to get me to the public hospital. I needed her, but she continued to board that bus and ride silently into white oblivion. Our lives were an endless cycle of good-byes and weary sighs.

I remember going to work with her once. I was seven. We rode the bus from Harlem to downtown Manhattan. It seemed like such a long ride. I sat silently with my nose pressed against the cool glass window and watched the world go by. I watched us go from one end of Harlem to the other. I watched Central Park unfold before my eyes. I had never seen the park before. I felt proud that part of it was in Harlem. But we kept on going, and soon all of the people in the streets were white and they were dressed in fine clothes and walking in a fancy way. I knew we weren't in Harlem any longer. We were way downtown—downtown in the white man's world. I looked around the bus; Mama and I were the only colored passengers left.

The white woman's home was as I had expected, very beautiful. There was even wall-to-wall carpeting and a brown-brick fireplace. Her son was also as I had expected, pink and round. His name was Jeffrey. He was five years old and I didn't like him. I thought he was dumb and spoiled. The range of his wit had, by age five, extended no further than the ability to play with toys and cry for the things he wanted but did not already have. Crying always seemed to work. But Mama suggested that I play with him and his toys, be nice to him, and not fight. So I did, and everything seemed to be going all right until Jeffrey, in his well-bred ignorance, found the nerve to ask Mama and me why we were "black." This was in 1957, when people of color were still being called "Negroes," so Mama didn't take to the idea of being called "black." She instructed Jeffrey and me to follow her into the kitchen. When we got there, she took a heavy, dark skillet down from one of the shelves and, holding it in front of Jeffrey, said, "This is black; we are brown," and left it at that. It was not long before I started pinching the little bastard real hard whenever Mama wasn't looking.

Keeping our tenement apartment "straightened up" soon became my responsibility. I knew that Mama worked all day keeping someone else's property spic and span, so I did not think it unreasonable of her to want to come home to an orderly place. She couldn't have expected much from my endeavors, because no matter how much "straightening up" or "putting away" I did, the apartment would still look depressing. Our furniture was cheap, the linoleum-covered floors were badly worn, and the plaster walls and ceilings were peeling. We even needed a new broom. But I "straightened up" anyway. I washed the dishes, swept the floors, made the bed, put away clothing, lined up the bath towels neatly on their racks, and took out the garbage. I often did my job in a hurry; there were even times when I dared not do it at all. Mama never fussed or whipped me; she just sighed that weary sigh of hers and then remained silent for the rest of the evening. Her silence made me feel more uncomfortable than any whipping ever could.

Harlem and all that came with it was home. It was all we knew. Rent was expensive for what we got, and what we got was what the rest of the city didn't want: poverty, hunger, disease, rats, and a high mortality rate. The tenement buildings were old and electrically unsafe, so there were numerous fires. The plumbing was so out of date and in need of repair that toilets were constantly broken and sinks were always backing up. The landlord rarely made repairs, and what usually resulted was the flooding of bathroom and kitchen floors and the eventual caving in of someone's ceiling. Such a thing happened to me when I was nine years old.

The leaking bathroom ceiling took a little getting used to. It had been a month or two since we last had problems with it, and we had once again gotten used to using the bathroom without having to run out every time we heard our upstairs neighbor flush his toilet. But the haphazard repairs that were made by the last visiting plumber had come undone.

The toilet water dribbled very slowly at first. A drip here, a drip there. Mama and I watched as the clear, round droplets squeezed through the cracked plaster. We waited, hoping that the leak was only the result of a simple toilet overflow. But by the third or fourth day, the water seeped through at a steady pace and the once random droplets had turned into an uninterrupted vertical stream of unclean toilet water. In the following three weeks, the paint and plaster began to peel and the ceiling began to rot.

Mama had been appealing to the landlord to make the necessary repairs for at least two months before the ceiling finally fell in. She had called his office several times and written a number of letters, politely stating the condition and requesting prompt repair. His only reply was a disconcerting, "All right, lady. I'll get somebody over there right away." No one ever came. After weeks of being put off and asked to "Please call back later," she began writing letters to the city health department and to the politicians of our district.

By this time, she had become very good at writing short, curt letters explaining the situation.

Dear Sir:

I am again writing in reference to the dangerous and unsanitary plumbing condition existing at 262 West 154th Street, Apartment #18. I have called the landlord's office and written numerous letters requesting the repair of our leaking bathroom ceiling. To date, no repairs have been made.

If action is not taken within five days to correct this condition, I shall make my complaints known to higher officials.

Sincerely,

Mrs. Helen R. King

She did. No one responded.

There was no time for me to run, no time to get out, no time to escape, before it felt as though the bathroom walls were closing in and sandwiching me between large chunks of plaster, toilet fixtures, and wood. It all happened so quickly. There was the loud, almost deafening sound of objects breaking through the crust of bathroom ceiling. Within seconds, I was knocked to the floor, my shoulders heavy with brittle, powder-white plaster, beams of brown-gray, stinking, splintered wood, and large, jagged, glasslike pieces of what used to be someone's porcelain toilet. I felt as though someone had dropped a bomb and it had landed directly on top of me. I felt so heavy. I had dirt and dust and splinters in my eyes, the taste of dry, bitter, unclean wood in my mouth. My body was numb. I was crying. I was trembling. Mama was screaming. Everyone who lived in the building was shouting and crowding around the narrow bathroom door. Someone tried to lift me out from under the heap of debris and rubble. The plaster began to roll from my back and arms and legs. Someone else called an ambulance and the police.

Two policemen arrived before the city ambulance did. They were big and white and dressed in blue. One of them stood by the apartment door trying to keep our neighbors out and answering their questions. The other came into the bathroom to inspect the "victim" and the "situation that had caused the accident." He looked down at me. I was scared and shaking and huddled on the rim of the bathtub. He looked up at the big, empty hole in the broken ceiling. He shook his head from side to side and muttered in a low, sympathetic tone, "That's a shame. That's a damn shame." He went on to say how I could have been killed and that those Jew landlords had no "human" right to make people live in such conditions. He then told Mama to tell me to tell the doctors that I had hurt my back. "There's no way they can prove it," he said. "Just tell 'em you hurt your back." He looked up at the hole again, then looked down and started pushing bits of plaster around the floor with his big black shoe. Two ambulance attendants arrived. They propped me up and began carrying me down the five flights of tenement stairs. All of our neighbors were in the hallway. They tried to comfort me and Mama as we passed by. When the two attendants lifted me into the ambulance, Mama was still crying, I was still scared, and the big, white, blue-suited policeman was still shaking his head and saying in a low voice, "That's a shame. That's a damn shame."

Mama filed a lawsuit against the landlord. She charged him with failure to make repairs. He fought the charge. The case took seven years. In the end, we got six hundred dollars. Mama paid the lawyer's fee and used the remaining money to move us out of Harlem.

Those remaining seven years in Harlem were the most agonizing and rage-filled years of my life. I saw more death, tasted more tears, fought more fights, and heard more tales of sorrow than I could ever again experience. I grew older, life grew harder. Life grew harder, I grew older; the two were inseparable. The Negro-infested streets were forever filled with the sounds of Harlem's people perfecting their game of survival. Life meant survival and, in that crowded area less than two miles square, survival was a brute impulse. It was an impulse that moved men toward killing and maiming each other, toward lying and cheating and stealing from each other, toward making fools of each other—and I was caught in the midst of it all.

Most of my years in school were spent in an angry frenzy. I was uncontrollable, destructive, stubborn, and mean. My fear, confusion, depression, and feelings of neglect were disguising themselves as a raging nine-year-old hurricane. I was soon labeled by the school officials "problem child" and "underachiever." One elementary school teacher went so far as to tell me that I was a masochist. "What's that?" I asked. "Go home and look it up," was her only reply. I didn't even know how to *spell* the word!

I had an endless list of things to do. I burned mailboxes, broke windows, pulled fire alarms, stole candy, fruit, and money; I harassed store keepers, and I even phoned in a bomb threat to my elementary school. Mama left for work early that day, and I had already decided to be late for school. I had a lot of extra time on my hands. I was smart enough to know that I couldn't use our private telephone to call in a bomb scare, so I started looking for a dime. I looked under the bed at first, then under the dresser and finally behind the sofa. When all three places failed me, I started searching through Mama's coat pockets. I found one. I used our telephone to call Helen, who was my best friend at the time. In a matter of minutes, we were on our way in search of a public telephone booth.

"Hurry, hurry—get the children out!" I said in my best Russian accent. Finally, all of those years of watching Bullwinkle, Boris, and Natasha were paying off! "Hurry, hurry—there's a bomb, a bomb in the school! Get the children out!" I hung up.

Trying to look extremely nonchalant, but also feeling very proud, Helen and I started walking toward school. When we reached the corner, we could hear the school fire-alarm bells ringing, and seconds later we saw all of the pupils and teachers come filing out in neatly assembled lines.

"Hot diggity!" I said.

"Whooo doggy!" Helen replied.

We found our class and took our places in line.

The fire department and bomb squad arrived. The whole inspection took a little more than two hours. Needless to say, no bomb was found. But no one seemed to mind. The teachers used the time to congregate in little groups. It was an outside coffee break for them, simply minus the coffee. The school day was cut short by two hours, and that was the whole idea.

Whenever I grew tired of my old routine, I would stop, catch my breath, backtrack my steps, and go looking for a fight. Fights were popular and easy to start:

"I heard you like my boyfriend."

"Maybe I do and maybe I don't."

"Well, alls I'm askin' is, 'Do you like my boyfriend or not?' "

"Maybe I do and maybe I don't."

"Well, I know what I heard. Do you or don't you?"

"Ain't none a' yo' business."

"Girl, you callin' me a liar?"

At this point an impatient child instigator would place his hand between us and say, "First one hits my hand starts the fight." And a fight would inevitably follow.

There were a number of things I would do to force a child to fight. Anything from laughing at him for having rats and roaches—only to have him mutter an embarrassing "I do not" and then get knocked in the teeth for lying—to making fun of someone for having holes in his socks: "Boy, your socks must go to church every day. They sure is the holiest socks I ever seen. Ain't your family got no needles and threads?" On occasion, when all else failed, I had simply to say something about another kid's mother. "Child, your mammy ain't got no underwear and can't cook worth beans." A fight in which a kid was defending his mother could last for days.

The fights must have looked hideous. Our small black bodies circled by a crowd of shouting children. We kicked, bit, pulled hair, and scratched each other. The only rules were that there were none. Our smooth brown legs were soon scraped by the pavement, and our hair would come undone. And when it was over, we would stand there with tearful eyes, scratched-up faces, bloody knees, torn dresses, untied shoes, and hair on end. I quickly made my own rules:

1. I would not fight with anyone who had long fingernails.
2. If I lost, I would stay home from school the next day, for the embarrassment would be more painful than the fight.

There were times when everyone in Harlem seemed to be fighting. Mothers fought with mothers over the same feud their children were fighting over. Fathers fought with their sons, each in an attempt to prove his masculinity. Brothers fought with sisters over food or clothing. Uncles fought with aunts over beer or liquor. Entire households fought over money and repairs. The anger at life and the frustration with being alive were evident everywhere. We were all so weary. So weary of the same old circumstances and of all the pain. And in our weariness, we lashed out not at our oppressors, but at the souls closest to us, our own Black selves. The brutality of it all was heartbreaking.

"Nigger, you fuck with me and I'll cut your throat."

"You're nothin' but tough shit."

"Say it again."

"You're nothin' but tough shit and a sleezy-ass motherfucker."

By this time a crowd had gathered. It was a rare occasion when anyone tried to stop a fight. I looked at Danny and I was afraid for him. I was afraid for him because he had always been so kind to me. He had always treated me with such respect, and now there he was, talking big because he was scared. This argument wasn't child's play.

"Boy, I been livin' twenty-four years and I ain't never took no shit from nobody and I sure as hell ain't startin' now."

"You fuckin' with the bad man now. You gonna get your throat cut. You gonna pay your dues."

"Come on, you jive-time nigger. Think you're so fuckin' much, don't ya? Think you're real hot shit, don't ya?"

"Nigger, I'm gonna kill you if I can."

No one moved. The two arguing men were silent for a while. Then someone let out with a disappointed, "Aw, man, they ain't gonna fight." That was all that was needed. Danny's opponent pulled a knife out from under his pants leg. The knife was long and smooth and shiny. I wanted Danny to stop. I wanted him to apologize. His opponent juggled the knife around in his big, brown hand, then said, "What did you say, man, huh, huh? What did you say?" And Danny said it again. He said it again and I knew it was too late. "I said you're a jive-time nigger and a sleezy-ass motherfucker."

The knife slashed Danny's face and then his chest. He moaned. His yellow knit shirt became stained with blood. Danny tried to hit the man. He tried to hit him, but he hit the knife blade instead. That man was good with his knife. He was sure of himself.

"I'm gonna kill you if I can, nigger. I'm gonna kill you if I can. I'm gonna kill you if I can, nigger. I'm gonna kill you if I can."

Danny was hunched over on the ground. The man was stabbing him and stabbing him and stabbing him. The man kept repeating his lines as though they were a death chant. Danny wiggled a little. His wiggling stopped. He didn't move anymore. He was dead.

I fell in love for the first time when I was twelve. He was seventeen. It was in the winter of 1962, the year the Drifters came out with "Up on the Roof," and Jerry and I spent most of our time standing in front of record shops and huddled together on park benches and in dingy tenement basements. We had nowhere to go. He couldn't take me home; I was too young. And if Mama knew that I was going around with someone who was five years my senior, she would just worry all day about my getting pregnant or something. She had enough to worry about, so I kept my relationship with Jerry a secret from her.

Jerry had processed hair, grown-up ways, and a group of friends who were not at all well liked by my neighbors. His friends drank a lot of wine. When the wine got hold of them, they would start to sing. The group knew a lot of tunes, but they seemed to favor "Blue Moon" and "You Belong to Me." Jerry also had a certain fascination with Jackie Wilson.

"I think I kinda look like him, myself."

"Look like who?" I asked.

"Jackie Wilson."

"Oh but, man, why do you process your hair?"

"Because I like it. Don't you like it?"

I wanted to change the subject. I didn't want to admit that I did like his hair. I couldn't let on that I liked him *that* much.

"Jerry Syphrett, where in hell did you ever get a name like that?"

"I kinda like it myself. It sounds like a white man's name."

He was very proud.

For the first time in my life, I was aware of my love for someone and of my frustration with Harlem. I was frustrated because time moved so slowly; we hoped for so much, and all that Harlem could yield was barren, half-worn. She sheltered us amidst her madness. Her tenements covered us as we loved. Her noise muffled our cries. Her song was sometimes one of love. I grew tired of going home and sleeping alone. Life was so bittersweet.

Two years later, Jerry was dead. He was dead and I felt hollow inside. I felt weightless, lifeless. He was dead and I was alive. I was alive and I would have to bear his death. I wanted to scream. I wanted to scream and cry and scream and cry until I was no more. Oh God, I wanted to be out of that misery. My Lord, how I wanted so not to *be*. The whisper of him was the strongest thing that had ever happened to me, and now he was dead.

No, I wasn't going to his funeral. I couldn't take any more pain. I couldn't be in that crowded parlor, moaning, "Lord God, please don't take him away." Oh no, I couldn't watch his mother cry. Lord Jesus, no, I couldn't watch them lay him in that hole in the ground. I would have gone insane. I didn't want any more death. No more dead and motionless black bodies. No more taste of tears.

Everything around me was dying, and for the first time I realized that if I did not leave, soon I would be dying too. And somehow I made it out. Somehow I am still alive. Somehow I am still sane, still whole. It is a wonder that my only scars are psychological.

Oh Life, you've been so hard, so cruel for so long. You've been so many things and worn so many faces. Endless chains of weary mothers coming home from working in some white woman's kitchen, coming home with aching feet in old hand-me-down shoes two sizes too small. Hungry and almost naked children with survival language, a knot on their heads, and a deep, fleshy scar for every year they've been alive. You've been cruel. You've been strung-out junkies standing on the corners, behind the stairs. Junkies, junkies everywhere, and the pungent smell of freshly coughed vomit. You've been roaches. Roaches in our cupboards, on our clothes, in our bed, in our food. You've been the smell of dead, decaying rats that died in the walls where we had no way of getting to them, so they would stay there and we would live with the smell. We would live with the smell until they didn't smell anymore. You've been hard. You've been our mothers, our brothers, our sisters, our lovers, found dead, and us not able to cry. No time for tears, just time to sit and wonder how soon before our lives would be done. You've been cruel. You've been grandparents and great-grandparents working, slaving five days and as many nights as could be arranged, scrubbing, chauffeuring, cleaning, serving, wiping up the white man's piss, and sewing his woman's dresses because rent was high, food was expensive, and our labor was cheap. You've been a struggle, for our dues have been paid a hundredfold.

White America, you have slaughtered my people. You slew us first in the fields, now in the slums and prisons. You throw us into cells, into tenements, into shacks, into situations that cause us to hate our brothers, to kill them—and then you sit back and watch. Life has been so much easier for you, for you make the guidelines, you make the rules, you stand up and tell us, "This is the way it's supposed to be," and in doing so, you further isolate the Black community from the mainstream of American life.

How long will it take before you realize that we are not white, that we have never been white? How long before you realize that it's hard for a people to remain sane when their work has no dignity, their children have no food, and they live in an overpriced, broken-down, rat-infested, five-flight walk-up flat or worse? How long before you realize that you are living your lives believing that the euphemism of Blackness is the true reality? How long before you realize that the real tragedy is *not* that a few have lived through the pain, but that *so many have died as a result of it?* So many mothers, so many fathers, so many children. So many innocent little children—knowing pain before they know love, tasting bondage before they taste freedom, dying before they even begin to live, dead before it's time to go, and few of them ever die easily.

I am Black. I am a woman. And I am angry.

Letter to Angela Davis

As a teenager George Jackson (1941–1971) fell into trouble with the police in his native Chicago. Because of this, his family moved to Los Angeles, but his troubles with the law continued, and by the time he was fifteen he was serving a prison term. At eighteen he was sentenced to from one year to life for stealing $70 from a gas station. He spent the rest of his life in prison. A self-educated revolutionary ("I met Marx, Lenin, Trotsky, Engels, and Mao when I entered prison and they redeemed me"), Jackson attempted to bring his fellow black prison mates to a revolutionary consciousness and claims to have been ". . . subjected to the most vicious reactionary violence by the state" as a result. He was vaulted to international fame when *Soledad Brother: The Prison Letters of George Jackson* was published in 1970. For many, including Angela Davis, he became a symbol of the oppression of American blacks and their attempt to be free. In 1968 Jackson and two other black inmates of Soledad were charged with the murder of a prison guard. In 1971, two days before the trial which would acquit his two co-defendants began, George Jackson was shot and killed by a prison guard at San Quentin in an alleged escape attempt.

1970

Angela,*

I am certain that they plan to hold me incommunicado. All of my letters except for a few to my immediate family have come back to me with silly comments on my choice of terms. The incoming mail is also sent back to the outside sender. The mail which I do receive is sometimes one or two weeks old. So, my sweet sister, when I reach you, it will be in this manner.

. . . I'm going to write on both sides of this paper, and when I make a mistake I'll just scratch over it and continue on. That is my style, completely informal.

Was that your sister with you in court? If so, she favored you. Both very beautiful people. You should have introduced me.

*Angela Y. Davis.

They are going to take your job, I know they are—anything else would be expecting too much. They can't, however, stop you from teaching in public institutions, can they?

They hate us, don't they? I like it that way, that is the way it's supposed to be. If they didn't hate me I would be doing something very wrong, and then I would have to hate myself. I prefer it this way. I get little hate notes in the folds of my newspaper almost every day now. You know, the racist stuff, traditional "Dear nigger" stuff, and how dead I am going to be one day. They think they're mad at me now, but it's nothing compared to how it will be when I really get mad myself. . . .

Pigs are punks, Angela. We've made a terrible mistake in overestimating these people. It reflects on us badly that we have allowed them to do the things they have done to us. Since they are idiots, what does that make us. I just read Bobby Seale's account of that scene in Chicago (*Ramparts*, June '70). It started in San Francisco with that flight to evade charge. One of the pigs commented that "this was so easy." But it shouldn't have been. Brothers like that are the best of us. It shouldn't have gone down like that. We should never make it easy for them—by relaxing—at this stage of the educational process. Examples are crucially important. Well that's the name of the game right now.

I have ideas, ten years' worth of them, I'd like all those brothers on Fiftieth Street to be aware of them. Tell Fay Stender to give you a copy of my thoughts on Huey Newton and politics. . . . At the end of these writings, titled "Letter to Huey Newton," there should be a note on revolutionary culture and the form it should take in the black American colonies. That was the best section. Without that section the power would be lost. Fay and I don't agree altogether on political method. But that is only because we are viewing things from very different levels of slavery. Mine is an abject slavery.

I think of you all the time. I've been thinking about women a lot lately. Is there anything sentimental or otherwise wrong with that? There couldn't be. It's never bothered me too much before, the sex thing. I would do my exercise and the hundreds of katas, stay busy with something . . . this ten years really has gone pretty quickly. It has destroyed me as a person, a human being that is, but it was sudden, it was a sudden death, it seems like ten days rather than ten years.

Would you like to know a subhuman. I certainly hope you have time. I'm not a very nice person. I'll confess out front, I've been forced to adopt a set of responses, reflexes, attitudes that have made me more kin to the cat than anything else, the big black one. For all of that I am not a selfish person. I don't think so anyway, but I do have myself in mind when I talk about us relating. You would be the generous one, I the recipient of that generosity.

GEORGE JACKSON / *Letter to Angela Davis*

They're killing niggers again down the tier, all day, every day. They are killing niggers and "them protesters" with small workings of mouth. One of them told a pig today that he was going to be awful disappointed with the pig if the pig didn't shoot some niggers or protesters this evening when he got off work. The pig found it very amusing. They went off on a twenty-minute political discussion, pig and his convict supporter. There is something very primitive about these people. Something very fearful. In all the time I've been down here on Maximum Row, no brother has ever spoken to one of these people. We never speak about them, you know, across the cells. Every brother down here is under the influence of the party line, and racist terms like "honky" have never been uttered. All of these are beautiful brothers, ones who have stepped across the line into the position from which there can be no retreat. All are fully committed. They are the most desperate and dauntless of our kind. I love them. They are men and they do not fight with their mouths. They've brought them here from prisons all over the state to be warehoused or murdered. Whichever is more expedient. That Brother Edwards who was murdered in that week in January told his lawyer that he would never get out of prison alive. He was at the time of that statement on Maximum Row, Death Row, Soledad, California. He was twenty-one years old. We have made it a point to never exchange words with these people. But they never relent. Angela, there are some people who will never learn new responses. They will carry what they incorporated into their characters at early youth to the grave. Some can never be educated. As an historian you know how long and how fervently we've appealed to these people to take some of the murder out of their system, their economics, their propaganda. And as an intelligent observer you must see how our appeals were received. We've wasted many generations and oceans of blood trying to civilize these elements over here. It cannot be done in the manner we have attempted it in the past. Dialectics, understanding, love, passive resistance, they won't work on an activistic, maniacal, gory pig. It's going to grow much worse for the black male than it already is, much, much worse. We are going to have to be the vanguard, the catalyst, in any meaningful change.

When generalizing about black women I could never include *you* in any of it that is not complimentary. But my mother at one time tried to make a coward of me, she did the same with Jon. She is changing fast under crisis situation and apocalyptic circumstance. John and Fleeta's mothers did the same to them, or I should say tried. And so did every brother's mother I've ever drawn out. I am reasonably certain that I can draw from every black male in this country some comments to substantiate that his mother, the black female, attempted to aid his survival by discouraging his violence or by turning it inward. The blacks of slave society, U.S.A., have always been a matriarchal subsociety. The implication is clear, black mama is going to have to put a

CHAPTER FOUR / *Survival*

sword in that brother's hand and stop that "Be a good boy" shit. Channel his spirit instead of break it, or help to break it I should say. Do you understand? *All* of the sisters I've ever known personally and through other brothers' accounts begged and bullied us to look for *jobs* instead of being satisfied with the candy-stick take. The strongest impetus a man will ever have, in an individual sense, will come from a woman he admires.

When "Soul" did that feature on you, I discussed you with some of the comrades. One of them asked me what my response would be if it were my job to guard your body (for the party) from the attack of ten armed pigs. I told them my response would be to charge. There would be eleven people hurting but you wouldn't be one of them. Everyone agreed it was the correct response.

As an individual, I am grateful for you. As the black male, I hope that since your inclination is to teach you will give serious consideration to redeeming this very next generation of black males by reaching for today's black female. I am not too certain about my generation. There are a few, and with these few we will keep something. But we have altogether too many pimps and punks, and black capitalists (who want a piece of the putrescent pie). There's no way to predict. Sometimes people change fast. I've seen it happen to brothers overnight. But then they have to learn a whole new set of responses and attack reflexes which can't be learned overnight. So cats like me who have no tomorrows have to provide examples. I have an ideal regarding tomorrow, but I live an hour at a time, right in the present, looking right over my nose for the trouble I know is coming.

There is so much that could be done, right now. . . . But I won't talk about those things right here. I will say that it should never be easy for them to destroy us. If you start with Malcolm X and count *all* of the brothers who have died or been captured since, you will find that not even one of them was really *prepared* for a fight. No imagination or fighting style was evident in any one of the incidents. But each one that died professed to know the nature of our enemies. It should never be so easy for them. Do you understand what I'm saying? Edward V. Hanrahan, Illinois State Attorney General, sent fifteen pigs to raid the Panther headquarters and murder Hampton and Clark. Do you have any idea what would have happened to those fifteen pigs if they had run into as many Viet Cong as there were Panthers in that building. The VC are all little people with less general education than we have. The argument that they have been doing it longer has no validity at all, because they were doing it just as well when they started as they are now. It's very contradictory for a man to teach about the murder in corporate capitalism, to isolate and expose the murderers behind it, to instruct that these madmen are completely without stops, are licentious—totally depraved—and then not make adequate preparations to defend himself from the madman's attack. Either they don't really believe their own spiel or they harbor some sort of subconscious death wish.

None of this should have happened as it did. I don't know if we'll learn in time or not. I am not well here. I pretend that all is well for the benefit of my family's peace of mind. But I'm going to cry to you, so you can let the people of Fiftieth Street know not to let this happen to them, and that they must resist that cat with *all* of their strength when he starts that jail talk.

When the menu reads steak we get a piece of rotten steer (I hope) the size of a quarter. When it reads cake we get something like cornbread. Those are the best things served. When two guys fight, the darker guy will get shot. To supplement their incomes the pigs will bring anything into the prison and sell it to the convict who smuggles money in from his visits. Now black people don't visit their kin in the joint much and those that do can't afford to give up any money. So we have less of everything that could make life more comfortable—and safe (weapons are brought in too). Pigs are fascist right out front, the white prisoner who is con-wise joins the Hitlerian party right here in the joint. He doesn't have to worry about the rules, he stays high. When he decides to attack us, he has the best of weapons (seldom will a pig give a con a gun, though. It has happened, however, in San Quentin three times to my knowledge. But they will provide cutlery and zip guns). The old convict code died years ago. These cons work right with the police against us. The only reason that I am still alive is because I take everything to the extreme, and they know it. I never let any of them get within arm's reach, and their hands must be in full view. When on the yard I would stay close to something to get under. Nothing, absolutely nothing comes as a surprise to me. There is much to be said about these places but I must let this go right now or I won't be able to post it until tomorrow. In the event that you missed it (my writing is terrible, I know), I think a great deal of you. This is one slave that knows how to love. It comes natural and runs deep. Accepting it will never hurt you. Free, open, honest love, that's me.

Should you run into Yvonne* tell her that I love her also and equally. Tell her that I want to see her, up close. Tell her I'm not a possessive cat, never demanding, always cool, never get upset until my (our) face and freedom get involved. But make her understand that I want to hold her (chains and all) and run my tongue in that little gap between her two front teeth. (That should make her smile.)

Power to the People!

George

*Yvonne is Angela Davis's middle name.

I Leave the Prison

One of the towering figures of world literature, Feodor Dostoyevsky (1821–1881) is also one of its most complex and interesting men. Born and raised in Moscow, he was a brilliant student at the College of Military Engineering in St. Petersburg and served his compulsory two years in the army before turning to writing. His first novel, *Poor Folk* (1846), brought him temporary fame, but his association with a group of tepid revolutionaries led to a turn of events that even the novelist Dostoyevsky at his most melodramatic would have been hard-pressed to match. He was arrested and sentenced to death on a vague suspicion of subversion, and on the night of December 22, 1849, he and two companions knelt, blindfolded and freezing, in the Russian winter night waiting for the death by firing squad that would never come. A planned last-minute reprieve in this grimly bizarre official charade saved the men from death, but sent Dostoyevsky to a Siberian prison camp, where he spent the next five years in hard labor. He depicts his prison life in *Memoirs from the House of the Dead* (1862), the last chapter of which is reprinted below. After his release, he was plunged into poverty chiefly because of his compulsive gambling. He produced brilliant novels like *Notes from the Underground* (1866) and *Crime and Punishment* (1866) at breakneck speed in order to pay his creditors. Epileptic, still unable to control his gambling, and in degrading poverty, he wrote *The Idiot* (1869) and *The Possessed* (1871). Dostoyevsky recognized in himself the inner conflict between good and evil and dramatized the complexities of that struggle in *Crime and Punishment* and *The Brothers Karamazov* (1881), in which he delved into the tragic contradictions in men's souls.

. . . I had already reached the last year of my penal servitude. This last year, and especially the very end of my time in the prison, is almost as clear in my memory as the first one. But why should I talk of the details? I recall only that during that year, in spite of all my impatience to come quickly to the end of my term, I found life easier than during all the preceding years of my exile. In the first place, among the prisoners I had by now many friends and well-wishers, who had finally decided that I was a good man. Many of them were devoted to my interests and genuinely fond of me. The Pioneer was very near tears when he accompanied my companion and me out of the prison and when afterwards, although we had been released, we were

From *Memoirs from the House of the Dead* by F. M. Dostoyevsky, translated by Jessie Coulson and published by Oxford University Press.

kept a whole month in a government building in the town, he called on us nearly every day, simply in order to see us. There were, however, also some characters who were unfriendly to the end and who, God knows why, seemed to find it a burden to exchange a word with me. There seemed to be a kind of barrier between them and me.

Towards the end I had more privileges than during all my time in prison. Some acquaintances of mine, and even some friends of my far-away school-days, turned up among the officers serving in the town. I renewed my acquaintance with them. Through them I was able to possess more money, to write home, and even to get books. For several years I had not read a single book, and it is difficult to convey the strange and disturbing effect produced on me by the first book I read in prison. I remember that I began reading in the evening when the barracks were locked, and read all through the night, until daybreak. It was a number of a magazine. It was as though news from that other world had come through to me; my former life rose before me in all its brightness, and I strove to guess from what I read whether I had lagged far behind that world, whether much had happened in my absence, what was exciting people there now, and what questions occupied their minds. I worried every word, tried to read between the lines, and strove to find hidden meanings and allusions to the past; I searched for traces of the things that had excited men before, in my time, and how sad it was for me to recognize to what extent I was now indeed a stranger to this new life, cut off and isolated. I should have to get used to new things and learn to know a new generation. I devoured particularly eagerly an article under which I found the name of a man I once knew intimately . . . But new names as well resounded now: new leaders had appeared, and I was greedily impatient to get to know them and fretted because I could see so few books in prospect and because it was so difficult to acquire them. Previously, indeed, under the old major, it had been dangerous to bring books into the prison. In the event of a search there would inevitably be questions: 'Where did the books come from?' 'When did you get them?' 'So you have connexions outside?' . . . And what could I have replied to such questions? So it was that, living without books, I had become wrapped up in myself, had set myself problems, tried to solve them, and sometimes tormented myself with them . . . But it is surely impossible to convey all this! . . .

I had entered the prison in winter, and therefore I was to emerge into freedom in winter, on the same day of the month as I had arrived. With what impatience I waited for the winter, with what joy, at the end of summer, I watched the leaves fade on the trees and the grass wither on the steppe. Now summer was already over, and the winds of autumn had begun to howl; now the first hesitant snowflakes began to drift down . . . At last the winter, so long awaited, had arrived. At times my heart would begin to beat thickly and heavily with the anticipation of freedom. But strange to say the more time went by and the nearer the end came, the more patient I became. During the very last few days I was even surprised, and reproached myself: it seemed to me that I had become callous and indifferent. Many of the prisoners, meeting me in the courtyard during our leisure time, talked to me and congratulated me.

'See now, Alexander Petrovich, sir, you'll be free soon, very soon. You are leaving us poor fellows all alone.'

'And will it be soon for you too, Martynov?' I would answer.

'Me? What a hope! I've got another seven years to drag through . . .'

And he would sigh and stand still, with an absent look, as though he were gazing into the future. It seemed to me that all of them had begun to be more friendly to me. I had visibly ceased to be one of themselves; they were already saying good-bye to me. One of the Polish gentlemen, a quiet and unassuming young man, was, like me, fond of walking in the yard in our leisure time. He thought the fresh air and exercise preserved his health and compensated for all the harm done by the stuffy nights in barracks. 'I am waiting impatiently for you to leave,' he said to me with a smile, meeting me once on his walk; 'when you leave, *I shall know* that I have exactly a year left before I get out.'

I will mention here in passing that, in consequence of our day-dreams and our long divorce from it, freedom somehow seemed to us freer than real freedom, the freedom, that is, that exists in fact, in real life. The prisoners exaggerated the idea of real freedom, and that is very natural and characteristic of all prisoners. Any ragamuffin of an officer's batman was for us all but a king, all but the ideal of the free man, compared with the prisoners, because he could go about unshaved and without fetters or guards.

On the eve of my release, at twilight, I walked *for the last time* round the prison stockade. How many thousand times I had walked round it during all those years! How, behind the barracks, I used to linger in my first year, solitary, friendless, and dejected! I remember calculating then how many thousand days still lay before me. Great God, how long ago it was! Here in this corner our eagle lived out his captivity; here Petrov and I often used to meet. Even now, he had not deserted me. He came running up and, as though guessing my thoughts, walked silently at my side, like a man wondering to himself about something. Mentally I took my leave of the blackened, rough-hewn timbers of the barracks. How unfriendly had been the impression they had made on me *then*, at first! Even they must have grown older since then, but I could see no sign of it. And how much youth had gone to waste within those walls, what great powers had perished uselessly there! For the whole truth must be told: these indeed were no ordinary men. Perhaps, indeed, they were the most highly gifted and the strongest of all our people. But these powerful forces were condemned to perish uselessly, unnaturally, wrongfully, irrevocably. And whose is the blame?

FEODOR DOSTOYEVSKY / *I Leave the Prison*

That is the question, whose is the blame?

Next morning early, before the prisoners went to their work, when it was just beginning to grow light, I went round all the barracks to say good-bye to all the prisoners. Many strong, calloused hands stretched out to me in friendship. Some shook mine like comrades, but they were not many. Others understood very well that I was on the point of becoming an entirely different man from them. They knew I had friends in the town and that I should go straight from them to the *bosses* and would sit down beside those bosses as their equal. They knew this, and said good-bye to me, though in a pleasant and friendly enough way, not at all as they would to a comrade, but as if to a gentleman. Some turned away from me and surlily refused to answer my farewell. A few even eyed me with something like hatred.

The drum beat, and everybody went off to work, but I remained behind. Sushilov that morning had been almost the first to get up and had worked anxiously and earnestly to make tea for me in time. Poor Sushilov! He cried when I gave him my old prison clothes, my shirts, my underfetters, and a little money.

'I don't want that, I don't want it!' he said, controlling his quivering lip with a great effort; 'how can I lose *you*, Alexander Petrovich? Who will be left for me here when you've gone?'

Last of all I said good-bye to Akim Akimovich.

'It will soon be your turn,' I said to him.

'I've got a long time, I've still got a very long time here,' he murmured, pressing my hand. I threw myself on his neck and we kissed.

Ten minutes after the prisoners, we too left the prison, never to return to it, I and the companion with whom I had arrived. We had to go straight to the smithy to have our fetters struck off. But there was no longer an armed guard to escort us: we went with a sergeant. It was our own prisoners who struck off our fetters in the engineering shops. I waited while my companion's fetters were removed, and then went up to the anvil. The smiths turned me round with my back to them, lifted my foot from behind, and put it on the anvil . . .

'The rivet, the rivet, turn the rivet first of all!' commanded the foreman. 'Hold it there, like that, that's right . . . Now strike it with the hammer . . .'

The fetters fell away. I lifted them up . . . I wanted to hold them in my hand and look at them for the last time. It seemed amazing now that it was my legs they had been on a moment ago.

'Well, God be with you, God be with you!' said the prisoners, in gruff, abrupt, yet pleased tones.

Yes, God was with us! Freedom, a new life, resurrection from the dead . . . What a glorious moment!

Letter to Theo

Vincent van Gogh's (1853–1890) was a tormented soul—intense, passionate, evangelical, and ultimately too much for him to bear. During his career as a painter, which spanned only the extraordinary last decade of his life, he broke fresh artistic ground in portraying his inner conflicts on canvas. He was also, literally, a man of letters. His voluminous correspondence to his adored and devoted brother Theo reveals a sensitive, eloquent writer and a troubled, compassionate man seeking to understand himself and to bring comfort to mankind through his art. The eldest child of a Dutch minister, van Gogh sold pictures for a time before turning his passion to religion. He became a missionary, working zealously for and sharing the lives of impoverished Belgian miners. His interest in painting flared when he began to draw the miners and their families. He studied painting in Brussels and Paris. Wanting a more peaceful atmosphere than turbulent Paris could provide, van Gogh moved to Arles in southern France, persuading Paul Gauguin to live with him. Their personal relationship was tempestuous, but each favorably influenced the other's painting. In Arles, van Gogh was subject to psychotic seizures. He was institutionalized several times before he succeeded in taking his own life. The following selection appears in *Dear Theo* (1937), Irving Stone's edition of van Gogh's letters to his brother.

———————————————————————————————————

Saint-Rémy, May, 1889

I think I have done well to come here, for by seeing the actual *truth* about the life of the various madmen and lunatics in this menagerie, I am losing the vague dread, the fear of the thing. And the change of surroundings is doing me good.

The idea of work as a duty is coming back very strong, and my faculties for work will also come back to me fairly quickly. Yet work often so absorbs me that I think I shall remain absent-minded and awkward in shifting for myself the rest of my life.

I have a little room with greenish-grey paper, with two curtains of sea-green with a design of very pale roses, brightened by slight touches of blood-red. These curtains, probably the relics of some rich and ruined defunct, are very pretty in design. From the same source probably comes a very worn armchair, recovered with an upholstery splashed like a Dias or a Monticelli, with brown, red, white, black, forget-me-not blue, and bottle green. Through the iron-barred window I see a square of corn in an enclosure, a perspective like van Goyen, above which I see in the morning the sun rising in his glory. In addition to this room—as there are more than thirty empty—I have one to work in.

The food is so-so. It naturally tastes rather mouldy, as in a shoddy restaurant in Paris or a boarding-house. As these poor souls do absolutely nothing (not a book; nothing but a game of bowls and a game of draughts), they have no other daily distraction than to stuff themselves with chick peas, haricots, lentils, and other groceries in set quantities and at fixed hours. The room where we stay on wet days is like a third-class waiting-room in some dead-alive village, the more so as there are some distinguished lunatics who always wear a hat, spectacles, cane, and travelling cloak.

Formerly I felt repulsion for these creatures, and it was a harrowing thought for me to reflect that so many of our profession, Troyon, Marchal, Meryon, Jundt, M. Maris, Monticelli, and heaps more had ended like this. Now I think of it all without fear; that is to say, I find it no more frightful than if they had been stricken with some other ailment. These artists, I see them take on their old serenity, and is it a little thing to rediscover the ancients of our profession? That is a thing I am profoundly thankful for.

Though there are some who howl or rave continually, in spite of that people get to know each other very well, and help each other when their attacks come on. They say we must put up with others so that others will put up with us; and between ourselves we understand each other very well. I can, for instance, sometimes chat with one of them who can only answer in incoherent sounds, because he is not afraid of me. And it is the same with those whose mania is to fly into frequent rages. The others interfere so that they do themselves no harm, and separate the combatants, if combat there is.

It is true there are some whose condition is more serious, who are either dirty or dangerous; these are in another courtyard.

There is another thing I am grateful for. I gather from others that they have heard during their attacks strange sounds and voices, as I have, and that to their eyes too things seemed to be changing. That lessens the horror that I had at first of my attacks, which when they come on one unawares cannot but frighten one beyond measure. Once you know that this is part of the disease, you take it like anything else. If I had not seen other lunatics close to, I should not have been able to free myself from constantly dwelling upon it.

Indeed, the anguish and suffering are no joke once you are caught by an attack. Most epileptics bite their tongue and wound themselves. Rey told me that he had seen a case where someone had wounded himself as I did, in the ear. Once you know what it is, once you are conscious of your condition, and of being subject to attacks, you can do something yourself not to be so taken aback by the suffering or the terror. For five months my suffering has been lessening, and I have good hopes of getting over it, or at least of not having attacks of such violence.

There is someone here who has been shouting and talking as I do *all the time* for a fortnight; he thinks he hears voices and words in the echoes of the corridors, probably because the nerves of the ear are diseased and oversensitive; in my case it was sight and hearing at once, which according to what Rey told me one day is usual in the beginning to epilepsy. The shock was such that it sickened me even to make a movement, and nothing would have pleased me better than never to have wakened again. At present this *horror of life* is less strong and the melancholy less acute. But from that to will and action there is still some way to go.

It is rather queer, perhaps, that as a result of this last terrible attack there is hardly any very definite desire or hope left in my mind, and I wonder if this is the way one thinks when, with the passions dying out, one descends the hill instead of climbing it. Of *will* I have none, and of everything belonging to ordinary life; the desire, for instance, to see my friends, although I keep thinking about them, I have almost none of. That is why I am not yet at the point when I can think of leaving here. I should have this depression anywhere. By staying here, the doctor will naturally be better able to see what is wrong, and will be more reassured as to my being allowed to paint.

I am having a bath now twice a week, and stay in it two hours; my stomach is infinitely better than it was a year ago, so as far as I know I have only to go on.

I do not notice in the others, either, any very definite desire to be somewhere else, but this may well come from the feeling that we are too thoroughly shattered for life outside. What I cannot quite understand is their absolute idleness; but that is the great fault of the South and its ruin. Yet what a lovely country, and what lovely blue, and what a sun! So far I have only seen the garden, and what I can look at through my window. When I am working in the garden they all come to look, and I assure you they have more sense, and the politeness to leave me alone, than the good people of the town of Arles.

It is a whole month since I came here. My hope is that at the end of a year I shall know better what I can do and what I want to do. Little by little the idea of a fresh start will come to me. To come back to Paris, or go anywhere at all, in no way takes my fancy at present.

Extreme enervation is what most of those who have been here for years suffer from. My work will in a certain measure preserve me from that. And though the pictures cost the price of canvas and paint, at the end of the month it is more profitable to spend a little more in this way and make use of what after all I have learnt, than to abandon them, since anyhow you have to pay for my keep. That is why I am working.

It is only too doubtful whether painting has any beauty or use. But what is to be done? There are people who love nature even though they are cracked or ill; those are the painters. Then there are those who like what is made by man's hands, and these even go so far as to like pictures.

Since I came here the deserted garden, planted with large pines beneath which grows the grass, tall and unkempt and mixed with various weeds, has sufficed for my work, and I have not yet gone outside. However, the country round Saint-Rémy is very beautiful, and bit by bit I shall go and stay at places.

When I send you the four canvases of the garden I have in hand you will see that considering life is spent mostly in the big garden, it is not so unhappy. Here at any rate we have splendid sunshine.

Yesterday I drew a very big, rather rare night moth called the death's head, its colouring of amazing distinction, black, grey, cloudy white tinged with carmine, or shading indistinctly to olive-green; it is very big. To paint it I had to kill it, and it was a pity, the insect was so beautiful.

What you say about the 'Woman Rocking' pleases me; it is very true that the common people, who are content with chromos and melt when they hear a barrel organ, are in some vague way right, perhaps more sincere than certain men about town who go to the Salon. I have a new canvas, once again as ordinary as a chromo in the little shops, which represents the eternal nests of greenery for lovers; some thick tree trunks covered with ivy, the ground also covered with ivy and periwinkle, a stone bench and a bush of roses pale in the cold shadow. The problem is to get distinction into it.

This morning I saw the country from my window a long time before sunrise, with nothing but the morning star, which looked very big. Daubigny and Rousseau have done just that, expressing in their work all that the scene has of intimacy, all its vast peace and majesty, but adding as well a feeling so individual, so heartbreaking. I have no aversion to that sort of emotion.

Give Gauguin, if he will accept it, a copy of the 'Woman Rocking,' and another to Bernard as a token of friendship. I hope that you will destroy a lot of the things that are too bad in the batch I have sent you from Arles, or at least only show what is most passable. As for the exhibition of the Independents, just act as if I weren't here; to avoid seeming indifferent, yet not exhibit anything too mad, perhaps the 'Starry Night' and the landscape with yellow leafage. Since these two are done with contrasting colours they might give somebody else the idea of doing such night effects better than I have.

I am always filled with remorse, terribly so, when I think of my work as so little in keeping with what I should have liked to do. I hope that in the long run this remorse will lead me to do better things.

I am going off tomorrow to see a little of the country, and since it is the season when there are plenty of flowers and consequently colour effects, it would perhaps be wise to send me five metres more of canvas. For the flowers are short-lived and will be replaced by the yellow cornfields. These especially I hope to catch better than I did at Arles. The mistral (since there are some mountains) seems much less tiresome here than there, where you always get it first-hand.

You absolutely must set your mind at rest about me now. My health is all right, so I feel happier with my work than I could be outside; I shall have learnt regular habits, and in the long run the result will be more order in my life and less susceptibility. That will be so much to the good. I went once, accompanied, to the village, but the mere sight of people and things had such an effect on me that I thought I was going to faint, and felt very ill. There must have been some all-powerful emotion within me to upset me like that, and I have no idea what can have caused it. Face to face with nature, it is the feeling for work that holds me.

I have two landscapes in hand, views taken among the hills; one is the country that I see from the window of my bedroom; in the foreground a field of corn ruined and dashed to the ground after a storm, a boundary wall, and beyond it the grey foliage of a few olive trees, some huts, and the hills. It is a landscape of extreme simplicity in colouring, it will make a companion-piece to the study of the 'Bedroom,' which has got damaged. When the thing represented is in point of character absolutely in agreement with the manner of representing it, isn't that just the element that gives a work of art its quality? This is why a mere loaf of bread, as far as painting goes, is especially good when it is painted by Chardin.

As I wish to preserve the study of the 'Bedroom,' I am going to repaint it. I wanted at first to have it recanvased, because I did not think I could do it again. But as my brain has grown calmer since, I can quite well do it up now. The thing is that among the number of things you make, there are always some that you felt more, or put more into, and that you want to keep in spite of everything.

joan didion

Goodbye to All That

Born and raised in Sacramento, California, Joan Didion (1934–   ) graduated from the University of California, Berkeley, in 1956. From there she went on to a career in New York journalism. She has been an associate editor of *Vogue* magazine, a columnist for the *Saturday Evening Post,* and a contributing editor to the *National Review.* In 1963 she won a Breadloaf Fellowship in fiction, and, as well as short stories, she has two published novels, *Run River* (1963) and *Play It As It Lays* (1970). The following essay appeared in a collection of her essays, *Slouching Towards Bethlehem* (1968).

How many miles to Babylon?
Three score miles and ten—
Can I get there by candlelight?
Yes, and back again—
If your feet are nimble and light
You can get there by candlelight.

It is easy to see the beginnings of things, and harder to see the ends. I can remember now, with a clarity that makes the nerves in the back of my neck constrict, when New York began for me, but I cannot lay my finger upon the moment it ended, can never cut through the ambiguities and second starts and broken resolves to the exact place on the page where the heroine is no longer as optimistic as she once was. When I first saw New York I was twenty, and it was summertime, and I got off a DC-7 at the old Idlewild temporary terminal in a new dress which had seemed very smart in Sacramento but seemed less smart already, even in the old Idlewild temporary terminal, and the warm air smelled of mildew and some instinct, programmed by all the movies I had ever seen and all the songs I had ever heard sung and all the stories I had ever read about New York, informed me that it would never be quite the same again. In fact it never was. Some time later there was a song on all the jukeboxes on the upper East Side that went "but where is the schoolgirl who used to be me," and if it was late enough at night I used to wonder that. I know now that almost everyone wonders something like that, sooner or later and no matter what he or she is doing, but one of the mixed blessings of being twenty and twenty-one and even twenty-three is the conviction that nothing like this, all evidence to the contrary notwithstanding, has ever happened to anyone before.

Of course it might have been some other city, had circumstances been different and the time been different and had I been different, might have been Paris or Chicago or even San Francisco, but because I am talking about myself I am talking here about New York. That first night I opened my window on the bus into town and watched for the skyline, but all I could see were the wastes of Queens and the big signs that said MIDTOWN TUNNEL THIS LANE and then a flood of summer rain (even that seemed remarkable and exotic, for I had come out of the West where there was no summer rain), and for the next three days I sat wrapped in blankets in a hotel room air-conditioned to 35° and tried to get over a bad cold and a high fever. It did not occur to me to call a doctor, because I knew none, and although it did occur to me to call the desk and ask that the air conditioner be turned off, I never called, because I did not know how much to tip whoever might come—was anyone ever so young? I am here to tell you that someone was. All I could do during those three days was talk long-distance to the boy I already knew I would never marry in the spring. I would stay in New York, I told him, just six months, and I could see the Brooklyn Bridge from my window. As it turned out the bridge was the Triborough, and I stayed eight years.

In retrospect it seems to me that those days before I knew the names of all the bridges were happier than the ones that came later, but perhaps you will see that as we go along. Part of what I want to tell you is what it is like to be young in New York, how six months can become eight years with the deceptive ease of a film dissolve, for that is how those years appear to me now, in a long sequence of sentimental dissolves and old-fashioned trick shots—the Seagram Building fountains dissolve into snowflakes, I enter a revolving door at twenty and come out a good deal older, and on a different street. But most particularly I want to explain to you, and in the process perhaps to myself, why I no longer live in New York. It is often said that New York is a city for only the very rich and the very poor. It is less often said that New York is also, at least for those of us who came there from somewhere else, a city for only the very young.

I remember once, one cold bright December evening in New York, suggesting to a friend who complained of having been around too long that he come with me to a party where there would be, I assured him with the bright resourcefulness of twenty-three, "new faces." He laughed literally until he choked, and I had to roll down the taxi window and hit him on the back.

"New faces," he said finally, "don't tell me about *new faces.*" It seemed that the last time he had gone to a party where he had been promised "new faces," there had been fifteen people in the room, and he had already slept with five of the women and owed money to all but two of the men. I laughed with him, but the first snow had just begun to fall and the big Christmas trees glittered yellow and white as far as I could see up Park Avenue and I had a new dress and it would be a long while before I would come to understand the particular moral of the story.

It would be a long while because, quite simply, I was in love with New York. I do not mean "love" in any colloquial way, I mean that I was in love with the city, the way you love the first person who ever touches you and never love anyone quite that way again. I remember walking across Sixty-second Street one twilight that first spring, or the second spring, they were all alike for a while. I was late to meet someone but I stopped at Lexington Avenue and bought a peach and stood on the corner eating it and knew that I had come out of the West and reached the mirage. I could taste the peach and feel the soft air blowing from a subway grating on my legs and I could smell lilac and garbage and expensive perfume and I knew that it would cost something sooner or later—because I did not belong there, did not come from there—but when you are twenty-two or twenty-three, you figure that later you will have a high emotional balance, and be able to pay whatever it costs. I still believed in possibilities then, still had the sense, so peculiar to New York, that something extraordinary would happen any minute, any day, any month. I was making only $65 or $70 a week then ("Put yourself in Hattie Carnegie's hands," I was advised without the slightest trace of irony by an editor of the magazine for which I worked), so little money that some weeks I had to charge food at Bloomingdale's gourmet shop in order to eat, a fact which went unmentioned in the letters I wrote to California. I never told my father that I needed money because then he would have sent it, and I would never know if I could do it by myself. At that time making a living seemed a game to me, with arbitrary but quite inflexible rules. And except on a certain kind of winter evening—six-thirty in the Seventies, say, already dark and bitter with a wind off the river, when I would be walking very fast toward a bus and would look in the bright windows of brownstones and see cooks working in clean kitchens and imagine women lighting candles on the floor above and beautiful children being bathed on the floor above that—except on nights like those, I never felt poor; I had the feeling that if I needed money I could always get it. I could write a syndicated column for teenagers under the name "Debbi Lynn" or I could smuggle gold into India or I could become a $100 call girl, and none of it would matter.

Nothing was irrevocable; everything was within reach. Just around every corner lay something curious and interesting, something I had never before seen or done or known about. I could go to a party and meet someone who called himself Mr. Emotional Appeal and ran The Emotional Appeal Institute or Tina Onassis Blandford or a Florida cracker who was then a regular on what he called "the Big C," the Southampton-El Morocco circuit ("I'm well-connected on the Big C, honey," he would tell me over collard greens on his vast borrowed terrace), or the widow of the celery king of the Harlem market or a piano salesman from Bonne Terre, Missouri, or someone who had already made and lost two fortunes in Midland, Texas. I could make promises to myself and to other people and there would be all the time in the world to keep them. I could stay up all night and make mistakes, and none of it would count.

You see I was in a curious position in New York: it never occurred to me that I was living a real life there. In my imagination I was always there for just another few months, just until Christmas or Easter or the first warm day in May. For that reason I was most comfortable in the company of Southerners. They seemed to be in New York as I was, on some indefinitely extended leave from wherever they belonged, disinclined to consider the future, temporary exiles who always knew when the flights left for New Orleans or Memphis or Richmond or, in my case, California. Someone who lives always with a plane schedule in the drawer lives on a slightly different calendar. Christmas, for example, was a difficult season. Other people could take it in stride, going to Stowe or going abroad or going for the day to their mothers' places in Connecticut; those of us who believed that we lived somewhere else would spend it making and canceling airline reservations, waiting for weatherbound flights as if for the last plane out of Lisbon in 1940, and finally comforting one another, those of us who were left, with the oranges and mementos and smoked-oyster stuffings of childhood, gathering close, colonials in a far country.

Which is precisely what we were. I am not sure that it is possible for anyone brought up in the East to appreciate entirely what New York, the idea of New York, means to those of us who came out of the West and the South. To an Eastern child, particularly a child who has always had an uncle on Wall Street and who has spent several hundred Saturdays first at F. A. O. Schwarz and being fitted for shoes at Best's and then waiting under the Biltmore clock and dancing to Lester Lanin, New York is just a city, albeit *the* city, a plausible place for people to live. But to those of us who came from places where no one had heard of Lester Lanin and Grand Central Station was a Saturday radio program, where Wall Street and Fifth Avenue and Madison Avenue were not places at all but abstractions ("Money," and "High Fashion," and "The Hucksters"), New York was no mere city. It was instead an infinitely romantic notion, the mysterious nexus of all love and money and power, the shining and perishable dream itself. To think of "living" there was to reduce the miraculous to the mundane; one does not "live" at Xanadu.

In fact it was difficult in the extreme for me to understand those young women for whom New York was not simply an ephemeral Estoril but a real place, girls who bought toasters and installed new cabinets in their apartments and committed themselves to some reasonable future. I never bought any furniture in New York. For a year or so I lived in other people's apartments; after that I lived in the Nineties in an apartment furnished entirely with things taken from storage by a friend whose wife had moved away. And when I left the apartment in the Nineties (that was when I was leaving everything, when it was all breaking up) I left everything in it, even my winter clothes and the map of Sacramento County I had hung on the bedroom wall to remind me who I was, and I moved into a monastic four-room floor-through on Seventy-fifth Street. "Monastic" is perhaps misleading here, implying some chic severity; until after I was married and my husband moved some furniture in, there was nothing at all in those four rooms except a cheap double mattress and box springs, ordered by telephone the day I decided to move, and two French garden chairs lent me by a friend who imported them. (It strikes me now that the people I knew in New York all had curious and self-defeating sidelines. They imported garden chairs which did not sell very well at Hammacher Schlemmer or they tried to market hair straighteners in Harlem or they ghosted exposés of Murder Incorporated for Sunday supplements. I think that perhaps none of us was very serious, *engagé* only about our most private lives.)

All I ever did to that apartment was hang fifty yards of yellow theatrical silk across the bedroom windows, because I had some idea that the gold light would make me feel better, but I did not bother to weight the curtains correctly and all that summer the long panels of transparent golden silk would blow out the windows and get tangled and drenched in the afternoon thunderstorms. That was the year, my twenty-eighth, when I was discovering that not all of the promises would be kept, that some things are in fact irrevocable and that it had counted after all, every evasion and every procrastination, every mistake, every word, all of it.

That is what it was all about, wasn't it? Promises? Now when New York comes back to me it comes in hallucinatory flashes, so clinically detailed that I sometimes wish that memory would effect the distortion with which it is commonly credited. For a lot of the time I was in New York I used a perfume called *Fleurs de Rocaille,* and then *L'Air du Temps,* and now the slightest trace of either can short-circuit my connections for the rest of the day. Nor can I smell Henri Bendel jasmine soap without falling back into the past, or the particular mixture of spices used for boiling crabs. There were barrels of crab boil in a Czech place in the Eighties where I once shopped. Smells, of course, are notorious memory stimuli, but there are other things which affect me the same way. Blue-and-white striped sheets. Vermouth cassis. Some faded nightgowns which were new in 1959 or 1960, and some chiffon scarves I bought about the same time.

I suppose that a lot of us who have been young in New York have the same scenes on our home screens. I remember sitting in a lot of apartments with a slight headache about five o'clock in the morning. I had a friend who could not sleep, and he knew a few other people who had the same trouble, and we would watch the sky lighten and have a last drink with no ice and then go home in the early morning light, when the streets were clean and wet (had it rained in the night? we never knew) and the few cruising taxis still had their headlights on and the only color was the red and green of traffic signals. The White Rose bars opened very early in the morning; I recall waiting in one of them to watch an astronaut go into space, waiting so long that at the moment it actually happened I had my eyes not on the television screen but on a cockroach on the tile floor. I liked the bleak branches above Washington Square at dawn, and the monochromatic flatness of Second Avenue, the fire escapes and the grilled storefronts peculiar and empty in their perspective.

It is relatively hard to fight at six-thirty or seven in the morning without any sleep, which was perhaps one reason we stayed up all night, and it seemed to me a pleasant time of day. The windows were shuttered in that apartment in the Nineties and I could sleep a few hours and then go to work. I could work then on two or three hours' sleep and a container of coffee from Chock Full O' Nuts. I liked going to work, liked the soothing and satisfactory rhythm of getting out a magazine, liked the orderly progression of four-color closings and two-color closings and black-and-white closings and then The Product, no abstraction but something which looked effortlessly glossy and could be picked up on a newsstand and weighed in the hand. I liked all the minutiae of proofs and layouts, liked working late on the nights the magazine went to press, sitting and reading *Variety* and waiting for the copy desk to call. From my office I could look across town to the weather signal on the Mutual of New York Building and the lights that alternately spelled out TIME and LIFE above Rockefeller Plaza; that pleased me obscurely, and so did walking uptown in the mauve eight o'clocks of early summer evenings and looking at things, Lowestoft tureens in Fifty-seventh Street windows, people in evening clothes trying to get taxis, the trees just coming into full leaf, the lambent air, all the sweet promises of money and summer.

Some years passed, but I still did not lose that sense of wonder about New York. I began to cherish the loneliness of it, the sense that at any given time no one need know where I was or what I was doing. I liked walking, from the East River over to the Hudson and back on brisk days, down around the Village on warm days. A friend would leave me the key to her apartment in the West Village when she was out of town, and sometimes I would just move down there, because by that time the telephone was beginning to bother me (the canker, you see, was already in the rose) and not many people had that number. I remember one day when someone who did have the West Village number came to pick me up for lunch there, and we both had hangovers, and I cut my finger opening him a beer and burst into tears, and we walked to a Spanish restaurant and drank Bloody Marys and *gazpacho* until we felt better. I was not then guilt-ridden about spending afternoons that way, because I still had all the afternoons in the world.

And even that late in the game I still liked going to parties, all parties, bad parties, Saturday-afternoon parties given by recently married couples who lived in Stuyvesant Town, West Side parties given by unpublished or failed writers who served cheap red wine and talked about going to Guadalajara, Village parties where all the guests worked for advertising agencies and voted for Reform Democrats, press parties at Sardi's, the worst kinds of parties. You will have perceived by now that I was not one to profit by the experience of others, that it was a very long time indeed before I stopped believing in new faces and began to understand the lesson in that story, which was that it is distinctly possible to stay too long at the Fair.

I could not tell you when I began to understand that. All I know is that it was very bad when I was twenty-eight. Everything that was said to me I seemed to have heard before, and I could no longer listen. I could no longer sit in little bars near Grand Central and listen to someone complaining of his wife's inability to cope with the help while he missed another train to Connecticut. I no longer had any interest in hearing about the advances other people had received from their publishers, about plays which were having second-act trouble in Philadelphia, or about people I would like very much if only I would come out and meet them. I had already met them, always. There were certain parts of the city which I had to avoid. I could not bear upper Madison Avenue on weekday mornings (this was a particularly inconvenient aversion, since I then lived just fifty or sixty feet east of Madison), because I would see women walking Yorkshire terriers and shopping at Gristede's, and some Veblenesque gorge would rise in my throat. I could not go to Times Square in the afternoon, or to the New York Public Library for any reason whatsoever. One day I could not go into a Schrafft's; the next day it would be Bonwit Teller.

I hurt the people I cared about, and insulted those I did not. I cut myself off from the one person who was closer to me than any other. I cried until I was not even aware when I was crying and when I was not, cried in elevators and in taxis and in Chinese laundries, and when I went to the doctor he said only that I seemed to be depressed, and should see a "specialist." He wrote down a psychiatrist's name and address for me, but I did not go.

Instead I got married, which as it turned out was a very good thing to do but badly timed, since I still could not walk on upper Madison Avenue in the mornings and still could not talk to people and still cried in Chinese laundries. I had never before understood what "despair" meant, and I am not sure that I understand now, but I understood that year. Of course I could not work. I could not even get dinner with any degree of certainty, and I would sit in the apartment on Seventy-fifth Street paralyzed until my husband would call from his office and say gently that I did not have to get dinner, that I could meet him at Michael's Pub or at Toots Shor's or at Sardi's East. And then one morning in April (we had been married in January) he called and told me that he wanted to get out of New York for a while, that he would take a six-month leave of absence, that we would go somewhere.

It was three years ago that he told me that, and we have lived in Los Angeles since. Many of the people we knew in New York think this a curious aberration, and in fact tell us so. There is no possible, no adequate answer to that, and so we give certain stock answers, the answers everyone gives. I talk about how difficult it would be for us to "afford" to live in New York right now, about how much "space" we need. All I mean is that I was very young in New York, and that at some point the golden rhythm was broken, and I am not that young any more. The last time I was in New York was in a cold January, and everyone was ill and tired. Many of the people I used to know there had moved to Dallas or had gone on Antabuse or had bought a farm in New Hampshire. We stayed ten days, and then we took an afternoon flight back to Los Angeles, and on the way home from the airport that night I could see the moon on the Pacific and smell jasmine all around and we both knew that there was no longer any point in keeping the apartment we still kept in New York. There were years when I called Los Angeles "the Coast," but they seem a long time ago.

1967

chapter five ─────────────────────

─────────────── *Relationships*

introduction

Our relationships with other human beings shape and guide our lives, whether we want them to or not. No matter how much we may cry out for freedom, personal independence, or the right to live our lives without being constrained by society's standards, few of us would willingly give up the source of most of our restrictions: our relationships with others. Although those relationships may be limiting, they can liberate us as well, enabling us to learn, to grow, to share in the lives of others as they share in ours. The material and psychological interdependences of human relationships have led to the extremes of love and war—and nearly everything else between them in human experience.

In this chapter Diane Walker and Richard Thurman write of childhood relationships which influenced their lives. Puzzled at first over the dominant role of her sister, Walker finally comes to understand the differences between her sister and herself. Thurman's friend Robert introduces him to some of the worldly delights of boyhood, but their friendship is cut off abruptly when Robert tells him more than he is prepared to know.

Given an assignment to write a paper that should "come out of you," Langston Hughes considers his own blackness and his instructor's whiteness:

> You are white—
> yet a part of me, as I am a part of you.
> That's American.

Nikos Kazantzakis' "The Irish Lass" flames with youthful passion in his portrayal of the fleeting romance that he enjoyed with the Irish girl. In contrast, Lillian Hellman relates the strength and depth of the love that bound her and Dashiell Hammett together for years in a unique relationship in which each retained an independent inner privacy while remaining unwaveringly devoted to the other until Hammett's death.

In "Zorba" Kazantzakis writes of his great friend who taught him to "love life and have no fear of death," a man whose influence on him he compares to that of Homer and Buddha and whose spirit inspired Kazantzakis to keep Zorba alive in literature after his death.

Theme for English B

Langston Hughes (1902–1967) stated that he wrote "to explain and illuminate the Negro condition in America," and throughout a writing career that spanned more than forty years, covered every genre, and produced over forty volumes, he worked toward that end. Born in Joplin, Missouri, Hughes spent his childhood and youth in many places in the Midwest. He attended Columbia University for a year before signing on as a mess boy on a freighter bound for Africa. From Africa he went to Europe and then returned to America to be "discovered" by writer Vachel Lindsay and vaulted into prominence as a poet. He was an essential part of the literary flowering of black writers in New York known as the Harlem Renaissance in the twenties. For the next thirty-five years he prolifically produced poetry, fiction, drama, history, and other assorted literary works. Hughes' most memorable character is Jesse B. Semple, who appears in many of his works and serves as Hughes' persona in his satiric barbs against racial oppression in America. Some of his volumes of poetry include *Weary Blues* (1926), *The Negro Mother* (1931), *The Dream Keeper* (1932), *Montage of a Dream Deferred* (1951)—in which the following selection appears—and *The Panther and the Lash* (1967). He wrote two volumes of autobiography, *The Big Sea* (1940) and *I Wonder as I Wander* (1956).

The instructor said,

Go home and write
a page tonight.
And let that page come out of you—
Then, it will be true.

I wonder if it's that simple?
I am twenty-two, colored, born in Winston-Salem.
I went to school there, then Durham, then here
to this college on the hill above Harlem.
I am the only colored student in my class.
The steps from the hill lead down into Harlem,
through a park, then I cross St. Nicholas,
Eighth Avenue, Seventh, and I come to the Y,

the Harlem Branch Y, where I take the elevator
up to my room, sit down, and write this page:

It's not easy to know what is true for you or me
at twenty-two, my age. But I guess I'm what
I feel and see and hear, Harlem, I hear you:
hear you, hear me—we two—you, me, talk on this page.
(I hear New York, too.) Me—who?
Well, I like to eat, sleep, drink, and be in love.
I like to work, read, learn, and understand life.
I like a pipe for a Christmas present,
or records—Bessie, bop, or Bach.
I guess being colored doesn't make me *not* like
the same things other folks like who are other races.
So will my page be colored that I write?
Being me, it will not be white.
But it will be

a part of you, instructor.
You are white—
yet a part of me, as I am a part of you.
That's American.
Sometimes perhaps you don't want to be a part of me.
Nor do I often want to be a part of you.
But we are, that's true!
As I learn from you,
I guess you learn from me—
although you're older—and white—
and somewhat more free.

This is my page for English B.

richard thurman _____

Not Another Word

Born in Salt Lake City, Utah, Richard Thurman (1921–   ) received his bachelor's degree with an English major from Utah State University. Although writing has been his chief continuing interest, Thurman has held diverse positions, including that of director of the University of Utah Press from 1963 to 1970. His short stories have appeared in such magazines as *Harper's*, the *Atlantic*, and the *Reader's Digest*. In 1956 he received one of the O. Henry Awards, which are presented for the best short stories published in American magazines. The following piece originally appeared in *The New Yorker* in 1957.

Because I was one of the bigger, healthier boys in the class—and also one of the biggest, smoothest liars, and thus apt to set an inspiring example for the others—Miss Devron would often begin the morning's inquisition with me. "Paul Adam," she would say, beaming down upon me, "would you be kind enough to tell us what you had for breakfast this morning?"

Even in the third grade, we were perceptive enough to sense that Miss Devron's inquiries into our daily breakfast menus sprang from something deeper than a mere interest in keeping us healthy. One look at her size and you knew what supreme importance food had in her life, and since we were her children—those she would never have herself, because of age, temperament, and general appearance—she apparently found it necessary to feel her way into our souls by following a glass of fruit juice and an egg and a slice of ham down our throats each morning. It wasn't just her zeal to know us personally through the food we ate that made us guard against her with a series of outrageous lies; she also wanted to know our families—their general way of life, their social and economic status in our small Utah town, and whether or not they lived in accordance with the Mormon doctrines, which were as inseparable from our lives as the mountain air we breathed. And she had a nasty way of pointing out any deviation from her set of standards by interrupting the stream of breakfast reports. "Hominy grits!" I remember her saying on one of the first mornings we were in her class. "Did you hear, class? Ronald Adair had hominy grits for breakfast."

She smiled her closed smile of wisdom and commiseration at Ronald, and placed the index finger of her left hand like a hot dog between her second and third chins while waggling her free hand scoldingly in his direction. "It's a lucky thing for you, young man, that your parents somehow had the energy to come out West, where you can get a new start in life," she said. "It's food like hominy grits that has kept the South backward so long. Out *here* we eat bacon and ham-and-eggs and hot cereal and fresh fruit juices and good buttered toast with jam. You're very lucky, young man! My, yes."

With such tactics she soon taught us to lie, and regardless of what each of us had eaten at home, there in Miss Devron's class we began to share a breakfast as monotonous as it was sumptuous. It was only a variation in quantity that crept into our diets from the first student's report to the last, for if one egg and a modest piece of ham were enough to start Miss Devron's fingers strolling contentedly over the terraces of her chins, it took considerably more than this to keep them happy and moving by the time the class was half through its recital, and by the time the last student's turn came, Miss Devron's wolfish appetite responded to nothing less than a gorge. Lila Willig was the last student on our class list. She looked as if she were made from five laths, and in the hectic flush of her unhealthiness—perhaps caused by near-starvation at home—she would sometimes get a little hysterical and report that she had eaten twenty-five eggs and a whole ham. I'm sure now that this was not because of any native waggishness in Lila, but we thought it was then, and we always laughed until Miss Devron had to pound the desk with her ruler.

"Now, stop that foolishness, Lila," she would say briskly. "Tell the class right out how many eggs you had for breakfast."

"Five," Lila would say, nervously scratching her frizzled yellow curls until they stood out like coiled wires. She could have said nothing else. The boy in front of her had just reported a breakfast of five eggs; anything less from Lila would have been picked up by Miss Devron as an example of parental neglect.

"That's better," the teacher would say, her fingers resuming their stroll. "And as I look over your faces this morning, class, I can already see the differences that good eating habits can make in one's life. How much brighter your eyes! How much stronger your backs!"

We simpered back at her, only vaguely and uneasily aware that she was a tyrant who was flattening our individuality with the weight of her righteous self-assurance. In less than a month under her, we were reduced to a spineless group of sycophantic ham, egg, and cereal eaters, with only Lila's occasional lapses to show us what a dull mold we had been crushed into. And then our integrity was rescued in an unexpected way.

The new boy who turned up in our class a month after the opening of school certainly looked like no hero. He was smaller than most of us, and while all of us boys were proudly wearing corduroy knickers, he still wore the short pants we scorned, and in the sharp air of that October morning his thin legs were mottled with a network of blue. We welcomed this pathetic figure with a fine generosity of spirit. "Where you from?" one of us asked him as we walked up to where he was standing, at the edge of the playground.

"New York."

"New York!" we said, and I now had an explanation of why he was such a puny-looking little rat. From the handful of Western movies and cowboy books I had already absorbed, I knew the kind of magic that enters into a man's blood when he is born west of the Mississippi River. His eye is clearer, his nerves are truer, his gait is more tireless, his aim is steadier, and in the very heart of his manliness there is a dimension that effete Easterners know nothing about. All this I knew as I looked down at the new boy's skinny blue legs.

"New York, eh?" I said menacingly, moving up to him until I could have rested my chin on top of his head.

"That's right," he said, lounging against the top rail of the playground fence and casually lifting one foot to rest it on the lower rail.

I eyed him with a steely coldness I had learned from a story about a man who had built the Union Pacific Railroad across the plains and who could drive a spike into a tie with two hammer blows. I put my fingers into my belt, just above where my six-shooters should have been. "Who's your old man voting for?" I asked. "Al Smith or Hoover?"

"Al Smith."

"Well, then, I guess I'll have to beat you up."

Perhaps nowadays, what with the broadened horizons brought on by the Second World War, Korea, UNESCO, and the stress on social-adjustment patterns in modern education, a new student from, say, Siam or Afghanistan can take his place unobtrusively in an American schoolroom. I don't know. But I do know that in my part of America in 1928 a new student had to fight his way into school, particularly if he had come to us from more than five blocks away. It will be understood, then, that I had no unusual political precocity or passion at the age of eight, and that this difference in our fathers' political views was only a pretext for me to beat up the new boy, who had offended every one of us by coming all the way from New York, with his short pants and blue skin.

We sized each other up for a second. Then he shrugged his thin shoulders and said "O.K.," and the quickness with which he squared away for battle gave me a little turn. We circled around each other, with everyone urging me to get in there and show him what was what. But just then the bell rang, and I felt a surge of relief that was just a bit disconcerting to anyone born as far west as I had been.

"I'll finish with you later," I said.

"O.K.," he said, with that same unnerving readiness.

Something more immediate than our father's political inclinations operated to bring us closer together that morning. Miss Devron put the new boy in the empty seat just in front of me, and I spent the first few minutes of class watching his blue neck turn pink in the warm room, while the pupils drearily went through their recital of breakfasts eaten that morning.

"And now the new boy, Robert Bloom," said Miss Devron, smiling down at him. "What did you have this morning?"

He had been listening carefully to what was going on, and once, when he turned his profile to me, I could see that he was enjoying himself. The rest of the pupils had answered from their seats, but he stood up in the aisle. He stood at attention like a soldier.

"I had a cup of coffee and a snail, Ma'am."

There was a stony quiet for a second, and then the dazzling irreverence of what he had said burst through us with shock waves of pure delight. Miss Devron pounded on the desk with the ruler, and her red chins trembled in front of her like molten lava. "Class!" she cried. "Class, we'll have order here! Come to order. Come to order this instant!"

But she was trying to calm down a madhouse.

"A cup of coffee and a snail, please!" somebody shouted.

"Give me a worm with mine!" somebody yelled back.

And on we went, up that enticing road of suggestibility, until we were eating snakes on muffins. The special delight, of course, was the coffee. *There* was the alluring evil and joy of what he had said, because most of us in that room, including Miss Devron, were Mormons, who felt, in a way beyond reason, that murder was no more than a high-spirited lark compared to drinking coffee or smoking. It wasn't until Miss Devron and her ruler and the powers of light finally triumphed over the dark joy in us that we began to realize the outrageousness of what he had said. We slunk back from debauchery to righteousness under Miss Devron's glowering eye, and finally he was left standing there, all alone before the glare of our joint indignation.

"We should never laugh at those who don't know better, class," Miss Devron began, in a carefully controlled voice. "We must share our knowledge with those less fortunate, and help them to know the truth. Robert comes from a part of the country where they don't know about health. Now then, Robert, that can't be all you had for breakfast, can it?" She looked at him with the pity, the heart-spoken prayer, and the tenderness of a missionary meeting with a cannibal for the first time.

"No, Ma'am," he said. "I had two cups of coffee."

The tight breath gathered in our throats again, but Miss Devron was in control now, and aside from a few blown cheeks and red faces there was no sign that we were not with her in spirit.

"Now, class," she continued, "I want to ask Robert's pardon for what I'm about to do, but I think we can all learn a great deal from what he has told us and from what we can see. Very soon now Robert will be as big and strong as any of you, because he will soon be eating the right foods. But look at him now. See how small he is? *This* is what comes from not eating the right foods and from drinking coffee."

We looked him over, almost seeming to pass him from desk to desk, as if he were a mounted disease-carrying bug we were studying. But what a happy, smiling bug! To judge from his face, he considered the attention we gave him an unexpectedly hearty welcome to his new school.

"I don't think it's the coffee, Ma'am," he suddenly added. "My dad says I steal too many of his cigarettes."

During the next couple of minutes, Miss Devron could have fired salvos of cannon shells over our heads without getting our attention. We were like an oppressed people hailing with insane joy the coming of a revolutionary leader. Even the girls in the room were caught up in the exultation of our victory. All the cigars, cigarettes, or drinking straws filled with grains of coffee that any of us had smoked in secret, all our uneasy past abandonments to appetite, curiosity, and lawlessness were suddenly recalled and made more glorious by Robert's cheerful confession. We worshipped him instantly, and at the end of the day a lot of us walked with him, proud to be seen with such a man. We were walking along with him, swearing, talking about smoking, and making faces at the girls on the other side of the street, when he stopped and tapped me on the arm.

"How about this place?" he said, pointing to a strip of grass between two houses.

"What do you mean?" I asked.

"Your old man's voting for Hoover, isn't he?"

"Sure, but . . ."

"Well, let's fight."

I wanted no part of the fight now, but Robert insisted. He proceeded to support his political views with a ferocity I couldn't seem to match, and it wasn't until he hit me a hard one in the eye that I brought any personal enthusiasm to the fight. From then on, my size and strength started getting the better of him, but no one in the group around us was shouting for me. Those who had been beside me that morning were now yelling for Robert to kill me, and I must say that he did his best. But I finally knocked him down and sat on top of him, and kept his shoulders pinned to the grass until he admitted that Hoover would win the election. When he was up again, he expressed some strong reservations about his opinion, but the election a few days later proved I was right, and, with our political differences out of the way, we became the best of friends.

For the next two or three weeks, Miss Devron tried her best to change Robert's breakfast habits, or at least to get him to lie a little in the interests of classroom harmony. But his incorruptible honesty soon inspired the rest of us to tell what we had really had for breakfast. Variety returned to the menu, and Miss Devron's discovery that some of the larger, healthier children, like me, frequently ate what tasted good for breakfast, instead of simply what was good for them, seemed to undermine her spirit. She acknowledged defeat one morning when she opened class by reading aloud to us from a book of dog stories by Albert Payson Terhune. Subsequently, she read to us whenever there were spare minutes in the day, and the breakfast lists were forgotten. From that time on, she was one of our favorite teachers.

My first idea about Robert's father was that he was a sailor in the United States Navy. Robert showed me pictures of him in a sailor suit—pictures in which he was leaning against a palm tree; laughing, with his arm around two girls; pulling a rope; scrubbing the deck of a ship; or standing on his hands, with a distant and smoking volcano framed between his spread legs. Then I learned that he was no longer in the Navy but was selling something—"selling something out on the road," as Robert described it. With only that imagination-tickling description, I developed the permanent expectation of turning a corner in the city someday and seeing Robert's father selling something right in the middle of the road. What he would be selling I couldn't imagine, nor had I a clear idea of how he would be doing it. Salesmen were never allowed in my own neighborhood, and the only prototype of Mr. Bloom I could conjure up was a man I had seen at the circus the year before. He had been standing outside one of the tents—a man with a dark face and a croaking voice, who kept urging us to come in, trying to scoop us up over his shoulder and into the dark tent with a dipping swing of his straw hat. "Selling, selling, selling!" my mother had said to my father. "It's plain disgusting." And so the man with the straw hat became Mr. Bloom, and I always had the feeling that Robert's house, too, was somehow disgusting. But it was also the most exciting house I had ever been in.

The excitement would hit me as soon as I entered the front door—usually in the form of Robert's dog, an overgrown mongrel lummox called Buddy. I think he was mostly a police dog, but any remnants of purebred respectability had worn thin through long association with the underworld of back alleys and garbage cans, and through personal vice, for the dog was a hopeless drunkard. At least once a week, Robert and I would take a bottle of beer from his refrigerator (and how thrilling it was for me to be in a house containing anything so illegal and wicked as a bottle of beer!) and pour some of it out into a saucer for the dog. He would go at it with a ravenous thirst, frothing the beer with slaps from his scooping tongue until the white suds were all over the floor and his muzzle. He looked as if he were mad, and soon he would act mad. He would lurch around the house, bumping into chairs and tables, and endangering ashtrays and bric-a-brac in his weaving course. I would hold him by the collar at one end of the living room while Robert

CHAPTER FIVE / *Relationships*

called him from the other end, and negotiating those fifteen feet of open rug held for him all the peril and adventure of a walk on a slippery deck in a typhoon. Once he made it to safety, he would sit down, brace himself against a chair, and look at us triumphantly. We would never get him drunk when Robert's mother was around, of course. That was the one thing I ever saw her really angry about. But she was a person of such unquenchable joy and good cheer that even the sight of Buddy drunk that one time didn't keep her angry for long.

She came home from town unexpectedly that day. Buddy's flank had just crashed into a floor lamp and Robert was juggling it back to equilibrium when his mother walked in the front door.

"Robert, have you got that dog drunk again?" she asked, after one look.

"Yes, Mom."

His truthfulness, both at school and at home, always amazed me. For me the truth was usually a fearful thing; my telling it often seemed to hurt my father or my mother, or someone else. But Robert was dauntless before it.

"I've *told* you not to, Robert," Mrs. Bloom said. "You know I have. Poor Buddy! Just look at him. That's no way to treat a dog."

We all looked at him, and I, at least, was conscience-stricken at what we had done. But none of us could remain remorseful for long. Deep in his cups, Buddy had misgauged the size and slipperiness of the low black leather hassock in front of the rocking chair, and though he managed to plant one haunch on it, it kept sliding off. He would edge it back momentarily, his happy face conveying to all of us his certainty that he was seated there four-square and in perfect dignity. I don't know what there was about him—perhaps a certain slack-jawed serenity—but we all started laughing helplessly at the same time. Robert's mother threw herself onto the couch, and Robert and I rolled on the floor in our laughter, while Buddy watched us out of one open eye.

She recovered enough after a time to continue her scolding, but she couldn't get more than a few words out without looking at Buddy, and then she would laugh again. Finally, she gave us some cookies and milk, and poured out a big saucerful of thick cream for Buddy, which she said would sober him faster than anything else. While Robert was drinking his milk at the kitchen table, she came up behind him and slipped her arms under his and clasped her hands on his chest. She kissed him on his neck and on his cheek and up into his hair, and all this time he went on eating his cookies and drinking his milk. I hardly dared to look at them, but I *had* to see the way she kissed him. She was a young woman, with long, dark hair, and black eyes that opened very suddenly at times, then closed very slowly, the lids seeming to take great pleasure in their long trip back down. The nails of her fingers, clasped on Robert's chest, were buffed to a high polish, and her lips were full and red, and looked wonderfully soft against Robert's cheek. I was the fifth, and youngest, child in my family, and I had only been pecked at gingerly by thin lips pulled tight against clenched teeth, and now I could almost feel that cushioned touch of Robert's mother's kiss on my own cheek. I had no name for the feeling it gave me. I was simply fascinated.

She straightened up, put her hand to the back of her hair, and walked to the refrigerator again. "Boys, boys, boys!" she said, "Little devils, all of you. Little heartless devils, getting dogs drunk, pulling girls' hair, fighting, swearing. You're no good, any of you." As she said it, she dug two big scoops of applesauce out of a bowl and slapped them into two dishes.

"So why do I like you so much?" she said to me as she leaned over the table to put a dish in front of me. She was wearing the kind of low dress she usually wore, but I didn't dare look away from her face. I just looked at her smile, and that was everywhere. Then she leaned over and kissed my forehead.

By the time I left for home, Buddy was on his feet and feeling well enough to walk to the corner with Robert and me.

"I like your mother," I said.

"Ah, she's all right," he said, leveling his toe at a rock and kicking it out into the street.

"You bet she's all right. I'd like to marry her when I grow up."

"She's already married."

"I know she is. My gosh, don't I know that? I just said I'd like to, that's all."

We stood on the corner and kicked a few more rocks into the street. And then we were just standing there. Suddenly there was between us a strip of that infinite desolation that surrounds and crisscrosses life, which children must face without the comfort of philosophy or the retreat of memory.

Robert slapped the dog on the side as hard as he could. "Come on, you," he said to him, and I stood and watched them run down the street. I wondered why he never seemed to like the dog except when we got him drunk. I would have given anything for him, but it had been made clear to me at home long before that our yard was too beautiful to be ruined by a "dirty dog."

Besides Buddy, and Robert's mother, with whom I fell more and more in love as I sampled her cakes, home-canned fruit, dill pickles, candy, sandwiches, and lemonade, there were other charms at Robert's house that made my own seem intolerably dreary. Although it was nearly Christmas and I had known Robert for more than two months, I still hadn't met his father, and yet I had come to feel that I knew him as well as my own, or even better. My father's actual physical arrival at home, after a day spent seeing patients in his office or operating at the hospital or attending a church meeting, was the main thing that impressed his existence upon me. He was so neat, so disciplined in his habits, and so completely without vices, eccentricities, or hobbies that he carried himself completely with him wherever he went. But Robert's father lay scattered about the house in the form of pipes, fishing equipment, shotguns, whiskey bottles locked in a glass-front cabinet, a tennis racket, a set of rusty golf clubs, and a three-foot-long Chinese beheading sword, with a dragon engraved on the length of the blade and a dull, pewtery stain on the bright steel, which Robert said was blood. His father had brought the sword home from China when he was in the Navy, and it hung, with its handle wrapped in cords of scarlet silk, above the bed that he and Robert's mother slept in. I was so taken by the sword at the time that I thought anyone would die of pride to have it hanging above his bed, but I now see what a generous concession to his male taste it was for her to have it there. I remember the room as delicately feminine in decor, but it was his room, too, and he had chosen the exact thing to put his mark on it that I would have chosen if I had been married to Robert's mother.

Mr. Bloom did come home occasionally, but even then I didn't get to see him. He was sleeping, Robert would say, going on to explain how tired a salesman becomes after several weeks on the road. On two or three such afternoons, Robert's mother was also not to be seen, and he told me that she, too, was taking a nap and that we were to tiptoe carefully when we went past the closed door to their bedroom.

Christmas morning came and I was downstairs at 5 A.M., tearing into my carefully wrapped presents with impatient, greedy hands. The unexpected child of my parents' middle age, with all my brothers and sisters grown up and living away from home, I had spent my early hours of the past three Christmases all by myself, and I am certain that the pain of a child getting up on Christmas morning to find nothing under the tree cannot be much worse than the pain of one who finds everything there but has no one to show it to. It was not that my parents were really unfeeling. Indeed, they carefully kept my belief in Santa Claus alive beyond the customary age of disillusionment, perhaps because I *was* the last and much youngest child—even telling me that all my Christmas presents, except for some clothing from my mother, had come from Santa Claus. But it never occurred to them to get up early on Christmas morning in order to share my excitement, and I can still remember the sick emptiness of the hour and a half between my discovery of my presents and the first sound of someone else stirring in the house. That year, as usual, I finally heard the maid come upstairs from her basement room, and for the next ten minutes I held her captive while I gloated over each new addition to my wealth.

"Santa was certainly generous to you," she said, and it was so true that I didn't at all mind her saying it in the middle of a yawn.

"Look what Santa Claus left me!" I was able to say to my parents at last, when they came down for breakfast. I had been particularly struck that year by the great number of things he had given me compared to what my mother had given me, and I emphasized this difference by putting his gifts to me and hers in two piles, side by side. But a peck on the cheek and a cursory smile were all the tribute my parents paid to me, Christmas, and Santa Claus's generosity before they opened their own small presents from me, with an air of rather hasty embarrassment, and then turned to the newspaper and to breakfast.

Still, this year I knew someone who would take a second look at what I had received. It took some tight crowding, but I managed to tie all my presents onto my new sled with my new lariat, and I departed for Robert's house. I wasn't disappointed. Not only did Robert's eyes pop at some of the individual presents and at the sheer mass of what I had been given but his mother and, yes, his father, too, were as excited as Robert himself. Mr. Bloom, who got down on the floor to play with my new hook-and-ladder fire engine, turned out to be just the sort of man I had expected. He liked the fire engine so much that I wanted to give it to him, except that the idea of giving it up hurt too much. Out of this dilemma came a sudden inspiration to ask him if he would like to trade his sword for my fire engine. I was circling carefully about this idea, trying to approach it in the best way, when something happened to destroy the notion utterly.

It was not surprising that none of us had paid much attention to Robert's gifts during the first few minutes I was there. All three of the Blooms were too polite not to have gone all out to admire a sledful of gifts dumped into the middle of their living room by a guest as greedy for appreciation as I was. They would have done this even if my presents had come from the ten-cent store. But my gifts were both costly and impressive, and the Blooms, in their modest circumstances, had no need to be just polite; quite simply, they all gave in to the dream of having enough money to buy what I spread out before them, and wholly enjoyed themselves with my presents. I was too far lost in their appreciation to remember that Robert had also had a Christmas that day. But he soon reminded me of it.

"Look!" he said to me. He held in his cupped hands a bright, gold-colored wheel, suspended on a silver axle within a framework of two intersecting wire circles.

"What the heck *is* it?" I asked.

Robert's mother and father were both down on the floor with us, and while Robert threaded a length of green string through a hole in the axle and then wound it carefully along the axle's length, I could feel their eyes looking from me to the wheel and back, excitedly waiting for my reaction. Then Robert gave the wound-up string a sudden vigorous pull, putting the muscles of his back and arm and the tension of his clenched teeth and closed eyes into it, and brought the top spinning to life. The golden wheel hummed softly within its unmoving world of wire circles. Robert placed the top carefully on the smooth surface of a box lid, and there it rested, poised on its projecting tip like a dancer on one leg.

"Watch," he said, and he picked up the wonderful toy and rested its cupped tip on the point of a pencil his father held up. Once the top was spinning there, Robert pushed it, a fraction of an inch at a time, until it was no longer a continuation of the pencil's length but was hanging horizontally out over space, held from falling only by the quiet humming and the touch of the pencil point on the cup.

"My *gosh!*" I said. "Where'd you get that?"

"Mom gave it to me."

"It's called a gyroscope," she said.

For the next five or ten minutes, we shared the excitement of watching the gyroscope ignore gravity in every position we could devise. I was ready to trade Robert all the solid excitement of my presents for the magic that I could feel spring to life when I pulled the green string. I held the gyroscope in my hand and laughed to feel that quiet, determined will fighting mine as I tipped the wheel away from the path it had chosen in the air. And then, suddenly, the magic would be gone and I would be left holding the toy dead in my hands.

"And what did your father give you?" I asked, staring down at the wheel.

"That Chinese beheading sword."

I gave him back the top, but I couldn't look at him. I could feel the cold, sharp edge of that sword in me.

"Where is it?" I asked at last.

"He hung it over my bed."

"Let's see it."

We stepped around the scattered toys and went into his bedroom. There it was, hanging over his bed, just as I had dreamed it might hang over mine.

"I'm not to touch it until I'm older, but she's all mine," Robert said.

I could easily have cried. My mother had given me ties, socks, gloves, shirts, pants, shoes, underwear—all the things a boy could easily do without. But Robert's mother had given him a gyroscope! And the sword had come from his father, while I didn't even think that my father had given me anything! I seemed to have only one real friend right then.

"What did Santa Claus bring you?" I asked.

"Santa Claus? *Santa Claus?*" he hooted. "There isn't any Santa Claus, you big dummy!"

I had heard there wasn't—but only speculatively, never with this final, crushing authority. I could think of only one way to defend myself against Robert's having everything and my not having even Santa Claus. I hit him twice, once on the chest and once in the face, and then I tied all my presents onto my sled with my lariat and started out of the living room, refusing to answer any of the questions his parents asked me. Robert followed me onto the porch, and when I was half a block away he called out to me, "What did you hit me for?"

"Shut up!" I yelled back, and I went home and put my presents under the tree for my relatives to see when they came around later.

Most of the rifts of childhood are as troubled, as tearing, and as quickly smoothed over as the wake of a small motorboat, and by the time Christmas vacation came to an end I had accepted the death of another illusion and Robert had forgotten my naïveté. We went on as before, with the abrasive honesty of his life wearing away at the hypocrisy of my own until I, too, occasionally knew some emotional truths. With that encouragement of truth which had been given him at home, he was quite free to say, for example, that he liked or disliked this or that person, this or that book, or a threatening gray or a clear blue sky. But I knew no such freedom. Caught within the attitude that this world was God's green acre and too sacred to be regarded critically by the likes of me, I wasn't free to decide whether I liked a dog better than a cat, or a mountain better than a rosebush. Any expression of vital choice on my part was seen as a blasphemous elevation and denigration of two aspects of the divine order, and, pressed down by the weight of my blasphemy, I lost the power to make any choice. But Robert restored this power during the next year of our friendship. He restored it with a series of shocks that showed me that what he said about something and what I felt about it, way down, were often related. How exhilarating it was to have him come out with a truth that my bones knew but my tongue could not say!

"What do you think of Miss Brown?" I might ask him, speaking about the elementary-school art teacher.

"She's a nice lady," he answered, "but she doesn't know anything about art."

My heart pounded with the truth of what he had said. I half knew she didn't know anything about art, but she had been put in our classroom by authority as an art teacher, so it was certain that I must be wrong about her. "What do you mean, she doesn't know anything about art?" I asked—on his side, of course, but still fearful.

"All she draws is mountains," he said disgustedly. "Never people, or dogs, or flowers, or trees, or boats, or water, or houses, or clouds, or *anything* but mountains. And it's always the same mountain. You should have seen the teacher I had in New York. She could draw a face on the board in two seconds and everyone knew who it was. Boy, was she an artist!"

If I was impressed at the time by the fearlessness of what Robert knew and said, it is only now that I can appreciate the full miracle of his freshness surviving the hothouse atmosphere of souls under cultivation for adulthood that existed in our third- and fourth-grade classrooms. Having known Robert, I now seriously believe that the right sort of parents can emotionally equip a child to survive the "civilizing" process of education. But my real appreciation of Robert came mostly in retrospect, and most of whatever I now know about truth I had to learn the hard way, for in the late winter of our fourth-grade year—about a year and a half after our friendship started—I cut myself off from the hope that Robert would go on indefinitely helping me to find truth.

It was one of those false spring days that sometimes appear toward the end of winter—a sad, nostalgic day, when the air teased our bodies with the promise of games and picnics, and the earth was still locked up and unavailable for our use, beneath two feet of grimy snow. Robert and I were walking home together. "Mom just put up some more dill pickles last night," he said, and suddenly the day came alive.

"First one who gets there gets the biggest," I said, and, with my longer legs, I was on the porch while Robert was still pounding up the sidewalk. We pushed the living-room door open, and when we weren't hit in the chest by a flying, dancing Buddy, we both understood the sign. Whenever Robert's father was out of town, his mother tried to keep Buddy in the house as a watchdog—I suppose on the theory that he might possibly trip up an intruder and break his neck as he frisked about him in indiscriminate welcome. But when Buddy was absent—off on some disreputable scavenging trip, no doubt—it usually meant that Mr. Bloom was home. Robert and I now peered out the back living-room window and saw the car in front of the garage, and he lifted his fingers to his lips. "Come on," he whispered. "Let's go into the kitchen."

We tiptoed past the closed door of his parents' bedroom and past the open door of his own bedroom. As usual, I looked in and saw the sword still hanging over his bed. The sharp pain of Robert's ownership of that sword had been replaced in me by a kind of dull wonder at his exasperating sense of honor. "No, I can't touch it until I'm twelve," he had insisted a dozen or more times that past year—times when nothing in the world but a three-foot-long Chinese beheading sword was appropriate to the game at hand. Now, in the kitchen, Robert whispered, "We better not have any pickles without asking Mom. Boy, was she ever mad the last time we ate them all! How about some apricot jam and bread?"

"Swell," I whispered back.

"Hey, would you rather have apricot or strawberry?" he whispered from the depths of the icebox.

"Let's have both," I said, regaining some of the excitement I had lost in my disappointment over the pickles.

He brought out the two jam jars, spooned large helpings of each kind into a bowl, and began whipping them together with a fork. I stared, hypnotized, at the clean colors as they ran together and faded to a pinkish tan. "Boy, are you ever lucky!" I said. "Eating any old thing you want when you want! Do you think my mother, or that old maid of ours, would let me eat *anything* between meals? No, sir! Our maid says you're spoiled because you're an only child and your mother doesn't know any better."

"Well, maybe," he said, shaking fist-size globs of jam onto the bread. "But Mom told me they're going to try and get me a baby brother or a baby sister pretty soon."

"A baby brother or sister? Which kind would you rather have?"

"Oh, I don't care. They're both O.K., I guess." He returned the jars to the icebox, and came back to the table and picked up his bread and jam. "How about taking these out on the front porch to eat?"

"O.K."

We crept past the closed bedroom door again and went out on the porch, being careful not to let the door slam behind us. When we were comfortably settled on the front steps, with our mouths full of bread and jam, I suddenly decided to ask him a question that had occurred to me many times. "Robert, is there something wrong with your mother and father?"

"What do you mean, 'something wrong'?" he asked.

"Well, you know. The way they're always resting when we come here. Are they sick?"

It seemed to me that they must certainly be sick, or something more than sick. For me, bed was a concept that changed entirely with the time of day. Bed at night was a completely respectable thing, both for myself and for my parents—so respectable, in fact, that I usually put up a spirited fight against going to it. But after the sun rose over the high, gray mountains east of town, bed instantly became something slack and irresponsible, even on week-end mornings, when there was no immediate reason for getting out of it. "What?" my father would say, standing over me at seven o'clock on a rainy Saturday morning. "Not up yet?" He never said it harshly but always with a friendly smile, kept just thin enough to give me the message that bed simply wasn't the place to be at that hour. So grave was this obscure crime that even when I was sick enough to stay in bed all day, I dreaded the long morning and afternoon hours there, and never wholly relaxed until it was 8 P.M. again and really time for bed. If there was one aspect of the irregularity of Robert's house that I did not enjoy, it was this matter of bed in the afternoon. There *was* something sick about it.

"Heck, no, they're not sick," Robert said. "Dad gets tired out on the road. I *told* you that. And Mom likes to be with him. They're just taking a nap. Or maybe they're trying to find me that baby brother."

I stopped in the middle of a bite and stared at him. If he had spoken the last words in Latin he could not have lost me more completely.

"They're trying to find a baby? In *there?*"

"Well, of course," he said, stuffing the last of his bread and jam into his mouth. And then the full extent of my darkness must have shown on my face. He swallowed with a little choking cough. "Oh, my gosh!" he said. "You don't know about *that*, either, do you?"

"Of course, I know about it," I said angrily. "I just didn't know what you meant."

But I couldn't cover up my ignorance or my need to know the truth, for he proceeded to tell me all about it. He told me in adequate detail and finished by saying that all babies were "found" in just this way.

"*All* babies?"

"Yep—me, you, everybody. That's the way everybody's parents get their children."

I jumped up, and, seeing the expression on my face, Robert stood up, too, and then I hit him twice—once on the chest to knock him down and once on the nose as he was falling. In its most impersonal sense, the idea he had given me was just barely tolerable, but in relation to my parents it was an unthinkable blasphemy. After all they had done for me, hitting him seemed the very least I could do. I stood over him, breathing hard and with my fists clenched. He looked up at me from the top step, where he had fallen, and slowly rubbed his nose.

"You big damn dumb!" he said at last. "I'll never tell you another thing as long as I live!"

"You just better not," I said. "You just better never say another word to me if you know what's good for you!"

And he never did. From that day forward, I was on my own.

Not a Runner

A native of New Zealand, Diane Walker (1938–   ) spent her first twenty years there, earning a teacher's certificate at Palmerston North Teachers' College and teaching elementary school for a year in a small country town. Subsequently she traveled in Europe, lived for a time in England, and taught again in Montreal, Canada. She came to California in 1969, enrolling at Laney College in Oakland the same year. She studied English at the California State College in Hayward and plans to teach in America after receiving her degree even if she has to "move to the wilderness" to get a teaching job.

On the last day of holidays, before she returned to school, my sister was always given a box of candy. I did not know this until shortly after my eleventh birthday, when the time came for me to be sent to school with her. "These are to take to school," said my father, handing me a box of assorted toffees. Candy, especially boxed, was reserved for special occasions like birthdays or Christmas, and I was so taken aback I took the box to my room, opened it, and while I pondered on the significance of such a gift, ate its entire contents. Later that evening my sister came into my room to check my packed suitcases. "Where's your candy?" she asked. I must have given her a guilty look, for "Find the box" was all she said, and left. She returned a few minutes later with an identical, unopened box, tore off the cellophane, divided the contents, tipped half into my box and tucked it into the bottom of my suitcase. "Everyone," she explained, "takes candy to school at the beginning of term."

I recall this incident not because it impressed me at the time: the fact that it did not is what impresses me now. That my sister had protected me from the slings and arrows of our small but sometimes outrageous world was something I had long taken for granted; she knew its pitfalls and put herself between them and me. Although she was only four years older than I, I can never remember her as anything but adult. In boarding school since her seventh year, she had apparently learned at an astonishingly early age to keep the child in herself well hidden. As far as I was concerned, she was related to God, all-knowing and all-good. With her on my side, who could be against me? With that faith and cheerful anticipation, I departed for

Original publication in this volume, by permission of the author.

Wellington, the nation's capital and home of the Samuel Marsden School for Girls.

Marsden School is situated in the hills of Karori, in what used to be one of the more fashionable suburbs of the city. The school buildings are not visible from the road, being set well back in the center of the grounds which are bounded by a high hedge. A long, sweeping driveway leads to two large buildings, the far one being the school itself, which draws most of its pupils from the city, and the near one housing the boarders, most of whom come from sheep stations or small country towns. On arrival my sister took me to a large sitting room where I was to wait, along with the other new girls, for that personage before whose very name even my own sister shrank, the headmistress.

Shortly, the door flew open and a woman entered. She was probably of medium height, or even less, but had a presence which made size irrelevant. Her hair was combed back severely and caught in a tight, rolled wave, and she had a mouth which reminded me of a capital "C" fallen flat on its face. I think we all felt the power of that woman because I can remember, and feel still, the tension she managed to produce in that brief initial meeting. After looking us over and checking as to who we were, she spoke. She would, she said, like to welcome us, and to express the hope that we would bring honor to the school. We were fortunate, as we all knew, in being able to attend, and she, Miss Neligan, hoped we would always remember this. She would, she said, like to have a brief word with us, singly, in her study before we settled in. We followed her and formed a line outside her study door. I was second or third in line, but she motioned for me to enter first. I stood in front of her desk while she sat and examined, for a moment, some papers.

"Now," she said, looking up, "we are pleased to have with us the sister of a girl in whom we have reason to feel much pride. No doubt," she continued, "we can hope to expect the same record from you that your sister has established at Marsden."

I thought of my sister's room at home: the row of cups, the wall of certificates and pendants. Why, I thought, the lady must be joking. She smiled at me a little, so I smiled back, sharing the joke.

"Well, tell me," she continued, "are you a runner?"

"No," I said, "I'm a Walker."

A quick frown showed her disapproval of my reply, and I shifted my feet uneasily.

"Are you good at sports?" she asked.

I said I didn't know; I didn't think so. I could swim well, but not fast.

"Well, what about tennis?" she asked.

I told her I hadn't played much tennis yet.

"We are establishing quite a name in competitive sports here," she said.

She asked me then about school work. Was I good in school, she wanted to know. I told her I thought I was about usual.

"Average," she said.

"Average," I echoed. "But," I added, "I'm pretty good at fishing."

"Fishing!" she cried. "Fishing! You won't be doing any of that here!"

The interview over, I was directed to my dormitory. My roommates were already there, sitting on their beds. They all had a pinched look, and one was sobbing quietly. "Listen," I said, "Do you know the headmistress's name?"

"It's Miss Neligan," one of them said.

"Hey," I chanted.

> "Miss Neligan, Miss Neligan,
> Her beak holds more than her belly can!"

We all started to giggle, when out of the corner of my eye I saw a shadow in the doorway. A tall girl, a badge-bearer, stood there, looking at me.

"Stand up!" she barked. "All of you. Stand up! And who, might I ask, are you?"

I told her my name.

"You must be . . ." she began.

"Yes," I said, "her sister."

"Rather big for your boots, aren't you?" she said. "But we shall soon fix that. Now, all of you, go down and line up for supper."

We filed down the corridor to the top of the stairwell, where groups of girls were milling around. A long wooden banister ran down one side of the staircase which led to the dining room. Prefects stood along the wall, hurrying us along, their badges shiny under the hall lights. One of them was my sister. I edged over to her. "Move along there," she was shouting. "Second bell is about to ring." I didn't think she had seen me, but she said, "You, too, Diane," very quietly. The prefect next to her looked at me.

"Hey," she said. "Is this skinny kid your sister?"

"Yes," my sister said.

"You don't look much to me," the other girl said. "How are you going to run on those peastick legs?"

At eleven I was very undersized. My weight, or lack of, had long been a family joke. My father said it must be all that standing in the water, holding a fishing line, had made me grow legs like a crane. Usually I took such remarks in good humor, but something in this girl's words made me unaccountably angry.

"Well," she persisted, "how?"

On sudden inspiration I answered her question.

"Like this!" I cried, throwing myself astride the banister railing, and before a startled audience, slid all the way to the bottom, where I made a spectacular and inelegant landing.

So began my career at Marsden. By the end of the first month I had achieved a notoriety that preceded me wherever I went. Not only had I organized a midnight feast, left the school grounds, skipped chapel, ruined the headmistress's ceiling (by overflowing a bath, directly overhead), but I had achieved an all-time record for accumulating "order marks." These were given for disciplinary purposes, and ranged from serious offences such as "answering back" (usually worth a double) down to "dust on dressing table" or "hairs in hairbrush." Order marks were an effective measure, used mainly by prefects, because once one received more than nine in a three-week period, the privilege of spending every third Saturday at the home of a relative or day pupil was taken away. The names of the girls who were "gated" were posted on the bulletin board on the Friday preceding "out Saturdays." My name caused a stir of unprecedented interest with a new and startling record of ninety. In class and out of it, my reputation grew. I was the despair of the staff, the horror of the prefects, a daily disappointment to all whose duty it was to bring me to heel.

"I can't understand it," the headmistress said. "Your sister is such a *nice* girl!"

My sister. Looking back, it's all so stunningly clear. I wonder how it was that I, and all those who struggled with me, could not see then what seems so obvious now. Of course, it may be that they did, and if so, what difference would it have made? To have to survive in the shadow of another is a poor survival at best. What is peculiar to children is their instinctive reaction toward preserving their individuality. It is primitive and swift, and does not seek compromise. Although I enjoyed a certain admiration among my peers for my daring and seemingly impervious nonchalance, I secretly trembled with fear lest someone would find a chink in the armor within which I hid the frightened little girl I really was. The only person I did not fight was she who was the source of all my troubles, my sister. Those times when we were forced into open conflict, we played our roles with perfect understanding. (I had to be at least as bad with her as with any other prefect. She, on the other hand, had to punish me with at least the same severity.) It was with some relief though, to both of us, that she left Marsden, and went off to begin life on the other side of those walls. Unfortunately for me, I had established my reputation so well I was unable to desert it. With adolescence, moreover, my innocence diluted and I developed the pains of anger, frustration, and remorse. Holidays became a nightmare, a week of waiting for my father to open my report and then of seeing the confusion and disappointment in his face. It was always the same: sighs would be followed by talks and, eventually, shouting. Afterwards, as I sat in the privacy of my room, I would hear my sister and father talking, and later she would come and sit with me. "Never mind," she would say. "Don't worry. It will all come out in the wash."

Actually it never does, quite. Once set in motion, the wheels that begin to turn us up a given path, although stopped, can never quite ignore the ground they have covered. That this was equally true of my sister, I never realized until our childhoods were long passed.

I was teaching in Canada, many years later, when I received a letter from my brother-in-law. My sister, he said, was not well, and would like to see me. A return ticket from Montreal to London, where they lived, was enclosed, and within a few days I was in England. Perhaps due to her weakened condition, my sister confided in me to a degree that was not typical of her, before or since. Among the many things she told me, one incident stands out with remarkable clarity. She described to me, in her matter-of-fact voice, an event in which I had taken part, but had absolutely no recollection of. We were, she said, aged three and seven. Our mother had recently died: her death, at twenty-nine, was sudden and unexpected, and our father was having difficulty coping with the situation. He took us, she said, down to the cemetery, where we stood by the graveside. Suddenly my father threw himself across the grave and wept uncontrollably. The effect on my sister was one of immediate horror and acute embarrassment. She said she vowed then and there she would never, not ever, display her own feelings, and, seeing the wide-eyed three-year-old watching, made a second decision. She would see to it that I would have, in her, the strength and protection my father was so obviously unable to offer.

I am not trying to say that, dramatic as it was, this event shaped our entire lives. It must, however, have provided a certain quality in the fabric of our destinies in that it lay down a pattern from which neither of us could escape. My sister condemned herself to being the "good one": strong, worthy, and successful. To match her success, I had to be as spectacularly "bad" as she was "good."

The Irish Lass

Nikos Kazantzakis (1885–1957) was born on the Greek island of Crete, a land that held an almost mystical grip on his imagination. A passionate man with an enormous zest for life, Kazantzakis was deeply intellectual as well. After completing studies in law at the University of Athens, he was a philosophy student of Henri Bergson in Paris. His first writings were philosophical treatises and literary criticism. He completed his education in literature and art in Italy and Germany. Although spiritually rooted in Crete, he was a tireless traveler, living for periods in Spain, England, Egypt, Israel, Russia, China, and Japan and writing travel books about the places he had been. It wasn't until later in his life that he began to write novels. Among his more than thirty volumes, the best-known works are *Zorba the Greek* (1946), *The Greek Passion* (1953), *The Odyssey: A Modern Sequel* (1958), *The Last Temptation of Christ* (1959), and his autobiography, *Report to Greco* (1965), in which the following selection appears.

I was still not entirely satisfied, however. I liked the road I had taken but felt I had to reach its furthest limits. That year an Irish girl had arrived in Kastro. She gave English lessons. The thirst for learning was aflame in me as always; I engaged her to tutor me. I wanted to learn the language and write manifestoes in English in order to enlighten those who lived outside Greece. Why should we let them remain in darkness? So I threw myself heart and soul into English, that strange magical world. What joy when I began to saunter through English lyric poetry with this Irish girl! The language, its vowels and consonants, had become so many warbling birds. I stayed at her house until late at night. We talked about music, read poetry, and the air between us caught fire. As I leaned over her shoulder following the lines of Keats and Byron, I breathed in the warm acrid smell of her armpits, my mind grew turbid, Keats and Byron disappeared, and two uneasy animals remained in the tiny room, one clothed in trousers, the other in a dress.

Now that I had finished the gymnasium, I was preparing to go to Athens to register at the university. Who could tell if I would ever see her again, this blue-eyed, slightly stooped but fluffily plump daughter of an Irish pastor. As our separation approached, I grew increasingly more uneasy. Just as when we view a ripe fig oozing with sweet syrup, and being hungry and thirsty we avidly stretch forth our hand to strip its rind, and as we strip it our mouth waters; so in the same way I cast furtive glances at this ripe Irish girl and stripped her in my imagination—like a fig.

One day in September I made my decision.

"Would you like to climb Psiloríti with me?" I asked her. "The whole of Crete is visible from the top, and there's a little chapel at the summit where we can spend the night and I can say goodbye to you."

Her ears turned crimson, but she accepted. What deep mystery that excursion involved, what sweetness and anxious anticipation—just like a honeymoon! We set out at night. The moon above our heads was truly dripping with honey; never again in my life did I see such a moon. That face, which had always seemed so sorrowful to me, laughed now and eyed us roguishly while advancing with us from east to west and descending by way of our opened blouses to our throats, and then down as far as our breasts and bellies.

We kept silent, afraid that words might destroy the perfect, tacit understanding achieved by our bodies as they walked one next to the other. Sometimes our thighs touched as we proceeded along a narrow path, but then each of us suddenly, abruptly, drew away from the other. It seemed that we did not wish to expend our unbearable desire in petty pleasures. We were keeping it intact for the great moment, and we marched hurriedly and with bated breath, not, so it seemed, like two friends, but like two implacable enemies: we were racing to the arena where we would come to grips, breast to breast.

Though we had uttered not a single amorous word before this time, though now, on this excursion, we had agreed on nothing, both of us knew full well where we were going and why. We were anxious to arrive—she, I felt, even more than I.

Daybreak found us in a village at the foot of Psiloríti. We were tired, and we went to lodge at the house of the village priest. I told him that my companion was the daughter of a pastor on a distant, verdant island, and that she desired to see the whole of Crete from the mountain's top. The priest's wife, the papadhiá, came to set the table. We ate. Then, sitting on the sofa, we engaged in small talk. First we discussed the Great Powers—England, France, America, Muscovy. Then vines and olives. Afterwards the priest spoke of Christ, who he said was Orthodox and would never turn Protestant no matter what was done to him. And he wagered that if the girl's father had been with us, he would have converted him to Orthodoxy in one night. But the blue eyes were sleepy, and the priest nodded to his wife.

"Fix her a bed so she can get some sleep. She's a woman, after all, and she's tired.

"But as for you," he continued, turning in my direction, "you're a man, a stalwart Cretan, and it's disgraceful for a Cretan to sleep during the day.

CHAPTER FIVE / *Relationships*

Come, let me show you my vineyards. There are still some unpicked grapes. We can eat them."

I was ready to drop from fatigue and lack of sleep, but what could I do? I was a Cretan and could not disgrace Crete. We went to the vineyards, ate the leftover grapes, then took a walk in the village. The retorts were boiling away in the courtyards, the liquor being removed. We drank more than enough raki, still warm, and returned home arm in arm, both staggering. It was evening already. The Irish girl had awakened, the papadhiá had killed a hen. We ate again.

"No talking tonight," declared the priest. "Go to sleep. At midnight I'll wake you up and give you my little shepherd as a guide, so you won't get lost."

Going out to the courtyard, he inspected the sky like an astronomer, then stepped back inside with a satisfied air. "You're in luck," he said. "Tomorrow will be gorgeous. Leave everything in God's hands. Good night."

Around midnight the priest seized me by the leg and awakened me. He also awakened the girl, by banging a copper roasting pan above her head. Awaiting us in the yard was a curly-haired shepherd boy with pointed ears and a fierce glance. He smelled of billy goats and cistus.

"Ready!" he said, raising his crook. "Quick march! We want to reach the summit in time for sunup."

The moon was at the zenith, still happy, still full of sweetness. It was cold out; we wrapped ourselves in our overcoats. The Irish girl's tiny nose had turned white, but her lips were richly red. I looked the other way in order not to see them.

It was a fierce mountain. Leaving the vineyards and olive groves behind us, then the oaks and wild cypresses, we reached bare rock. Our shoes lacked spikes; we kept slipping. The Irish girl fell two or three times but got up unaided. We were no longer cold; sweat drenched our bodies. Clenching our lips together to keep from gasping, we advanced in silence, the little shepherd boy leading, the Irish girl in the middle, and myself bringing up the rear.

The sky began to turn bluish white. The crags became visible; the first hawks hovered in the blue-black air in search of prey. And when at last we set foot on the summit, the east was gleaming rosy-red. But I could see nothing in the distance. A thick mist lay all around us, shrouding land and sea. Crete's entire body was covered. Shivering from the frightful cold, we pushed open the chapel's little door and went inside. The shepherd, meanwhile, began to search all about to find dry twigs in order to light a fire.

The chapel was built of stones laid up without cement. We remained alone inside, the Irish lass and myself. Christ and the Virgin gazed at us from the humble iconostasis, but we did not gaze at them. Demons opposed to Christ and Virgin, antichrists, antivirgins, had risen within us. Extending my hand, I seized the Irish lass by the nape of the neck. She inclined submissively—this is what she had been waiting for—and the two of us rolled down together onto the flagstones.

A black trap door opened to swallow me, and I perished within. When I raised my lids, I discovered Christ eying me furiously from the iconostasis. The green sphere He held in His right hand was swaying, as though about to be hurled at me. I felt terrified, but the woman's arms wrapped themselves around me and I plunged anew into chaos.

My knees were shaking when we opened the door to go outside; my hand trembled as it drew back the bolt. I had suddenly been possessed by an age-old fear: God would hurl a thunderbolt to reduce both of us, the Irish girl and myself—Adam and Eve—to ashes. To be sure, it is not with impunity that one defiles the house of the Lord directly in front of the Virgin's eyes. . . . I gave the door a push and bounded outside. Whatever happens, I said to myself, may it happen quickly and let's be done with it. But as I ran outside and saw: Oh, what immense joy, what a miracle this was that stretched before me! The sun had appeared, the mist had lifted, and the entire island of Crete from one end to the other gleamed white, green, and rose—fully naked—surrounded by her four seas. With her three high summits, the White Mountains, Psiloríti and Dhíkti, Crete was a triple-masted schooner sailing in the foam. She was a sea monster, a gorgon with myriad breasts, stretched supine on the waves and sunning herself. In the morning sun I distinctly saw her face, hands, feet, tail, and erect breasts. . . . A goodly number of pleasures have fallen to my lot in the course of a lifetime; I have no reason to complain. But this, the sight of the entire island of Crete upon the billows, was one of the greatest. I turned to look at the Irish girl. She was leaning against the little church, chewing a piece of chocolate and calmly, indifferently, licking her lips, which were covered with my bites.

The return to Kastro was dismal. At last we came near; there stood the famous Venetian ramparts with their winged lions of stone. The tired Irish girl drew close in order to lean against my arm, but I could not endure her odor or her leaden eyes—the apple she fed me had covered my lips and teeth with ashes. Moving away brusquely, I refused to let her approach. She, without a word, fell one pace behind me. I heard her sobs. I wanted to turn, clasp her in my arms, and say a kind word to her, but instead I quickened my pace and remained silent. Finally we reached her house. She withdrew the key from her pocket and opened the door. Then she stood waiting on the threshold. Head bowed, she stood waiting. Would I come in or not? Unbearable compassion and a multitude of joyful and sorrowful words rose in me, reaching as far as my throat. But I pressed my lips tightly together and did not speak. I gave her my hand; we separated. The following day I departed for Athens. I had no monkey to give her as a keepsake, but through one of her students I sent her a little dog which liked to snap, a dog I loved. Its name was Carmen.

Dashiell Hammett

One of America's leading dramatists, Lillian Hellman (1905–   ) was born and raised in New Orleans. She attended New York University, though she has stated that college meant very little to her. She entered the literary world through a job with the Liveright publishing house, and later she was a script reader for MGM in Hollywood. Her most prominent plays include *The Children's Hour* (1934), *The Little Foxes* (1939), *Another Part of the Forest* (1946), *Watch on the Rhine* (1941), and *Toys in the Attic* (1960). The last two won New York Drama Critics' Circle Awards for being the best plays of their years. Miss Hellman has written for the screen, and several of her plays were also made into films. She has been called one of the best craftsmen in the American theatre for the precision of her language and the perceptiveness of her characterizations. *An Unfinished Woman* (1969), her autobiography, won the National Book Award. The record of her long relationship with writer Dashiell Hammett is reprinted from it.

For years we made jokes about the day I would write about him. In the early years, I would say, "Tell me more about the girl in San Francisco. The silly one who lived across the hall in Pine Street."

And he would laugh and say, "She lived across the hall in Pine Street and was silly."

"Tell more than that. How much did you like her and how—?"

He would yawn. "Finish your drink and go to sleep."

But days later, maybe even that night, if I was on the find-out kick, and I was, most of the years, I would say, "O.K., be stubborn about the girls. So tell me about your grandmother and what you looked like as a baby."

"I was a very fat baby. My grandmother went to the movies every afternoon. She was very fond of a movie star called Wallace Reid and I've told you all this before."

I would say I wanted to get everything straight for the days after his death when I would write his biography and he would say that I was not to bother writing his biography because it would turn out to be the history of Lillian Hellman with an occasional reference to a friend called Hammett.

The day of his death came on January 10, 1961. I will never write that biography because I cannot write about my closest, my most beloved friend. And maybe, too, because all those questions through all the thirty-one on and off years, and the sometime answers, got muddled, and life changed for both of us and the questions and answers became one in the end, flowing together from the days when I was young to the days when I was middle-aged. And so this will be no attempt at a biography of Samuel Dashiell Hammett, born in St. Mary's County, Maryland, on May 27, 1894. Nor will it be a critical appraisal of his work. In 1966 I edited and published a collection of his stories. There was a day when I thought all of them very good. But all of them are not good, though most of them, I think, are very good. It is only right to say immediately that by publishing them at all I did what Hammett did not want to do: he turned down all offers to republish the stories, although I never knew the reason and never asked. I did know, from what he said about "Tulip," the unfinished novel that I included in the book, that he meant to start a new literary life and maybe didn't want the old work to get in the way. But sometimes I think he was just too ill to care, too worn out to listen to plans or read contracts. The fact of breathing, just breathing, took up all the days and nights.

In the First World War, in camp, influenza led to tuberculosis and Hammett was to spend years after in army hospitals. He came out of the Second World War with emphysema, but how he ever got into the Second World War at the age of forty-eight still bewilders me. He telephoned me the day the army accepted him to say it was the happiest day of his life, and before I could finish saying it wasn't the happiest day of mine and what about the old scars on his lungs, he laughed and hung up. His death was caused by cancer of the lungs, discovered only two months before he died. It was not operable—I doubt that he would have agreed to an operation even if it had been—and so I decided not to tell him about the cancer. The doctor said that when the pain came, it would come in the right chest and arm, but that the pain might never come. The doctor was wrong: only a few hours after he told me, the pain did come. Hammett had had self-diagnosed rheumatism in the right arm and had always said that was why he had given up hunting. On the day I heard about the cancer, he said his gun shoulder hurt him again, would I rub it for him. I remember sitting behind him, rubbing the shoulder and hoping he would always think it was rheumatism and remember only the autumn hunting days. But the pain never came again, or if it did he never mentioned it, or maybe death was so close that the shoulder pain faded into other pains.

He did not wish to die and I like to think he didn't know he was dying. But I keep from myself even now the possible meaning of a night, very late, a short time before his death. I came into his room, and for the only time

288

CHAPTER FIVE / *Relationships*

in the years I knew him there were tears in his eyes and the book was lying unread. I sat down beside him and waited a long time before I could say, "Do you want to talk about it?"

He said, almost with anger, "No. My only chance is not to talk about it."

And he never did. He had patience, courage, dignity in those last, awful months. It was as if all that makes a man's life had come together to prove itself: suffering was a private matter and there was to be no invasion of it. He would seldom even ask for anything he needed, and so the most we did—my secretary and Helen, who were devoted to him, as most women always had been—was to carry up the meals he barely touched, the books he now could hardly read, the afternoon coffee, and the martini that I insisted upon before the dinner that wasn't eaten.

One night of that last year, a bad night, I said, "Have another martini. It will make you feel better."

"No," he said, "I don't want it."

I said, "O.K., but I bet you never thought I'd urge you to have another drink."

He laughed for the first time that day. "Nope. And I never thought I'd turn it down."

Because on the night we had first met he was getting over a five-day drunk and he was to drink very heavily for the next eighteen years, and then one day, warned by a doctor, he said he would never have another drink and he kept his word except for the last year of the one martini, and that was my idea.

We met when I was twenty-four years old and he was thirty-six in a restaurant in Hollywood. The five-day drunk had left the wonderful face looking rumpled, and the very tall thin figure was tired and sagged. We talked of T. S. Eliot, although I no longer remember what we said, and then went and sat in his car and talked at each other and over each other until it was daylight. We were to meet again a few weeks later and, after that, on and sometimes off again for the rest of his life and thirty years of mine.

Thirty years is a long time, I guess, and yet as I come now to write about them the memories skip about and make no pattern and I know only certain of them are to be trusted. I know about that first meeting and the next, and there are many other pictures and sounds, but they are out of order and out of time, and I don't seem to want to put them into place. (I could have done a research job, I have on other people, but I didn't want to do one on Hammett, or to be a bookkeeper of my own life.) I don't want modesty for either of us, but I ask myself now if it can mean much to anybody but me that my second sharpest memory is of a day when we were living on a small island off the coast of Connecticut. It was six years after we had first met: six full, happy, unhappy years during which I had, with help from

Hammett, written *The Children's Hour,* which was a success, and *Days to Come,* which was not. I was returning from the mainland in a catboat filled with marketing and Hammett had come down to the dock to tie me up. He had been sick that summer—the first of the sicknesses—and he was even thinner than usual. The white hair, the white pants, the white shirt made a straight, flat surface in the late sun. I thought: Maybe that's the handsomest sight I ever saw, that line of a man, the knife for a nose, and the sheet went out of my hand and the wind went out of the sail. Hammett laughed as I struggled to get back the sail. I don't know why, but I yelled angrily, "So you're a Dostoevsky sinner-saint. So you are." The laughter stopped, and when I finally came in to the dock we didn't speak as we carried up the packages and didn't speak through dinner.

Later that night, he said, "What did you say that for? What does it mean?" I said I didn't know why I had said it and I didn't know what it meant.

Years later, when his life had changed, I did know what I had meant that day: I had seen the sinner—whatever is a sinner—and sensed the change before it came. When I told him that, Hammett said he didn't know what I was talking about, it was all too religious for him. But he did know what I was talking about and he was pleased.

But the fat, loose, wild years were over by the time we talked that way. When I first met Dash he had written four of the five novels and was the hottest thing in Hollywood and New York. It is not remarkable to be the hottest thing in either city—the hottest kid changes for each winter season—but in his case it was of extra interest to those who collect people that the ex-detective who had bad cuts on his legs and an indentation in his head from being scrappy with criminals was gentle in manner, well educated, elegant to look at, born of early settlers, was eccentric, witty, and spent so much money on women that they would have liked him even if he had been none of the good things. But as the years passed from 1930 to 1948, he wrote only one novel and a few short stories. By 1945, the drinking was no longer gay, the drinking bouts were longer and the moods darker. I was there off and on for most of those years, but in 1948 I didn't want to see the drinking anymore. I hadn't seen or spoken to Hammett for two months until the day when his devoted cleaning lady called to say she thought I had better come down to his apartment. I said I wouldn't, and then I did. She and I dressed a man who could barely lift an arm or a leg and brought him to my house, and that night I watched delirium tremens, although I didn't know what I was watching until the doctor told me the next day at the hospital. The doctor was an old friend. He said, "I'm going to tell Hammett that if he goes on drinking he'll be dead in a few months. It's my duty to say it, but it won't do any good." In a few minutes he came out of Dash's room and said, "I told him. Dash said O.K., he'd go on the wagon forever, but he can't and he won't."

But he could and he did. Five or six years later, I told Hammett that the doctor had said he wouldn't stay on the wagon.

Dash looked puzzled. "But I gave my word that day."

I said, "Have you always kept your word?"

"Most of the time," he said, "maybe because I've so seldom given it."

He had made up honor early in his life and stuck with his rules, fierce in the protection of them. In 1951 he went to jail because he and two other trustees of the bail bond fund of the Civil Rights Congress refused to reveal the names of the contributors to the fund. The truth was that Hammett had never been in the office of the Congress, did not know the name of a single contributor.

The night before he was to appear in court, I said, "Why don't you say that you don't know the names?"

"No," he said, "I can't say that."

"Why?"

"I don't know why. I guess it has something to do with keeping my word, but I don't want to talk about that. Nothing much will happen, although I think we'll go to jail for a while, but you're not to worry because"—and then suddenly I couldn't understand him because the voice had dropped and the words were coming in a most untypical nervous rush. I said I couldn't hear him, and he raised his voice and dropped his head. "I hate this damn kind of talk, but maybe I better tell you that if it were more than jail, if it were my life, I would give it for what I think democracy is, and I don't let cops or judges tell me what I think democracy is." Then he went home to bed, and the next day he went to jail.

July 14, 1965

It is a lovely summer day. Fourteen years ago on another lovely summer day the lawyer Hammett said he didn't need, didn't want, but finally agreed to talk to because it might make me feel better, came back from West Street jail with a message from Hammett that the lawyer had written on the back of an old envelope. "Tell Lilly to go away. Tell her I don't need proof she loves me and don't want it." And so I went to Europe, and wrote a letter almost every day, not knowing that about one letter in ten was given to him, and never getting a letter from him because he wasn't allowed to write to anybody who wasn't related to him. (Hammett had, by this time, been moved to a federal penitentiary in West Virginia.) I had only one message that summer: that his prison job was cleaning bathrooms, and he was cleaning them better than I had ever done.

I came back to New York to meet Hammett the night he came out of jail. Jail had made a thin man thinner, a sick man sicker. The invalid figure was trying to walk proud, but coming down the ramp from the plane he was holding tight to the railing, and before he saw me he stumbled and stopped to rest. I guess that was the first time I knew he would now always be sick. I felt too bad to say hello, and so I ran back into the airport and we lost each other for a few minutes. But in a week, when he had slept and was able to eat small amounts of food, an irritating farce began and was to last for the rest of his life: jail wasn't bad at all. True, the food was awful and sometimes even rotted, but you could always have milk; the moonshiners and car thieves were dopes but their conversation was no sillier than a New York cocktail party; nobody liked cleaning toilets, but in time you came to take a certain pride in the work and an interest in the different cleaning materials; jail homosexuals were nasty-tempered, but no worse than the ones in any bar, and so on. Hammett's form of boasting was always to make fun of trouble or pain. We had once met Howard Fast on the street and he told us about his to-be-served jail sentence. As we moved away, Hammett said, "It will be easier for you, Howard, and you won't catch cold, if you first take off the crown of thorns." So I should have guessed that Hammett would talk about his own time in jail the way many of us talk about college.

I do not wish to avoid the subject of Hammett's political beliefs, but the truth is that I do not know if he was a member of the Communist party and I never asked him. If that seems an odd evasion between two people we did not mean it as an evasion: it was, probably, the product of the time we lived through and a certain unspoken agreement about privacy. Now, in looking back, I think we had rather odd rules about privacy, unlike other peoples' rules. We never, for example, asked each other about money, how much something cost or how much something earned, although each of us gave to the other as, through the years, each of us needed it. It does not matter much to me that I don't know if Hammett was a Communist party member: most certainly he was a Marxist. But he was a very critical Marxist, often contemptuous of the Soviet Union in the same hick sense that many Americans are contemptuous of foreigners. He was often witty and biting sharp about the American Communist party, but he was, in the end, loyal to them. Once, in an argument with me, he said that of course a great deal about Communism worried him and always had and that when he found something better he intended to change his opinions. And then he said, "Now please don't let's ever argue about it again because we're doing each other harm." And so we did not argue again, and I suppose that itself does a kind of harm or leaves a moat too large for crossing, but it was better than the arguments we had been having—they had started in the 1940's—when he knew that I could not go his way. I think that must have pained him, but he never said so. It pained me, too, but I knew that, unlike many radicals, whatever he believed in, whatever he had arrived at, came from reading and thinking.

He took time to find out what he thought, and he had an open mind and a tolerant nature.

Hammett came from a generation of talented writers. The ones I knew were romantic about being writers: it was a good thing to be, a writer, maybe the best, and you made sacrifices for it. I guess they wanted money and praise as much as writers do today, but I don't think the diseased need was as great, nor the poison as strong. You wanted to have money, of course, but you weren't in competition with merchants or bankers, and if you threw your talents around you didn't throw them to the Establishment for catching. When I first met Dash he was throwing himself away on Hollywood parties and New York bars: the throwing away was probably no less damaging but a little more forgivable because those who were there to catch could have stepped from *The Day of the Locust*. But he knew what was happening to him, and after 1948 it was not to happen again. It would be good to say that as his life changed the productivity increased, but it didn't. Perhaps the vigor and the force had been dissipated. But good as it is, productivity is not the only proof of a serious life, and now, more than ever, he sat down to read. He read everything and anything. He didn't like writers very much, he didn't like or dislike most people, but he was without envy of good writers and was tender about all writers, probably because he remembered his own early struggles.

I don't know when Hammett first decided to write, but I know that he started writing after he left army hospitals in the 1920's, settling with his wife and daughter—there was to be another daughter—in San Francisco. (He went back to work for Pinkerton for a while, although I am not sure if it was this period or later.) Once, when I asked him why he never wanted to go to Europe, why he never wanted to see another country, he said he had wanted to go to Australia, maybe to stay, but on the day he decided to leave Pinkerton forever he decided to give up the idea of Australia forever. An Australian boat, out of Sydney for San Francisco, carrying two hundred thousand dollars in gold, notified its San Francisco insurance broker that the gold was missing. The insurance company was a client of Pinkerton's, and so Hammett and another operative met the boat as it docked, examined all sailors and officers, searched the boat, but couldn't find the gold. They knew the gold had to be on the boat, and so the agency decided that when the boat sailed home Hammett should sail with it. A happy man, going free where he had always dreamed of going, packed his bags. A few hours before sailing time, the head of the agency suggested they give a last, hopeless search. Hammett climbed a smokestack he had examined several times before, looked down and shouted, "They moved it. It's here." He said that as the words came out of his mouth, he said to himself, "You haven't sense enough even to be a detective. Why couldn't you have discovered the gold one day out to sea?" He fished out the gold, took it back to the Pinkerton office, and resigned that afternoon.

With the resignation came a series of jobs, but I don't remember what he said they were. In a year or so, the tuberculosis started to cut up again and hemorrhages began. He was determined not to go back to army hospitals, and since he thought he had a limited amount of time to live, he decided to spend it on something he wanted to do. He moved away from his wife and children, lived on soup, and began to write. One day the hemorrhages stopped, never to reappear, and sometime in this period he began to earn a small living from pulp magazines and squibs and even poems sold to Mencken's *Smart Set*. I am not clear about this time of Hammett's life, but it always sounded rather nice and free and 1920's Bohemian, and the girl on Pine Street and the other on Grant Street, and good San Francisco food in cheap restaurants, and dago red wine, and fame in the pulp magazine field, then and maybe now a world of its own.

July 18, 1965

This memory of Hammett is being written in the summer. Maybe that's why most of what I remember about him has to do with summer, although like all people who live in the country, we were more closely thrown together in winter. Winter was the time of work for me and I worked better if Hammett was in the room. There he was, is, as I close my eyes and see another house, reading *The Autumn Garden*. I was, of course, nervous as I watched him. He had always been critical, I was used to that and wanted it, but now I sensed something new and was worried. He finished the play, came across the room, put the manuscript in my lap, went back to his chair and began to talk. It was not the usual criticism: it was sharp and angry, snarling. He spoke as if I had betrayed him. I was so shocked, so pained that I would not now remember the scene if it weren't for a diary that I've kept for each play. He said that day, "You started as a serious writer. That's what I liked, that's what I worked for. I don't know what's happened, but tear this up and throw it away. It's worse than bad—it's half good." He sat glaring at me and I ran from the room and went down to New York and didn't come back for a week. When I did come back I had torn up the play, put the scraps in a briefcase, put the briefcase outside his door. We never mentioned the play again until seven months later when I had rewritten it. I was no longer nervous as he read it: I was too tired to care and I went to sleep on the couch. I woke up because Hammett was sitting beside me, patting my hair, grinning at me and nodding.

After he had nodded for a long time, I said, "What's the matter with you?"

"Nice things. Because it's the best play anybody's written in a long time. Maybe longer. It's a good day. A good day."

I was so shocked with the kind of praise I had never heard before that I started out of the door to take a walk.

He said, "Nix. Come on back. There's a speech in the last act went sour. Do it again."

I said I wasn't going to do it again. He said O.K., he'd do it, and he did, working all through the night.

When *The Autumn Garden* was in rehearsal Dash came almost every day, even more disturbed than I was that something was happening to the play, life was going out of it, which can and does happen on the stage and once started can seldom be changed.

Yesterday I read three letters he wrote to a friend about his hopes for the play, the rehearsals and the opening. His concern for me and the play was very great, but in time I came to learn that he was good to all writers who needed help, and that the generosity had less to do with the writer than with writing and the pains of writing. I knew, of course, about the generosity long before, but generosity and profligacy often intertwine and it took me a long time to tell them apart.

A few years after I met Dash the large Hollywood money was gone, given away, spent on me who didn't want it and on others who did. I think Hammett was the only person I ever met who really didn't care about money, made no complaints and had no regrets when it was gone. Maybe money is unreal for most of us, easier to give away than things we want. (But I didn't know that then, maybe confused it with showing off.) Once, years later, Hammett bought himself an expensive crossbow at a time when it meant giving up other things to have it. It had just arrived that day and he was testing it, fiddling with it, liking it very much, when friends arrived with their ten-year-old boy. Dash and the boy spent the afternoon with the crossbow and the child's face was awful when he had to leave it. Hammett opened the back door of the car, put in the crossbow, went hurriedly into the house, refusing all cries of "No, no" and such.

When our friends had gone, I said, "Was that necessary? You wanted it so much."

Hammett said, "The kid wanted it more. Things belong to people who want them most."

And thus it was, certainly, with money, and thus the troubles came, and suddenly there were days of no dinners, rent unpaid and so on; there they were, the lean times, no worse than many other people have had, but the contrast of no dinner on Monday and a wine feast on Tuesday made me a kind of irritable he never understood.

When we were very broke, those first years in New York, Hammett got a modest advance from Knopf and began to write *The Thin Man*. He moved to what was jokingly called the Diplomat's Suite in a hotel run by our friend Nathanael West. It was a new hotel, but Pep West and the depression had managed to run it down immediately. Certainly Hammett's suite had never seen a diplomat, because even the smallest Oriental could not have functioned well in the space. But the rent was cheap, the awful food could be charged, and some part of my idle time could be spent with Pep snooping around the lives of the other rather strange guests. I had known Dash when he was writing short stories, but I had never been around for a long piece of work. Life changed: the drinking stopped, the parties were over. The locking-in time had come and nothing was allowed to disturb it until the book was finished. I had never seen anybody work that way: the care for every word, the pride in the neatness of the typed page itself, the refusal for ten days or two weeks to go out even for a walk for fear something would be lost. It was a good year for me and I learned from it and was, perhaps, frightened by a man who now did not need me. So it was a happy day when I was given half the manuscript to read and was told that I was Nora. It was nice to be Nora, married to Nick Charles, maybe one of the few marriages in modern literature where the man and woman like each other and have a fine time together. But I was soon put back in place—Hammett said I was also the silly girl in the book and the villainess. I don't know if he was joking, but in those days it worried me: I was very anxious that he think well of me. Most people wanted that from him. Years later, Richard Wilbur said that as you came toward Hammett to shake his hand in the first meeting, you wanted him to approve of you. There are such people and Hammett was one of them. I don't know what makes this quality in certain men—something floating around them that hasn't much to do with who they are or what they've done—but maybe it has to do with reserves so deep that we know we cannot touch them with charm or jokes or favors. It comes out as something more than dignity and shows on the face. In jail the guards called Hammett "sir" and out of jail other people came close to it. One night in the last years of his life, we walked into a restaurant, passing a group of young writers that I knew but he didn't. We stopped and I introduced him: these hip young men suddenly turned into deferential schoolboys and their faces became what they must have been at ten years old. It took me years of teasing to force out of Hammett that he knew what effect he had on many people. Then he told me that when he was fourteen years old and had his first job working for the Baltimore and Ohio Railroad, he had come late to work each day for a week. His employer told him he was fired. Hammett said he nodded, walked to the door, and was called back by a puzzled man who said, "If you give me your word it won't happen again, you can keep the job." Hammett said, "Thank you, but I can't do that." After a silence the man said, "O.K., keep the job anyway." Dash said that he didn't know what was right about what he had done, but he did know that it would always be useful.

When *The Thin Man* was sold to a magazine—most of the big slick magazines had turned it down for being too daring, although what they meant by daring was hard to understand—we got out of New York fast. We got drunk for a few weeks in Miami, then moved on to a primitive fishing camp in the Keys where we stayed through the spring and summer, fishing every day, reading every night. It was a fine year: we found out that we got along best without people, in the country. Hammett, like many Southerners, had a deep feeling for isolated places where there were animals, birds, bugs and sounds. He was easy in the woods, an excellent shot, and later when I bought the farm, he would spend the autumn days in the woods, coming back with birds or rabbits, and then, when the shooting season was over, would spend many winter days sitting on a stool in the woods watching squirrels or beavers or deer, or ice fishing in the lake. (He was, as are most sportsmen, obsessively neat with instruments, and obsessively messy with rooms.) The interests of the day would carry into the nights when he would read *Bees: Their Vision and Language* or *German Gunmakers of the Eighteenth Century* or something on how to tie knots, or inland birds, and then leave such a book for another book on whatever he had decided to learn. It would be impossible now for me to remember all that he wanted to learn, but I remember a long year of study on the retina of the eye; how to play chess in your head; the Icelandic sagas; the history of the snapping turtle; Hegel; would a hearing aid—he bought a very good one—help in detecting bird sounds; then from Hegel, of course, to Marx and Engels straight through; the shore life of the Atlantic; and finally, and for the rest of his life, mathematics. He was more interested in mathematics than in any other subject except baseball. Listening to television or the radio, he would mutter about the plays and the players to me who didn't know the difference between a ball and a bat. Often I would ask him to stop it, and then he would shake his head and say, "All I ever wanted was a docile woman and look what I got," and we would talk about docility, how little for a man to want, and he would claim that only vain or neurotic men needed to have "types" in women—all other men took what they could get.

The hit and miss reading, the picking up of any book, made for a remarkable mind, neat, accurate, respectful of fact. He took a strong and lasting dislike to a man who insisted mackerel were related to herring, and once he left my living room when a famous writer talked without much knowledge of existentialism, refusing to come down to dinner with the writer because, he said, "He's a waste of time. Liars are bores." A neighbor once rang up to ask him how to stop a leak in a swimming pool, and he knew; my farmer's son asked him how to make a pair of snowshoes, and he knew; born a Maryland Catholic (but having long ago left the Church), he knew more about Judaism than I did, and more about New Orleans music, food and architecture than my father, who had grown up there. Once I wanted to know about early glassmaking for windows and was headed for the encyclopedia, but Hammett told me before I got there; he knew a great deal about birds and insects, and for a month he studied the cross-pollination of corn, and for many, many months tried plasma physics. It was more than reading: it was a man at work. Any book would do, or almost any—he was narrowly impatient when I read letters or criticism and would refer to them as my "carrying" books, good only for balancing yourself as you climbed the stairs to bed. It was always strange to me that he liked books so much and had so little interest in the men who wrote them. (There were, of course, exceptions: he liked Faulkner and we had fine drinking nights together during Faulkner's New York visits in the '30's.) Perhaps it is more accurate to say that he had a good time with writers when they talked about books, but would usually leave them when they talked about anything else. He was deeply moved by painting—he himself tried to paint until the last summer of his life when he could no longer stand at an easel, and the last walk we ever took was down the block to the Metropolitan Museum—and by music. But I never remember his liking a painter or a musician, although I do remember his saying that he thought most of them peacocks. He was never uncharitable toward simple people, he was often too impatient with famous people.

There are, of course, many men who are happy in an army, but up to the Second World War I had never known any and didn't want to. I was, therefore, shocked to find that Hammett was one of them. I do not know why an eccentric man who lived more than most Americans by his own standards found the restrictions, the disciplines, and the hard work of an army enlisted man so pleasant and amusing. Maybe a life ruled over by other people solved some of the problems, allowed a place for a man who by himself could not seek out people, maybe gave him a sense of pride that a man of forty-eight could stand up with those half his age; maybe all that, and maybe simply that he liked his country and felt that this was a just war and had to be fought. Whatever Hammett's reasons, the miseries of the Aleutian Islands were not miseries to him. I have many letters describing their beauty and for years he talked of going back to see them again. He conducted a training program there for a while and edited a good army newspaper: the copy was clean, the news was accurate, the jokes were funny. He became a kind of legend in the Alaska-Aleutian army. I have talked to many men who served with him, and have a letter from one of them: "I was a kid then. We all were. The place was awful but there was Hammett, by the time I got there called Pop by some and Grandpop by others, editor of the paper, with far more influence on us, scaring us more in a way than the colonel, although I think he also scared the colonel. . . . I remember best that we'd come into the hut screaming or complaining and he'd be lying on his bunk reading. He'd look up and smile and we'd all shut up. Nobody would go near the bed or disturb him. When money was needed or help he'd hear about it and there he was. He paid for the leave and marriage of one kid. When another of us ran up a scarey bar bill in Nome, he gave the guy who cleaned the Nome toilets money to pay it and say it was his bill if anybody in the army asked him. . . . A lot of kids did more than complain—they went half to nuts. And why not? We had the worst weather in the most desolate hole, no fighting, constant williwaws when you had to crawl to the latrines because if you stood up the wind would take you to Siberia, and an entertainment program which got mixed up between Olivia de Haviland and recordings of W. H. Auden. But the main worry was women. When you'd been there a year all kinds of rumors went around about what happened to you without them. I remember nightly bull sessions in our hut about the dangers of celibacy. Hammett would listen for a while, smile, go back to reading or when the talk got too loud he'd sigh and go to sleep. (Because of the newspaper his work hours started around two A.M.) One night when the session was extra loud crazy and one kid was yelling, Hammett got off his bunk to go to work. The kid yelled, 'What do you think, Pop? Say something.' Hammett said, 'O.K. A woman would be nice, but not getting any doesn't cause your teeth or hair to fall out and if you go nuts you'd have gone anyway and if you kiddies don't stop this stuff I'm going to move into another hut and under my bed is a bottle of Scotch so drink it and go to sleep.' Then he walked out to go to work. We got so scared about losing him that we never said another word like that in front of him."

But, as I have said, the years after the war, from 1945 to 1948, were not good years; the drinking grew wilder and there was a lost, thoughtless quality I had never seen before. I knew then that I had to go my own way. I do not mean that we were separated, I mean only that we saw less of each other, were less close to each other. But even in those years there still were wonderful days on the farm of autumn hunting and squirrel pies and sausage making and all the books he read as I tried to write a play. I can see him now, getting up to put a log on the fire and coming over to shake me. He swore that I would always say, "I haven't been sleeping. I've been thinking." He would laugh and say, "Sure. You've been asleep for an hour, but lots of people think best when they're asleep and you're one of them."

In 1952 I had to sell the farm. I moved to New York and Dash rented a small house in Katonah. I went once a week to see him, he came once a week to New York, and we talked on the phone every day. But he wanted to be alone—or so I thought then, but am now not so sure because I have learned that proud men who can ask for nothing may be fine characters, but they are difficult to live with or to understand. In any case, as the years went on he became a hermit, and the ugly little country cottage grew uglier with books piled on every chair and no place to sit, the desk a foot high with unanswered mail. The signs of sickness were all around: now the phonograph was unplayed, the typewriter untouched, the beloved, foolish gadgets unopened in their packages. When I went for my weekly visits we didn't talk much and when he came for his weekly visits to me he was worn out from the short journey.

Perhaps it took me too long to realize that he couldn't live alone anymore, and even after I realized it I didn't know how to say it. One day, immediately after he had made me promise to stop reading "L'il Abner," and I was laughing at his vehemence about it, he suddenly looked embarrassed—he always looked embarrassed when he had something emotional to say—and he said, "I can't live alone anymore. I've been falling. I'm going to a Veterans Hospital. It will be O.K., we'll see each other all the time, and I don't want any tears from you." But there were tears from me, two days of tears, and finally he consented to come and live in my apartment. (Even now, as I write this, I am still angry and amused that he always had to have things on his own terms: a few minutes ago I got up from the typewriter and railed against him for it, as if he could still hear me. I know as little about the nature of romantic love as I knew when I was eighteen, but I do know about the deep pleasure of continuing interest, the excitement of wanting to know what somebody else thinks, will do, will not do, the tricks played and unplayed, the short cord that the years make into rope and, in my case, is there, hanging loose, long after death. I am not sure what Hammett would feel about the rest of these notes about him, but I am sure that he would be pleased that I am angry with him today.) And so he lived with me for the last four years of his life. Not all of that time was easy, indeed some of it was very bad, but it was an unspoken pleasure that having come together so many years before, ruined so much, and repaired a little, we had endured. Sometimes I would resent the understated or seldom stated side of us and, guessing death wasn't too far away, I would try for something to have afterwards. One day I said, "We've done fine, haven't we?"

He said, "Fine's too big a word for me. Why don't we just say we've done better than most people?"

On New Year's Eve, 1960, I left Hammett in the care of a pleasant practical nurse and went to spend a few hours with friends. I left their house at twelve-thirty, not knowing that the nurse began telephoning for me a few minutes later. As I came into Hammett's room, he was sitting at his desk, his face as eager and excited as it had been in the drinking days. In his lap was the heavy book of Japanese prints that he had bought and liked many years before. He was pointing to a print and saying to the nurse, "Look at it, darling, it's wonderful." As I came toward him, the nurse moved away, but he caught her hand and kissed it, in the same charming, flirtatious way of the early days, looking up to wink at me. The book was lying upside down and so the nurse didn't need to mumble the word "irrational." From then on—we took him to the hospital the next morning—I never knew and will now not ever know what irrational means. Hammett refused all medication, all aid from nurses and doctors in some kind of mysterious wariness. Before the night of the upside-down book our plan had been to move to Cambridge because I was to teach a seminar at Harvard. An upside-down book should have told me the end had come, but I didn't want to think that way, and so I flew to Cambridge, found a nursing home for Dash, and flew back that night to tell him about it. He said, "But how are we going to get to Boston?" I said we'd take an ambulance and I guess for the first time in his life he said, "That will cost too much." I said, "If it does, then we'll take a covered wagon." He smiled and said, "Maybe that's the way we should have gone places anyway."

And so I felt better that night, sure of a postponement. I was wrong. Before six o'clock the next morning the hospital called me. Hammett had gone into a coma. As I ran across the room toward his bed there was a last sign of life: his eyes opened in shocked surprise and he tried to raise his head. He was never to think again and he died two days later.

But I do not wish to end this book on an elegiac note. It is true that I miss Hammett, and that is as it should be. He was the most interesting man I've ever met. I laugh at what he did say, amuse myself with what he might say, and even this many years later speak to him, often angry that he still interferes with me, still dictates the rules.

But I am not yet old enough to like the past better than the present, although there are nights when I have a passing sadness for the unnecessary pains, the self-made foolishness that was, is, and will be. I do regret that I have spent too much of my life trying to find what I called "truth," trying to find what I called "sense." I never knew what I meant by truth, never made the sense I hoped for. All I mean is that I left too much of me unfinished because I wasted too much time. However.

Zorba

For biographical information on Nikos Kazantzakis (1885–1957), see page 283. The selection reprinted below is from his autobiography, *Report to Greco* (1965).

My life's greatest benefactors have been journeys and dreams. Very few people, living or dead, have aided my struggle. If, however, I wished to designate which people left their traces embedded most deeply in my soul, I would perhaps designate Homer, Buddha, Nietzsche, Bergson, and Zorba. The first, for me, was the peaceful, brilliantly luminous eye, like the sun's disk, which illuminated the entire universe with its redemptive splendor; Buddha, the bottomless jet-dark eye in which the world drowned and was delivered. Bergson relieved me of various unsolved philosophical problems which tormented me in my early youth; Nietzsche enriched me with new anguishes and instructed me how to transform misfortune, bitterness, and uncertainty into pride; Zorba taught me to love life and have no fear of death.

If it had been a question in my lifetime of choosing a spiritual guide, a *guru* as the Hindus say, a *father* as say the monks at Mount Athos, surely I would have chosen Zorba. For he had just what a quill-driver needs for deliverance: the primordial glance which seizes its nourishment arrow-like from on high; the creative artlessness, renewed each morning, which enabled him to see all things constantly as though for the first time, and to bequeath virginity to the eternal quotidian elements of air, ocean, fire, woman, and bread; the sureness of hand, freshness of heart, the gallant daring to tease his own soul, as though inside him he had a force superior to the soul; finally, the savage bubbling laugh from a deep, deep wellspring deeper than the bowels of man, a laugh which at critical moments spurted redemptively from Zorba's elderly breast, spurted and was able to demolish (did demolish) all the barriers—morality, religion, homeland—which that wretched poltroon, man, has erected around him in order to hobble with full security through his miserable smidgen of life.

When I think what nourishment books and teachers fed me for so many years in an attempt to satisfy a famished soul, and of the solid, leonine brain fed me by Zorba for just a few months, I find it difficult to endure my bitterness and indignation. How can I avoid heartfelt excitement when I recall the words he spoke to me, the dances he danced for me, the santir he played for me on that Cretan shore where we spent six months digging with a mass of laborers, supposedly to find lignite? We both knew full well that this practical aim was dust to mislead the eyes of the world. We waited anxiously for the sun to set and the laborers to stop work, so that the two of us could lay our dinner out on the beach, eat our delicious peasant meal, drink our tart Cretan wine, and begin to talk.

I rarely opened my mouth. What could an "intellectual" say to an ogre? I listened to him tell me about his village on the flanks of Mount Olympus, about snow, wolves, komitadjis, Saint Sophia, lignite, women, God, patriotism, death—and when words became too constricting for him and he felt suffocated, he leaped to his feet and began to dance on the shore's coarse pebbles. Spare, vigorous, with a tall, erect body and small circular eyes like a bird's, he danced with inclined head, and shrieked and stamped his big feet on the shore line, sprinkling my face with sea water.

If I had listened to his voice—not his voice, his cry—my life would have acquired value. I would have experienced with blood, flesh, and bone what I now ponder like a hashish-smoker and effectuate with paper and ink. But I did not dare. I watched Zorba dance and whinny in the middle of the night, heard him call me to leap up in my own turn from the agreeable haven of prudence and custom in order to depart with him on great voyages from which there was no return, and there I sat, motionless and shivering.

I have been ashamed many times in my life because I caught my soul not daring to do what supreme folly—the essence of life—called me to do. But I never felt so ashamed of my soul as I did in front of Zorba.

The lignite enterprise went to the devil. Laughing, playing, conversing, Zorba and I did all we could to reach the catastrophe. We did not dig to find lignite; that was a pretext meant for the naïve and prudent—"to keep them from barraging us with lemon rinds," Zorba always said, bursting into laughter. "As for us, boss" (he used to call me boss and laugh), "we have other aims, great ones."

"What are they, Zorba?" I asked him.

"It seems we're digging to see what devils we have inside us."

In no time we devoured what my poor dear of an uncle had given me to open (supposedly) an office. Dismissing the workmen, we roasted a lamb, filled a little barrel with wine, spread our meal at the water's edge, the site of our quarry, and began to eat and drink. Zorba took up his santir. Stretching his elderly throat, he commenced an amané. We ate and drank. I can never remember being in such good spirits. "God forgive the dear departed," we shouted. "God forgive the late enterprise—and long life to ourselves! To the devil with lignite!"

We parted at dawn. I headed for paper and ink again, incurably wounded by the bloody dart which, not knowing what else to call it, we term *spirit;* he went north and landed in Serbia, near Skopje, at a mountain where it seems he unearthed a rich vein of magnesite, wrapped various nabobs around his little finger, purchased tools, recruited workers, and began to open galleries in the earth again. He dynamited boulders, constructed roads, brought water, built a house and, succulent old man that he was, married a pretty, fun-loving widow named Lyuba, and had a child by her.

Whereupon one day I received a telegram: "Found most beautiful green stone. Come immediately. Zorba." It was the period when the first distant rumblings of the Second World War could be heard, the tempest which had already begun to drive down upon the earth. Millions of people trembled as they saw the oncoming hunger, slaughter, and madness. All the devils in men were awake and thirsting for blood.

It was in those venomous days that I received Zorba's telegram. At first I grew angry. The world was perishing; honor, man's soul, life itself, were in danger, and here of all things was a telegram asking me to set out and travel a thousand miles to see a beautiful green stone! Beauty be damned! I said. It is heartless, and cares nothing for man's pain.

But I suddenly felt afraid. My anger had already evaporated; now I had the horrible feeling that this inhuman cry of Zorba's corresponded to another inhuman cry inside my own being. A savage vulture within me was beating its wings in order to leave. But I did not leave; once more I did not dare. I did not depart to make the journey, did not follow the divinely brutal inner cry, did not perform a valiant, preposterous act. Following the cold human voice of reason, I took up my pen and wrote to Zorba, explaining to him . . .

He answered me: "Forgive me for saying so, boss, but you're just a pen-pusher. Here you had the chance of a lifetime to see a beautiful green stone, and you didn't see it. By God, sometimes when I have nothing better to do, I sit down and ask myself, Is there a hell or isn't there? But yesterday when I received your letter, I said, There sure is a hell for certain pen-pushers!"

Years went by, long, terrible years in which the times gathered momentum and seemed to go mad, years when geographical frontiers danced and states expanded and contracted like accordions. Zorba and I lost each other in the storm. Now and then, only, I received a brief card from him, from Serbia: "I'm still alive. It's devilishly cold here, so I had to get married. Turn the card over to see her little mug. Quite a piece, eh? Her belly is a trifle inflated because she's already getting a little Zorbadhaki ready for me. Her name is Lyuba. The overcoat I'm wearing with the fox-fur collar is part of my wife's dowry. They're an odd breed; she also gave me a sow with seven piglets! Love and kisses, Alexis Zorba, ex-widower!"

Another time he sent me an embroidered Montenegrin cap from Serbia. It had a silver bell on its pompon. "Wear it, boss," he wrote to me, "when you write the hooey you write. I wear the same cap when I work. People laugh. 'Are you crazy, Zorba?' they ask. 'Why do you wear that bell?' But I chuckle and refuse to answer them. The two of us, boss, we know why we wear the bell."

Meanwhile, I had harnessed myself again to paper and ink. I had come to know Zorba too late. At this point there was no further salvation for me; I had degenerated into an incurable pen-pusher.

I began to write. But no matter what I wrote—poems, plays, novels—the work always acquired, without conscious effort on my part, a dramatic *élan* and form—full of mutually clashing forces, struggle, indignation, revolt, the pursuit of a lost equilibrium; full of portents and sparks from the approaching tempest. No matter how much I struggled to give a balanced form to what I wrote, it quickly assumed a vehement dramatic rhythm. In spite of my wishes, the peaceful voice I desired to emit became a cry. That is why I kept finishing one work, finding that it did not unburden me, and desperately beginning another, always with the hope of being able to reconcile the dark and luminous forces which were then in a state of war, and of divining what form their future harmony would take.

Dramatic form makes it possible for creative literature to formulate the unbridled forces of our times and of our souls by incarnating them in the work's vying heroes. As faithfully and intensely as I could, I attempted to experience the important age in which I happened to be born.

The Chinese have a strange malediction: "I curse you; may you be born in an important age." We have been born in an important age full of kaleidoscopic experiments, adventures, and clashes, not only between the virtues and the vices, as formerly, but rather—and this is the most tragic of all—between the virtues themselves. The old, recognized virtues have begun to lose their authority; they are no longer able to fulfill the religious, moral, intellectual, and social demands of the contemporary soul. Man's soul seems to have grown bigger; it cannot fit any longer within the old molds. A pitiless civil war has broken out in the vitals of our age, has broken out, whether consciously or unconsciously, in the vitals of every man abreast of his times—a civil war between the old, formerly omnipotent myth which has vented its strength, yet which fights desperately to regulate our lives a while longer, and the new myth which is battling, still awkwardly and without organization, to govern our souls. That is why every living man is racked today by the dramatic fate of his times.

And the creator most of all. There are certain sensitive lips and fingertips which feel a tingling at a tempest's approach, as though they were being pricked by thousands of needles. The creator's lips and fingertips are of this kind. When the creator speaks with such certainty of the tempest which is bearing down upon us, what speaks is not his imagination but the lips and fingertips which have already begun to receive the tempest's initial sparks. We must reconcile ourselves heroically to the fact that peace, carefree joy, and so-called happiness belong to other ages, past or future, not to our own. Our age has long since entered the constellation of anguish.

In formulating this anguish, however, I was fighting without conscious effort to·surpass it and find (or create) a form of deliverance. In what I wrote, I often took my pretext from ancient times and legends, but the substance was modern and living, racked by contemporary problems and present-day agonies.

But I was tormented and enticed less by these agonies than by certain still-indefinite, vacillatory hopes whose countenances I struggled to stabilize, the great hopes which enable us to hold ourselves still erect and to gaze confidently before us, past the tempest, at the destiny of man.

I was troubled by concern not so much for present-day man in his state of decomposition as—this above all—for future man in his state of composition and gestation. I reflected that if today's creative artist formulated his deepest inner presentiments with integrity, he would aid future man to be born one hour sooner, one drop more integrally.

I kept divining the creator's responsibility with ever-increasing clarity. Reality, I said to myself, does not exist independent of man, completed and ready; it comes about with man's collaboration, and is proportionate to man's worth. If we open a riverbed by writing or acting, reality may flow into that riverbed, into a course it would not have taken had we not intervened. We do not bear the full responsibility, naturally, but we do bear a great part.

Writing may have been a game in other ages, in times of equilibrium. Today it is a grave duty. Its purpose is not to entertain the mind with fairy tales and make it forget, but to proclaim a state of mobilization to all the luminous forces still surviving in our age of transition, and to urge men to do their utmost to surpass the beast.

The heroes in ancient Greek tragedies were no more or less than Dionysus's scattered limbs, clashing among themselves. They clashed because they were fragments. Each represented only one part of the deity; they were not an intact god. Dionysus, the intact god, stood invisible in the center of the tragedy and governed the story's birth, development, and catharsis. For the initiated spectator, the god's scattered limbs, though battling against one another, had already been secretly united and reconciled within him. They had composed the god's intact body and formed a harmony.

I always considered that in just this way the future harmony must be elevated in today's tragedy, above the enmity and battle, intact amid the fragmented, antagonistic heroes. This is an extremely difficult task, perhaps one still incapable of achievement. We find ourselves in a moment of universal destruction and creation in which even the most valiant individual attempts are in most cases condemned to miscarry. These miscarriages are fertile, however—not for us, but for those yet to come. They open a road and aid the future to enter.

As I wrote in the peace of my family home, wrote away in a transport, this terrible responsibility never left my mind. Verily, in the beginning was the Word. Before action. The Son, only Son, of God; the spermatic Word which creates both the visible and invisible world.

Gradually, exultantly, I found myself engulfed in ink. Great shadows jammed around the pit of my heart and sought to drink the warm blood which would bring them back to life—Julian the Apostate, Nicephorus Phocas, Constantine Palaeologus, Prometheus. Great tormented souls that had suffered and loved exceedingly in their lives, and had impudently contended against God and destiny. I fought to drag them up from Hades in order to glorify their pain and struggle—mankind's pain and struggle—in front of living men. In order to gain courage myself.

I know that what I write will never be artistically consummate, because I intentionally struggle to surpass the boundaries of art, and thus harmony, the essence of beauty, is distorted.

The more I wrote the more deeply I felt that in writing I was struggling, not for beauty, but for deliverance. Unlike a true writer, I could not gain pleasure from turning an ornate phrase or matching a sonorous rhyme; I was a man struggling and in pain, a man seeking deliverance. I wanted to be delivered from my own inner darkness and to turn it into light, from the terrible bellowing ancestors in me and to turn them into human beings. That was why I invoked great figures who had successfully undergone the most elevated and difficult of ordeals: I wanted to gain courage by seeing the human soul's ability to triumph over everything. This is what I knew, what I saw: the same eternal battle which had broken out before my eyes when I was a child was still breaking out uninterruptedly inside me, breaking out uninterruptedly in the world at large. It was the inexhaustible motif of my life. This is why in all my work these two wrestlers, and these alone, were always the protagonists. If I wrote, it was because my writings, alas, were the only means I had to aid the struggle. Crete and Turkey, good and evil, light and darkness, were wrestling uninterruptedly inside me, and my purpose in writing, a purpose at first unconscious and afterwards conscious, was to do my utmost to aid Crete, the good and the light, to win. My purpose in writing was not beauty, it was deliverance.

I chanced to be born in an age when this struggle was so intense and the need of help so imperative that I could quickly see the identity between my individual struggle and the great struggle of the contemporary world. We were alike in our battle to be delivered, I from my dark ancestors, it from the old iniquitous world, both from darkness.

World War II had been declared, the whole earth had gone mad. Now

I plainly saw that each age has its demon. This demon governs, not we. The demon of our age is a bloodthirsty carnivore, as is always the case when a world rots and must disappear. It seems that an inhuman, superhuman Mind aids the spirit to deliver itself from putrescent man and ascend; when it sees a world stepping in the way, it dispatches the carnivorous demon of havoc to demolish this world and clear a road, always a bloody one, so that the spirit may pass.

Now, without respite, I saw and heard the world around me being demolished. Everyone saw it being demolished. The purest souls tried to resist, but the demon puffed upon them and they lost their wings.

I took to the Cretan mountains again when war was declared, knowing that only there could I find, not peace or consolation, but the pride a man needs in difficult moments to keep him from becoming worthless. Once I saw an aged campaigner sitting on the church stoop one Sunday after the service and advising young men in the stratagems of manly valor. "Look fear straight in the eye if you can," I heard him say, "and the fear will feel afraid and run away." I took my staff, therefore, slung a rucksack over my shoulders, and headed for the mountains. It was the time when the Germans were forcing their way into Norway and fighting to subjugate it.

One midday I heard a savage voice high above me as I was traversing the foot of Psiloríti. "Hey, neighbor, wait a minute! I want to ask you something!"

Lifting my head, I perceived a man draw away from a boulder and come tumbling down. He descended with giant strides from rock to rock; the stones rolled away under his feet, a great clamor began, the entire mountain seemed to be tumbling down with him. Now I could distinctly see that he was an immense, elderly shepherd. I stopped and waited for him. What could he want with me, I asked myself, and why such eagerness?

He came close to me, halting on a rock. His uncovered chest was hairy and steaming.

"Hey, neighbor, how is Norway getting on?" he asked with panting breath.

He had heard that a country was in danger of being enslaved. He had no real idea what Norway was, where it was located or what kind of people lived there. The one thing he clearly understood was that liberty was in danger.

"Better, grandpa, better. No need to worry," I answered.

"Thank God," roared the old shepherd, making the sign of the cross.

"Want a cigarette?" I asked him.

"Bah! What do I want with a cigarette? I don't want anything. If Norway's all right, that's enough for me!"

Saying this, he swung out his crook and climbed up again to find his flock.

The Greek air is truly holy, I thought to myself; surely freedom was born here. I do not know if the ordeal of a remote and unknown land fighting for its freedom could have been experienced with as much anguish and disinterestedness by any other peasant or shepherd in the world. Norway's struggle had become this Greek shepherd's struggle, because liberty, for him, was like his own daughter.

Such was the combative assignment I gave my duty as I wrote in the peacefulness of my family home, trying to play my part in the eternal battle. But sometimes I abandoned paper and ink in order to take the olive- and vine-surrounded road which leads to Knossos. When this unforeseen Cretan miracle first rose like spring out of the soil, when I first saw the stone stairways, the columns, courtyards, and frescoes, I was overwhelmed by inexpressible gladness and sorrow for this extraordinary world which had perished, for the doom of every human exploit: to maintain itself a split second in the light and then plunge into chaos for all eternity. To the degree to which the royal palace was reconstructed, loomed again in the Cretan sunlight, and the bullfights and the women with high, exposed breasts, painted lips, and curled unruly tresses came to life again on the half-demolished walls, to this same degree a Last Judgment loomed before me; age-old unknown ancestors rose from the soil, the men mute, jolly, and cunning, the women wearing skirts embroidered with stars from the sky, stars from the sea, flowers from the earth, and dandling God's poisonous snakes in their arms.

But one day when I took the verdurous road again, reached the Last Judgment's sacred hill, and strolled for hours among the crumbling miracles, one painting shook me above all. It was as though I had seen it for the first time. Doubtlessly, this painting must have corresponded to my soul's present concerns and hopes; that was why I understood its hidden meaning on this day for the first time. Numerous fish were cruising in the water with lifted tails, frolicking happily, whereupon a flying fish in their midst suddenly spread its little fins, took a leap and bounded out of the sea in order to breathe air. Too big for its slavish piscine nature it was, too big to live all its life in the water. It suddenly longed to transcend its destiny, breathe free air, and become a bird—for a flash only, as long as it could endure. But that was enough; this flash was eternity. That is the meaning of eternity.

I experienced great agitation and fellow feeling as I gazed at this flying fish, as though it was my own soul I saw on that palace wall painting which had been made thousands of years before. "This is Crete's sacred fish," I murmured to myself, "the fish which leaps in order to transcend necessity and breathe freedom." Did not Christ, the ICHTHYS, seek the same thing: to transcend man's destiny and unite with God, in other words with absolute freedom? Does not every struggling soul seek the same thing: to smash frontiers? What good fortune, I reflected, that Crete should have been perhaps the first place on earth to see the birth of this symbol of the soul fighting and dying for freedom! The flying fish—behold the soul of struggling, indomitable man!

I observed the flying fish venture the fatal leap out of the water, observed the svelte, narrow-waisted man and woman playing happily with the bull in the stone-paved arenas, observed the lioness sleeping peacefully among the lilies, and struggled to find their hidden meaning. What was the source of such valor and joy? What prayer were the woman's triumphant arms offering, and to whom—those bare arms entwined by black snakes? This indestructible thirst for life and this heroic fearless smile in the face of danger and death awakened fatal ancestral feats of derring-do in me, long-desired encounters with death. Bull and man, death and the soul, seemed to be friends; both naked, both anointed like athletes with aromatic oil, they were playing for one hour, two hours, as long as the sunlight lasted. Shaken and disturbed, I reflected that it is here in this terrible moment of confrontation between the Cretan and the abyss that Crete's secret lies concealed. I had to find this secret.

Christ, Buddha, and Lenin had paled inside me; I had been swept away by the soil of Crete. Without looking behind me now, I lifted my eyes to gaze with longing and fright upon an invisible peak still enveloped in clouds—a God-trodden peak of Sinai where, armed with thunderbolts and stern commandments (such was my presentiment) my God had his abode.

I sensed new strength, new responsibility, swelling my veins. My soul seemed to have been enriched along with the Cretan soil; it felt kneaded from more of the age-old laughter and tears. Once again I realized how intensely and with what secret assurance soil feels its correspondence to the soul. Similarly, a flower must surely have an inner awareness of the mud which rises from its roots and is transformed into aroma and color.

I saw my soul expanding in my blood like a mysterious miniature of Crete. It had the same contour of a three-masted schooner; it lived through the same centuries, the same terrors and joys, cruising in the middle of the three continents—the three violent, spermatic winds—of saintly Asia, ardent Africa, and sober Europe. The conscious or unconscious longing I had for years awoke even more imperatively inside me now: the longing to harmonize these three disparate desires and drives, and to reach the supreme exploit—the synthesis, the sacred trihypostatic Monad.

In me, the world-wide religious symbol of the Holy Trinity was transposed to another, less symbolic plane. It became burning imperious reality, an immediate, supreme duty. "This or nothing!" was the inner vow I took in a moment of rapture. This Trinity was not given me ready-made from on high; I had to create it myself. This was my duty, this and only this! I told myself that it was not for nought that Crete was situated in the middle of three great Breaths, not for nought that my soul assumed Crete's contours and destiny. It was my duty to take what Crete had cried out over the centuries, with her people, her mountains, the frothy seas around her, with her body and soul, in her sleeping hours and waking hours, to take this and turn it into an integrated message. Was I not her son? Was I not of her soil? Was it not she, now when I confronted her most ancient splendor, who had commanded me to find the hidden meaning of her struggle, and why she had been crying out for so many centuries, and what—what Cretan message all her own—she was toiling to deliver to mankind?

I took the road leading back to my house. When did I pass the olive groves and vineyards, when did I enter Megalo Kastro and reach home? I saw nothing. The flying fish kept desperately leaping in front of my eyes. I thought to myself, would that I could fashion a soul able to leap and to smash man's boundaries if only for a split second, able to escape necessity if only for a split second, to leave joys, sorrows, ideas, and gods behind it, and to breathe unsoiled, uninhabited air!

A letter with a mourning band on the envelope was awaiting me at home. It bore a Serbian stamp; I understood. I held it in my trembling hand. Why should I open it? I had surmised the bitter news at once. "He's dead, he's dead," I murmured, and the world grew dark.

For a long time I looked through the window at the descending night. The pots in the yard must have been watered that evening; the soil was fragrant. The evening star suspended itself from the acacia's thorny branches like a drop of dew. The evening was lovely; life seemed very sweet to me. For an instant I forgot the sorrowful letter I held in my hand.

Suddenly I realized that in regarding the world's beauty I had been attempting to forget death. Feeling ashamed, I ripped the envelope open with a violent movement. At first the letters danced, but then they settled little by little into immobility, and I was able to read:

I am the village schoolmaster. I am writing in order to inform you of the sad news that Alexis Zorba, who ran a magnesite mine here, passed away last Sunday at six o'clock in the evening. He called for me during his death agony and said, "Come here, teacher. I have a certain friend in Greece. When I die, write him that I'm dead and that I was in my right mind to the very last, all my wits about me, and was thinking of him. And that no matter what I did, I don't regret it. Tell him I hope he stays well, and that it's high time he put some sense into his head. . . . And if any priest comes to confess me and give me communion, tell him to make himself scarce, and may he give me his curse! I did this, that, and the other thing in my life, yet I did very little. Men like me should live a thousand years. Good night!"

I closed my eyes and felt the tears rolling slowly, warmly down my cheeks. "He's dead, dead, dead . . ." I murmured. "Zorba is gone, gone forever. The laughter is dead, the song cut off, the santir broken, the dance on the seaside pebbles has halted, the insatiable mouth that questioned with such incurable thirst is filled now with clay, never will a more tender and accomplished hand be found to caress stones, sea, bread, women. . . ."

I was carried away, not by grief, but by anger. "Unjust! Unjust!" I cried. "Such souls should not die. Will earth, water, fire, and chance ever be able to fashion a Zorba again?"

Although I had gone without news from him for many months, I had not been worried. It was as though I believed him to be immortal. I said to myself, How can a fountain like that ever run dry? How can Charon force such a cunning antagonist to bite the dust? At the last moment won't he find a laugh, a dance, a maneuver to trip up Charon and escape him?

I was unable to close my eyes that entire night. Memories had set out in haste, one straddling the next, to ascend anxious and panting into my mind, as though they wished to gather Zorba up from the ground and air in order to keep him from scattering. Even the most insignificant incidents connected with him gleamed clear, quick-moving, and precious in my memory, like colorful fish in a transparent summertime ocean. Inside me nothing of his had died. It seemed that whatever Zorba touched had become immortal.

All night long I kept thinking, What can I do, what can I do to exorcise death—his death?

The trap door to my vitals swung open and the irate memories sprang out, jostling one another in their haste to encircle my heart. Working their lips, they called me to gather Zorba up from earth, sea, air, and bring him back to life. Was this not the heart's duty? Did not God create the heart for this very purpose: to resurrect dear ones, bring them back to life?

Resurrect him!

The human heart is surely a deep, closed, blood-filled pit. When it opens, all the thirsting, inconsolable shades we have loved run to drink and be revived; they grow continually denser around us, blackening the air. Why do they run to drink the blood of our hearts? Because they realize that no other resurrection exists. On this day Zorba was running in front of all the rest with his great strides, pushing aside the other shades, because he knew that, of all those I loved in my life, I loved him most.

By morning I had made my decision. I felt suddenly calm, as though the resurrection had already begun inside me, as though my heart were a Magdalene speeding to the tomb and resurrecting.

I had remained in bed later than usual. The cheerful springtime sun entered my room and illuminated the beloved bas-relief above my bed. My father had found this relief somehow and had hung it over my head while I was still a child. I do not believe in coincidence; I believe in destiny. This bas-relief divulged the secret of my life with astonishing simplicity, perhaps the secret of Zorba's life as well. It was a copy of an ancient tombstone carving. A naked warrior, who has not abandoned his helmet, not even in death, is kneeling on his right knee and squeezing his breast with both palms, a tranquil smile flitting around his closed lips. The graceful motion of the powerful body is such that you cannot distinguish whether this is a dance or death. Or is it a dance and death together?

Even if it is death, we shall transform it into a dance, I said to myself, encouraged by the happy sun falling upon the warrior and bringing him to life. You and I, my heart, let us give him our blood so that he may be brought back to life, let us do what we can to make this extraordinary eater, drinker, workhorse, woman-chaser, and vagabond live a little while longer—this dancer and warrior, the broadest soul, surest body, freest cry I ever knew in my life.

chapter six ———————————————

——————————— *Looking Outward*

introduction

The importance of introspection cannot be exaggerated, but some occasions call for divorcing our consciousness from our inner selves to view the external world with computerlike detachment. Most of the time, however, our perceptions of external reality are filtered through the self. The authors of the essays in this final chapter recognize the self as man's eternal reference point, and they look outward from and through it, using their experiences to illustrate and connect with ideas and experiences outside themselves, discovering the links which bind us to each other and to the cosmos.

George Orwell and James Baldwin show us both sides of oppression. In "Shooting an Elephant" Orwell crystallizes the phenomenon of colonialism in the microcosm of his experience as a colonial officer ironically trapped by his own authority into doing what the colonials demand of him. Baldwin illustrates the oppression of blacks in America through his father's and his own experiences, showing how his personal psychological explosion is magnified thousands of times in the Harlem riots.

In "Seven Up" Thomas Healy seeks escape from being stifled by the old and familiar by desperately taking to the road and following the sun. His search for freedom and renewal is only partially fulfilled, however, in the vast spaces of the West.

Joan Didion looks first to herself and then extends her experience to general principle in discussing an old-fashioned virtue, self-respect, which she infuses with new moral life.

In reviewing a long and varied public career, Simone de Beauvoir is struck by the reality that, no matter how rich the life, it can never be lived over but must end in aging and death. She concludes the essay with bitter sadness, realizing "with stupor how much I was gypped."

Virginia Woolf and Loren Eiseley find large implications in seemingly trivial incidents. Woolf sees the limits of mortality in the death of a moth, and Eiseley, in the closing essay, makes the grandest connection of all. Spurred by his backyard explorations, he speculates on the scientific research into the origin of life and decides that the mystery is in no danger of being solved.

Shooting an Elephant

One critic has called George Orwell (1903–1950) "the conscience of his generation," but if this description suggests a moralistic rhetorician it is misleading, for Orwell's ideas are founded solidly in his often harsh and bitter experiences. Suspicious of the vague or abstract, especially in politics, left or right, Orwell warned against the curtailment of freedom through deception in deed or language in essays like "Politics and the English Language" (1946) and in his best-known books, *Animal Farm* (1945) and *Nineteen Eighty-Four* (1949). The second child of an Anglo-Indian family, he attended school in England but returned to the East to serve in the Indian Imperial Police Force in Burma, leaving it after five years chiefly because he could no longer tolerate imperialism. He spent the next few years in Paris and London writing without being published, making ends meet by washing dishes, tutoring, selling books, and hoboing. His experiences during these years are chronicled in *Down and Out in Paris and London* (1933). Seeking to act on his moral and political convictions, he joined the Loyalist forces against Franco in the Spanish Civil War in 1936. He served for four months on the Aragon front, but the infighting among the leftist Loyalist forces instilled in Orwell "a horror for politics." *Homage to Catalonia* (1938) is the record of his exploits in the Spanish Civil War. Orwell wrote several novels, but almost all of them were chiefly concerned with social and political issues rather than with individual characters. As an essayist Orwell has few peers in the English language, and his literary reputation will probably ultimately point to the pre-eminence of his essays. The following selection is reprinted from *Shooting an Elephant and Other Essays* (1950).

In Moulmein, in Lower Burma, I was hated by large numbers of people—the only time in my life that I have been important enough for this to happen to me. I was sub-divisional police officer of the town, and in an aimless, petty kind of way anti-European feeling was very bitter. No one had the guts to raise a riot, but if a European woman went through the bazaars alone somebody would probably spit betel juice over her dress. As a police officer I was an obvious target and was baited whenever it seemed safe to do so. When a nimble Burman tripped me up on the football field and the referee (another Burman) looked the other way, the crowd yelled with hideous laughter. This happened more than once. In the end the sneering yellow faces of young men that met me everywhere, the insults hooted after me when I was at a safe distance, got badly on my nerves. The young Buddhist priests were the worst of all. There were several thousands of them in the town and none of them seemed to have anything to do except stand on street corners and jeer at Europeans.

All this was perplexing and upsetting. For at that time I had already made up my mind that imperialism was an evil thing and the sooner I chucked up my job and got out of it the better. Theoretically—and secretly, of course—I was all for the Burmese and all against their oppressors, the British. As for the job I was doing, I hated it more bitterly than I can perhaps make clear. In a job like that you see the dirty work of Empire at close quarters. The wretched prisoners huddling in the stinking cages of the lock-ups, the grey, cowed faces of the long-term convicts, the scarred buttocks of the men who had been flogged with bamboos—all these oppressed me with an intolerable sense of guilt. But I could get nothing into perspective. I was young and ill-educated and I had had to think out my problems in the utter silence that is imposed on every Englishman in the East. I did not even know that the British Empire is dying, still less did I know that it is a great deal better than the younger empires that are going to supplant it. All I knew was that I was stuck between my hatred of the empire I served and my rage against the evil-spirited little beasts who tried to make my job impossible. With one part of my mind I thought of the British Raj as an unbreakable tyranny, as something clamped down, in *saecula saeculorum*, upon the will of prostrate peoples; with another part I thought that the greatest joy in the world would be to drive a bayonet into a Buddhist priest's guts. Feelings like these are the normal by-products of imperialism; ask any Anglo-Indian official, if you can catch him off duty.

One day something happened which in a roundabout way was enlightening. It was a tiny incident in itself, but it gave me a better glimpse than I had had before of the real nature of imperialism—the real motives for which despotic governments act. Early one morning the sub-inspector at a police station the other end of the town rang me up on the 'phone and said that an elephant was ravaging the bazaar. Would I please come and do something about it? I did not know what I could do, but I wanted to see what was happening and I got on to a pony and started out. I took my rifle, an old .44 Winchester and much too small to kill an elephant, but I thought the noise might be useful *in terrorem*. Various Burmans stopped me on the way and told me about the elephant's doings. It was not, of course, a wild elephant, but a tame one which had gone "must." It had been chained up, as tame elephants always are when their attack of "must" is due, but on the previous night it had broken its chain and escaped. Its mahout, the only person who could manage it when it was in that state, had set out in pursuit, but had taken the wrong direction and was now twelve hours' journey away, and in the morning the elephant had suddenly reappeared in the town. The Burmese population had no weapons and were quite helpless against it. It had already destroyed somebody's bamboo hut, killed a cow and raided some fruit-stalls and devoured the stock; also it had met the municipal rubbish van and, when the driver jumped out and took to his heels, had turned the van over and inflicted violences upon it.

The Burmese sub-inspector and some Indian constables were waiting for me in the quarter where the elephant had been seen. It was a very poor quarter, a labyrinth of squalid bamboo huts, thatched with palm-leaf, winding all over a steep hillside. I remember that it was a cloudy, stuffy morning at the beginning of the rains. We began questioning the people as to where the elephant had gone and, as usual, failed to get any definite information. That is invariably the case in the East; a story always sounds clear enough at a distance, but the nearer you get to the scene of events the vaguer it becomes. Some of the people said that the elephant had gone in one direction, some said that he had gone in another, some professed not even to have heard of any elephant. I had almost made up my mind that the whole story was a pack of lies, when we heard yells a little distance away. There was a loud, scandalized cry of "Go away, child! Go away this instant!" and an old woman with a switch in her hand came round the corner of a hut, violently shooing away a crowd of naked children. Some more women followed, clicking their tongues and exclaiming; evidently there was something that the children ought not to have seen. I rounded the hut and saw a man's dead body sprawling in the mud. He was an Indian, a black Dravidian coolie, almost naked, and he could not have been dead many minutes. The people said that the elephant had come suddenly upon him round the corner of the hut, caught him with its trunk, put its foot on his back and ground him into the earth. This was the rainy season and the ground was soft, and his face had scored a trench a foot deep and a couple of yards long. He was lying on his belly with arms crucified and head sharply twisted to one side. His face was coated with mud, the eyes wide open, the teeth bared and grinning with an expression of unendurable agony. (Never tell me, by the way, that the dead look peaceful. Most of the corpses I have seen looked devilish.) The friction of the great beast's foot had stripped the skin from his back as neatly as one skins a rabbit. As soon as I saw the dead man I sent an orderly to a friend's house nearby to borrow an elephant rifle. I had already sent back the pony, not wanting it to go mad with fright and throw me if it smelt the elephant.

The orderly came back in a few minutes with a rifle and five cartridges, and meanwhile some Burmans had arrived and told us that the elephant was in the paddy fields below, only a few hundred yards away. As I started forward practically the whole population of the quarter flocked out of the houses and followed me. They had seen the rifle and were all shouting excitedly that I was going to shoot the elephant. They had not shown much interest in the elephant when he was merely ravaging their homes, but it was different now that he was going to be shot. It was a bit of fun to them, as it would be to an English crowd; besides they wanted the meat. It made me vaguely uneasy. I had no intention of shooting the elephant—I had merely sent for the rifle to defend myself if necessary—and it is always unnerving to have a crowd following you. I marched down the hill, looking and feeling a fool, with the rifle over my shoulder and an ever-growing army of people jostling at my heels. At the bottom, when you got away from the huts, there was a metalled road and beyond that a miry waste of paddy fields a thousand yards across, not yet ploughed but soggy from the first rains and dotted with coarse grass. The elephant was standing eight yards from the road, his left side towards us. He took not the slightest notice of the crowd's approach. He was tearing up bunches of grass, beating them against his knees to clean them and stuffing them into his mouth.

I had halted on the road. As soon as I saw the elephant I knew with perfect certainty that I ought not to shoot him. It is a serious matter to shoot a working elephant—it is comparable to destroying a huge and costly piece of machinery—and obviously one ought not to do it if it can possibly be avoided. And at that distance, peacefully eating, the elephant looked no more dangerous than a cow. I thought then and I think now that his attack of "must" was already passing off; in which case he would merely wander harmlessly about until the mahout came back and caught him. Moreover, I did not in the least want to shoot him. I decided that I would watch him for a little while to make sure that he did not turn savage again, and then go home.

But at that moment I glanced round at the crowd that had followed me. It was an immense crowd, two thousand at the least and growing every minute. It blocked the road for a long distance on either side. I looked at the sea of yellow faces above the garish clothes—faces all happy and excited over this bit of fun, all certain that the elephant was going to be shot. They were watching me as they would watch a conjurer about to perform a trick. They did not like me, but with the magical rifle in my hands I was momentarily worth watching. And suddenly I realized that I should have to shoot the elephant after all. The people expected it of me and I had got to do it; I could feel their two thousand wills pressing me forward, irresistibly. And it was at this moment, as I stood there with the rifle in my hands, that I first grasped the hollowness, the futility of the white man's dominion in the East. Here was I, the white man with his gun, standing in front of the unarmed native crowd—seemingly the leading actor of the piece; but in reality I was only an absurd puppet pushed to and fro by the will of those yellow faces behind. I perceived in this moment that when the white man turns tyrant it is his own freedom that he destroys. He becomes a sort of hollow, posing dummy, the conventionalized figure of a sahib. For it is the condition of his rule that he shall spend his life in trying to impress the "natives," and so in every crisis he has got to do what the "natives" expect of him. He wears a mask, and his face grows to fit it. I had got to shoot the elephant. I had committed myself to doing it when I sent for the rifle. A sahib has got to act like a sahib; he has got to appear resolute, to know his own mind and do definite things. To come all that way, rifle in hand, with two thousand people marching at my heels, and then to trail feebly away, having done nothing—no, that was impossible. The crowd would laugh at me. And my whole life, every white man's life in the East, was one long struggle not to be laughed at.

But I did not want to shoot the elephant. I watched him beating his bunch of grass against his knees, with that preoccupied grandmotherly air that elephants have. It seemed to me that it would be murder to shoot him. At that age I was not squeamish about killing animals, but I had never shot an elephant and never wanted to. (Somehow it always seems worse to kill a *large* animal.) Besides, there was the beast's owner to be considered. Alive, the elephant was worth at least a hundred pounds; dead, he would only be worth the value of his tusks, five pounds, possibly. But I had got to act quickly. I turned to some experienced-looking Burmans who had been there when we arrived, and asked them how the elephant had been behaving. They all said the same thing: he took no notice of you if you left him alone, but he might charge if you went too close to him.

It was perfectly clear to me what I ought to do. I ought to walk up to within, say, twenty-five yards of the elephant and test his behavior. If he charged, I could shoot; if he took no notice of me, it would be safe to leave him until the mahout came back. But also I knew that I was going to do no such thing. I was a poor shot with a rifle and the ground was soft mud into which one would sink at every step. If the elephant charged and I missed him, I should have about as much chance as a toad under a steam-roller. But even then I was not thinking particularly of my own skin, only of the watchful yellow faces behind. For at that moment, with the crowd watching me, I was not afraid in the ordinary sense, as I would have been if I had been alone. A white man mustn't be frightened in front of "natives"; and so, in general, he isn't frightened. The sole thought in my mind was that if anything went wrong those two thousand Burmans would see me pursued, caught, trampled on and reduced to a grinning corpse like that Indian up the hill. And if that happened it was quite probable that some of them would laugh. That would never do. There was only one alternative. I shoved the cartridges into the magazine and lay down on the road to get a better aim.

The crowd grew very still, and a deep, low, happy sigh, as of people who see the theatre curtain go up at last, breathed from innumerable throats. They were going to have their bit of fun after all. The rifle was a beautiful German thing with cross-hair sights. I did not then know that in shooting an elephant one would shoot to cut an imaginary bar running from ear-hole to ear-hole. I ought, therefore, as the elephant was sideways on, to have aimed straight at his ear-hole; actually I aimed several inches in front of this, thinking the brain would be further forward.

When I pulled the trigger I did not hear the bang or feel the kick—one never does when a shot goes home—but I heard the devilish roar of glee that went up from the crowd. In that instant, in too short a time, one would have thought, even for the bullet to get there, a mysterious, terrible change had come over the elephant. He neither stirred nor fell, but every line of his body had altered. He looked suddenly stricken, shrunken, immensely old, as though the frightful impact of the bullet had paralysed him without knocking him down. At last, after what seemed a long time—it might have been five seconds, I dare say—he sagged flabbily to his knees. His mouth slobbered. An enormous senility seemed to have settled upon him. One could have imagined him thousands of years old. I fired again into the same spot. At the second shot he did not collapse but climbed with desperate slowness to his feet and stood weakly upright, with legs sagging and head drooping. I fired a third time. That was the shot that did for him. You could see the agony of it jolt his whole body and knock the last remnant of strength from his legs. But in falling he seemed for a moment to rise, for as his hind legs collapsed beneath him he seemed to tower upward like a huge rock toppling, his trunk reaching skywards like a tree. He trumpeted, for the first and only time. And then down he came, his belly towards me, with a crash that seemed to shake the ground even where I lay.

I got up. The Burmans were already racing past me across the mud. It was obvious that the elephant would never rise again, but he was not dead. He was breathing very rhythmically with long rattling gasps, his great mound of a side painfully rising and falling. His mouth was wide open—I could see far down into caverns of pale pink throat. I waited a long time for him to die, but his breathing did not weaken. Finally I fired my two remaining shots into the spot where I thought his heart must be. The thick blood welled out of him like red velvet, but still he did not die. His body did not even jerk when the shots hit him, the tortured breathing continued without a pause. He was dying, very slowly and in great agony, but in some world remote from me where not even a bullet could damage him further. I felt that I had got to put an end to that dreadful noise. It seemed dreadful to see the great beast lying there, powerless to move and yet powerless to die, and not even to be able to finish him. I sent back for my small rifle and poured shot after shot into his heart and down his throat. They seemed to make no impression. The tortured gasps continued as steadily as the ticking of a clock.

In the end I could not stand it any longer and went away. I heard later that it took him half an hour to die. Burmans were bringing dahs and baskets even before I left, and I was told they had stripped his body almost to the bones by the afternoon.

Afterwards, of course, there were endless discussions about the shooting of the elephant. The owner was furious, but he was only an Indian and could do nothing. Besides, legally I had done the right thing, for a mad elephant has to be killed, like a mad dog, if its owner fails to control it. Among the Europeans opinion was divided. The older men said I was right, the younger men said it was a damn shame to shoot an elephant for killing a coolie, because an elephant was worth more than any damn Coringhee coolie. And afterwards I was very glad that the coolie had been killed; it put me legally in the right and it gave me a sufficient pretext for shooting the elephant. I often wondered whether any of the others grasped that I had done it solely to avoid looking a fool.

james baldwin _____

Notes of a Native Son

Born in Harlem, James Baldwin (1924–   ) has written much about his childhood and youth in *The Fire Next Time* and in the essay reprinted here from *Notes of a Native Son*. His gift for public speaking led him into a career as a teen-aged minister, but he dropped it when he recognized the falsity of that life. Strongly influenced by the writing and example of Richard Wright, Baldwin, like Wright, left America to live and write in Paris. During a ten-year stay he published two novels, *Go Tell It on the Mountain* (1952) and *Giovanni's Room* (1956), and the collection of essays *Notes of a Native Son* (1955). After his return to America, Baldwin's writing turned angrier than it had been before. Some of his best work, the novel *Another Country* (1962) and two collections of essays, *Nobody Knows My Name* (1961) and *The Fire Next Time* (1963), were written in the years soon after his return. His latest novel is *No Name in the Street* (1972). Baldwin is able to relate his personal life to larger social issues of the day, illuminating both as few writers in America can. The following essay is one of the best examples of that talent.

On the 29th of July, in 1943, my father died. On the same day, a few hours later, his last child was born. Over a month before this, while all our energies were concentrated in waiting for these events, there had been, in Detroit, one of the bloodiest race riots of the century. A few hours after my father's funeral, while he lay in state in the undertaker's chapel, a race riot broke out in Harlem. On the morning of the 3rd of August, we drove my father to the graveyard through a wilderness of smashed plate glass.

The day of my father's funeral had also been my nineteenth birthday. As we drove him to the graveyard, the spoils of injustice, anarchy, discontent, and hatred were all around us. It seemed to me that God himself had devised, to mark my father's end, the most sustained and brutally dissonant of codas. And it seemed to me, too, that the violence which rose all about us as my father left the world had been devised as a corrective for the pride of his eldest son. I had declined to believe in that apocalypse which had been central to my father's vision; very well, life seemed to be saying, here is something that will certainly pass for an apocalypse until the real thing comes along.

I had inclined to be contemptuous of my father for the conditions of his life, for the conditions of our lives. When his life had ended I began to wonder about that life and also, in a new way, to be apprehensive about my own.

I had not known my father very well. We had got on badly, partly because we shared, in our different fashions, the vice of stubborn pride. When he was dead I realized that I had hardly ever spoken to him. When he had been dead a long time I began to wish I had. It seems to be typical of life in America, where opportunities, real and fancied, are thicker than anywhere else on the globe, that the second generation has no time to talk to the first. No one, including my father, seems to have known exactly how old he was, but his mother had been born during slavery. He was of the first generation of free men. He, along with thousands of other Negroes, came North after 1919 and I was part of that generation which had never seen the landscape of what Negroes sometimes call the Old Country.

He had been born in New Orleans and had been a quite young man there during the time that Louis Armstrong, a boy, was running errands for the dives and honky-tonks of what was always presented to me as one of the most wicked of cities—to this day, whenever I think of New Orleans, I also helplessly think of Sodom and Gomorrah. My father never mentioned Louis Armstrong, except to forbid us to play his records; but there was a picture of him on our wall for a long time. One of my father's strong-willed female relatives had placed it there and forbade my father to take it down. He never did, but he eventually maneuvered her out of the house and when, some years later, she was in trouble and near death, he refused to do anything to help her.

He was, I think, very handsome. I gather this from photographs and from my own memories of him, dressed in his Sunday best and on his way to preach a sermon somewhere, when I was little. Handsome, proud, and ingrown, "like a toe-nail," somebody said. But he looked to me, as I grew older, like pictures I had seen of African tribal chieftains: he really should have been naked, with war-paint on and barbaric mementos, standing among spears. He could be chilling in the pulpit and indescribably cruel in his personal life and he was certainly the most bitter man I have ever met; yet it must be said that there was something else in him, buried in him, which lent him his tremendous power and, even, a rather crushing charm. It had something to do with his blackness, I think—he was very black—with his blackness and his beauty, and with the fact that he knew that he was black but did not know that he was beautiful. He claimed to be proud of his blackness but it had also been the cause of much humiliation and it had fixed bleak boundaries to his life. He was not a young man when we were growing up and he had already suffered many kinds of ruin; in his outrageously demanding and protective way he loved his children, who were black like him and menaced, like him; and all these things sometimes showed in his face when he tried, never to my knowledge with any success, to establish contact with any of us. When he took one of his children on his knee to play, the child always became fretful and began to cry; when he tried to help one of us with our homework the absolutely unabating tension which emanated from him caused our minds and our tongues to become paralyzed, so that he, scarcely knowing why, flew into a rage and the child, not knowing why, was punished. If it ever entered his head to bring a surprise home for his children, it was, almost unfailingly, the wrong surprise and even the big watermelons he often brought home on his back in the summertime led to the most appalling scenes. I do not remember, in all those years, that one of his children was ever glad to see him come home. From what I was able to gather of his early life, it seemed that this inability to establish contact with other people had always marked him and had been one of the things which had driven him out of New Orleans. There was something in him, therefore, groping and tentative, which was never expressed and which was buried with him. One saw it most clearly when he was facing new people and hoping to impress them. But he never did, not for long. We went from church to smaller and more improbable church, he found himself in less and less demand as a minister, and by the time he died none of his friends had come to see him for a long time. He had lived and died in an intolerable bitterness of spirit and it frightened me, as we drove him to the graveyard through those unquiet, ruined streets, to see how powerful and overflowing this bitterness could be and to realize that this bitterness now was mine.

When he died I had been away from home for a little over a year. In that year I had had time to become aware of the meaning of all my father's bitter warnings, had discovered the secret of his proudly pursed lips and rigid carriage: I had discovered the weight of white people in the world. I saw that this had been for my ancestors and now would be for me an awful thing to live with and that the bitterness which had helped to kill my father could also kill me.

He had been ill a long time—in the mind, as we now realized, reliving instances of his fantastic intransigence in the new light of his affliction and endeavoring to feel a sorrow for him which never, quite, came true. We had not known that he was being eaten up by paranoia, and the discovery that his cruelty, to our bodies and our minds, had been one of the symptoms of his illness was not, then, enough to enable us to forgive him. The younger children felt, quite simply, relief that he would not be coming home anymore. My mother's observation that it was he, after all, who had kept them alive all these years meant nothing because the problems of keeping children alive are not real for children. The older children felt, with my father gone, that they could invite their friends to the house without fear that their friends would be insulted or, as had sometimes happened with me, being told that their friends were in league with the devil and intended to rob our family of everything we owned. (I didn't fail to wonder, and it made me hate him, what on earth we owned that anybody else would want.)

His illness was beyond all hope of healing before anyone realized that he was ill. He had always been so strange and had lived, like a prophet, in such unimaginably close communion with the Lord that his long silences which were punctuated by moans and hallelujahs and snatches of old songs while he sat at the living-room window never seemed odd to us. It was not until he refused to eat because, he said, his family was trying to poison him that my mother was forced to accept as a fact what had, until then, been only an unwilling suspicion. When he was committed, it was discovered that he had tuberculosis and, as it turned out, the disease of his mind allowed the disease of his body to destroy him. For the doctors could not force him to eat, either, and, though he was fed intravenously, it was clear from the beginning that there was no hope for him.

In my mind's eye I could see him, sitting at the window, locked up in his terrors; hating and fearing every living soul including his children who had betrayed him, too, by reaching towards the world which had despised him. There were nine of us. I began to wonder what it could have felt like for such a man to have had nine children whom he could barely feed. He used to make little jokes about our poverty, which never, of course, seemed very funny to us; they could not have seemed very funny to him, either, or else our all too feeble response to them would never have caused such rages. He spent great energy and achieved, to our chagrin, no small amount of success in keeping us away from the people who surrounded us, people who had all-night rent parties to which we listened when we should have been sleeping, people who cursed and drank and flashed razor blades on Lenox Avenue. He could not understand why, if they had so much energy to spare, they could not use it to make their lives better. He treated almost everybody on our block with a most uncharitable asperity and neither they, nor, of course, their children were slow to reciprocate.

The only white people who came to our house were welfare workers and bill collectors. It was almost always my mother who dealt with them, for my father's temper, which was at the mercy of his pride, was never to be trusted. It was clear that he felt their very presence in his home to be a violation: this was conveyed by his carriage, almost ludicrously stiff, and by his voice, harsh and vindictively polite. When I was around nine or ten I wrote a play which was directed by a young, white schoolteacher, a woman, who then took an interest in me, and gave me books to read and, in order to corroborate my theatrical bent, decided to take me to see what she somewhat tactlessly referred to as "real" plays. Theater-going was forbidden in our house, but, with the really cruel intuitiveness of a child, I suspected that the color of this woman's skin would carry the day for me. When, at school, she suggested taking me to the theater, I did not, as I might have done if she had been a Negro, find a way of discouraging her, but agreed that she should pick me up at my house one evening. I then, very cleverly, left all the rest to my mother, who suggested to my father, as I knew she would, that it would not be very nice to let such a kind woman make the trip for nothing. Also, since it was a schoolteacher, I imagine that my mother countered the idea of sin with the idea of "education," which word, even with my father, carried a kind of bitter weight.

Before the teacher came my father took me aside to ask *why* she was coming, what *interest* she could possibly have in our house, in a boy like me. I said I didn't know but I, too, suggested that it had something to do with education. And I understood that my father was waiting for me to say something—I didn't quite know what; perhaps that I wanted his protection against this teacher and her "education." I said none of these things and the teacher came and we went out. It was clear, during the brief interview in our living room, that my father was agreeing very much against his will and that he would have refused permission if he had dared. The fact that he did not dare caused me to despise him: I had no way of knowing that he was facing in that living room a wholly unprecedented and frightening situation.

Later, when my father had been laid off from his job, this woman became very important to us. She was really a very sweet and generous woman and went to a great deal of trouble to be of help to us, particularly during one awful winter. My mother called her by the highest name she knew: she said she was a "christian." My father could scarcely disagree but during the four or five years of our relatively close association he never trusted her and was always trying to surprise in her open, Midwestern face the genuine, cunningly hidden, and hideous motivation. In later years, particularly when it began to be clear that this "education" of mine was going to lead me to perdition, he became more explicit and warned me that my white friends in high school were not really my friends and that I would see, when I was older, how white people would do anything to keep a Negro down. Some of them could be nice, he admitted, but none of them were to be trusted and most of them were not even nice. The best thing was to have as little to do with them as possible. I did not feel this way and I was certain, in my innocence, that I never would.

But the year which preceded my father's death had made a great change in my life. I had been living in New Jersey, working in defense plants, working and living among southerners, white and black. I knew about the south, of course, and about how southerners treated Negroes and how they expected them to behave, but it had never entered my mind that anyone would look at me and expect *me* to behave that way. I learned in New Jersey that to be a Negro meant, precisely, that one was never looked at but was simply at the mercy of the reflexes the color of one's skin caused in other people. I acted in New Jersey as I had always acted, that is as though I thought a great deal of myself—I had to *act* that way—with results that were, simply, unbelievable. I had scarcely arrived before I had earned the enmity, which was extraordinarily ingenious, of all my superiors and nearly all my co-workers. In the beginning, to make matters worse, I simply did not know what was happening. I did not know what I had done, and I shortly began to wonder what *anyone* could possibly do, to bring about such unanimous, active, and unbearably vocal hostility. I knew about jim-crow but I had never experienced it. I went to the same self-service restaurant three times and stood with all the Princeton boys before the counter, waiting for a hamburger and coffee; it was always an extraordinarily long time before anything was set before me; but it was not until the fourth visit that I learned that, in fact, nothing had ever been set before me: I had simply picked something up. Negroes were not served there, I was told, and they had been waiting for me to realize that I was always the only Negro present. Once I was told this, I determined to go there all the time. But now they were ready for me and, though some dreadful scenes were subsequently enacted in that restaurant, I never ate there again.

It was the same story all over New Jersey, in bars, bowling alleys, diners, places to live. I was always being forced to leave, silently, or with mutual imprecations. I very shortly became notorious and children giggled behind me when I passed and their elders whispered or shouted—they really believed that I was mad. And it did begin to work on my mind, of course; I began to be afraid to go anywhere and to compensate for this I went places to which I really should not have gone and where, God knows, I had no desire to be. My reputation in town naturally enhanced my reputation at work and my working day became one long series of acrobatics designed to keep me out of trouble. I cannot say that these acrobatics succeeded. It began to seem that the machinery of the organization I worked for was turning over, day and night, with but one aim: to eject me. I was fired once, and contrived, with the aid of a friend from New York, to get back on the payroll; was fired again, and bounced back again. It took a while to fire me for the third time, but the third time took. There were no loopholes anywhere. There was not even any way of getting back inside the gates.

That year in New Jersey lives in my mind as though it were the year during which, having an unsuspected predilection for it, I first contracted some dread, chronic disease, the unfailing symptom of which is a kind of blind fever, a pounding in the skull and fire in the bowels. Once this disease is contracted, one can never be really carefree again, for the fever, without an instant's warning, can recur at any moment. It can wreck more important things than race relations. There is not a Negro alive who does not have this rage in his blood—one has the choice, merely, of living with it consciously or surrendering to it. As for me, this fever has recurred in me, and does, and will until the day I die.

My last night in New Jersey, a white friend from New York took me to the nearest big town, Trenton, to go to the movies and have a few drinks. As it turned out, he also saved me from, at the very least, a violent whipping. Almost every detail of that night stands out very clearly in my memory. I even remember the name of the movie we saw because its title impressed me as being so patly ironical. It was a movie about the German occupation of France, starring Maureen O'Hara and Charles Laughton and called *This Land Is Mine*. I remember the name of the diner we walked into when the movie ended: it was the "American Diner." When we walked in the counterman asked what we wanted and I remember answering with the casual sharpness which had become my habit: "We want a hamburger and a cup of coffee, what do you think we want?" I do not know why, after a year of such rebuffs, I so completely failed to anticipate his answer, which was, of course, "We don't serve Negroes here." This reply failed to discompose me, at least for the moment. I made some sardonic comment about the name of the diner and we walked out into the streets.

This was the time of what was called the "brown-out," when the lights in all American cities were very dim. When we re-entered the streets something happened to me which had the force of an optical illusion, or a nightmare. The streets were very crowded and I was facing north. People were moving in every direction but it seemed to me, in that instant, that all of the people I could see, and many more than that, were moving toward me, against me, and that everyone was white. I remember how their faces gleamed. And I felt, like a physical sensation, a *click* at the nape of my neck as though some interior string connecting my head to my body had been cut. I began to walk. I heard my friend call after me, but I ignored him. Heaven only knows what was going on in his mind, but he had the good sense not to touch me—I don't know what would have happened if he had—and to keep me in sight. I don't know what was going on in my mind, either; I certainly had no conscious plan. I wanted to do something to crush these white faces, which were crushing me. I walked for perhaps a block or two until I came to an enormous, glittering, and fashionable restaurant in which I knew not even the intercession of the Virgin would cause me to be served. I pushed through the doors and took the first vacant seat I saw, at a table for two, and waited.

I do not know how long I waited and I rather wonder, until today, what I could possibly have looked like. Whatever I looked like, I frightened the waitress who shortly appeared, and the moment she appeared all of my fury flowed towards her. I hated her for her white face, and for her great, astounded, frightened eyes. I felt that if she found a black man so frightening I would make her fright worth-while.

She did not ask me what I wanted, but repeated, as though she had learned it somewhere, "We don't serve Negroes here." She did not say it with the blunt, derisive hostility to which I had grown so accustomed, but, rather, with a note of apology in her voice, and fear. This made me colder and more murderous than ever. I felt I had to do something with my hands. I wanted her to come close enough for me to get her neck between my hands.

So I pretended not to have understood her, hoping to draw her closer. And she did step a very short step closer, with her pencil poised incongruously over her pad, and repeated the formula: ". . . don't serve Negroes here."

Somehow, with the repetition of that phrase, which was already ringing in my head like a thousand bells of a nightmare, I realized that she would never come any closer and that I would have to strike from a distance. There was nothing on the table but an ordinary watermug half full of water, and I picked this up and hurled it with all my strength at her. She ducked and it missed her and shattered against the mirror behind the bar. And, with that sound, my frozen blood abruptly thawed, I returned from wherever I had been, I *saw*, for the first time, the restaurant, the people with their mouths open, already, as it seemed to me, rising as one man, and I realized what I had done, and where I was, and I was frightened. I rose and began running for the door. A round, potbellied man grabbed me by the nape of the neck just as I reached the doors and began to beat me about the face. I kicked him and got loose and ran into the streets. My friend whispered, *"Run!"* and I ran.

My friend stayed outside the restaurant long enough to misdirect my pursuers and the police, who arrived, he told me, at once. I do not know what I said to him when he came to my room that night. I could not have said much. I felt, in the oddest, most awful way, that I had somehow betrayed him. I lived it over and over and over again, the way one relives an automobile accident after it has happened and one finds oneself alone and safe. I could not get over two facts, both equally difficult for the imagination to grasp, and one was that I could have been murdered. But the other was that I had been ready to commit murder. I saw nothing very clearly but I did see this: that my life, my *real* life, was in danger, and not from anything other people might do but from the hatred I carried in my own heart.

I had returned home around the second week in June—in great haste because it seemed that my father's death and my mother's confinement were both but a matter of hours. In the case of my mother, it soon became clear that she had simply made a miscalculation. This had always been her tendency and I don't believe that a single one of us arrived in the world, or has since arrived anywhere else, on time. But none of us dawdled so intolerably about the business of being born as did my baby sister. We sometimes amused ourselves, during those endless, stifling weeks, by picturing the baby sitting within in the safe, warm dark, bitterly regretting the necessity of becoming a part of our chaos and stubbornly putting it off as long as possible. I understood her perfectly and congratulated her on showing such good sense so soon. Death, however, sat as purposefully at my father's bedside as life stirred within my mother's womb and it was harder to understand why he so lingered in that long shadow. It seemed that he had bent, and for a long time, too, all of his energies towards dying. Now death was ready for him but my father held back.

All of Harlem, indeed, seemed to be infected by waiting. I had never before known it to be so violently still. Racial tensions throughout this country were exacerbated during the early years of the war, partly because the labor market brought together hundreds of thousands of ill-prepared people and partly because Negro soldiers, regardless of where they were born, received their military training in the south. What happened in defense plants and army camps had repercussions, naturally, in every Negro ghetto. The situation in Harlem had grown bad enough for clergymen, policemen, educators, politicians, and social workers to assert in one breath that there was no "crime wave" and to offer, in the very next breath, suggestions as to how to combat it. These suggestions always seemed to involve playgrounds, despite the fact that racial skirmishes were occurring in the playgrounds, too. Playground or not, crime wave or not, the Harlem police force had been augmented in March, and the unrest grew—perhaps, in fact, partly as a result of the ghetto's instinctive hatred of policemen. Perhaps the most revealing news item, out of the steady parade of reports of muggings, stabbings, shootings, assaults, gang wars, and accusations of police brutality, is the item concerning six Negro girls who set upon a white girl in the subway because, as they all too accurately put it, she was stepping on their toes. Indeed she was, all over the nation.

I had never before been so aware of policemen, on foot, on horseback, on corners, everywhere, always two by two. Nor had I ever been so aware of small knots of people. They were on stoops and on corners and in doorways, and what was striking about them, I think, was that they did not seem to be talking. Never, when I passed these groups, did the usual sound of a curse or a laugh ring out and neither did there seem to be any hum of gossip. There was certainly, on the other hand, occurring between them communication extraordinarily intense. Another thing that was striking was the unexpected diversity of the people who made up these groups. Usually, for example, one would see a group of sharpies standing on the street corner, jiving the passing chicks; or a group of older men, usually, for some reason, in the vicinity of a barber shop, discussing baseball scores, or the numbers, or making rather chilling observations about women they had known. Women, in a general way, tended to be seen less often together—unless they were church women, or very young girls, or prostitutes met together for an unprofessional instant. But that summer I saw the strangest combinations: large, respectable, churchly matrons standing on the stoops or the corners with their hair tied up, together with a girl in sleazy satin whose face bore the marks of gin and the razor, or heavy-set, abrupt, no-nonsense older men, in company with the most disreputable and fanatical "race" men, or these same "race" men with the sharpies, or these sharpies with the churchly women. Seventh Day Adventists and Methodists and Spiritualists seemed to be hobnobbing with Holyrollers and they were all, alike, entangled with the most flagrant disbelievers; something heavy in their stance seemed to indicate that they had all, incredibly, seen a common vision, and on each face there seemed to be the same strange, bitter shadow.

The churchly women and the matter-of-fact, no-nonsense men had children in the Army. The sleazy girls they talked to had lovers there, the sharpies and the "race" men had friends and brothers there. It would have demanded an unquestioning patriotism, happily as uncommon in this country as it is undesirable, for these people not to have been disturbed by the bitter letters they received, by the newspaper stories they read, not to have been enraged by the posters, then to be found all over New York, which described the Japanese as "yellow-bellied Japs." It was only the "race" men, to be sure, who spoke ceaselessly of being revenged—how this vengeance was to be exacted was not clear—for the indignities and dangers suffered by Negro boys in uniform; but everybody felt a directionless, hopeless bitterness, as well as that panic which can scarcely be suppressed when one knows that a human being one loves is beyond one's reach, and in danger. This helplessness and this gnawing uneasiness does something, at length, to even the toughest mind. Perhaps the best way to sum all this up is to say that the people I knew felt, mainly, a peculiar kind of relief when they knew that their boys were being shipped out of the south, to do battle overseas. It was, perhaps, like feeling that the most dangerous part of a dangerous journey had been passed and that now, even if death should come, it would come with honor and without the complicity of their countrymen. Such a death would be, in short, a fact with which one could hope to live.

It was on the 28th of July, which I believe was a Wednesday, that I visited my father for the first time during his illness and for the last time in his life. The moment I saw him I knew why I had put off this visit so long. I had told my mother that I did not want to see him because I hated him. But this was not true. It was only that I *had* hated him and I wanted to hold on to this hatred. I did not want to look on him as a ruin: it was not a ruin I had hated. I imagine that one of the reasons people cling to their hates so stubbornly is because they sense, once hate is gone, that they will be forced to deal with pain.

We traveled out to him, his older sister and myself, to what seemed to be the very end of a very Long Island. It was hot and dusty and we wrangled, my aunt and I, all the way out, over the fact that I had recently begun to smoke and, as she said, to give myself airs. But I knew that she wrangled with me because she could not bear to face the fact of her brother's dying. Neither could I endure the reality of her despair, her unstated bafflement as to what had happened to her brother's life, and her own. So we wrangled and I smoked and from time to time she fell into a heavy reverie. Covertly, I watched her face, which was the face of an old woman; it had fallen in, the eyes were sunken and lightless; soon she would be dying, too.

In my childhood—it had not been so long ago—I had thought her beautiful. She had been quick-witted and quick-moving and very generous with all the children and each of her visits had been an event. At one time one of my brothers and myself had thought of running away to live with her. Now she could no longer produce out of her handbag some unexpected and yet familiar delight. She made me feel pity and revulsion and fear. It was awful to realize that she no longer caused me to feel affection. The closer we came to the hospital the more querulous she became and at the same time, naturally, grew more dependent on me. Between pity and guilt and fear I began to feel that there was another me trapped in my skull like a jack-in-the-box who might escape my control at any moment and fill the air with screaming.

She began to cry the moment we entered the room and she saw him lying there, all shriveled and still, like a little black monkey. The great, gleaming apparatus which fed him and would have compelled him to be still even if he had been able to move brought to mind, not beneficence, but torture; the tubes entering his arm made me think of pictures I had seen when a child, of Gulliver, tied down by the pygmies on that island. My aunt wept and wept, there was a whistling sound in my father's throat; nothing was said; he could not speak. I wanted to take his hand, to say something. But I do not know what I could have said, even if he could have heard me. He was not really in that room with us, he had at last really embarked on his journey; and though my aunt told me that he said he was going to meet Jesus, I did not hear anything except that whistling in his throat. The doctor came back and we left, into that unbearable train again, and home. In the morning came the telegram saying that he was dead. Then the house was suddenly full of relatives, friends, hysteria, and confusion and I quickly left my mother and the children to the care of those impressive women, who, in Negro communities at least, automatically appear at times of bereavement armed with lotions, proverbs, and patience, and an ability to cook. I went downtown. By the time I returned, later the same day, my mother had been carried to the hospital and the baby had been born.

For my father's funeral I had nothing black to wear and this posed a nagging problem all day long. It was one of those problems, simple, or impossible of solution, to which the mind insanely clings in order to avoid the mind's real trouble. I spent most of that day at the downtown apartment of a girl I knew, celebrating my birthday with whiskey and wondering what to wear that night. When planning a birthday celebration one naturally does not expect that it will be up against competition from a funeral and this girl had antici-pated taking me out that night, for a big dinner and a night club afterwards. Sometime during the course of that long day we decided that we would go out anyway, when my father's funeral service was over. I imagine *I* decided it, since, as the funeral hour approached, it became clearer and clearer to me that I would not know what to do with myself when it was over. The girl, stifling her very lively concern as to the possible effects of the whiskey on one of my father's chief mourners, concentrated on being conciliatory and practically helpful. She found a black shirt for me somewhere and ironed it and, dressed in the darkest pants and jacket I owned, and slightly drunk, I made my way to my father's funeral.

The chapel was full, but not packed, and very quiet. There were, mainly, my father's relatives, and his children, and here and there I saw faces I had not seen since childhood, the faces of my father's one-time friends. They were very dark and solemn now, seeming somehow to suggest that they had known all along that something like this would happen. Chief among the mourners was my aunt, who had quarreled with my father all his life; by which I do not mean to suggest that her mourning was insincere or that she had not loved him. I suppose that she was one of the few people in the world who had, and their incessant quarreling proved precisely the strength of the tie that bound them. The only other person in the world, as far as I knew, whose relationship to my father rivaled my aunt's in depth was my mother, who was not there.

It seemed to me, of course, that it was a very long funeral. But it was, if anything, a rather shorter funeral than most, nor, since there were no overwhelming, uncontrollable expressions of grief, could it be called—if I dare to use the word—successful. The minister who preached my father's funeral sermon was one of the few my father had still been seeing as he neared his end. He presented to us in his sermon a man whom none of us had ever seen—a man thoughtful, patient, and forbearing, a Christian inspiration to all who knew him, and a model for his children. And no doubt the children, in their disturbed and guilty state, were almost ready to believe this; he had been remote enough to be anything and, anyway, the shock of the incontrovertible, that it was really our father lying up there in that casket, prepared the mind for anything. His sister moaned and this grief-stricken moaning was taken as corroboration. The other faces held a dark, non-committal thoughtfulness. This was not the man they had known, but they had scarcely expected to be confronted with *him;* this was, in a sense deeper than questions of fact, the man they had not known, and the man they had not known may have been the real one. The real man, whoever he had been, had suffered and now he was dead: this was all that was sure and all that mattered now. Every man in the chapel hoped that when his hour came he, too, would be eulogized, which is to say forgiven, and that all of his lapses, greeds, errors, and strayings from the truth would be invested with coherence and looked upon with charity. This was perhaps the last thing human beings could give each other and it was what they demanded, after all, of the Lord. Only the Lord saw the midnight tears, only He was present when one of His children, moaning and wringing hands, paced up and down the room. When one slapped one's child in anger the recoil in the heart reverberated through heaven and became part of the pain of the universe. And when the children were hungry and sullen and distrustful and one watched them, daily, growing wilder, and further away, and running headlong into danger, it was the Lord who knew what the charged heart endured as the strap was laid to the backside; the Lord alone who knew what one *would* have said if one had had, like the Lord, the gift of the living word. It was the Lord who knew of the impossibility every parent in that room faced: how to prepare the child for the day when the child would be despised and how to *create* in the child—by what means?—a stronger antidote to this poison than one had found for oneself. The avenues, side streets, bars, billiard halls, hospitals, police stations, and even the playgrounds of Harlem—not to mention the houses of correction, the jails, and the morgue—testified to the potency of the poison while remaining silent as to the efficacy of whatever antidote, irresistibly raising the question of whether or not such an antidote existed; raising, which was worse, the question of whether or not an antidote was desirable; perhaps poison should be fought with poison. With these several schisms in the mind and with more terrors in the heart than could be named, it was better not to judge the man who had gone down under an impossible burden. It was better to remember: *Thou knowest this man's fall; but thou knowest not his wrassling.*

While the preacher talked and I watched the children—years of changing their diapers, scrubbing them, slapping them, taking them to school, and scolding them had had the perhaps inevitable result of making me love them, though I am not sure I knew this then—my mind was busily breaking out with a rash of disconnected impressions. Snatches of popular songs, indecent jokes, bits of books I had read, movie sequences, faces, voices, political issues—I thought I was going mad; all these impressions suspended, as it were, in the solution of the faint nausea produced in me by the heat and liquor. For a moment I had the impression that my alcoholic breath, inefficiently disguised with chewing gum, filled the entire chapel. Then someone began singing one of my father's favorite songs and, abruptly, I was with him, sitting on his knee, in the hot, enormous, crowded church which was the first church we attended. It was the Abyssinia Baptist Church on 138th Street. We had not gone there long. With this image, a host of others came. I had forgotten, in the rage of my growing up, how proud my father had been of me when I was little. Apparently, I had had a voice and my father had liked to show me off before the members of the church. I had forgotten what he had looked like when he was pleased but now I remembered that he had always been grinning with pleasure when my solos ended. I even remembered certain expressions on his face when he teased my mother—had he loved her? I would never know. And when had it all begun to change? For now it seemed that he had not always been cruel. I remembered being taken for a haircut and scraping my knee on the footrest of the barber's chair and I remembered my father's face as he soothed my crying and applied the stinging iodine. Then I remembered our fights, fights which had been of the worst possible kind because my technique had been silence.

I remembered the one time in all our life together when we had really spoken to each other.

It was on a Sunday and it must have been shortly before I left home. We were walking, just the two of us, in our usual silence, to or from church. I was in high school and had been doing a lot of writing and I was, at about this time, the editor of the high school magazine. But I had also been a Young Minister and had been preaching from the pulpit. Lately, I had been taking fewer engagements and preached as rarely as possible. It was said in the church, quite truthfully, that I was "cooling off."

My father asked me abruptly, "You'd rather write than preach, wouldn't you?"

I was astonished at his question—because it was a real question. I answered, "Yes."

That was all we said. It was awful to remember that that was all we had *ever* said.

The casket now was opened and the mourners were being led up the aisle to look for the last time on the deceased. The assumption was that the family was too overcome with grief to be allowed to make this journey alone and I watched while my aunt was led to the casket and, muffled in black, and shaking, led back to her seat. I disapproved of forcing the children to look on their dead father, considering that the shock of his death, or, more truthfully, the shock of death as a reality, was already a little more than a child could bear, but my judgment in this matter had been overruled and there they were, bewildered and frightened and very small, being led, one by one, to the casket. But there is also something very gallant about children at such moments. It has something to do with their silence and gravity and with the fact that one cannot help them. Their legs, somehow, seem *exposed*, so that it is at once incredible and terribly clear that their legs are all they have to hold them up.

I had not wanted to go to the casket myself and I certainly had not wished to be led there, but there was no way of avoiding either of these forms. One of the deacons led me up and I looked on my father's face. I cannot say that it looked like him at all. His blackness had been equivocated by powder and there was no suggestion in that casket of what his power had or could have been. He was simply an old man dead, and it was hard to believe that he had ever given anyone either joy or pain. Yet, his life filled that room. Further up the avenue his wife was holding his newborn child. Life and death so close together, and love and hatred, and right and wrong, said something to me which I did not want to hear concerning man, concerning the life of man.

After the funeral, while I was downtown desperately celebrating my birthday, a Negro soldier, in the lobby of the Hotel Braddock, got into a fight with a white policeman over a Negro girl. Negro girls, white policemen, in or out of uniform, and Negro males—in or out of uniform—were part of the furniture of the lobby of the Hotel Braddock and this was certainly not the first time such an incident had occurred. It was destined, however, to receive an unprecedented publicity, for the fight between the policeman and the soldier ended with the shooting of the soldier. Rumor, flowing immediately to the streets outside, stated that the soldier had been shot in the back, an instantaneous and revealing invention, and that the soldier had died protecting a Negro woman. The facts were somewhat different—for example, the soldier had not been shot in the back, and was not dead, and the girl seems to have been as dubious a symbol of womanhood as her white counterpart in Georgia usually is, but no one was interested in the facts. They preferred the invention because this invention expressed and corroborated their hates and fears so perfectly. It is just as well to remember that people are always doing this. Perhaps many of those legends, including Christianity, to which the world clings began their conquest of the world with just some such concerted surrender to distortion. The effect, in Harlem, of this particular legend was like the effect of a lit match in a tin of gasoline. The mob gathered before the doors of the Hotel Braddock simply began to swell and to spread in every direction, and Harlem exploded.

The mob did not cross the ghetto lines. It would have been easy, for example, to have gone over Morningside Park on the west side or to have crossed the Grand Central railroad tracks at 125th Street on the east side, to wreak havoc in white neighborhoods. The mob seems to have been mainly interested in something more potent and real than the white face, that is, in white power, and the principal damage done during the riot of the summer of 1943 was to white business establishments in Harlem. It might have been a far bloodier story, of course, if, at the hour the riot began, these establishments had still been open. From the Hotel Braddock the mob fanned out, east and west along 125th Street, and for the entire length of Lenox, Seventh, and Eighth avenues. Along each of these avenues, and along each major side street—116th, 125th, 135th, and so on—bars, stores, pawnshops, restaurants, even little luncheonettes had been smashed open and entered and looted—looted, it might be added, with more haste than efficiency. The shelves really looked as though a bomb had struck them. Cans of beans and soup and dog food, along with toilet paper, corn flakes, sardines, and milk tumbled every which way, and abandoned cash registers and cases of beer leaned crazily out of the splintered windows and were strewn along the avenues. Sheets, blankets, and clothing of every description formed a kind of path, as though people had dropped them while running. I truly had not realized that Harlem *had* so many stores until I saw them all smashed open; the first time the word *wealth* ever entered my mind in relation to Harlem was when I saw it scattered in the streets. But one's first, incongruous impression of plenty was countered immediately by an impression of waste. None of this was doing anybody any good. It would have been better to have left the plate glass as it had been and the goods lying in the stores.

It would have been better, but it would also have been intolerable, for Harlem had needed something to smash. To smash something is the ghetto's chronic need. Most of the time it is the members of the ghetto who smash each other, and themselves. But as long as the ghetto walls are standing there will always come a moment when these outlets do not work. That summer, for example, it was not enough to get into a fight on Lenox Avenue, or curse out one's cronies in the barber shops. If ever, indeed, the violence which fills Harlem's churches, pool halls, and bars erupts outward in a more direct fashion, Harlem and its citizens are likely to vanish in an apocalyptic flood. That this is not likely to happen is due to a great many reasons, most hidden and powerful among them the Negro's real relation to the white American. This relation prohibits, simply, anything as uncomplicated and satisfactory as pure hatred. In order really to hate white people, one has to blot so much out of the mind—and the heart—that this hatred itself becomes an exhausting and self-destructive pose. But this does not mean, on the other hand, that love comes easily: the white world is too powerful, too complacent, too ready with gratuitous humiliation, and, above all, too ignorant and too innocent for that. One is absolutely forced to make perpetual qualifications and one's own reactions are always canceling each other out. It is this, really, which has driven so many people mad, both white and black. One is always in the position of having to decide between amputation and gangrene. Amputation is swift but time may prove that the amputation was not necessary—or one may delay the amputation too long. Gangrene is slow, but it is impossible to be sure that one is reading one's symptoms right. The idea of going through life as a cripple is more than one can bear, and equally unbearable is the risk of swelling up slowly, in agony, with poison. And the trouble, finally, is that the risks are real even if the choices do not exist.

"But as for me and my house," my father had said, "we will serve the Lord." I wondered, as we drove him to his resting place, what this line had meant for him. I had heard him preach it many times. I had preached it once myself, proudly giving it an interpretation different from my father's. Now the whole thing came back to me, as though my father and I were on our way to Sunday school and I were memorizing the golden text: *And if it seem evil unto you to serve the Lord, choose you this day whom you will serve; whether the gods which your fathers served that were on the other side of the flood, or the gods of the Amorites, in whose land ye dwell: but as for me and my house, we will serve the Lord.* I suspected in these familiar lines a meaning which had never been there for me before. All of my father's texts and songs, which I had decided were meaningless, were arranged before me at his death like empty bottles, waiting to hold the meaning which life would give them for me. This was his legacy: nothing is ever escaped. That bleakly memorable morning I hated the unbelievable streets and the Negroes and whites who had, equally, made them that way. But I knew that it was folly, as my father would have said, this bitterness was folly. It was necessary to hold on to the things that mattered. The dead man mattered, the new life mattered; blackness and whiteness did not matter; to believe that they did was to acquiesce in one's own destruction. Hatred, which could destroy so much, never failed to destroy the man who hated and this was an immutable law.

It began to seem that one would have to hold in the mind forever two ideas which seemed to be in opposition. The first idea was acceptance, the acceptance, totally without rancor, of life as it is, and men as they are: in the light of this idea, it goes without saying that injustice is a commonplace. But this did not mean that one could be complacent, for the second idea was of equal power: that one must never, in one's own life, accept these injustices as commonplace but must fight them with all one's strength. This fight begins, however, in the heart and it now had been laid to my charge to keep my own heart free of hatred and despair. This intimation made my heart heavy and, now that my father was irrecoverable, I wished that he had been beside me so that I could have searched his face for the answers which only the future would give me now.

joan didion ————————————————————————————————

On Self-Respect

For biographical information on Joan Didion (1934–   ), see page 250. The following selection is from her collection of essays, *Slouching Towards Bethlehem*.

Once, in a dry season, I wrote in large letters across two pages of a notebook that innocence ends when one is stripped of the delusion that one likes oneself. Although now, some years later, I marvel that a mind on the outs with itself should have nonetheless made painstaking record of its every tremor, I recall with embarrassing clarity the flavor of those particular ashes. It was a matter of misplaced self-respect.

I had not been elected to Phi Beta Kappa. This failure could scarcely have been more predictable or less ambiguous (I simply did not have the grades), but I was unnerved by it; I had somehow thought myself a kind of academic Raskolnikov, curiously exempt from the cause-effect relationships which hampered others. Although even the humorless nineteen-year-old that I was must have recognized that the situation lacked real tragic stature, the day that I did not make Phi Beta Kappa nonetheless marked the end of something, and innocence may well be the word for it. I lost the conviction that lights would always turn green for me, the pleasant certainty that those rather passive virtues which had won me approval as a child automatically guaranteed me not only Phi Beta Kappa keys but happiness, honor, and the love of a good man; lost a certain touching faith in the totem power of good manners, clean hair, and proven competence on the Stanford-Binet scale. To such doubtful amulets had my self-respect been pinned, and I faced myself that day with the nonplused apprehension of someone who has come across a vampire and has no crucifix at hand.

Although to be driven back upon oneself is an uneasy affair at best, rather like trying to cross a border with borrowed credentials, it seems to me now the one condition necessary to the beginnings of real self-respect. Most of our platitudes notwithstanding, self-deception remains the most difficult deception. The tricks that work on others count for nothing in that very well-lit back alley where one keeps assignations with oneself: no winning smiles will do here, no prettily drawn lists of good intentions. One shuffles flashily but in vain through one's marked cards—the kindness done for the wrong reason, the apparent triumph which involved no real effort, the seemingly heroic act into which one had been shamed. The dismal fact is that self-respect has nothing to do with the approval of others—who are, after all, deceived easily enough; has nothing to do with reputation, which, as Rhett Butler told Scarlett O'Hara, is something people with courage can do without.

To do without self-respect, on the other hand, is to be an unwilling audience of one to an interminable documentary that details one's failings, both real and imagined, with fresh footage spliced in for every screening. *There's the glass you broke in anger, there's the hurt on X's face; watch now, this next scene, the night Y came back from Houston, see how you muff this one.* To live without self-respect is to lie awake some night, beyond the reach of warm milk, phenobarbital, and the sleeping hand on the coverlet, counting up the sins of commission and omission, the trusts betrayed, the promises subtly broken, the gifts irrevocably wasted through sloth or cowardice or carelessness. However long we postpone it, we eventually lie down alone in that notoriously uncomfortable bed, the one we make ourselves. Whether or not we sleep in it depends, of course, on whether or not we respect ourselves.

To protest that some fairly improbable people, some people who *could not possibly respect themselves,* seem to sleep easily enough is to miss the point entirely, as surely as those people miss it who think that self-respect has necessarily to do with not having safety pins in one's underwear. There is a common superstition that "self-respect" is a kind of charm against snakes, something that keeps those who have it locked in some unblighted Eden, out of strange beds, ambivalent conversations, and trouble in general. It does not at all. It has nothing to do with the face of things, but concerns instead a separate peace, a private reconciliation. Although the careless, suicidal Julian English in *Appointment in Samarra* and the careless, incurably dishonest Jordan Baker in *The Great Gatsby* seem equally improbable candidates for self-respect, Jordan Baker had it, Julian English did not. With that genius for accommodation more often seen in women than in men, Jordan took her own measure, made her own peace, avoided threats to that peace: "I hate careless people," she told Nick Carraway. "It takes two to make an accident."

Like Jordan Baker, people with self-respect have the courage of their mistakes. They know the price of things. If they choose to commit adultery, they do not then go running, in an access of bad conscience, to receive absolution from the wronged parties; nor do they complain unduly of the unfairness, the undeserved embarrassment, of being named co-respondent. In brief, people with self-respect exhibit a certain toughness, a kind of moral nerve; they display what was once called *character,* a quality which, although approved in the abstract, sometimes loses ground to other, more instantly negotiable virtues. The measure of its slipping prestige is that one tends to think of it only in connection with homely children and United States senators who have been defeated, preferably in the primary, for reelection. Nonetheless, character—the willingness to accept responsibility for one's own life—is the source from which self-respect springs.

Self-respect is something that our grandparents, whether or not they had it, knew all about. They had instilled in them, young, a certain discipline, the sense that one lives by doing things one does not particularly want to do, by putting fears and doubts to one side, by weighing immediate comforts against the possibility of larger, even intangible, comforts. It seemed to the nineteenth century admirable, but not remarkable, that Chinese Gordon put on a clean white suit and held Khartoum against the Mahdi; it did not seem unjust that the way to free land in California involved death and difficulty and dirt. In a diary kept during the winter of 1846, an emigrating twelve-year-old named Narcissa Cornwall noted coolly: "Father was busy reading and did not notice that the house was being filled with strange Indians until Mother spoke about it." Even lacking any clue as to what Mother said, one can scarcely fail to be impressed by the entire incident: the father reading, the Indians filing in, the mother choosing the words that would not alarm, the child duly recording the event and noting further that those particular Indians were not, "fortunately for us," hostile. Indians were simply part of the *donnée*.

In one guise or another, Indians always are. Again, it is a question of recognizing that anything worth having has its price. People who respect themselves are willing to accept the risk that the Indians will be hostile, that the venture will go bankrupt, that the liaison may not turn out to be one in which *every day is a holiday because you're married to me*. They are willing to invest something of themselves; they may not play at all, but when they do play, they know the odds.

That kind of self-respect is a discipline, a habit of mind that can never be faked but can be developed, trained, coaxed forth. It was once suggested to me that, as an antidote to crying, I put my head in a paper bag. As it happens, there is a sound physiological reason, something to do with oxygen, for doing exactly that, but the psychological effect alone is incalculable: it is difficult in the extreme to continue fancying oneself Cathy in *Wuthering Heights* with one's head in a Food Fair bag. There is a similar case for all the small disciplines, unimportant in themselves; imagine maintaining any kind of swoon, commiserative or carnal, in a cold shower.

But those small disciplines are valuable only insofar as they represent larger ones. To say that Waterloo was won on the playing fields of Eton is not to say that Napoleon might have been saved by a crash program in cricket; to give formal dinners in the rain forest would be pointless did not the candlelight flickering on the liana call forth deeper, stronger disciplines, values instilled long before. It is a kind of ritual, helping us to remember who and what we are. In order to remember it, one must have known it.

To have that sense of one's intrinsic worth which constitutes self-respect is potentially to have everything: the ability to discriminate, to love and to remain indifferent. To lack it is to be locked within oneself, paradoxically incapable of either love or indifference. If we do not respect ourselves, we are on the one hand forced to despise those who have so few resources as to consort with us, so little perception as to remain blind to our fatal weaknesses. On the other, we are peculiarly in thrall to everyone we see, curiously determined to live out—since our self-image is untenable—their false notions of us. We flatter ourselves by thinking this compulsion to please others an attractive trait: a gist for imaginative empathy, evidence of our willingness to give. *Of course* I will play Francesca to your Paolo, Helen Keller to anyone's Annie Sullivan: no expectation is too misplaced, no role too ludicrous. At the mercy of those we cannot but hold in contempt, we play roles doomed to failure before they are begun, each defeat generating fresh despair at the urgency of divining and meeting the next demand made upon us.

It is the phenomenon sometimes called "alienation from self." In its advanced stages, we no longer answer the telephone, because someone might want something; that we could say *no* without drowning in self-reproach is an idea alien to this game. Every encounter demands too much, tears the nerves, drains the will, and the specter of something as small as an unanswered letter arouses such disproportionate guilt that answering it becomes out of the question. To assign unanswered letters their proper weight, to free us from the expectations of others, to give us back to ourselves—there lies the great, the singular power of self-respect. Without it, one eventually discovers the final turn of the screw: one runs away to find oneself, and finds no one at home.

1961

thomas healy ————————————————————— ——

Seven Up

Thomas Healy (1950–   ) grew up in New England—first in Boston, then in Lewiston, Maine, on a farm that "offered me varied stretches of solitude and exploratory labor. It stuck to me like those misty, cool thorns that adorn every Maine season." After three semesters at the University of Maine, Healy left school "to get my attitudes beaten into different directions from college" and took a job in a textile factory. Eventually he made his way to California, where he lived for a time in the High Sierras before returning to school at Laney College in Oakland and at the University of California in Berkeley.

Turn on the mikes, turn on the radio . . . better begin the last take and get it right because this time there won't be any going back. The car and I are a very long way from home, burning out along the turnpike just west of Cleveland, trying to reach Flagstaff before another baby is born, before my memory realizes I am gone, and before my spirit for escape is arrested. To find dividends for my ambitions will be dependent upon whether or not the present and past are united in forcing me on, for giving me nothing more than initiative, or whether the future is an empty shaft, good only for falling into. Their respective strengths will decide which I choose to honor. In one of them I must find strength.

I left Maine with an ambition for time suspension . . . just to jump out and see. But people seem to get uglier, and the clocks are still turning. All their faces are foreign: uncontrollable, mysterious, and distant. In my vehicle, though, the big hand is frozen at a dash past eight. Outside it is almost quarter of. I'm doing just fine. I know myself. But will the hour unhinge and pass? Will the season change as I race to escape it?

High gear is holding well . . . lineal acceleration straight away from my trailing memory exhaust. Seventy-five miles per hour.

I am headed south. South to the broad-hat border under the sun where that one bright element continuously keeps the dust loose and moving, as people everywhere must jump and squirm from time to time, although here the changes are lazy and noncompulsory. I must become oblivious in comfort, lost with yearlong gentle leisure. The sun's heat is what I crave, hoping its

Original publication in this volume, by permission of the author.

ceaseless glare will make every day of the year the same, hoping it will accept my moving as my home cannot, hoping it will erase my memory.

Got to lose my sense of binding time before it is too late, before a messenger element of the earth grabs me, calls for me to give it up, to come back, to remember. I passed Buffalo at dawn this morning. The speedometer broke at the state line, so seventy-five does not matter. There are so many lines to cross.

Back home one cool summer day a neighbor told me in clichés and smiles about home. I did the same. Those things were all around, all the time. That crusty street poked at every spring by the water-company machines. Mud and slippery boots. Sitting in class with sweating feet, unable to get off to the basement where you always hit your head until all the marbles have been counted. Bringing the woolen pants in off the line, flat-hard as a pile of boards from the cold. Like sitting with the neighbor, sipping lemonade and talking of faded flavors. Sitting there. . . .

It comes back to me now as fleeting, full parentheses that have realized I have fled their bounds and are groping for the course of my escape.

Maine home. It's all for solid values, each attached to its own separate season, like hand-holds, to keep one close by to the tumultuous turning of the year. The seasons don't change as do slow, hot sand curves: they break out when backs are turned, jackets forgotten. They do it just to get away from the previous season, as when you leave and get on the road, suspend yourself in the hopeful hazard of a land of one season for a mile and hour. Crash into Arizona when no one is expecting you. All the lights are green. Home paddocks, yes, gotta bound away into a different, gentle parade and cadence.

At least two days of impulse and upshifting take me down into the Southwest, where those lonesomely perpetual trucks come for miles from the horizon and take their gleam and square roar solidly away, all the way away, amid low piles of desolation and western kick-out. I have to accustom myself to this continuous expanse. My foot is to the boards.

But why am I not expected here? Aren't the same songs playing on the radio? They aren't new to me, but their Main Street manifestations are. I should not slow down; several indictments are right behind me. What about those expectations of this place, what about my frozen moment, what about my memory?

No time for retrospection. Clouds and untold fadings would be everywhere in front of me. Out around the car, blankets of sunlight are constant, lasting longer than a day. Even when the stars are popping, the massively silent desert wind is tremendous in its prevalent element mind. The earth is powerful everywhere upon its surface, but it is the desert that kept me up nights in Maine, checking maps. Surely location decides what impulses will be captured from the desert wind and element mind; but if I could have felt that wind and expanse by staying back there, rationalization of that static situation would have come easy. That is why I am gone. Rationality is no bargain.

Perhaps I did wrong to leave. My memory is strong, and the spring and summer, fall and winter, will catch me whenever I forget the bad, get out, and attempt to live only in the good of the earth. My position might be in this present escapist moment, or in memory, or in the darkness up ahead. It is certainly somewhere close, undecided.

But I drive into the unknown and it becomes my moment, and I am not welcome here. These Arizona people are invisible, for it is impossible that we relate our dreams. We must remain strangers in a constant present. That is all we are allowed, being strangers. Perhaps they know it already. My dreams and memories belong to the earth in part, for it created them. These people have values for their particular moment, for they have decided. I have not. How can I tell these people that the earth has us all?

Gas. Down off the ramp amid purple sky-droppings of clear night and into hometown Arizona. The town bulges bright up ahead, not much more than filling stations and swishing automatic transmissions. There are no trees, except those green puffy pops planted on the sidewalks by municipal order. A few light poles and other lights approach, fluctuating. The car rolls down in neutral as we are tied into the speed limit. No hurry through these intersections. Watch closely, I need some gas.

An angry yellow light blots the green . . . the cables click under the road, punched by an interfering pedestrian button. I get on the brake and suck up to the line. Gas on the next corner is cheap. Across my headlights crooks an ancient lady, pulling a two-wheel shopping cart, going to market this evening. She must have been the one who punched the stop lights, cued the click under the concrete and grease, heat and travel. She is after a few last, late bargains, but she made all the lights in my face come up bright, made them finally outright hostile.

Lights come up on the dash, making me aware of the gauges. One is broken, the other is low. Like the snap of an unpulled alarm, the clamping threshold is awakened and my difficulties are seen in all their futility. The future is now locked to the present.

No more hope. The distant question is answered, and my exercise is revealed in all its flailings. All the pieces I tossed up and aside at the start have come into place exactly as they had been. The impulse is lost. My very own retrospection has checked my room and has come after me. Captured. And it did not take much to tie my hands. I am again its partner—only now, far removed from the Maine throne, in desert dunes and sunlit-moonlit severity, the partnership is only in mind and passion. Going back would only force me to do this thing again. I had to get out.

Horns sound behind me, their lights close and hounding. The car kicks up off the start, shudders, and stalls. The red gas-gauge arrow is far below E.

These people . . . I can escape these people through silence (I have become very good at it), but it is then that the earth speaks in its greatest tones. When I pause on these bright western streets, silent, memory becomes brazen. Admittedly, it is a valuable process within my constitution. If those memory elements are unavoidable and unshakable, let them remain. . . .

Where is the snow and blister wind now?

Encompassing passion, in distant alliance with textures recalled . . . to wallow in glacial mud up through my pores; to find a season, any or all seasons, and immerse myself in them; to drain my components into the Maine rock soil; to be blown into vapor; to careen up and above my memory street and then to drop in gray sheets upon an embracing earth; to drip into the ground and be divided there once again. Then to be frozen, to cry for the cold to stop, so that I can push a purple head out of a muddy drudge grave, with the traveling clouds correctly above me, to greet the spring as a wailing wayward mud flower, too early to be lost . . . my purple head popping for a place in the sun.

Epilogue to Force of Circumstance

Born in Paris and educated at the Sorbonne, Simone de Beauvoir (1908–   )
taught philosophy in various places in France from 1931 until 1943, when she began
writing full-time. Her best-known novel, *The Mandarins* (1953), whose subject was
the French literary and intellectual community, won the prestigious Prix Goncourt.
The book she claims has given her the most satisfaction, however, is *The Second
Sex* (1953), in which she writes angrily and incisively about the second-class status
of women in society. In 1959 she began her autobiography, which has now gone
to four volumes: *Memoirs of a Dutiful Daughter* (1959), *The Prime of Life* (1962),
Force of Circumstance (1963), and *A Very Easy Death* (1964). Her most recent
work, *The Coming of Age* (1972), concerns growing old. For over forty years she
and Jean-Paul Sartre have shared a personal and intellectual relationship that married
couples anywhere might envy, but on principle they have refused to marry, attributing
much of the lasting success of their relationship to the fact that they are not married.

There has been one undoubted success in my life: my relationship with Sartre.
In more than thirty years, we have only once gone to sleep at night disunited.
These years spent side by side have not decreased the interest we find in
each other's conversation: a woman friend[1] has observed that we always listen
to each other with the closest attention. Yet so assiduously have we always
criticized, corrected or ratified each other's thought that we might almost
be said to think in common. We have a common store of memories, knowledge
and images behind us; our attempts to grasp the world are undertaken with
the same tools, set within the same framework, guided by the same touchstones.
Very often one of us begins a sentence and the other finishes it; if someone
asks us a question, we have been known to produce identical answers. The
stimulus of a word, a sensation, a shadow, sends us both traveling along
the same inner path, and we arrive simultaneously at a conclusion—a memory,
an association—completely inexplicable to a third person. We are no longer
astonished when we run into each other even in our work; I recently read
some reflections noted down by Sartre in 1952 which I had not known about

[1]Maria-Rosen Oliver in an interview she gave to an Argentine newspaper.

till now; there were passages in them which occur again, almost word for word, in my *Memoirs*, written ten years later. Our temperaments, our directions, our previous decisions, remain different, and our writings are on the whole almost totally dissimilar. But they have sprung from the same plot of ground.

This relationship has been stigmatized by some as a contradiction of the views on morality expressed in *The Second Sex:* I insist that women be independent, yet I have never been alone. The two words are not synonymous; but before I explain myself further on that point, there are a few stupid misconceptions I should like to dispose of.

It has been said by some people that Sartre writes my books. The day after I was awarded the Goncourt, someone advised me with no malicious intention whatever: "If you give any interviews, make it quite clear that you did write *Les Mandarins;* you know what people are saying: that Sartre stands behind you . . ." It has also been said that he made me as a writer. The only thing he ever did in this line was to pass two of my manuscripts on to Brice Parrain, one of which was in any case rejected. Let it pass. Long before I came on the scene they were saying that Colette "slept her way" to fame; so anxious is our society to maintain the accepted status of members of my sex as secondary beings, reflections, toys or parasites of the all-important male.

Even more strongly held is the belief that all my convictions were put into my head by Sartre. "With someone else, she would have been a mystic," wrote Jean Guitton; and quite recently a critic, Belgian if I remember rightly, mused in print: "If it had been Brasillach she had met up with!" In a broadsheet called the *Tribune des Assurances,* I read: "If instead of being a pupil of Sartre, she had come under the influence of a theologian, she would have been a passionate theist." Fifty years have gone by, but this is still the same old idea my father held: "A woman is what her husband makes her." He was deceiving himself; he never altered by so much as a hairsbreadth the beliefs of the pious young lady formed by the Couvent des Oiseaux. Even the gigantic personality of Jaurès shattered against the stubborn piety of his wife. Youth has its own specific gravity, its own resilience; how could the girl I was at twenty possibly have succumbed to the influence of a believer or a Fascist? But people in our society really do believe that a woman thinks with her uterus—what low-mindedness, really! I did come across Brasillach and his clique; they filled me with horror. I could only have become attached to a man who was hostile to all that I loathed: the Right, conventional thinking, religion. It was no matter of chance that I chose Sartre; for after all I did choose him. I followed him joyfully because he led me along the paths I wanted to take; later, we always discussed our itinerary together. I remember that, in 1940, receiving his last letter from Brumath, written hurriedly, slightly obscure, there was one sentence as I read it through for the first time that filled me with terror: was Sartre about to compromise? During the instant that the fear gripped me, I knew from the way I stiffened, from the pain I felt, that if I could not dissuade him we were doomed to spend the rest of our lives in opposite camps.

This does not alter the fact that philosophically and politically the initiative has always come from him. Apparently some young women have felt let down by this fact; they took it to mean that I was accepting the "relative" role I was advising them to escape from. No. Sartre is ideologically creative, I am not; this bent forced him into making political choices and going much more profoundly into the reasons for them than I was interested in doing. The real betrayal of my liberty would have been a refusal to recognize this particular superiority on his part; I would then have ended up a prisoner of the deliberately challenging attitude and the bad faith which are at once an inevitable result of the battle of the sexes and the complete opposite of intellectual honesty. My independence has never been in danger because I have never unloaded any of my own responsibilities onto Sartre. I have never given my support to any idea, any decision, without first having analyzed it and accepted it on my own account. My emotions have been the product of a direct contact with the world. My own work has demanded from me a great many decisions and struggles, a great deal of research, perseverance and hard work. He has helped me, as I have helped him. I have not lived through him.

As a matter of fact, this accusation is just one of the weapons in my adversaries' well-stocked arsenal. For the story of my public life is that of my books, my successes, my failures; and also of the attacks that have been launched against me.

In France, if you are a writer, to be a woman is simply to provide a stick to be beaten with. Especially at the age I was when my first books were published. If you are a very young woman they indulge you, with an amused wink. If you are old, they bow respectfully. But lose the first bloom of youth and dare to speak before acquiring the respectable patina of age: the whole pack is at your heels! If you are conservative, if you yield with grace before the accepted superiority of the male, if you seem insolent and in fact say nothing, then they'll leave you unscathed. I am of the Left, I had things I was trying to say; among others, that women are not just a tribe of moral cripples from birth.

"You've won. You've made all the right enemies," Nelson Algren said to me in the spring of 1960. Yes; the insults I received from *Rivarol*, from *Preuves*, from *Carrefour*, from Jacques Laurent, delighted me. The snag is that ill will spreads like oil in water. Slanders are quick to produce answering echoes, if not in people's hearts at least in their mouths! No doubt this is just one of the forms of the dissatisfaction we all feel to some extent at being no more than we are. We are capable of understanding, but we prefer to belittle. Writers are a favorite target of this sort of spite; the public treats them with reverence, knowing full well that they are people just like anybody else, and then feels resentful toward them because of this contradiction; all the outward signs of their common humanity are entered on the debit side of the ledger drawn up against them. An American critic, and one quite well disposed toward me, in his review of *The Prime of Life* said that despite all my efforts I had brought Sartre down off his pedestal: what pedestal? He ended by adding that even if Sartre had lost a bit of his prestige, at least he had been made more lovable. Generally speaking, if the public finds out that you are not superhuman then it classes you down among the lowest of the low—a monster. Between 1945 and 1952, we were particularly subject to such distortions because we were so difficult to classify. Left-wing but not Communists, in fact in very bad odor with the Communist Party, we were also not "bohemians"; I was criticized for living in a hotel, and Sartre for living with his mother; at the same time we rejected middle-class life, we were not part of "society," we had money but we didn't live in style; our lives were intimately linked without either of us being in any way subjected to the other. This complete bypassing of all their touchstones disconcerted and irritated people. I was struck for example by the fact that *Samedi-Soir* should have waxed so indignant over the price we had paid for a taxi from Bou Saâda to Djelfa: to hire a car for a thirty-mile journey is less of a luxury than to own an automobile of one's own. Yet no one criticized me later on when I bought my Aronde; the price of buying a car is a classic expense perfectly acceptable by bourgeois standards.

One of the factors that contributes most to distorting writers' public images is the number of people who include us in their fantasy lives. At one time my sister moved about a great deal in society, where she was always introduced by her husband's name. She used to be stunned by the things that were said when the conversation got onto the subject of me and my work. "I know her very well . . . she's a great friend of mine . . . I happened to have dinner with her only last week"; this from people I had never even set eyes on. There was a wealth of comments too. With a smile, she stood and listened to a lady who assured her: "She's a fishwife! Swears like a trooper, you know." One year, in New York, Fernand and Stépha asked me reproachfully: "Why have you hidden your marriage to Sartre from us?" I denied that we were married; they laughed. "Oh come now! Our friend Sauvage was a witness at the ceremony; he told us all about it himself." I had to show them my passport to convince them. In about 1949, France Roche featured us in the *France-Dimanche* gossip column: Sartre and I had bought a country house called La Berle and carved two hearts on a tree there. Sartre sent a letter denying it, which was not published, and she told a friend: "But

I know it's a fact because it was passed on to me by Z., who had tea with them in their garden." I also remember the young woman who came up to me timidly once in the Deux Magots. "Excuse me for disturbing you, but I'm a very good friend of Bertrand G." I looked at her questioningly and she seemed astonished. "Bertrand G., who has lunch with you every week." I felt awful for her and said hastily: "I expect you've got the names mixed up. My sister's a painter, she's called Hélène de Beauvoir, I expect he's one of her friends . . ."—"No," she said, "it wasn't your sister he meant. I understand now. Excuse me . . ." She left in complete confusion, and the suddenness with which her eyes had been opened was obviously so painful to her that I felt almost guilty. Obviously such people's fantasies are only interesting if they've got some pretty worthwhile facts—such as a secret marriage, or else a spicy detail or two—to divulge. It's not difficult for them to find an audience; the public likes gossip. There are some maniacs for whom no fact is really true unless it has been seen through a keyhole. I recognize that there is some excuse for this peculiarity; official accounts and portraits are always patently full of lies, so people imagine that truth must have its mysteries, its initiates, its hidden channels. Our enemies exploit this credulity.

Two images of me are current: I am a madwoman, an eccentric. (The newspapers in Rio reported in a tone of surprise: "We were expecting an eccentric; we were rather let down to be introduced to a woman dressed like anyone else.") My morals are extremely dissolute; in 1945, a Communist woman told the story that during my youth in Rouen I had been seen dancing naked on the tops of barrels; I have assiduously practiced every vice, my life is a perpetual orgy, etc.

Or, flat heels, tight bun, I am a chieftainess, a lady manager, a schoolmistress (in the pejorative sense given to this word by the Right). I spend my existence with books and sitting at my worktable, pure intellect. "She doesn't live," I've heard a young woman journalist say. "If I were invited to Mme T.'s Mondays I'd be there like a shot." The magazine *Elle*, depicting various categories of women for the benefit of its readers, gave my photograph the caption: *Exclusively intellectual life.*

Apparently a combination of these two portraits involves no contradiction. I can also be an egg-headed whore or a lubricious manageress; the essential is that the figure I cut should be abnormal. If my censors are trying to say that I am different from them, then I take it as a compliment. The fact is that I am a writer—a woman writer, which doesn't mean a housewife who writes but someone whose whole existence is governed by her writing. It's as good a life as any other. It has its reasons, its order and its ends, which one must misunderstand completely in order to think of it as extravagant. Was mine really ascetic, purely cerebral? God knows I don't get the impression that my contemporaries are getting all that much more amusement out of this world of ours than I, or that their experience is any larger. In any case, looking back over my past, there is no one I envy.

I trained myself when young not to care for public opinion. Since then, I have had Sartre and solid friendships to protect me. All the same, there have been certain whispers, certain looks that I have found it hard to bear: the sneering laughter of Mauriac and the young people with him in the Deux Magots. For several years I loathed showing myself in public; I stopped going to cafés, I avoided theater openings and all "Parisian" entertainments. This reserve was in accordance with my distaste for publicity: I have never appeared on television, never talked about myself on the radio, almost never given an interview. I have already explained my reasons for accepting the Goncourt and nevertheless refused even then to exhibit myself in any way. I wished to owe any success I might have to my own efforts and not to outside influences. And I knew that the more the press talked about me, the more I should be misrepresented. It was my desire to establish the truth of these matters that was largely responsible for my writing these memoirs, and many readers have in fact said that the ideas they entertained of me beforehand could scarcely have been more false. I still have my enemies; I should be very worried if I hadn't. But with time my books have lost their flavor of scandal; age, alas! has conferred on me a certain respectability; and above all I have won for myself a public that listens when I talk to them. At this stage, I am largely spared the unpleasant aspects of notoriety.

As a beginner, I experienced only the pleasures it brings, and even in the years since then they have always come in far fuller measure than the disadvantages. Fame gave me what I desired: that people should like my books, and through them me; that they should listen to me and let me serve them by showing them the world as I saw it. I have known these joys since the day *She Came to Stay* was published. I have not avoided being deceived by false illusions, I have experienced vanity: it flowers as soon as one smiles at one's own image, as soon as one shivers at the sound of one's name. At least I have never become self-important.

I have always taken my failures well; they were nothing but shots off target, never obstacles in my path. My successes, until recent years, have given me pleasures without reserve; for me, the approval of my readers always carried more weight than the praises of the professional critics: letters received, sentences overheard, the traces of an influence, in a book, in someone's life. Since the publication of the *Memoirs of a Dutiful Daughter,* and even more so since that of *The Prime of Life,* my relationship to the public has become ambiguous because the horror my class inspires in me has been brought to white heat by the Algerian war. There is no hope for reaching the wider reading public if one's books are not the sort they like; one is only printed in a cheap edition if the normal first-run edition has sold well. So, willy-nilly, it is the middle classes one is writing for. And among them there are some of course who have torn themselves away from their class, or are at least trying to—intellectuals, young people; with them I am on the same wavelength. But I feel ill at ease if the middle class as a whole gives me a good reception. There were too many women who read the *Memoirs of a Dutiful Daughter* because they enjoyed the accuracy with which I had depicted a milieu they recognized, but without being at all interested in the effort I had made to escape from it. As for *The Prime of Life,* many's the time I've stood gritting my teeth as people congratulated me: "It's bracing, it's dynamic, it's optimistic," when I was so sickened by everything that I would rather have been dead than alive.

I am by no means insensitive to praise or blame. Yet, if I dig down into myself, it is not long before I reach a bedrock of almost total indifference to the extent of my success. There was a time, as I have said, when pride and caution prevented me from making an estimate of my powers; today, I no longer have any idea of what standard of measurement I should use. Should it be with reference to the public, to the critics, to a few selected judges, to my deep personal convictions, to my publicity, to the lack of it? And what would this estimate be *of?* Fame or quality, influence or talent? And then again: what do those words mean? Not only the possible answers to them, but these questions themselves now strike me as inane. My detachment goes deeper than that; it has its roots in a childhood devoted to the absolute: I have remained convinced of the vanity of earthly successes. My apprenticeship to the world strengthened this disdain; I discovered in the world an amount of misery too immense for me to disturb myself unduly over the place I hold in it or over the rights I may or may not have to occupy a place in it.

Despite this undertow of disenchantment, though all idea of duty, of mission, of salvation has collapsed, no longer sure for whom or for what I write, the activity itself is now more necessary to me than ever. I no longer believe it to be a "justification," but without it I should feel mortally unjustified. There are days so beautiful that you want to shine like the sun, I mean to splash bright words over all the world; there are hours so black that no other hope is left but the cry that you would like to vent. Whence does it come, no less urgent now at fifty-five than it was when I was twenty, this extraordinary power of the Word? I say: "Nothing takes place but the place," or "One and one make one: what a misunderstanding!" and in my throat rises a flame that as it burns exalts me. Words without doubt, universal, eternal, presence of all in each, are the only transcendent power I recognize and am affected by; they vibrate in my mouth, and with them I can communicate with humanity. They wrench tears, night, death itself from the moment, from contingency, and then transfigure them. Perhaps the most profound desire

I entertain today is that people should repeat in silence certain words that I have been the first to link together.

There are obvious advantages in being a well-known writer; no more bread-and-butter jobs, but work you are doing because you want to, meeting people, travel, a more direct grip on events than before. The support of the French intellectuals is sought by a great many foreigners at variance with their own governments; we are often asked as well to demonstrate our solidarity with friendly nations. We are all a bit crushed by the weight of the manifestoes, protests, resolutions, declarations, appeals and messages that we have to draw up or sign. It is impossible to take part in all the committees, conferences, discussions and meetings to which we are invited. But in exchange for the time we do give them, the people who ask for our support keep us informed in a much more detailed, more exact and above all more living way than any newspaper about what is happening in their country: in Cuba, in Guinea, in the Antilles, in Venezuela, in Peru, in the Cameroons, in Angola, in South Africa. However modest my contribution to their struggles is, it gives me the feeling that I do have some little effect on history. Instead of being "well-connected" in the usual sense, I have connections with the world as a whole. An old friend once said reproachfully: "You live in a convent." Perhaps I do; but I spend a great deal of time in the parlor talking to my visitors.

Yet it was with nostalgia and with anxiety that I discovered the full bloom of Sartre's celebrity and my own budding fame. The carefree days were over the moment we became public persons and were always forced to take this new objectivity into account; the adventurous side of our earlier trips was lost forever; we had to give up all sudden whims, all wandering where we chose. To protect our private lives we had to erect barriers—leave hotel and café life behind—and I found it weighed on me to be cut off like that, I had so loved living mixed up together with everyone else. I see a great many people; but most of them no longer talk to me as they would to just anyone, my relations with them have been falsified. "Sartre is never to be seen with anyone except the people who are to be seen with Sartre," Claude Roy wrote once. The same is true of me. I run the risk of understanding them less well simply because I no longer entirely share their lot with them. This difference between us is simply a product of celebrity and of the material ease that follows in its train.

Economically I belong to a privileged class. Since 1954, my books earn me a great deal of money; in 1952 I bought myself an automobile, and in 1955 an apartment. I don't go out, I don't entertain; I still retain the repugnance to glamorous luxury places that I felt when I was twenty; I dress without ostentation, I eat sometimes very well, usually very little; but all such things I leave to the caprice of the moment—I never deliberately deprive myself.

There are censorious critics who reproach me for the comfort of my life: right-wingers, it goes without saying; on the Left, no one ever condemns another left-wing member on the score of wealth, even if he be a millionaire;[1] they are simply grateful to him for being on the Left. Marxist ideology has nothing to do with Evangelical morality, it demands neither asceticism nor poverty of any individual; to tell the truth, it is not concerned with your private life. The Right is so persuaded of the legitimacy of its claims that its adversaries can justify themselves in its eyes only by making martyrs of themselves; then too, its choices are all dictated by economic interests and it has difficulty in conceiving that the two could possibly be dissociated: a Communist with money, in their estimation, could not possibly be sincere. Finally, and most important, as far as the Right is concerned any stick will do to beat a dog, when it comes to attacking their Leftist enemies. One critic, who was doing his best to be impartial moreover, wrote after reading *The Prime of Life* that I had a taste for "low life" because at a time when I was very poor during the war I lived in sordid hotels; what wouldn't they find to say now if I elected to move into some cheap tavern! A warm topcoat is a concession to the middle class; a neglected appearance would be construed as affectation or as unseemly behavior. You are accused either of throwing money down every drain or of being a miser. And don't think you can escape by trying to stick to some happy medium or other: they'd soon have a name for that too—petty-mindedness, for example. The only solution is to follow your own conscience and let them say what they will.

Which doesn't mean that I accept my situation with a light heart. The uneasiness it caused me around 1946 still persists. I know that I am a profiteer, and that I am one primarily because of the education I received and the possibilities it opened up for me. I exploit no one directly; but the people who buy my books are all beneficiaries of an economy founded upon exploitation. I am an accomplice of the privileged classes and compromised by this connection; that is the reason why living through the Algerian war was like experiencing a personal tragedy. When one lives in an unjust world there is no use hoping by some means to purify oneself of that injustice; the only solution would be to change the whole world, and I don't have that power. To suffer from these contradictions serves no good purpose; to blind oneself to them is mere self-deception. On this point too, since I have no solution, I trust to my mood of the moment. But the consequence of my attitude is that I live in what approaches isolation; my objective condition cuts me off from the proletariat, and the way in which I experience it subjectively makes me an enemy of the middle classes. This relatively monastic life suits me quite well because I am always short of time; but it does deprive me of

[1]There are left-wing millionaires in South America.

a certain warmth—which I was able to re-experience with such joy during the demonstrations of the past few years—and also, a more serious matter for me, it sets limits to my experience.

To these mutilations of my life, which are only the reverse aspect of my good fortune, must be added another for which I can discern no compensation. Since 1944, the most important, the most irreparable thing that has happened to me is that—like Zazie—I have grown old. That means a great many things. To begin with, that the world around me has changed: it has become smaller and narrower. I can no longer forget that the surface of the earth is finite, finite the number of its inhabitants, of its different plants and animal species, finite too the books, the pictures and the monuments set there. Each element of it can be explained with relation to that whole and refers back only to it; its richness too is limited. When young, Sartre and I often used to meet "personalities on a higher level than our own," which meant that they were impervious to our powers of analysis and so were still endowed in our eyes with some of the magical prestige of childhood. This core of mystery is now dissolved. There are no more oddities, madness is no longer holy, crowds have lost the power to intoxicate me; youth, which once fascinated me, seems now no more than a prelude to maturity. Reality still interests me, but it no longer reveals itself like an awful lightning flash. Beauty yes, beauty remains; even though it no longer stuns me with its revelations, even though most of its secrets have gone flat, there are still moments when it can make time stop. But often I loathe it too. The evening after a massacre, I was listening to a Beethoven andante and stopped the record halfway through in anger: all the pain of the world was there, but so magnificently sublimated and controlled that it seemed justified. Almost all beautiful works have been created for the privileged and by privileged people who, even if they have suffered, have always had the possibility of expressing their sufferings; they are disguising the horror of misery in its nakedness.[1] Another evening, after another massacre—there have been so many—I longed for all such lying beauty to be utterly destroyed. Today, that feeling of horror has died down. I can listen to Beethoven. But neither he nor anyone else will ever again be able to give me that feeling I used to have of having reached some absolute.

For now I know the truth of the human condition: two-thirds of mankind are hungry. My species is two-thirds composed of worms, too weak ever to rebel, who drag their way from birth to death through a perpetual dusk of

[1] Popular art and certain works that I should qualify as "untamed" constitute exceptions to this rule; for example, I have heard the chant of a rabbi for the dead at Auschwitz, and another sung by a Jewish child telling the story of a pogrom. And yet, even in these cases, the very fact that relief has been sought in communication already tends to place one at a remove from the horror, which is, by definition, evil's absolute irrecoverability.

despair. In my dreams, ever since my youth, there are objects that have always recurred, in appearance inert, but receptacles of suffering: the hands of a watch that begin to race, no longer moved by a mechanism but by a secret and appalling organic disorder; a piece of wood bleeds beneath the blow of the ax, in a moment a disgustingly mutilated being will be discovered beneath the woody carapace. I feel the terror of these nightmares in my waking hours, if I call to mind the walking skeletons of Calcutta or those little gourds with human faces—children suffering from malnutrition. That is the only point at which I touch infinity: it is the absence of everything, with consciousness. They will die, and that is all that will have happened. The void frightens me less than misery made absolute.

I no longer have much desire to go traveling over this earth emptied of its marvels; there is nothing to expect if one does not expect everything. But I should very much like to know the sequel to our story. The young of today are simply future adults, but I am interested in them; the future is in their hands, and if in their schemes I recognize my own, then I feel that my life will be prolonged after I am in the grave. I enjoy being with them; and yet the comfort they bring me is equivocal: they perpetuate our world, and in doing so they steal it from me. Mycenae will be theirs, Provence and Rembrandt, and all the *piazze* of Rome. Oh, the superiority of being alive! All the eyes that rested before mine on the Acropolis seem to me already to have sunk into the abyss. In the eyes of those twenty-year-olds, I see myself already dead and mummified.

But whom do I see thus? To grow old is to set limits on oneself, to shrink. I have fought always not to let them label me; but I have not been able to prevent the years from enmeshing me. I shall live for a long time in this little landscape where my life has come to rest. I shall remain faithful to the old friendships; my stock of memories, even if there are some additions still to come, will stay as it is now. I have written certain books, not others. And at this point, suddenly, I feel strangely disconcerted. I have lived stretched out toward the future, and now I am recapitulating, looking back over the past. It's as though the present somehow got left out. For years I thought my work still lay ahead, and now I find it is behind me: there was no moment when it took place. It's a bit like the number in mathematics which has no place in either of the two series it separates. I was learning all the time so that one day I could put my store of knowledge to good use. I have forgotten an enormous amount, and for all that still floats on the surface of my memory I can see no possible use. As I retrace the story of my past, it seems as though I was always just approaching or just beyond something that never actually was accomplished. Only my emotions seem to have given me the experience of fulfillment.

The writer nevertheless has the good fortune to be able to escape his own petrifaction at the moments when he is writing. Every time I start on a new book, I am a beginner again. I doubt myself, I grow discouraged, all the work accomplished in the past is as though it never was, my first drafts are so shapeless that it seems impossible to go on with the attempt at all, right up until the moment—always imperceptible, there, too, there is a break—when it has become impossible not to finish it. Each page, each sentence, makes a fresh demand on the powers of invention and requires an unprecedented choice. Creation is adventure, it is youth and liberty.

But then, once my worktable is left behind, time past closes its ranks behind me. I have other things that I must think; suddenly, I collide again with my age. That ultramature woman is my contemporary. I recognize that young girl's face belatedly lingering amid the withered features. That hoary-headed gentleman, who looks like one of my great-uncles, tells me with a smile that we used to play together in the gardens of the Luxembourg. "You remind me of my mother," I am told by a woman of about thirty or so. At every turn the truth jumps out at me, and I find it hard to understand by what trick it manages to attack me thus from the outside when it lives inside me all the time.

Old age. From a distance you take it to be an institution; but they are all young, these people who suddenly find that they are old. One day I said to myself: "I'm forty!" By the time I recovered from the shock of that discovery I had reached fifty. The stupor that seized me then has not left me yet.

I can't get around to believing it. When I read in print Simone de Beauvoir, it is a young woman they are telling me about, and who happens to be me. Often in my sleep I dream that in a dream I'm fifty-four, I wake and find I'm only thirty. "What a terrible nightmare I had!" says the young woman who thinks she's awake. Sometimes, too, just before I come back to reality, a giant beast settles on my breast: "It's true! It's my nightmare of being more than fifty that's come true!" How is it that time, which has no form nor substance, can crush me with so huge a weight that I can no longer breathe? How can something that doesn't exist, the future, so implacably calculate its course? My seventy-second birthday is now as close as the Liberation Day that happened yesterday.

To convince myself of this, I have but to stand and face my mirror. I thought, one day when I was forty: "Deep in that looking glass, old age is watching and waiting for me; and it's inevitable, one day she'll get me." She's got me now. I often stop, flabbergasted, at the sight of this incredible thing that serves me as a face. I understand La Castiglione, who had every mirror smashed. I had the impression once of caring very little what sort of figure I cut. In much the same way, people who enjoy good health and always have enough to eat never give their stomachs a thought. While I was able to look at my face without displeasure I gave it no thought, it could look after itself. The wheel eventually stops. I loathe my appearance now:

the eyebrows slipping down toward the eyes, the bags underneath, the excessive fullness of the cheeks, and that air of sadness around the mouth that wrinkles always bring. Perhaps the people I pass in the street see merely a woman in her fifties who simply looks her age, no more, no less. But when I look, I see my face as it was, attacked by the pox of time for which there is no cure.

My heart too has been infected by it. I have lost my old power to separate the shadows from the light, to pay the price of the tornadoes and still make sure I had the radiance of clear skies between. My powers of revolt are dimmed now by the imminence of my end and the fatality of the deteriorations that troop before it; but my joys have paled as well. Death is no longer a brutal event in the far distance; it haunts my sleep. Awake, I sense its shadow between the world and me: it has already begun. That is what I had never foreseen: it begins early and it erodes. Perhaps it will finish its task without much pain, everything having been stripped from me so completely that this presence I have so longed to retain, my own, will one day not be present anywhere, not be, and allow itself to be swept away with indifference. One after the other, thread by thread, they have been worn through, the bonds that hold me to this earth, and they are giving way now, or soon will.

Yes, the moment has come to say: Never again! It is not I who am saying good-bye to all those things I once enjoyed, it is they who are leaving me; the mountain paths disdain my feet. Never again shall I collapse, drunk with fatigue, into the smell of hay. Never again shall I slide down through the solitary morning snows. Never again a man. Now, not my body alone but my imagination too has accepted that. In spite of everything, it's strange not to be a body any more. There are moments when the oddness of it, because it's so definitive, chills my blood. But what hurts more than all these deprivations is never feeling any new desires: they wither before they can be born in this rarefied climate I inhabit now. Once, the days slipped by with no sense of haste. I was going even faster than they, drawn into the future by all my plans. Now, the hours are all too short as they whirl me on in the last furious gallop to the tomb. I try not to think: In ten years, in a year. Memories grow thin, myths crack and peel, projects rot in the bud; I am here, and around me circumstances. If this silence is to last, how long it seems, my short future!

And what threats it includes! The only thing that can happen now at the same time new and important is misfortune. Either I shall see Sartre dead, or I shall die before him. It is appalling not to be there to console someone for the pain you cause by leaving him. It is appalling that he should abandon you and then not speak to you again. Unless I am blessed by a most improbable piece of good fortune, one of these fates is to be mine. Sometimes I want to finish it all quickly so as to shorten the dread of waiting.

Yet I loathe the thought of annihilating myself quite as much now as I ever did. I think with sadness of all the books I've read, all the places I've seen, all the knowledge I've amassed and that will be no more. All the music, all the paintings, all the culture, so many places: and suddenly nothing. They made no honey, those things, they can provide no one with any nourishment. At the most, if my books are still read, the reader will think: There wasn't much she didn't see! But that unique sum of things, the experience that I lived, with all its order and its randomness—the Opera of Peking, the arena of Huelva, the *candomblé* in Bahía, the dunes of El-Oued, Wabansia Avenue, the dawns in Provence, Tiryns, Castro talking to five hundred thousand Cubans, a sulphur sky over a sea of clouds, the purple holly, the white nights of Leningrad, the bells of the Liberation, an orange moon over the Piraeus, a red sun rising over the desert, Torcello, Rome, all the things I've talked about, others I have left unspoken—there is no place where it will all live again. If it had at least enriched the earth; if it had given birth to . . . what? A hill? A rocket? But no. Nothing will have taken place, I can still see the hedge of hazel trees flurried by the wind and the promises with which I fed my beating heart while I stood gazing at the gold mine at my feet: a whole life to live. The promises have all been kept. And yet, turning an incredulous gaze toward that young and credulous girl, I realize with stupor how much I was gypped.

June 1960–March 1963

The Death of the Moth

Few writers have been as naturally directed to a literary career as was Virginia Woolf (1882–1941). Her father, Leslie Stephen, an eminent Victorian man of letters, educated his daughter in his magnificent library, and as a child she became a favorite of her father's friends and associates, the cream of the British intelligentsia. She married social and literary critic Leonard Woolf in 1912, and their house in the Bloomsbury section of London became the center of the "Bloomsbury group," a circle of writers and intellectuals that included biographer Lytton Strachey, economist John Maynard Keynes, and novelist E. M. Forster. For their own amusement the Woolfs founded the Hogarth Press in 1917, a venture that quickly grew from an amateur project to a commercially successful publishing house which put out the early works of emerging writers like T. S. Eliot, Katherine Mansfield, and Forster, as well as all of Mrs. Woolf's works. As a writer, Virginia Woolf is best known for the stream-of-consciousness technique which she mastered in novels like *Mrs. Dalloway* (1925) and *To the Lighthouse* (1927). In addition to nine novels, she wrote reviews and critical essays covering a wide range of literature in a personal, informal style. These essays have been collected in *The Common Reader* (1925), *The Second Common Reader* (1932), *The Death of the Moth and Other Essays* (1942), whose title essay appears below, and *Granite and Rainbow* (1958). In 1953 Leonard Woolf published *A Writer's Diary*, excerpts from his wife's journals concerning her writing.

Moths that fly by day are not properly to be called moths; they do not excite that pleasant sense of dark autumn nights and ivy-blossom which the commonest yellow-underwing asleep in the shadow of the curtain never fails to rouse in us. They are hybrid creatures, neither gay like butterflies nor sombre like their own species. Nevertheless the present specimen, with his narrow hay-coloured wings, fringed with a tassel of the same colour, seemed to be content with life. It was a pleasant morning, mid-September, mild, benignant, yet with a keener breath than that of the summer months. The plough was already scoring the field opposite the window, and where the share had been, the earth was pressed flat and gleamed with moisture. Such vigour came rolling in from the fields and the down beyond that it was difficult to keep the eyes strictly turned upon the book. The rooks too were keeping one of their annual festivities; soaring round the tree tops until it looked as if a vast net with thousands of black knots in it had been cast up into the air; which, after a few moments sank slowly down upon the trees until every twig seemed to have a knot at the end of it. Then, suddenly, the net would be thrown into the air again in a wider circle this time, with the utmost clamour and vociferation, as though to be thrown into the air and settle slowly down upon the tree tops were a tremendously exciting experience.

The same energy which inspired the rooks, the ploughmen, the horses, and even, it seemed, the lean bare-backed downs, sent the moth fluttering from side to side of his square of the window-pane. One could not help watching him. One was, indeed, conscious of a queer feeling of pity for him. The possibilities of pleasure seemed that morning so enormous and so various that to have only a moth's part in life, and a day moth's at that, appeared a hard fate, and his zest in enjoying his meagre opportunities to the full, pathetic. He flew vigorously to one corner of his compartment, and, after waiting there a second, flew across to the other. What remained for him but to fly to a third corner and then to a fourth? That was all he could do, in spite of the size of the downs, the width of the sky, the far-off smoke of houses, and the romantic voice, now and then, of a steamer out at sea. What he could do he did. Watching him, it seemed as if a fibre, very thin but pure, of the enormous energy of the world had been thrust into his frail and diminutive body. As often as he crossed the pane, I could fancy that a thread of vital light became visible. He was little or nothing but life.

Yet, because he was so small, and so simple a form of the energy that was rolling in at the open window and driving its way through so many narrow and intricate corridors in my own brain and in those of other human beings, there was something marvellous as well as pathetic about him. It was as if someone had taken a tiny bead of pure life and decking it as lightly as possible with down and feathers, had set it dancing and zigzagging to show us the true nature of life. Thus displayed one could not get over the strangeness of it. One is apt to forget all about life, seeing it humped and bossed and garnished and cumbered so that it has to move with the greatest circumspection and dignity. Again, the thought of all that life might have been had he been born in any other shape caused one to view his simple activities with a kind of pity.

After a time, tired by his dancing apparently, he settled on the window ledge in the sun, and, the queer spectacle being at an end, I forgot about him. Then, looking up, my eye was caught by him. He was trying to resume his dancing, but seemed either so stiff or so awkward that he could only flutter to the bottom of the window-pane; and when he tried to fly across it he failed. Being intent on other matters I watched these futile attempts for a time without thinking, unconsciously waiting for him to resume his flight, as one waits for a machine, that has stopped momentarily, to start again without considering the reason of its failure. After perhaps a seventh attempt he slipped from the wooden ledge and fell, fluttering his wings, on to his back on the window sill. The helplessness of his attitude roused me. It flashed upon me that he was in difficulties; he could no longer raise himself; his legs struggled vainly. But, as I stretched out a pencil, meaning to help him to right himself, it came over me that the failure and awkwardness were the approach of death. I laid the pencil down again.

The legs agitated themselves once more. I looked as if for the enemy against which he struggled. I looked out of doors. What had happened there? Presumably it was midday, and work in the fields had stopped. Stillness and quiet had replaced the previous animation. The birds had taken themselves off to feed in the brooks. The horses stood still. Yet the power was there all the same, massed outside indifferent, impersonal, not attending to anything in particular. Somehow it was opposed to the little hay-coloured moth. It was useless to try to do anything. One could only watch the extraordinary efforts made by those tiny legs against an oncoming doom which could, had it chosen, have submerged an entire city, not merely a city, but masses of human beings; nothing, I knew, had any chance against death. Nevertheless after a pause of exhaustion the legs fluttered again. It was superb this last protest, and so frantic that he succeeded at last in righting himself. One's sympathies, of course, were all on the side of life. Also, when there was nobody to care or to know, this gigantic effort on the part of an insignificant little moth, against a power of such magnitude, to retain what no one else valued or desired to keep, moved one strangely. Again, somehow, one saw life, a pure bead. I lifted the pencil again, useless though I knew it to be. But even as I did so, the unmistakable tokens of death showed themselves. The body relaxed, and instantly grew stiff. The struggle was over. The insignificant little creature now knew death. As I looked at the dead moth, this minute wayside triumph of so great a force over so mean an antagonist filled me with wonder. Just as life had been strange a few minutes before, so death was now as strange. The moth having righted himself now lay most decently and uncomplainingly composed. O yes, he seemed to say, death is stronger than I am.

The Secret of Life

A scientist with illustrious credentials, Loren Eiseley (1907–   ) is also the envy of many writers for the eloquence and clarity of his prose style. Born in Lincoln, he obtained his B.A. there at the University of Nebraska. He received graduate degrees in anthropology at the University of Pennsylvania, where, after teaching at many universities including Columbia, Harvard, and the University of California, he is now professor of anthropology and the history of science. Recipient of a host of awards and honorary degrees, Eiseley is past president of the American Institute of Human Paleontology. He has contributed to numerous scientific journals as well as to more popular periodicals such as *Horizon, Saturday Review,* and *Harper's.* Among his books are *Darwin's Century* (1958), *The Firmament of Time* (1960), and *The Immense Journey* (1953), whose last chapter is reprinted below.

I am middle-aged now, but in the autumn I always seek for it again hopefully. On some day when the leaves are red, or fallen, and just after the birds are gone, I put on my hat and an old jacket, and over the protests of my wife that I will catch cold, I start my search. I go carefully down the apartment steps and climb, instead of jump, over the wall. A bit further I reach an unkempt field full of brown stalks and emptied seed pods.

By the time I get to the wood I am carrying all manner of seeds hooked in my coat or piercing my socks or sticking by ingenious devices to my shoestrings. I let them ride. After all, who am I to contend against such ingenuity? It is obvious that nature, or some part of it in the shape of these seeds, has intentions beyond this field and has made plans to travel with me.

We, the seeds and I, climb another wall together and sit down to rest, while I consider the best way to search for the secret of life. The seeds remain very quiet and some slip off into the crevices of the rock. A woolly-bear caterpillar hurries across a ledge, going late to some tremendous transformation, but about this he knows as little as I.

It is not an auspicious beginning. The things alive do not know the secret, and there may be those who would doubt the wisdom of coming out among discarded husks in the dead year to pursue such questions. They might say the proper time is spring, when one can consult the water rats or listen to little chirps under the stones. Of late years, however, I have come to suspect that the mystery may just as well be solved in a carved and intricate seed case out of which the life has flown, as in the seed itself.

In autumn one is not confused by activity and green leaves. The underlying apparatus, the hooks, needles, stalks, wires, suction cups, thin pipes, and iridescent bladders are all exposed in a gigantic dissection. These are the essentials. Do not be deceived simply because the life has flown out of them. It will return, but in the meantime there is an unparalleled opportunity to examine in sharp and beautiful angularity the shape of life without its disturbing muddle of juices and leaves. As I grow older and conserve my efforts, I shall give this season my final and undivided attention. I shall be found puzzling over the saw teeth on the desiccated leg of a dead grasshopper or standing bemused in a brown sea of rusty stems. Somewhere in this discarded machinery may lie the key to the secret. I shall not let it escape through lack of diligence or through fear of the smiles of people in high windows. I am sure now that life is not what it is purported to be and that nature, in the canny words of a Scotch theologue, "is not as natural as it looks." I have learned this in a small suburban field, after a good many years spent in much wilder places upon far less fantastic quests.

The notion that mice can be generated spontaneously from bundles of old clothes is so delightfully whimsical that it is easy to see why men were loath to abandon it. One could accept such accidents in a topsy-turvy universe without trying to decide what transformation of buckles into bones and shoe buttons into eyes had taken place. One could take life as a kind of fantastic magic and not blink too obviously when it appeared, beady-eyed and bustling, under the laundry in the back room.

It was only with the rise of modern biology and the discovery that the trail of life led backward toward infinitesimal beginnings in primordial sloughs, that men began the serious dissection and analysis of the cell. Darwin, in one of his less guarded moments, had spoken hopefully of the possibility that life had emerged from inorganic matter in some "warm little pond." From that day to this biologists have poured, analyzed, minced, and shredded recalcitrant protoplasm in a fruitless attempt to create life from nonliving matter. It seemed inevitable, if we could trace life down through simpler stages, that we must finally arrive at the point where, under the proper chemical conditions, the mysterious borderline that bounds the inanimate must be crossed. It seemed clear that life was a material manifestation. Somewhere, somehow, sometime, in the mysterious chemistry of carbon, the long march toward the talking animal had begun.

A hundred years ago men spoke optimistically about solving the secret, or at the very least they thought the next generation would be in a position to do so. Periodically there were claims that the emergence of life from matter had been observed, but in every case the observer proved to be self-deluded. It became obvious that the secret of life was not to be had by a little casual experimentation, and that life in today's terms appeared to arise only through the medium of preëxisting life. Yet, if science was not to be embarrassed by some kind of mind-matter dualism and a complete and irrational break between life and the world of inorganic matter, the emergence of life had, in some way, to be accounted for. Nevertheless, as the years passed, the secret remained locked in its living jelly, in spite of larger microscopes and more formidable means of dissection. As a matter of fact the mystery was heightened because all this intensified effort revealed that even the supposedly simple amoeba was a complex, self-operating chemical factory. The notion that he was a simple blob, the discovery of whose chemical composition would enable us instantly to set the life process in operation, turned out to be, at best, a monstrous caricature of the truth.

With the failure of these many efforts science was left in the somewhat embarrassing position of having to postulate theories of living origins which it could not demonstrate. After having chided the theologian for his reliance on myth and miracle, science found itself in the unenviable position of having to create a mythology of its own: namely, the assumption that what, after long effort, could not be proved to take place today had, in truth, taken place in the primeval past.

My use of the term *mythology* is perhaps a little harsh. One does occasionally observe, however, a tendency for the beginning zoological textbook to take the unwary reader by a hop, skip, and jump from the little steaming pond or the beneficent chemical crucible of the sea, into the lower world of life with such sureness and rapidity that it is easy to assume that there is no mystery about this matter at all, or, if there is, that it is a very little one.

This attitude has indeed been sharply criticized by the distinguished British biologist Woodger, who remarked some years ago: "Unstable organic compounds and chlorophyll corpuscles do not persist or come into existence in nature on their own account at the present day, and consequently it is necessary to postulate that conditions were once such that this did happen although and in spite of the fact that our knowledge of nature does not give us any warrant for making such a supposition . . . It is simple dogmatism—asserting that what you want to believe did in fact happen."

Yet, unless we are to turn to supernatural explanations or reinvoke a dualism which is scientifically dubious, we are forced inevitably toward only two possible explanations of life upon earth. One of these, although not entirely disproved, is most certainly out of fashion and surrounded with greater obstacles to its acceptance than at the time it was formulated. I refer, of course,

CHAPTER SIX / *Looking Outward*

to the suggestion of Lord Kelvin and Svante Arrhenius that life did not arise on this planet, but was wafted here through the depths of space. Microscopic spores, it was contended, have great resistance to extremes of cold and might have come into our atmosphere with meteoric dust, or have been driven across the earth's orbit by light pressure. In this view, once the seed was "planted" in soil congenial to its development, it then proceeded to elaborate, evolve, and adjust until the higher organisms had emerged.

This theory had a certain attraction as a way out of an embarrassing dilemma, but it suffers from the defect of explaining nothing, even if it should prove true. It does not elucidate the nature of life. It simply removes the inconvenient problem of origins to far-off spaces or worlds into which we will never penetrate. Since life makes use of the chemical compounds of this earth, it would seem better to proceed, until incontrovertible evidence to the contrary is obtained, on the assumption that life has actually arisen upon this planet. The now widely accepted view that the entire universe in its present state is limited in time, and the apparently lethal nature of unscreened solar radiation are both obstacles which greatly lessen the likelihood that life has come to us across the infinite wastes of space. Once more, therefore, we are forced to examine our remaining notion that life is not coterminous with matter, but has arisen from it.

If the single-celled protozoans that riot in roadside pools are not the simplest forms of life, if, as we know today, these creatures are already highly adapted and really complex, though minute beings, then where are we to turn in the search for something simple enough to suggest the greatest missing link of all—the link between living and dead matter? It is this problem that keeps me wandering fruitlessly in pastures and weed thickets even though I know this is an old-fashioned naturalist's approach, and that busy men in laboratories have little patience with my scufflings of autumn leaves, or attempts to question beetles in decaying bark. Besides, many of these men are now fascinated by the crystalline viruses and have turned that remarkable instrument, the electron microscope, upon strange molecular "beings" never previously seen by man. Some are satisfied with this glimpse below the cell and find the virus a halfway station on the road to life. Perhaps it is, but as I wander about in the thin mist that is beginning to filter among these decaying stems and ruined spider webs, a kind of disconsolate uncertainty has taken hold of me.

I have come to suspect that this long descent down the ladder of life, beautiful and instructive though it may be, will not lead us to the final secret. In fact I have ceased to believe in the final brew or the ultimate chemical. There is, I know, a kind of heresy, a shocking negation of our confidence in blue-steel microtomes and men in white in making such a statement. I would not be understood to speak ill of scientific effort, for in simple truth

I would not be alive today except for the microscopes and the blue steel. It is only that somewhere among these seeds and beetle shells and abandoned grasshopper legs I find something that is not accounted for very clearly in the dissections to the ultimate virus or crystal or protein particle. Even if the secret is contained in these things, in other words, I do not think it will yield to the kind of analysis our science is capable of making.

Imagine, for a moment, that you have drunk from a magician's goblet. Reverse the irreversible stream of time. Go down the dark stairwell out of which the race has ascended. Find yourself at last on the bottommost steps of time, slipping, sliding, and wallowing by scale and fin down into the muck and ooze out of which you arose. Pass by grunts and voiceless hissings below the last tree ferns. Eyeless and earless, float in the primal waters, sense sunlight you cannot see and stretch absorbing tentacles toward vague tastes that float in water. Still, in your formless shiftings, the *you* remains: the sliding particles, the juices, the transformations are working in an exquisitely patterned rhythm which has no other purpose than your preservation—you, the entity, the ameboid being whose substance contains the unfathomable future. Even so does every man come upward from the waters of his birth.

Yet if at any moment the magician bending over you should cry, "Speak! Tell us of that road!" you could not respond. The sensations are yours but not—and this is one of the great mysteries—the power over the body. You cannot describe how the body you inhabit functions, or picture or control the flights and spinnings, the dance of the molecules that compose it, or why they chose to dance into that particular pattern which is you, or, again, why up the long stairway of the eons they dance from one shape to another. It is for this reason that I am no longer interested in final particles. Follow them as you will, pursue them until they become nameless protein crystals replicating on the verge of life. Use all the great powers of the mind and pass backward until you hang with the dire faces of the conquerors in the hydrogen cloud from which the sun was born. You will then have performed the ultimate dissection that our analytic age demands, but the cloud will still veil the secret and, if not the cloud, then the nothingness into which, it now appears, the cloud, in its turn, may be dissolved. The secret, if one may paraphrase a savage vocabulary, lies in the egg of night.

Only along the edges of this field after the frost there are little whispers of it. Once even on a memorable autumn afternoon I discovered a sunning blacksnake brooding among the leaves like the very simulacrum of old night. He slid unhurriedly away, carrying his version of the secret with him in such a glittering menace of scales that I was abashed and could only follow admiringly from a little distance. I observed him well, however, and am sure he carried his share of the common mystery into the stones of my neighbor's wall, and is sleeping endlessly on in the winter darkness with one great coil locked around that glistening head. He is guarding a strange, reptilian darkness which is not night or nothingness, but has, instead, its momentary vision of mouse bones or a bird's egg, in the soft rising and ebbing of the tides of life. The snake has diverted me, however. It was the dissection of a field that was to occupy us—a dissection in search of secrets—a dissection such as a probing and inquisitive age demands.

Every so often one encounters articles in leading magazines with titles such as "The Spark of Life," "The Secret of Life," "New Hormone Key to Life," or other similar optimistic proclamations. Only yesterday, for example, I discovered in the *New York Times* a headline announcing: "Scientist Predicts Creation of Life in Laboratory." The Moscow-date-lined dispatch announced that Academician Olga Lepeshinskaya had predicted that "in the not too distant future, Soviet scientists would create life." "The time is not far off," warns the formidable Madame Olga, "when we shall be able to obtain the vital substance artificially." She said it with such vigor that I had about the same reaction as I do to announcements about atomic bombs. In fact I half started up to latch the door before an invading tide of Russian protoplasm flowed in upon me.

What finally enabled me to regain my shaken confidence was the recollection that these pronouncements have been going on for well over a century. Just now the Russian scientists show a particular tendency to issue such blasts—committed politically, as they are, to an uncompromising materialism and the boastfulness of very young science. Furthermore, Madame Lepeshinskaya's remarks as reported in the press had a curiously old-fashioned flavor about them. The protoplasm she referred to sounded amazingly like the outmoded *Urschleim* or *Autoplasson* of Haeckel—simplified mucoid slimes no longer taken very seriously. American versions—and one must remember they are often journalistic interpretations of scientists' studies rather than direct quotations from the scientists themselves—are more apt to fall into another pattern. Someone has found a new chemical, vitamin, or similar necessary ingredient without which life will not flourish. By the time this reaches the more sensational press, it may have become the "secret of life." The only thing the inexperienced reader may not comprehend is the fact that no one of these items, even the most recently discovered, is *the* secret. Instead, the substance is probably a part, a very small part, of a larger enigma which is well-nigh as inscrutable as it ever was. If anything, the growing list of catalysts, hormones, plasma genes, and other hobgoblins involved in the work of life only serves to underline the enormous complexity of the secret. "To grasp in detail," says the German biologist Von Bertalanffy, "the physico-chemical organization of the simplest cell is far beyond our capacity."

It is not, you understand, disrespect for the laudable and persistent patience of these dedicated scientists happily lost in their maze of pipettes, smells, and gas flames, that has led me into this runaway excursion to the wood. It is rather the loneliness of a man who knows he will not live to see the mystery solved, and who, furthermore, has come to believe that it will not be solved when the first humanly synthesized particle begins—if it ever does—to multiply itself in some unknown solution.

It is really a matter, I suppose, of the kind of questions one asks oneself. Some day we may be able to say with assurance, "We came from such and such a protein particle, possessing the powers of organizing in a manner leading under certain circumstances to that complex entity known as the cell, and from the cell by various steps onward, to multiple cell formation." I mean we may be able to say all this with great surety and elaboration of detail, but it is not the answer to the grasshopper's leg, brown and black and saw-toothed here in my hand, nor the answer to the seeds still clinging tenaciously to my coat, nor to this field, nor to the subtle essences of memory, delight, and wistfulness moving among the thin wires of my brain.

I suppose that in the forty-five years of my existence every atom, every molecule that composes me has changed its position or danced away and beyond to become part of other things. New molecules have come from the grass and the bodies of animals to be part of me a little while, yet in this spinning, light and airy as a midge swarm in a shaft of sunlight, my memories hold, and a loved face of twenty years ago is before me still. Nor is that face, nor all my years, caught cellularly as in some cold precise photographic pattern, some gross, mechanical reproduction of the past. My memory holds the past and yet paradoxically knows, at the same time, that the past is gone and will never come again. It cherishes dead faces and silenced voices, yes, and lost evenings of childhood. In some odd nonspatial way it contains houses and rooms that have been torn timber from timber and brick from brick. These have a greater permanence in that midge dance which contains them than ever they had in the world of reality. It is for this reason that Academician Olga Lepeshinskaya has not answered the kind of questions one may ask in an open field.

If the day comes when the slime of the laboratory for the first time crawls under man's direction, we shall have great need of humbleness. It will be difficult for us to believe, in our pride of achievement, that the secret of life has slipped through our fingers and eludes us still. We will list all the chemicals and the reactions. The men who have become gods will pose austerely before the popping flashbulbs of news photographers, and there will be few to consider—so deep is the mind-set of an age—whether the desire to link life to matter may not have blinded us to the more remarkable characteristics of both.

As for me, if I am still around on that day, I intend to put on my old